300 YEARS OF RACING AT BELLEWSTOWN

THE HISTORY OF THE RACECOURSE
1726 TO 2013

JOHN KIRWAN AND BELLEWSTOWN HERITAGE GROUP

© John Kirwan 2013 and Bellewstown Heritage Group

First published in 2013

ISBN No. 978-0-9576528-0-4

All rights reserved. No parts of this book may be reprinted or reproduced or utilised in any electronic, mechanical or other means, now known or hereafter invented, including photocopying or recording or otherwise, without the prior permission of the publishers

The authors have asserted their moral rights in this work

PUBLISHED BY

BELLEWSTOWN HERITAGE GROUP, HONEYSUCKLE COTTAGE, BELLEWSTOWN, DROGHEDA, CO. MEATH, IRELAND

300 YEARS OF RACING AT BELLEWSTOWN

List of Contents   Page

BELLEWSTOWN: THE EIGHTEENTH CENTURY
Racing in the eighteenth century   10

BELLEWSTOWN: THE NINETEENTH CENTURY
Bellewstown Races in 1864   16
Racing in the nineteenth century   17
Abd-el-Kadir   22
The Lord Lieutenant attends Bellewstown races Thursday 25 June 1835   23
Opening of the Dublin and Drogheda Railway Line   27
Ladies at the Races   28
Entertainment at the Races   29
Getting there   33
The Society at Bellewstown Races 1868 from the Drogheda Argus   35
Daniel O'Connell at Bellewstown Racecourse 15 April 1843   36
Improvements at Bellewstown in the 19th century   38
Opening of the Gormanston Stand   41
Law and Order at the Races   42
Bellewstown: Stewards in the nineteenth century   45

BELLEWSTOWN: THE TWENTIETH CENTURY
Racing in the twentieth century   48
Improvements in the twentieth century   51
Recalling Bellewstown races in the 1920s   53
Jockey Steve Donoghue on racing in Bellewstown   55
A Perfect Day's Racing in the 1930s   57
Clerks and Secretaries of the Course   59
Stewards of the twentieth century   60
There's one born every tick of the clock by Alfred Woods   61
Kay Crozier looks back fondly at the races in her young days   62
Thimble Rigger   64
Jim Curley remembers tips for betting in his younger days   65
A journalist attends the races in the eighties   69
The Sport of Kings   70
250th Anniversary of Bellewstown Races   72
Report Card on Bellewstown   73
Ladies Day at Bellewstown   75

BELLEWSTOWN: MANAGING THE RACECOURSE
Jim Corcoran interview   78
Bellewstown Memories and Management: Kevin Coleman   81
Joe Collins: Modernising Bellewstown Racecourse   86

	Page
Managing in the Old Days at Bellewstown, John Purfield looks back	89
Roy Craigie remembers	92
Legends at Bellewstown	93
Tony Redmond, jockey and trainer	95
James Black, groundsman	98
Locals look back	100

BELLEWSTOWN RACING ROUND-UP
An account of meetings 1900-1999   103

BELLEWSTOWN'S BIG RACING COUP
A first-hand account of Barney Curley's Racing Coup 1975   174

BELLEWSTOWN MISCELLANY

Little Grange Harriers	186
A few famous local horses	190
Ten of the Best Horses to win at Bellewstown	191
Brigadier Boylan	194
The Delany Family	195
Bellewstown People in Racing	196
Workers at the Racecourse	197

BELLEWSTOWN STATISTICS   201

INTRODUCTION

Held on the hill of Crockafotha since the seventeenth century, the Bellewstown Races have always been hugely important to the communities of Meath and Louth. Through stories, newspaper archives and personal recollections, the rich tapestry of horse racing intertwined with local history has been collated and preserved in '300 Years of Racing at Bellewstown'. Ireland has an enviable reputation as the 'land of the horse', producing some of the best thoroughbreds in the world, and home to supremely talented trainers, jockeys and the most picturesque of racecourses. The history of the Bellewstown Races showcases the impact of a small racecourse on society, economically, socially and culturally.

All classes enjoyed attending the races, as reported in the Drogheda Conservative Journal, from the "numerous and elegant assemblage of beauty and fashion" to the "peasantry, whose peaceful and unoffending demeanour was gratifying". Highlighting the importance of good transport links, the book describes the opening of the railway line between Dublin and Drogheda in 1844, as the transformation of Bellewstown, "bringing droves of people from Dublin to enjoy a day out in the country at the races". The Railway Company became the first company to sponsor an Irish horse race and their decision to allow horses to be ferried to and from the racecourse free of charge, greatly assisted the rejuvenation of racing in Bellewstown. Just as prize-money is hugely important today, it was a central element to racing at Bellewstown, with prizes of Plates of £5 and £10 advertised in 1726 and in the nineteenth century the King's Plate race had an impressive prize fund of 100 guineas.

As is the case with racecourses around Ireland today, the re-development of Bellewstown Racecourse and its facilities in 1868 was seen as significant and news-worthy. The building of the Gormanston grandstand on the crown of Crockafotha, with views of Louth, Meath, Dublin, Monaghan, Cavan and Down was reported as a huge success – "the occasional exclamations of admiration must have been very gratifying to the gallantry of the gentlemen who originated this great improvement in the course".

As well as revealing local memories and interesting characters connected to Bellewstown, the book delves into the management of the racecourse over the years, including interviews with Jim Corcoran, Kevin Coleman and Joe Collins and stewards such as John Purfield and Roy Craigie. The stories of local jockeys and trainers like Tony Redmond are also told and there are many wonderful photos, particularly from the 1900's, along with a complete index of all results.

Preserving memories and tales is vitally important and '300 Years of Racing at Bellewstown 1726-2013' provides an invaluable resource for this and future generations. Taking the reader through the ages, with stories, interviews, articles and images it provides a fascinating insight into the names and personalities who helped to shape horse racing in Ireland as we know it today.

Joe Keeling, Chairman Horse Racing Ireland

MESSAGE FROM JIM CORCORAN

CHAIRMAN OF BELLEWSTOWN RACE COMMITTEE

One of life's great pleasures is memories of times past.

Unfortunately few people commit these memories to paper and as a result these moments in time are lost forever.

I am delighted that John Kirwan and Bellewstown Heritage Group have put pen to paper to record three hundred years of history and memories of Bellewstown.

Over all these years, thousands of people have enjoyed the racing and fun on The Hill and I hope many more will enjoy this book.

Jim Corcoran

Bellewstown Heritage Group is delighted to be associated with this marvellous publication of 300 YEARS OF RACING IN BELLEWSTOWN.

John Kirwan is a founding member of Bellewstown Heritage Group and has been its treasurer since its inception in 2007. A very well-known resident of Bellewstown, with a keen interest in horse racing, John has attended the annual races on the local track here in Bellewstown every year of his life. In the past decade, he has become even more actively involved since taking over as racecourse groundsman in 2002.

He has previously compiled the history of the houses of Bellewstown and co-written The Story of Bellewstown Old National School (2010); The History of Hilltown House (2011) and The Baddies of Bellewstown and the RIC Barracks (2012). For the past few years, when he was not to be found on the racecourse, he was most likely in the National Library, poring over accounts of races in the nineteenth century. It is great to see all of this research come at last to fruition, with the help of Fiona Ahern, also a member of Bellewstown Heritage Group, who compiled the social history of the racecourse, managed the project and edited the book. Other members of the heritage group who assisted were Sheila Scanlan who conducted interviews, Paul Black who collected photographs, John Bellew who restored the photographs, Colin Byrne who helped with statistics and Tommy Arnold, Jim Cahill, Helena Kelly, Willie Ludlow and John Moore who shared their early memories of the races.

John has been to every racecourse in Ireland but has only been to Cheltenham once. However, with the book finished and now that he has finally got a passport, he may be over there more often!

Bernadette McGuinness
Chairperson Bellewstown Heritage Group

Acknowledgements

We are immensely grateful to Kevin Coleman who contacted so many people for us, and who interviewed, proof-read and enthusiastically assisted with the organisation of so many details of the book. We are very grateful also to Joe Collins who generously allowed us access to his personal archive on racing in Bellewstown in the 1970s and 80s, supplied many photographs and loaned racing books and proof-read sections of the book.

A very big thank you to the following people who shared their memories of racing at Bellewstown with us: Tommy Arnold, James Black, Desmond Boylan, Kevin Coleman, Joe Collins, Jim Corcoran, Noel Coogan, Roy Craigie, Kay Crozier, Jim Curley, Peadar Flanagan, Willie Ludlow, John Purfield, Tony Redmond, Jackie Tallon, Tom Winters, Nora Wiseman/nee Crinion, Noreen Wiseman, Alfred Woods. The interviews were carried out by John Kirwan, Sheila Scanlan, Kevin Coleman and Fiona Ahern.

Many thanks to Barney Curley for allowing us to reproduce his own account of his big gambling coup at Bellewstown in 1975, from his book *Giving a Little Back* (1999), pp 152-172, pub. CollinsWillow. A new updated version of this book, including the Bellewstown story, *The Sure Thing, the Greatest Coup in Horse Racing History* will be published by Century early in 2014.

Sincere thanks to Paul Black for assembling so many photographs for the book and to John Bellew who recovered so many old damaged photographs. We are very grateful to the following people who generously supplied us with photographs: The Misses Barry (Dunboyne), Ann Bellew, John Bellew, Marie Brennan/nee Collins, Larry Brien, Jim Cahill, Kevin Coleman, Tony Collier, Joe Collins, Jim Curley, Jack Gogarty, Austin Greene, Ita Hoey, Philip Kirwan, Peter Leonard, Tom McCourt, John Moore, John Purfield, Angela Sheridan, Irene Townley, Noreen Wiseman, Alfred Woods and many other Bellewstown people. Thank you also to Healy Photographers for permission to use so many of their photographs in the coloured section of the book. Racecards and memorabilia were loaned by Dick Brabazon, Joe Collins, Paddy Curley, Dessie Dorey, Phyllis Mangan, Larry McDonald, Rosaleen McEnteggart, Andrew Moore, Frank Mulryan, Nick O'Toole, Betty and Eimear Tallon.

A big thank-you to John's sister, Betty Devereaux, who typed so many articles, interviews and statistics. Thank you also to Colin Byrne for all the typing of statistics and to Sheila Scanlan and Eleanor McGuinness who typed up oral interviews for us. Thank you also to Deirdre Ahern who proof-read sections of the book.

Many thanks to Padraic Kierans, of Anglo Printers, for all his advice and assistance in producing such a beautiful record of Bellewstown Races and to Aisling Murphy for her terrific work on the cover and photograph sections, not to mention the statistics. We are grateful for the assistance of the staff of the National Library, who were haunted by John Kirwan for the past two years in his non-stop search for material on Bellewstown Races. Thank you also to Dr Tom French, Meath County Library Archivist, for his advice and encouragement.

This project has been assisted by Bellewstown Race Committee and by Noel French of the Meath Heritage Centre, Trim, Co. Meath. The Meath Heritage Centre gratefully acknowledges the support of Trim Forum for Employment, Fas, Meath County Council, Trim Town Council and the local community.

Fiona Ahern
Editor

BELLEWSTOWN: THE EIGHTEENTH CENTURY

Situated in the beautiful rustic setting of the tiny village of Bellewstown, Co. Meath, Bellewstown Racecourse stands on the commonage of the Hill of Crockafotha, with wonderful views sweeping north over Drogheda, the river Boyne and the Mourne Mountains and east to where the Irish Sea laps the coastline of Bettystown, Laytown and Gormanstown. Discoveries in Newgrange show that horses have been in Co. Meath since the early Bronze Age and Bellewstown Racecourse is believed to be one of the oldest in Europe. Tradition has it that horse sports first took place in Bellewstown during the reign of King Conary the Great, High King of Ireland, about two thousand years ago, when the king is believed to have hunted deer on the Hill. Perhaps that is where the name of Crockafotha or Hill of the Playing Field (Cnoc an Faoite) derives. Nowadays long summer evenings attract a holiday crowd to the racing festival, where punters revel in the traditional rural and informal atmosphere of the venue and where each meeting has a feeling almost of a family re-union about it. Neighbours and locals catch up on the news, while the children enjoy all the fun of the amusements and afterwards the party spills over into the pub and its car-park, where singing, dancing, drinking and enjoyment continue to the wee hours.

A section of the crowd at Bellewstown Races in 1909

Bellewstown Races 1789 (*Finn's Leinster Journal* 11 July, 1789
Monday, June 29
£50 for three years old, three 1 ½ mile heats, carrying 7st. 7lb.
Mr Kirwan's b.c. *Sir Oliver*   1 2 2
Mr Greydon's b.c. *Sir Peter*   2 3 3
Colonel Lumm's c.m. *Aurora* 3 1 1
The closest and best running ever seen on Bellewstown-hill; the mare won but by half a length
Tuesday, June 30
£50 for 4 and 5 years old; 4 years old, 7 st. 7 lb.; 5 years old 8 st. 7 lb. – three mile heats.
Colonel Lumm's c.h. *Honest Tom*   1 1
Mr Hamilton's g.c. *Oldcastle*   2 2
Two to one on *Honest Tom*
Wednesday July 1
£50 for 5 years old and aged – 6 years old 8 st 10 lb.; aged - 9 st. four-mile heats
Colonel Lumm's c.h. *Honest Tom* walked over the course.
Thursday July 2
£50 for hunters that never started for a racing plate – four-mile heats
Mr Fallan's g.h. *Drunkard*   1 1
Mr Denis's c.h. *Chance*   2 2
Two to one at starting on *Chance* – good running – after the first heat, even betting.
Friday, July 3
Colonel Lumm's b.m. *Trifle*   1 1
Mr Callaghan's b.m. *Pinkeen* 2 2

Racing is known to have taken place in Bellewstown since, at least, the seventeenth century, although such races were not publicised in newspapers at that time. The first written record of a meeting taking place in Bellewstown seems to have been in 1726, when a three-day event was arranged and publicised in the *Dublin Gazette and Weekly Courant* of 31 August 1726, with prizes of Plates of £10 and £5.

There is a Plate of £10 value to be run for on September 21st on the course at Bellewstown, by any horse, mare or gelding that does not exceed 14 hands and that never won above the value of £6 by Plate or Match, nor started for above the value of £10; also a Plate of £5 on the 23rd of the same month. The Articles at large are printed and delivered in Coffee Houses and in the country.
(*Dublin Gazette and Weekly Courant* 31 August 1726)

Racing obviously continued on a regular basis at Bellewstown but races were not advertised regularly in the newspapers. The first man named in connection with the races was Mr. Pat Smith, the local innkeeper, who acted as Clerk of the Course and Receiver of Entries. In an advertisement placed in *Faulkner's Dublin Journal* in August 1734, Mr Smith sought entries for a £10 Plate, the best of three heats.

Bellewstown Races

Entries with their colours, marks and owner's names to be made three days before the races and each owner, not being a subscriber, shall pay one guinea for each horse entered, with five shillings and five pence for scales and straw and no man shall enter or start

more than one horse either in his own name or trust. To start precisely at two o'clock and be allowed half an hour between each heat for rubbing. Judges to be named by the majority of the subscribers in the field and to decide and determine any differences that may arise. No jostling but by the foremost horses the last half mile of every heat.
(*Faulkner's Dublin Journal* August 1734)

In 1745, *Faulkner's Dublin Journal* carried the following advertisement for Bellewstown:

Bellewstown Race-course: On Thursday the twelfth of September inst., will be run for upon the Hill aforesaid, a five pound Plate by any horse, mare or gelding, not exceeding 14 hands high, that never won the value of four pounds sterling at any one time and to carry eight stone; each horse or mare or gelding to be entered the first Inst. with Patrick Smith, at the Publick House on said Hill, paying each one English Crown Entrance; Two rounds of the course, one Hate and the best of three hates for the Plate. There will also be the same day, a Free Saddle to be run for, by any horse, mare or gelding running Hates for the same and a good match in the forenoon of said day.
(*Faulkner's Dublin Journal* 7-10 September 1745)

The Turf Club had not been founded at that time so horses had to be registered with Patrick Smith, owner of the pub in Bellewstown and Clerk of the Course. Over the years, they appear to have raced both left-handed and right-handed. In the eighteenth century, the course was the entire circuit of the hill, not the present-day half circuit. The enclosure was at Crockafotha, with the medieval mound (still there today) serving as the stand. The races consisted of several heats and the prize-money increased to a purse of twenty guineas as can be seen in the following advertisement for racing in Bellewstown in 1750:

John Pond, an auctioneer, established *The Sporting Kalendar,* which published the Rules of Racing. In 1751 the Kalendar gave the results of three races at Bellewstown. The first race, run on 26 August, 1751, was won by Mr Arthur Mervyn, an important flour-miller from the Naul, whose bay gelding *Geoseberry* won a purse of £40. On August 28th, Mr Burrass's mare, *Sprightly Peggy,* won a purse of £30 and on the 30th August, Mr Rowley's mare, *Comely,* won a damask table-cloth, valued at £20. Mr Arthur Mervyn, who was president of the Irish Jockey Club, which later evolved into the Turf Club, also owned a horse named *Skewball,* out of *Godolphin Arabian,* one of the outstanding Irish horses in the eighteenth century. *Skewball* won also at Bellewstown and achieved fame through his defeat of Sir Ralph Gore's grey mare *Miss Sportly* in a 300 guineas-a-side match at the Curragh in the Spring of 1752. Sir Ralph Gore was later Ranger of the Curragh from 1756-60 and co-incidentally also a President of the Jockey Club. This Jockey Club sent out invitations to members to dine together as early as 1758, when the following advertisement appeared in the *Universal Advertiser*

Jockey Club: The Jockey Club intend to dine at the Rose and Bottle in Dame Street on Friday the 9th of June. Signed: Arthur Mervyn, President.
(*Universal Advertiser* 27 May 1758)

The following year it was Sir Ralph Gore who, as president, invited the Jockey Club members to dine with him, adding 'All Gentlemen are requested to attend.'
(Abstracted from *Horses, Lords and Racing Men*, Fergus D'Arcy, p. 2.)

By 1754, Bellewstown Races were so successful that a second meeting was held in October, the highlight of which was a substantial 500 guinea-a-side match race between Sir Patrick Bellew's horse and a horse called *Black and All Black*. Sir Patrick's horse was beaten. A two-horse race was a tremendous attraction and by this time the fame of Bellewstown's racing had spread, so that it became one of the leading racecourses in Ireland and England. Huge crowds gathered on race-days, and by 1771, the race meeting had stretched to six days, with generous purses of fifty and sixty shillings as prizes. County Meath was home to numerous country gentlemen, who nearly all hunted and raced. Competition was keen among them as to who owned the best horse and many two-horse matches were decided at Bellewstown racecourse. Bellewstown became a fashionable venue, with visitors coming from far and wide, many of them spending the week in the houses of the local gentry and attending the Assemblies at night in Drogheda.

Bellewstown Races 1771
On Monday the 24th June will be run for over the Course of Bellewstown, a purse of 50 pounds, given by the Town of Drogheda, for any Four-Year-Old Horse, Mare or Gelding to carry 8st. 7 lb.; 3 lb. to be allowed to mares and geldings, Bridle and Saddle included, the best of three 2-mile Heats. On Tuesday the 25th June, a purse of 50 pounds, for any Six-Years-Old Horse etc. to carry 9st.; 3 lb. to be allowed to mares and geldings, Bridle and Saddle included, the best of three 4-mile Heats. On Wednesday the 26th June, a purse of 40 pounds, for any Five-Years-Old Horse etc. to carry 9st.; 3 lb. to be allowed to mares and geldings, Bridle and Saddle included, the best of three 3-mile Heats. On Thursday the 27th June, a purse of 50 pounds, for any aged Horse etc. to carry 9st. 3 lb. to be allowed to mares and geldings, Bridle and Saddle included, the best of three 4-mile Heats. On Friday the 28th June, a purse of 25 pounds, given by the Town of Drogheda, for real Hunters that never won anything but a Hunter's Plate (Matches excepted) etc. to carry 12st.; Bridle and Saddle included, the best of three 4-mile Heats. On Saturday the 29th June, a purse of 60 pounds, to be run for Weight for Age; Four Years Old to carry 7st.; Five Years Old 7st. 12 lb.; Six Years Old 8st. 8 lb.; Aged 9st.; Bridle and Saddle included, the best of three 4-mile Heats. The Qualifications of the Horses etc. to be certified under the Owner's Hand or upon Oath if required. And the winning Horse of any of the above prizes is not allowed to start for a second. All horses etc. to run according to the King's Plate Articles and to be shewn and entered with Mr William Collins, Clerk of the Course, eight clear Days before the respective Dates of starting or running, paying one shilling in the pound entrance, if a subscriber, if not, double, at his house on the Race Ground. Each Horse Sec. To pay Five shillings for scales and straw, the winning horse to pay double. Double Entrance at the Post. Every wine tent on or near the Race Course, to pay Half a Guinea to William Collins and every Ale Tent, five British Shillings. Good ORDINARIES (dinners) every day in Drogheda at the House of Pat. Baratt and John Sydal. ASSEMBLIES each night.
Horses etc. to start each Day precisely at One O'Clock, Grooms are desired to be ready at the Hour, as the Clerk of the Course has positive orders to start those that appear at the hour appointed. All disputes to be determined by the Judges that shall be appointed each day. *(Faulkner's Dublin Journal* June 1771*)*

A set of damask linen, value twenty-five guineas, was donated by the Corporation of Drogheda as a prize in 1775.

In 1781 the racecourse was used as a gathering place, not for horses, but for the Volunteers, protesting about the severity of the Penal Laws. 3000 troops assembled, consisting of cavalry, infantry and artillery. In charge of the artillery was James Napper Tandy, then residing in Lisdornan, Bellewstown. Other prominent locals were Thomas Trotter, of Duleek House, Hamilton Gorges of Kilbrew, Ashbourne, Graves Chamney of Plattin Hall, and John and James Montgomery-Lyons of Beaulieu House, all leaders of the local Volunteer movement.

A £50 Plate was given by the Town of Drogheda in 1788 for hunters that were 'fairly hunted, to the death of two brace of foxes or four brace of hares last season.'

Some of the attendance in the carriage enclosure at Bellewstown in the early 1900s

BELLEWSTOWN: THE NINETEENTH CENTURY

Bellewstown Races in 1864
There was a time when the races on this far-famed spot extended over a week and when they were patronised by the highest in the land, whose glittering array of equipages, as they flanked the ropes or dashed through the long stretch of beautiful heath that stretches away on every side, gave an extremely picturesque touch to the scene. On the day all the turmoil and troubles are dashed aside for the nonce. The shopkeeper or employer lets business mind itself and the artisans pour forth en masse and seem, while washing away the smoke or dust of the workshop and casting off their working clothes, to be determined to leave their cares behind them. And then the bustle and excitement in Drogheda, which lies on the principal route to the Hill. Vehicles of almost every description come in from the rural districts and continue on their course without pausing. Hackney cars, their number vastly increased by an influx of jarveys from other parts of the country, line the streets, stalwart men and blooming girls crowd round. All is haste, a well of a car is lifted, a hamper containing an abundance of good things is crammed in, seats are taken and away flies the car which is rapidly followed by another and another and so on, while their places are being as quickly filled by those who have left their passengers off at the course. From the time Drogheda is left behind until the journey's end you are continually encountering and pursuing long lines of vehicles, which in themselves indicate the various positions filled by their occupants. Here whirls along the fine lady and rich gentleman in their splendid carriage, the trappings glittering in the brilliant sunshine, the horses, as if conscious of their superiority, arching their necks and dashing on proudly. Then we have the hackney car, occupied by the artisan or comfortable shopkeeper, the joyous laugh and merry jest shortening the distance, as it were, to their destination. Then we have the numerous rude and primitive vehicles which carry the rustic portion of the motley mass. There is the far-famed Irish low-backed car, rattling and jogging along, the passengers, light-hearted and happy. A sack of straw or hay is placed on each side to mollify the jolting, for the labourer and his cherry-lipped lass, who both exhibit a redundancy of health and spirits. As we ascend the eminence, the vast and ever increasing panorama of wood and pasture, mansion and cottage stretching away beneath and around is interesting and beautiful in the extreme. But on gaining the table-land of the course, the traveller is wrapt in wonder at the magnificent prospect that bursts upon his vision. Miles away, to the left, as we debouch from the Drogheda road, lies the Irish Sea, blue as ether, as seemingly calm and undisturbed as the cerulean sky above and beyond. The view embraces the Boyne viaduct and Millmount in Drogheda, which stand out in bold relief, commanding the attention of all. We now proceed to take a view of the race course. About the centre are ranged upwards of a score of roomy tents and in passing those we are attracted by the incessant noise of voices, mingled with roars of laughter and the inspiring sounds of violin or bagpipes. In these the younger and more light-hearted portion of the assemblage passed the greater part of the day on the 'light fantastic toe.' Pursuing our way, as we pass between the ropes which bound the course in the vicinity of the Stand House and along on either side, cars and carriages are thickly ranged, containing an array of beauty and fashion such as is seldom met with. Dull our care would be, if we didn't hear the incessant beating of the drums from the show boxes. There were five of those temples of the legitimate drama to claim the attention of young men from the country. The rival claims seemed to be settled by which could make the greatest din. Decidedly, the best part of the performance was to be seen outside, where the companies put on all their strength. A real nigger, none of your lamp-black articles, put himself to the unnecessary trouble of grimacing in order to increase his evident ugliness, while he yelled a negro melody, to the delight of the gaping outsiders, while a ballad singer claimed their attention by detailing how a love-lorn

maiden appealed to her lover: 'Arrah, Jemmy, dear, don't murder me, or else I'll surely die.' Commingling her description of historic incidents was an ancient lady with a strong Munster 'brogue' who presided over a peep show and told those who paid for a peep: "Now look to the right and you have a splendid view of northern Ireland, divil a bit of me knows where, and here you have Mount Vesuvius and on the right you see nobility in great grandeur and splendour while the country is going to blazes. There you have Pharoah's daughter finding Moses by the river Nile. There he is and a thundering fine boy he is and there's General McClellan and the American army." And next you have roulette tables, inviting the ingenuous youth to stake five on the blue and eight on the yellow. Aunt Sally has gone, leaving a legacy in the shape of broken glass and china behind her, which will ensure her blessings in the shape of curses. Drogheda Argus 9 July 1864

Racing in the nineteenth century

The success of racing at Bellewstown continued into the nineteenth century, much assisted by the securing of a prestigious King's Plate for the meeting. In March 1800, George Tandy, former Lord Mayor of Drogheda, headed a successful delegation to petition the Duke of Richmond for an annual grant of £100 towards the races, leading to the foundation of the annual King's Plate race with a prize of 100 guineas, held by Bellewstown thereafter. This race began that same year.

On Thursday, June 30, was run over the course of Bellewstown, His Majesty's Plate of 100 guineas, weight for age, 3-mile heats and was won by Mr Daly's *Cornelius,* 5 years old and carrying 8st. 9 lb. (*Faulkner's Dublin Journal* July 1800).

Bellewstown had its first racing under *Rules* in 1805, when Drogheda Corporation supported it with a Plate. In the following year, Bellewstown racegoers enjoyed two meetings, with Robert Hunter acting as judge. Although there was no meeting in 1807, Bellewstown secured a King's Plate of 100 guineas in 1808.

Racing was becoming more and more popular throughout Ireland in the nineteenth century. The proliferation of race meetings and the resulting clash of fixture dates for the various racing venues, that had become established all over Ireland, led to intervention by the Turf Club. In order to regulate fixtures, in October 1812 the Stewards of the Turf Club announced:

We very strongly recommend to the different stewards of the following meetings that they should appoint them to take place at the following periods:

Bellewstown	last full week in June
Derry	Monday, second July
Carlow	tenth July
Westport	twenty-third July
Tuam	first August
Monaghan	second week in August
Maryborough	week after Curragh September Meeting
Birr	week after Maryborough

(*Horses, Lords and Racing Men* (1991) by Fergus D'Arcy p. 35-36)

The *Drogheda Conservative Journal* reported that 'a numerous and elegant assemblage of beauty and fashion thronged the course' in 1823, adding that 'as great a concourse as we have witnessed on a similar occasion assembled.' Despite the crush and the high spirits engendered by a day off work, 'great order and regularity were observed by the peasantry, whose peaceful and unoffending demeanour was gratifying.' The reporter also commented on the private matches which took place alongside the official programme.

'Amongst the many private matches which took place, none appeared to afford more entertainment than that between Messrs Mansfield and Guscock and although the result proved unfavourable to the latter gentleman, yet the determined manner of riding he exhibited excited universal admiration and called forth loud and reiterated applauses.'

The Bellewstown Races (Paddy Whack, *The Drogheda Journal* 1828)
I upon you all will frown if you go to Bellewstown
Consider well the dire disgrace of being parties to a race

The company with whom you'll mix is not worse beyond the Styx
Fiddlers, pickpockets and women, in the gulf of ruin swimmin'

Blacklegs, jockeys and rakes, looking at the Pentland Stakes
Betting, gambling and dice, whiskey, peppermint and vice

Loss of money, broken heads, Consumption got from unmade beds
Drunken blackguards shooting cats, balls lit up with mutton fats
Tough beefsteaks at derepas, and thousands of etceteras

This lecture surely should persuade you or I'll think the devil made you
Win my smile, avoid my frown, go not, I say, to Bellewstown

Go not I say to Bellewstown!

BELLEWSTOWN RACES.

The races of Bellewstown commenced on Monday se'nnight and terminated on Friday. The course each day exhibited a numerous assemblage of beauty and fashion; but on Thursday the crowd exceeded any that had been witnessed there for many years. The Stewards were indefatigable in the discharge of their duties, and by their excellent management, the utmost order and regularity prevailed throughout the week.

The Ball on Thursday evening exceeded that of the preceding year. It was opened by Anthony Dopping, Esq., and Mrs. Vesey. One hundred and sixty persons sat down to a splendid supper, which afforded every delicacy that could be procured, and fully sustained the character for good taste heretofore enjoyed by the Misses Smith. Dancing was resumed after supper, and kept up with great spirit and vivacity until four o'clock; and the whole passed off in a manner to give general satisfaction.

Freeman's Journal **30 June 1824**

In 1825, a huge crowd attended the races, as it was a special holy day in Drogheda and the workers had a free day. 'No accident occurred. This being St Peter's Day, every vehicle was in requisition and a multitude of beings went to witness the amusement'. 'Enough cannot be said for the exertions of our worthy stewards and for their attention to those rules of order and etiquette which have always been so strongly adhered to by them.' Again in 1826, the stewards were praised by the reporter from the *Drogheda Journal*. 'The Stewards were highly efficient, owing to their judicious arrangements, no accidents occurred and all the parties, high and low, seemed anxious to obey their dictates.' Improvements to the layout of the race-course, with more space allotted to the carriages and other vehicles, were greatly appreciated by the race-goers.

The Stewards afforded general satisfaction to the subscribers particularly from the arrangements made by railing in a portion of the course for their carriages and cars, a plan which we recommend should be continued in future. The police, under the command of Captain Henderson, attended the course daily but we are happy to say their interference to preserve order was not required.
(*Drogheda Conservative Journal* 26 June 1830)

Results
Monday 27 June 1825
Sweepstakes of 10 guineas, half forfeit with £60 added. For Hunters, Race-horses admitted; 2 mile heats.

Mr Hunter's b.c.	*Telemarque*	6st 12 lb.	1	1
Mr Logan's b.g.	*Dandy*	7 st 12 lb.	0	2
Mr Hunter's b.c.	*Hypocrite*	7 st 8 lb.	0	3
Mr Callwell's br.m.	*Mary Anne*	8 st 3 lb.	3	4
Mr Battersby's b.f.	*Jemima*	6 st 6 lb.	0	0
ch.h	*Irishman*	10 st 0 lb.	pd fr	

Results Tuesday 28 June 1825
Sweepstakes of £5 to which stewards added £40 for Hunters that never started for a racing Plate or Sweepstake

Mr Stackpoole's	*Violet*	1	1
Mr Dowdall's	*D O'Connor*	4	2
Mr Evoy's	*Miss Stephens*	3	5
Mr Fitzpatrick's		2	4

Mr Ferguson's horse bolted the first heat. Three others started but not placed.
Sweepstakes of £3 for Hunters and Racehorses 2 mile heats
Won by Mr Callwell's *Mary Anne* beating five others.

EXPENSES OF RACING AT BELLEWSTOWN IN 1829

On the 17th of June 1829, James Farrell, who managed the Curragh stables of Martin J. Blake, Brook Lodge, Tuam, a steward of the Turf Club at the time, recorded his expenses for his entry of Blake's horses at the Bellewstown Meeting in June and submitted his account to Blake. It took until December 1839, ten years later, after exhaustive pleas by his solicitor, for Farrell to be paid by Blake for these expenses and many more, amounting to the huge sum of £1,656 8s 6d:

Expenses to Bellewstown	3s 4d
Back to Clane	3s 4d
Turnpikes	4d
Carriage Hire	15s 0d
Entrance for two horses	£2 2s 0d
Clerk of Course	10s 0d
Scales and Straw	£2 1s 0d
Certificate	5s 0d
Livery	10s 0d

Dress-making for Bellewstown Races (27 June 1846 *Drogheda Argus*)
On Wednesday morning, the 25th, as some girls were proceeding at an early hour to milk their cows, their attention was attracted by a large brilliant and very extraordinary object, in a field belonging to Mr Richard Sheil of Ardcath. When they ventured to approach this very novel object, they perceived, as they thought, that it was constructed of beautiful striped silk. What splendid dresses it would make for the next races of Bellewstown. Most carefully was the prize conveyed to the nearest cabin, where after due deliberation, the scissors were applied, when lo! the secret came to light, the gas escaped, the balloon collapsed and their hopes, like fairy gifts, faded away, for the striped silk was metamorphosed into striped oil paper! It is supposed that this balloon is one of those 'pilots' as they are called, that ascended those few evenings past from the Rotundo Gardens (Dublin), as the wind was favourable for its conveyance thence to Ardcath, sixteen miles from Dublin.

SPORTING INTELLIGENCE.

BELLEWSTOWN RACES.

THIRD DAY—WEDNESDAY, JUNE 25.

Sweepstakes of Ten Pounds—half forfeit—Fifty Pounds added by the Stewards, for Hunters, Race Horses admitted. Two mile heats.

Mr. Batersby's Sloven, 3 yrs. old, 6s. 2lb.	1	1
Mr. Caldwell's Queensberry, 5 yrs. 7 t. 7lb.	2	2
Mr. Hunter's Fisherman, 5 yrs. 7st. 10lb.	3	3

THURSDAY, 26.

King's Plate of 100 Gs. for Irish bred Horses—weight for age.—Three mile heats.

Mr. Blake's Napoleon, 4 years old, 8st. 10lb.	1	1
Mr Savage's Mount Loftus, 5 yrs. old, 8st. 8lb.	2	dr.
Mr. Caldwell's Johnny Bush, 6 yrs. old, 8st. 13lb.	3	dr.

SAME DAY.

Handicap Race—For Hunters, Race Horses admitted. Two mile Heats—£25 added.

Mr. Savage's Mount Loftus, 5 yrs. 9st. 0lb.	1	2	1
Mr. Batersby's Seaford, aged, 8st. 7lb.	2	1	2

FRIDAY, 27.

Sweepstakes of Two Pounds, to which the Stewards added the Ladies Purse and 20l., for the beaten Hunters of the week; Race Horses admitted.

Mr. Caldwell's Queensberry, 5 yrs. old, 9st.	1	1
Mr. Seeley's Johnny Bush, 6 yrs. 8st. 10lb.	2	2
Mr. Osborne's mare paid.		
Mr Bodkin's Peverel, paid.		

The Course each day was crowded with an immense concourse of people from the surrounding counties. Several handsome equipages, filled with lovely and fashionably attired females, graced the scene. The Stewards were indefatigable in their exertions to preserve order and obtain for the spectators an extended view. We are gratified in stating that no accident of a serious nature occurred.

The Ball on Thursday night was opened by Mr. VESEY and Miss CODDINGTON. Nearly 300 persons sat down to supper. The tables were covered with all the delicacies the season afforded, and reflect great credit on the taste and liberality of the Misses SMITH. Dancing was resumed and continued with life and spirit until five o'clock. The rooms were not perfectly cleared until six. Several Officers of the 17th Lancers from Dundalk were present.

Our Subscribers, whose accounts have been repeatedly furnished of late, are earnestly requested to discharge their arrears. We trust this appeal will be more successful than our applications by post have hitherto been.

BIRTHS.

At Crawfordsburn, near Bangor, at the seat of her father, William S. Crawford, Esq., the Lady of Henry B. Coddington, of Old bridge, Esq., of a son and heir.

In Eccles-street, Dublin, the Lady of Charles James Adams, Esq. of Retreat, in the County Cavan of a son.

MARRIED.

In the Chapel of Ease at Moy, by the Rev. Charles Richardson, and afterwards by the Rev. Mr. Montagne, Parish Priest of Clonfecle, Mr Henry Griffin, to Miss Marks, sister to Benjamin Marks, Esq , both of Moy.

Advertisement for Bellewstown Races in *The Drogheda Journal*, June 1828.

Abd-el-Kadir

Henry Osborne, of Dardistown Castle, in 1829, bought a dam being used to draw a stage-coach, hoping for a win at Bellewstown races. She won her race and went on to produce nine foals, one of them, a gelding of 15 hands, was called *Abd-el-Kadir*, known locally as *Little Ab*. In 1850, *Abd-el-Kadir* won the Aintree Grand National, ridden by Chris Greene. The following year, *Abd-el-Kadir* won the Grand National again, this time partnered by Jimmy Abbot, making *Little Ab* the first horse to win the double in the history of Aintree.

Joseph Osborne

By 1834, the meeting at Bellewstown was being described as 'always being of more or less benefit to the shopkeepers of Drogheda', and as offering 'a few days of rational amusement to the town and the neighbourhood.' But it was acknowledged that if it were not for the exertions of young Joseph Osborne of nearby Dardistown Castle, the races could not have taken place at all. Joseph Osborne had recently become a member of the Turf Club and had exerted himself to ensure that as many noblemen and gentlemen, as well as important officials of the Turf Club attended the meeting that year. As a result, the racing of 1834 was most successful.

Bellewstown Races attracted such a diverse range of punters that, by 1835, Osborne felt that a small police presence was necessary to preserve law and order. He wrote to the Chief Secretary at Dublin Castle:

> Myself and brother stewards think it advisable for the preservation of order at the ensuing Bellewstown Races to apply for a small body of Police; not that we apprehend any resistance, but merely to have them as a check on some disorderly individuals who, last year, attempted to disturb the meeting. (State Papers SPOI/CSORP 1835/2014)

Osborne was correct to enlist police protection, as can be clearly seen from the section on Law and Order at the Races at the end of this chapter. It would be 1849 before a permanent police presence was established in Bellewstown, with the opening of the R.I.C. barracks early in that year. Joseph Osborne continued his letter by boldly issuing an invitation to the new Lord Lieutenant to attend the races, assuring him that 'nothing would be wanting on our part or the part of the gentry of the county, in paying him every respect.' So with due pomp and ceremony, the Lord Lieutenant, Constantine Phipps, 2nd Earl Musgrave, attended Bellewstown Races on Thursday 25 June 1835, to witness the running of the King's Plate of 100 guineas.

The Lord Lieutenant attends Bellewstown races Thursday 25 June 1835

This day his Excellency the Lord Lieutenant arrived at the course at two o'clock, in a carriage and four, escorted by a party of the 15th Hussars, and accompanied by Captain Williams and the Hon. R.E. Boyle, Aides de Camp. A stand was prepared for the accommodation of his Excellency to which he was led by the Earl of Howth and the Stewards, Joseph Osborne and J. Young, Esqrs. A handsome marquee was erected in which the Lord Lieutenant partook of refreshments. His Excellency returned to town after the second race – he was enthusiastically cheered on his arrival and departure by the populace. (*Drogheda Journal*)

Osborne's gratitude to the Lord Lieutenant for attending the Bellewstown races was expressed by his naming a horse *Maria* after the Marchioness of Normanby, the Lord Lieutenant's wife. The filly was the produce of *Sir Hercules* and Osborne's senior mare *The Pleiad*.

Attending the races in Bellewstown in the late 1960s, locals Joe Sherry, Mary Kirwan, Sadie Littlefield, Eileen Murphy, Eileen Murphy, Betty Kirwan.

In 1843, Nicholas Boylan of Hilltown House, Bellewstown was local big land-owner, manager of the Gormanston estate, judge and personal friend, fund-raiser and devoted supporter of Daniel O'Connell. He also found time to act as secretary and treasurer of the racecourse. He inserted the following advertisement for the races in the *Drogheda Conservative Journal* in June of that year:

Bellewstown Meeting
Stewards Sir W. Somerville, Bart., M.P.
        The Mayor of Drogheda
        Henry Grattan Esq., M.P.
        Matthew Corbally Esq., M.P.
        John Preston Esq.
        Nicholas Boylan Esq.

Tuesday June 27
1. Trial Stakes
2. Drogheda Tradesmen's Plate
3. A Scurry Sweepstakes

Wednesday June 28
1. Bellewstown Stakes
2. The Selling Stakes
3. Consolidation Stakes
4. The Queen's Plate

Nicholas Boylan Esq., Treasurer, Hilltown House, Drogheda.
N.B. From a deficiency in the Fund necessary to support the Bellewstown Meeting, the stewards will be obliged to charge for admittance to the course as follows: For every 4-wheeled carriage 2s/0d; for every 2-wheel car or gig 1s/0d; Saddle Horses 0s/6d.
(*Drogheda Conservative Journal* 24 June 1843)

Bellewstown Races 8th July 1863

In 1863 the Stewards were The Mayor of Drogheda; the Most Noble the Marquis Conyngham; Rt. Hon. Viscount Gormanstown; M.E. Corbally, Esq., M.P.; James McCann, Esq., J.P.; Richard Langan, Esq., Treasurer; Hon. Secs. – Robert B. Daly, Esq.; Edward Markey, Esq.; Mr Robert J. Hunter, Judge; Mr J. H. Coatsworth, Clerk of the Course and Handicapper.

There was a capital day's racing at Bellewstown Hill and the course from the late rains was in capital running order and the attendance was good.
The Steward's Plate for two and three years old. Weight for Age. Two yrs old 7 st.; three yrs, 9 st. 4 lb. About three-quarters of a mile. 3 sovs each, 30 added. Winners in 1863 of any race, value £50, 5 lb. extra; if two of that amount, or any of £100, 7 lb. extra. Horses that have started for any race in 1863 and not won, allowed 5 lb.; 3 lb. allowed to fillies and geldings. Six subscribers or no race. The winner to pay 3 sovereigns to the fund. £1 10s entrance.

Captain Machell's *Bacchus* by *Claret,* 2 yrs, 6 st. 9 lb, D. Wynne   1
Captain Jones's *Iced Cream,* 2 yrs, 6 st. 9 lb., M. Conolly   2
Marquis of Conyngham's *Armstrong's Gun* 3 yrs, 8 st. 13 lb., Murphy   3
Mr Kinsella's *Colleen Rhue,* 3 yrs, 8 st. 10 lb., Midgley   0
Betting 6 to 4 on *Bacchus*; 5 to 2 agst *Colleen Rhue*

Bacchus jumped off with the lead, but soon resigned it to *Armstrong's Gun,* who carried on the running to the distance when *Bacchus* passed him, and won easily by three parts of a length; two lengths between second and third. *Colleen Rhue* bolted soon after starting and was pulled up.

The Drogheda Tradesmen's Plate of 80 sovs, added to a Handicap Sweepstakes of 5 sovs each. The winner to pay 5 sovs to the fund. Second horse to save his stake. 2 miles.

Mr Keary's *Outcast,* 6 yrs, 7 st. 8 lb, Dunne	1
Mr Longfield's *Redskin,* 4 yrs, 8 st. 10 lb., Moran	2
Mr Conlan's *Toggery,* 6 yrs, 8 st. 4 lb., Lennon	3
Mr Disney's *Troublesome,* 4 yrs, 8 st. 3 lb., D. Doyle	4
Lord de Freyne's *O'Connell,* aged, 8 st., J. Doyle	0
Mr Flood's *Emotion,* 4 yrs, 7st. 7lb., M. Murphy	0
Mr O. Cummin's *Harvey Birch,* 3 yrs, 7 st. 4 lb., D Wynne	0

The Misses Maura and Eithne Callan, Drogheda, Mrs Noel Ryan, Piltown and Mrs B. Lenehan, Navan, enjoyed the races in the 1950s

Letter to the editor of the Drogheda Argus 1863

Dear Editor

In all your life did you ever see a people can jump on their legs so quick as the Irish? – Three bad years nearly knocked the fun out of all of us; the wet blanket, sure enough, covered us from head to heels; but glory be to Providence, when things come to the worst, they always mend; and now let me ask you, did you ever enjoy anything with better heart than Wednesday and Thursday at the Hill?

The devil such racing, courting, pick-nicking or dancing, went on these twenty years, as on the Queen's Plate Day. The sun shone, the girls laughed, the horses, the creatures, felt it too, it was very hard to hould them on the road or anywhere; and as for the boys, it's very well some of them kept in their skins. Just to give you a little example of what I mean – Coming down the course on Thursday, I spied a most grave and staid burgess of our wonderful borough – when at home you might as well ask him for a drop of his precious blood as a coin of the realm – he was bantering with a strawberry lass from Dublin, who was persuading him he was a regular lady-killer, in exchange for a sixpence, when he turns around and catches me by the hand. 'Well Mick', says he, 'do you want money for the races?' 'Does a duck swim?' says I, when to my bewitchment, he takes a half sovereign and spins it at me as if it was a rap halfpenny; he then claps me on the back and earnestly and affectionately takes me into Byrne and Sheridan's tent where he placed the disposal of all the viands in that renowned restaurant at my command.

The weather was delightful, the running was good – good humour prevailed; beauty, love and hope joined on this festive occasion; the sons and daughters of Erin, as seen on Thursday, from the highest to the lowest, would bear comparison with any similar gathering on the face of this earth; and as they clapped their hands in exultation and made the valleys resound with joy, there was no mistaking the wish upon every lip: long life to Old Bellewstown Hill and the sky over it.

Yours etc.

The Opening of the Dublin and Drogheda Railway Line 1844
The completion of the railway line from Dublin to Drogheda in 1844 transformed Bellewstown racing, bringing droves of people from Dublin to enjoy a day out in the country at the races. The *Drogheda Conservative Journal* in June 1844 reported that 'the attendance on the Hill was never so large in our recollections.' The newly established railway company, the Dublin and Drogheda Railway Company, in 1844 became the first railway company in Ireland to sponsor an Irish horse-race when it added 25 sovereigns to a Handicap Sweepstakes of 5 sovereigns at Bellewstown on June 26, 1844. In 1845 and again in 1846, the same company provided 40 sovereigns for the Railway Stakes at Bellewstown, after which it gave up its sponsorship, although it continued to carry hundreds of patrons down to Drogheda each summer for the Bellewstown festival. However, following improvements to the racecourse, in 1874 the Railway Company greatly assisted the rejuvenation of racing in Bellewstown by its generous decision to ferry horses by train to and from the meeting, free of charge.

1847
Not even the outbreak of the worst famine Ireland had ever experienced interfered with the running of Bellewstown races, although the meeting was postponed for a few months, on account of the 'miserable state of the country'.

Bellewstown Races Tuesday September 21st 1847
Stewards: Sir William Somerville, Bart., M.P.; Matthew E. Corbally, Esq., M.P.; Henry Grattan, Esq., M.P.; the Mayor of Drogheda; Nicholas Boylan, Esq.; J.J. Preston, Esq.,; and Captain Armitt. These ever far-famed sports were, under a variety of circumstances, chiefly dependant on the miserable state of the country, postponed from the usual period this year, but we are extremely glad to find that no fears can now be entertained of the withdrawal of the Royal Prize from a locality so pre-eminently distinguished not merely for good racing but a 'world of fun' besides. The results achieved by a very few gentlemen in getting up the races at this late period of the year and under circumstances not a little discouraging, proves that by securing the active interference of half a dozen thorough sportsmen for the next season to undertake the management – including of course those who were efficient this year, the ancient prestige of Bellewstown shall be fully restored.
(*Drogheda Journal*)

Ladies at the Races

From the very beginning of racing at Bellewstown, ladies came along to enjoy the day and to see and be seen. The reporter from The Drogheda Journal enthused about the crowds of women attending the races in June 1823.

A numerous and elegant assemblage of beauty and fashion thronged the course, particularly on Wednesday, upon which day as great a concourse as we have witnessed on a similar occasion assembled. *(Drogheda Journal* June 1823)

In June 1825, the same reporter wrote of the women arriving by carriage.

The course was fashionably though not numerously attended. Yesterday the Hunter's Plate attracted number: several handsome carriages, gigs and jaunting-cars filled with the lovely daughters of the Emerald Isle met the eye in all directions.
(*Drogheda Journal* 1825)

Race-goers on the steps of Hilltown House 1908

By 1878 the Turf Correspondent got carried away and broke into verse when thinking of the lovely ladies at Bellewstown:

The reserved stand was well patronised by lady visitors and during the afternoon not a few pretty toilettes (dresses) and prettier faces graced the scene. Indeed the presence of so many ladies so tastefully and so elegantly attired, combined with the lovely scenery which delights the eye in every direction around this popular resort of the race-goer reminds one not a little of the unrivalled attractions of Glorious Goodwood. The ladies dresses at the Ducal meet may be richer but not more graceful than those worn by our fair sisters at home:

Lesbia wears a robe of gold, but all so close the Nymph hath lac'd it
Not a charm of beauty's mould presumes to stay where Nature plac'd it.
Oh! My Nora's gown for me, that floats as wild as mountain breezes,
Leaving every beauty free to sink or swell as Heaven pleases.

In personal charms Erin's fair daughters need yield to those of no other clime, and the fairest and loveliest of which our land can boast were well represented today. But this is a dangerous subject for a Turf writer to enter upon and descending from such a high elevation we must be content to take a lower level and treat of matters speculative, horsy and prosy. (*The Drogheda Journal* June 1879)

However, by the end of the nineteenth century, the reporter from *The Irish Sportsman* was rather taken aback by the brazen betting of the ladies. He wrote in 1889,

I fear the bishops and deans would be thrown into a bad state of health had they heard some of the ladies asking for the good things and getting their 'bit on' after one of the many oracles had imparted the desired information. The weakness of speculation seems to have firm hold of the sex. And I see by a Society journal that Irish servant girls have taken to backing horses!
(*The Irish Sportsman* July 1889)

Entertainment at the Races
1853 We would be doing an act of injustice were we to omit noticing the admirable arrangements of Simcock's Refreshment Marquee. Indeed with the exception of the favourable state of the weather on the first day and the large and fashionable attendance on the second, it was the *only* redeeming feature of the meeting. Everything was of the best quality – served in the most tasteful style – and at a cost, not exceeding the ordinary charges in town. Disappointment in the racing transactions was to some extent atoned for by this circumstance; if the eye was not feasted, there was ample provision for the 'inward man' and many and loud were the gratulations that the attention and liberality of Mrs Simcocks had supplied such an acceptable set off to the scanty 'bill of fare' on the turf. (*Drogheda Journal*)

It was traditional to provide some light musical entertainment for the crowds during the races. In 1825, for example, the scene was enlivened by an elegant band which in the intervals between the heats played many delightful airs. The classical music programme, outlined below and performed by the officer band of the 18th Hussars under the baton of Bandmaster J. Englefield, must have added greatly to the festive air of the Races. The programme was as follows:

Quadrille, New Promenade, Coote
Overture, Schubert, Suppe
Waltz, Visions d'Amour, Delbruck
Fantasia, Patience, Sir A. Sullivan
Waltz, Gloire de Dijon, Andrew
Mazurka, Azalien, Faust
Ballet music in William Tell, Rossini
Waltz, Fedora, Bucalossi
Gallop, Wie der Wind, Faust
God Save the Queen.

Many people brought a picnic hamper in their carriage to the races or at least some bread and a hunk of cheese to ward off the hunger pangs. Bellewstown was ideally situated on a height, suitable for fashionable picnics, while many landowners had their own tents or marquees. Others were wined and dined by the Stewards in special marquees. Some people, however, who had neglected to provide themselves with a lunch, were more than a little disgruntled by the catering provided to the general public, as observed here by the racing correspondent of *The Irish Sportsman and Farmer*

' The general arrangements are now excellent but we must mention that for a meeting of this class the refreshment department was about the worst that ever came under our experience. This is a matter that inflicts considerable hardship on the general public and is well worthy the attention of all racing executives.'

The starving journalist, however, heaped praise on 'the capital dinner provided each evening at the Drogheda Railway station refreshment rooms. This came as a boon and a blessing to many after the miserable style in which the catering was done at the course'.

1840 'The races commenced on Tuesday and the attendance both of sporting characters and nags was superior to that of last year – the several prizes being closely contested. There were a number of tents on the ground and, as a proof of the progress of Temperance in this district, we need only say that there were several of them erected for the 'Teetotallers'. A great concourse of people attended each day and the greatest order and good humour prevailed. The interest taken in getting up these races by Nicholas Boylan Esq., Hilltown, the acting steward, is highly creditable to that gentleman.'
(*Drogheda Argus*)

BELLEWSTOWN RACES

MICHAEL GARRETTY begs leave to inform his
Friends and the Public, that he will have a good and
comfortable ORDINARY at his House each day of the
Meeting – Dinners bespoke for select parties, to be ready
at any hour they may appoint. The Ordinary to be served
immediately after the last Race each day.
Dinners bespoke......................2s 0d.
Ordinary................................1s 6d.
N.B. – Gentlemen intending dining at Garretty's will please leave their names
at the bar, at or before 3 o'clock.
Bellewstown Hill, 23rd June 1827.

Late night entertainment

In the evening, after a day spent at Bellewstown, a select crowd dined and danced in Drogheda. In 1823, the Drogheda Conservative Journal reported that

The Ball on Thursday evening exceeded any of preceding years. The ballroom exhibited a striking coup d'oeil. Dancing commenced at an early hour and was kept up with great spirit and vivacity until five o'clock. One hundred and seventy-five persons sat down to supper and the evening was passed off in a manner to give general satisfaction.
(*Drogheda Conservative Journal* July 1823)

Again, in 1826, two hundred patrons had supper together in Drogheda. The nightly entertainments were even better in 1830, as again described in the Drogheda Journal:

The Ordinary was numerously and respectably attended in the Mayoralty House, the use of which was kindly afforded by the mayor for the purpose. We feel that Mr Murphy could not be sufficiently compensated for his exertions and liberality in supplying superabundantly. Every luxury and comfort that the season could afford was stocked. The wines, consisting of claret, champagne etc. were supplied by Mr Smith, wine merchant of the town and were of the choicest description. The Ball on Thursday in the Mayoralty House was attended by nearly two hundred and fifty persons. Dancing commenced at half past ten and was kept up by a succession of quadrilles until an early hour in the morning. The ordinary and the supper were supplied by Mr Murray, 37 Nassau Street, Dublin.
(*Drogheda Conservative Journal* July 1830)

RACE BALLS

THE MISS SMITHS beg to acquaint their Friends and the Public that there will be a BALL and SUPPER, at the Mayoralty House on Tuesday the 24th and Thursday the 26th and a CARD ASSEMBLY on Wednesday the 25th and Friday the 27th of June next; when they hope for that Support they have so amply experienced.

Admittance to Balls and Suppers:

Ladies 5s 5d. Gentlemen 11s 5 ½ d

Admittance to Card assemblies

Ladies 2s 2d Gentlemen 3s 3d.

Drogheda Journal 31st May 1806

Bellewstown Races

If a respite you'd borrow from turmoil or sorrow
I'll tell you the secret of how it is done:
Tis found in this version of all the diversion
That Bellewstown knows when the races come on.
Make one of a party whose spirits are hearty
Get a seat on a trap that is safe not to spill
In its well, pack a hamper – then off for a scamper –
And hurroo! For the glories of Bellewstown Hill.

On the road how they dash on, rank, beauty and fashion,
It Banagher bangs, be the table o'war;
From the coach of the quality, down to the jollity
Jogging along on an ould low-back car,
Though straw cushions are placed, two foot thick at the least
Its concussive jollity to mollify still;
O! The cheeks of my Nelly are shaking like jelly
From the jolting she gets as she jogs to the Hill.

Arrived at the summit, the view that you come at
From etherealised Mourne to where Tara ascends
There's no scene in our sireland – dear Ireland, old Ireland –
To which Nature more exquisite loveliness lends.
And the sod 'neath your feet has a memory sweet,
The Patriot's deeds, they hallow it still;
Eighty-two's Volunteers (would today saw their peers!)
Marched past in review upon Bellewstown Hill.

But hark! There's a shout 'The horses are out!'
Along the ropes on the stand, what a hullabaloo!
To auld Crockafotha, the people that dot the
Broad plateau around are all off for a view.
'Come Ned, me tight fellow! I'll bet on the yellow!'
'Success to the green! Faith we'll stand by it still!'
The uplands and hollows, they're skimming like swallows,
'Til they dash by the post upon Bellewstown Hill.

In the tents play the pipers, the fiddlers, the fifers,
Those rollicking lilts such as Ireland best knows;
While Paddy is prancing, his colleen is dancing
Demure, with her eyes quite intent on his toes.
'More power to you Mickey! Faith your foot isn't sticky,
But bounds from the boards like a pay from a quill!'
O! 'twould cure a rheumatic – he'd jump up ecstatic
At the 'Tatter Jack Walsh' upon Bellewstown Hill.

Oh! Tis there, 'neath the haycocks, all splendid like paycocks –
In chattering groups that the quality dine
Sitting cross-legged like tailors, the gintleman dealers
In flattery spout and come out mighty fine
And the gentry from Navan and Cavan are having
Neath the shade of green trees, an exquisite quadrille –
All we read in the pages of pastoral ages
Tells of no scene like this upon Bellewstown Hill.

Getting there

1860 *'About twelve o'clock, the rain ceased to pour and the sun began to shine out delightfully, thus promising the timid that they might prepare to enjoy the sports of the day. Soon cars were ready and along the road from Drogheda to the hill were to be seen every species of vehicle from the light and graceful dray to the low-backed car, bearing many a bright-eyed Mary. Those itinerant characters who frequent fairs, thimble-riggers, trick o' the loop men, and even the proprietors of that aristocratic game 'Aunt Sally' were to be seen treading their way along with their gambling apparatus on their back; also were to be seen those proprietors of baskets of fruit, ginger-beer and half-and-half, who quench many a poor fellow's thirst with their delicious beverages. It was certainly a grand sight to view the course from the stand-house and see it so immensely thronged with persons, who, moving in masses, seemed like the waves of the ocean, when influenced by the winds. The number of carriages was extremely large but there were not so many ladies upon the course as on the previous day, owing to the threatening character of the morning. The running throughout the day was admirable, as good as any we ever saw before.'*

In the days before motor-cars in the nineteenth century, people travelled to Bellewstown races on foot, by carriage or cart, or quite often by train from Dublin and thence by horse and cab out to Bellewstown. The journalist from *The Irish Sportsman and Farmer* described his journey from Dublin to Bellewstown in 1870 as follows:

Bellewstown Races are events which are annually awaited with considerable interest by the great majority of racing men as well as by a large number of the citizens of Dublin. To the latter they afford two very agreeable holidays in the midst of all that is lovely in "Royal Meath". A trip to Drogheda en route to the famous Hill of Bellewstown is in every respect most enjoyable, particularly at this time of the year, when Nature on all sides presents her most charming appearances. Even to the most careless observer, it would have been plainly visible that some unusually interesting matters were about coming off, as through town early this morning a deal of bustle and hurrying was visible. No doubt the regatta at Kingstown contributed largely to this busy aspect which affairs partook of. But the large number of vehicles which were to be seen making their way for the road to Drogheda showed plainly that 'the races' were the more popular event. For some days before, parties were formed who elected to enjoy the pleasure of a drive, more than a trip by rail, and as the day was one in every respect suited to a drive, we fancy those that chose that mode of conveyance had good reason to congratulate themselves for patronising the jarvies. The Dublin and Drogheda Railway Company arranged to run a 'special' at 9.15 and at that hour a comparatively small number assembled at the Amiens Street Terminus, to find a few carriages attached to a cattle-train! Not a doubt of it, reader. This was the accommodation provided. As is usual, the train travelled at a sickening rate and in truth it was most disagreeable to be jogging along at the pace we went. The only thing that counteracted the effects of these abominable arrangements was that the country looked on every side, most delightful. On one side the Bay of Dublin was so beautiful to view that it was worthy of the pencil of any artist; on the other, the crops were all in their emerald hues and would truly be worthy of a visit from our agricultural editor. Until we had neared Laytown there were no visible signs of people making their way to the racecourse, but after that station being passed there might be seen batches of

people, attired in their holiday costume, wending their way to the 'scene of action'. After an exceedingly slow journey we arrived at Drogheda about 11.30; and at that place were an immense number of cars awaiting the arrival of the train to convey parties to the course. Never have we passed through a more charming country than that which separates Drogheda from the racecourse. In the first place the most beauteous hedgerows clothed in their summer garb are passed; and outside these is to be seen some of the richest land that 'Royal Meath' can boast of. It would have been vain for us to try to describe the scenery for we confess a hand more skilled than ours would be requisite. The course is situate about four miles from the town and therefore necessitates about a three-quarter's hour drive. Through the kindness of Mr Boylan a considerable distance is saved by his allowing parties to cross through his demesne on the private drive. Were it for no other purpose, a visit to this place would well repay a journey. The road leads from the demesne directly onto the course. Messrs Byrne and Sheridan had a splendid marquee erected, where the best drinks were dispensed throughout the day. Near the principal entrance was a marquee, in which the stewards had a first-class luncheon and to which a large number of their friends were invited (including ourselves).
The Irish Sportsman and Farmer July 1870

Racing at Bellewstown in the 1970s

Fashionable Society at Bellewstown Races 1868
(from the Drogheda Argus)

In the lawn near the haycocks, all splendid like paycocks
In chattering groups, see the quality dine
Sitting cross-legged like tailors, the gentlemen dealers
In flattery spout and come out mighty fine
And the gentry from Navan and Cavan are having
'Neath the shade of green trees, an exquisite quadrille
All we read in the pages of pastoral ages
Tells of no scene like this upon Bellewstown Hill.

Taking the attendance on both days, never perhaps has there been a more fashionable and crowded company assembled on the memorable old course.

Amongst those who attended were: - Lords Gormanstown, Bellew, Howth; Benjamin Whitworth M.P.; James Matthews J.P., Mount Hanover; Gustavus W. Lambert, Beauparc; Thomas Greene, Mayor of Drogheda; Francis Brodigan, J.P., Piltown House; James Gartlan, Mountjoy Square, Dublin; John Gradwell, J.P., Platten House; J.P. Culverwell, Secretary Dublin and Drogheda Railway; Wm. Whitworth, Drogheda; Peter Verdun, J.P., Bayview House; Dr. R.J. Kelly, West Street, Drogheda; J.J. Gormley, T.C., Drogheda; Eugene Clarke, Drogheda; Captain Gardiner, SI; E.J. Bannon, R.M.; Dr. McIver, Ardee; Messrs Thunder, Lagore; Barnwall, Crofton, Drogheda; Nicholas Hammond, Malahide; James Boylan, CE, Dublin; Edward Markey, PLG, The Naul; Capt. Holt, 21st Fusiliers; R. Smith, Newtown; J.D. Matthews, Mount Hanover; R. Gradwell, J.P., Dowth; Major Smith, Annesbrook; J.S. Healy, solr., Drogheda; Nicholas Flynn, ditto; R. Clinton, ditto; Malachi Hussey, M. Kelsh, Fennor; F. Osborne, Smithstown; Wm. Morton, Drogheda; O. Osborne, Rosnaree; Thos Boylan, J.P., Hilltown House; J.A. Flanagan, T.C., Drogheda; Peter O'Neill, Secretary Drogheda Steam Packet Company; M. Saurin, PLG; J.A. Clarke, Drogheda; P.V.M. Saurin, Garballa; G. Butterly, sub-sheriff, Drogheda; John Hughes, Proprietor *Argus*; Messrs Halfpenny, Ardee; Joseph Dean, Drogheda; M. Reynolds, Thos. McEvoy, Balmarino House; O.J. Carragher, Dardistown; Dr Darby, Duleek; Thos Simcocks, T.C., Drogheda; Captains Branigan, Bowden, Drogheda Staem Packet Company; Henry Garnett, Greenpark; Thomas Jackson, Lisnaboe; E. McDonough, Drogheda; Patk. Kenny, Rocksavage; James Levins, T.C., Drogheda; M. Butler, Brownstown; J. Murphy, Drogheda; N. Ennis, Claremount; John Costello, *Argus,;* J.W. Greene, Cooper Hill; P. Reilly, Drogheda; James Bradley, ditto; J. Kelly, T.C., ditto; M. Jones, Dublin; Thomas Mullen, Navan; M. Verdun, solicitor; Dr. Adrien, Julianstown; J. Manley, Tara; Mr Jones, Drogheda; Gordon Jackson, L. Kieran, Ashville; A. Ternan, Janesville; J. Dolan, Dysart; Thos. Dolan, Ardee; Dr. Moyle, Navan, etc, etc. (*Drogheda Argus* July 1868)

Daniel O'Connell at Bellewstown Racecourse 15 April 1843

Having successfully achieved Catholic Emancipation in 1829 by peaceful means, Daniel O'Connell turned his attention to the question of Repeal of the Act of Union, which had been passed in 1800. He began by holding a series of large peaceful political rallies and declared 1843 to be Repeal Year. These mass rallies were known as Monster Meetings. Daniel O'Connell was actively supported in his endeavours by the Catholic clergy, who exhorted their parishioners to support O'Connell, pay the 'Repeal Rent' and attend the monster meetings. Nicholas Boylan of Hilltown House, Bellewstown was soon to the forefront of the Repeal Movement, not alone in Bellewstown where he collected the Repeal Rent but also in Co. Meath. He chaired the monster meetings in Navan and Drogheda and also in Bellewstown, as can be read below in the extract from *The Nation* newspaper. Approximately twenty-five thousand people turned out to greet Daniel O'Connell in Bellewstown, despite the terrible weather. One hundred thousand had been expected if the day were fine. The Liberator addressed the people from the balcony of the pub, which was then owned by Geraty's. Nicholas Boylan welcomed the large assembly, as did several priests from the area. Nicholas Boylan subsequently lost his job as Justice of the Peace because of his political involvement, despite his pleas that he was entitled to protest peacefully. Daniel O'Connell, in one of the grand gestures for which he was famed, arranged for a collection to be taken up in support of Nicholas Boylan's stance and a silver salver was presented to him in late 1843, inscribed as follows:

To Nicholas Boylan, Esq. of Hilltown House, by 1100 Repealers to record their disapprobation of the Arbitrary conduct of the government in dismissing him from the commission of the peace, for exercising the constitutional right of the subject and to endite their admiration of his eminent private virtues as well as his high-toned public spirit and uncompromising patriotism, A.D. 1843.

(This salver is now in the collection of the National Museum, Collins Barracks)

GREAT REPEAL DEMONSTRATION AT BELLEWSTOWN

Notwithstanding the extreme inclemency of the day, the meeting at Bellewstown on Sunday was a great and glorious demonstration. During the previous night, and the early part of the morning, the rain fell in torrents and in the brief intermissions, the sombre appearance of the sky gave no promise of a continued improvement; yet, with all this, the brave and hardy men of the district around the hill were there in tens of thousands, more, the district around Bellewstown comprises within it perhaps a greater number of wealthy, intelligent, bold and independent gentlemen farmers than any other district in Ireland – they were there in hundreds – and as a still stronger evidence of the extent to which the question of Repeal has spread and become fixed in the public mind, not only was the large room in the rear of the platform crowded by the highly respectable and decidedly beautiful ladies of this district, but even many of them who could not find room within, remained upon the platform during the proceedings, notwithstanding the heavy pouring of rain which continued with little pause during the entire day. Between showers, the sun shone brilliantly upon the beautiful landscape around the hill.

About ten o'clock, the Trades of Drogheda, preceded by an excellent band, marched in procession from Drogheda, with their gorgeous banners, and accompanied by a long train of jaunting cars and an immense train of pedestrians. They proceeded to Clinstown, the residence of Peter Arnold, Esq., where the Liberator slept the previous night. About one o'clock, the cortege proceeded from Clinstown to the Hill. As they neared the hill, the clouds were overcast and a most tremendous shower of hail and rain fell; yet such was the enthusiasm of the people, that the line of march was unbroken until Mr O'Connell's carriage reached the platform, where he was received with the most thrilling applause. As soon as the storm had somewhat subsided, Mr O'Connell presented himself on the platform and was greeted with renewed cheers. The platform selected was the large and permanent balcony attached to Geraty's on the hill. Around it was an immense mass of people, numbering between 20,000 and 25,000 persons; and we have no hesitation in stating that if it was not for the inclemency of the weather, 100,000 would have been there. On the platform we observed, besides the Liberator, N. Boylan, Esq. J.P.; Rev. Mr Hanlon, P.P., Duleek; Rev. T. Matthews, C.C., Duleek; Mr Walsh, P.P., Rosnaree; Rev. J. Langan, P.P., Ardcath; Rev. T. Langan, C.C., Ardcath; Rev Mr Breggy, C.C., Stamullen; Rev. Mr Smith, Balbriggan; Rev. Mr Kealy, Navan; Rev. Mr O'Farrell, diocese of Kilmore; Messrs T. Boylan, Pat Mathews, Peter Mathews, William Boylan, L. Ball, P. Langan, Nicholas Markey, Owen Markey, R. Langan, Alderman Rogers, Alderman Simcox; Joseph McCann, T.C.; P. Boylan, T.C.; William Campbell, T.C.; Daniel Brady, T.C.; P. Kelly, T.C.; P. Byrne, T. C.; James Levine, T.C.; J Connolly, T.C.; P. Conway, T.C.; A Keapock, T.C.; M. Walsh, T.C.; P. Verdun, T.C.; J. Collins T.C.; S. Drew, T.C.; J. Finnegan, T.C.; P. Ward, J. Langan, J. Curtis, Robert Daly, Dr Lynch, P. Arnold, W. Arnold, W. Grace, R. Sheil, T. Brennan, Robert Horgan, P. Gargan, T. Gargan, P. Gargan, J. Gargan, J. Markey, W. A. McKenna, P. Markey, Bernard Finegan, Edward S. Markey, L. Frayne, J. O'Brien, N. Fitzpatrick, P. Ennis, John Carty, J. Ennis, R. Ennis, B. Ennis, jun., J Curtis, J. O'Neill, J. Ketch, M. Hughes, J. Hughes, Thomas Johnson, and many other gentlemen, besides a number of beautiful ladies.

On the motion of P. Mathews, seconded by the unanimous roar of the multitude, N. Boylan, Esq., J.P., Hilltown House was called to the chair. Thomas Boylan moved that John Gargan Esq. be appointed to act as secretary to the meeting. Carried unanimously. Mr Gargan returned thanks for the honour of being appointed secretary at so numerous and so respectable a meeting. Mr Boylan, on being called to the chair, addressed the meeting in eloquent and appropriate terms and concluded as follows: 'We have this day collected 50 pounds and some odd shillings Repeal Rent and the Liberator will take this sum with him as a proof of the sincerity of the men of this part of Meath, in the cause of their country's salvation.' Mr Boylan sat down, loudly applauded. The Rev. Mr Hanlon came forward to the front of the platform and was loudly cheered. He proposed the first resolution. The Rev. Mr Mathews, in seconding the motion, said 'Mr Chairman and fellow-countrymen, in seconding the resolution just proposed, allow me to express my sincere delight at witnessing this day, your peaceful determination to unite with your countrymen in the constitutional struggle for national independence. That resolution requires but little argument to secure your concurrence in its being carried. Turn your eyes wherever you will, go to the north or the south, the east or the west of the island and you will also discover innumerable sorrowful evidences of the fatal effects of the union. (Cries of hear, hear). Let us rally then around the standard of our victorious leader, let us enrol ourselves members of the Loyal National Repeal Association. He is still able to conduct us to another glorious victory, though the snow of more than sixty years is upon him, he still possesses the vigour of manhood, and the blush of health still mantles on his cheek, and you will join in a fervent prayer, may it long continue. (Cheers) Let all dissension and differences among Irishmen be based in a generous oblivion and let us reflect in our lives the words of the poet.' (*The Nation* 15 April 1843)

BELLEWSTOWN RACE MEETING
Pony Race Objection 1886

The following is a copy of the objection lodged with Mr Brindley.

I object to Small Fry being declared the winner of the Pony Plate at Bellewstown, on the ground that she was not qualified according to the article, she not having been trained for the last six months in Ireland. I also object to Modesty, who was placed second, on the ground that she did not carry the proper weight. And I claim the race for Lady Superior, who was placed Third by the judge. Leonard Sheil 38, Lr Leeson Street.

Improvements at Bellewstown in the 19th century

The racing correspondent of the *Irish Sportsman* newspaper acted almost as an inspector down the years and felt it was his duty to draw attention to the deficiencies of the racecourse, constantly chivvying the committee to improve conditions for the punters. He commented on the weather, the dust, the train-service, the habit of the jarveys of over-charging race-goers travelling from Drogheda station to Bellewstown; he decried the late starting times, the quality of the food on offer, the length of time the special took to get from Dublin to Drogheda, the height of the steps on the stand, the tan on the road etc. He constantly called for an improvement in the entertainment being offered, describing flat racing as being old-fashioned, the heats-system as lacking in entertainment value etc. And the Race Committee responded well to these criticisms, each year improving somewhat on its previous performance.

In the nineteenth century, the stewards's committee was dominated by titled gentlemen originally but as racing moved into the 1870s, a more professional approach was adopted. The *Irish Times* reported in May 1864 that only two men had shown up at a meeting called to arrange that year's racing in Bellewstown, Mr Thomas McCann and Mr R.B. Daly. These two gentlemen had shouldered almost the entire responsibility for the previous year's meeting, which had been very successful. However, because of the apathy exhibited towards the organisation of the races, they feared that the 1864 fixture might have to be abandoned, with the subsequent withdrawal of Her Majesty's Plate. This disaster was obviously averted. Gradually specific jobs emerged and became more specialised. A Mr R. Hunter acted as judge for many years, every other duty falling on the shoulders of the secretary. The first manager, Mr T.G. Waters was appointed in 1871, followed in 1873 by the appointment of a starter, Mr Osborne. Shortly afterwards in 1876, the first handicapper, Mr G.T. Watts-Waters, came on board and this was followed by the appointment of a clerk of the scales, Mr L. Hunter. In 1878, Mr G.T. Waters combined the jobs of manager and clerk of the course. While the management committee became more professional, at the request of several owners, the course distances were also altered to suit all classes of horses.

Bellewstown Hill 1868
This stand is raised upon the famous hill of Crockafotha and commands without exception the grandest and most inspiring views to be had from any other spot, even in our lovely island. Many travellers ascend the Alpine range and seek in vain upon foreign shores to find anything like the rich, varied and ennobling scenes which stretch out panorama-like before the eye as one stands upon this magnificent elevation. The bays of Drogheda, Carlingford and Dundalk – the Newry and Mourne mountain ranges – the counties of Louth, Down, Monaghan and Cavan – the rich plains of Meath, with Tara of the Kings – the fine Dublin county, taking in the background the mountains of Wicklow – the beautifully dotted seaboard, all beneath the feet of the enraptured beholder. Add to all this the table-cloth laid, the lamb, the salad and the darling girls – who is the misanthropic wretch who will be absent from the Hill this year; and who is the sordid being who will refuse a sovereign when called upon next week?

A new concrete stand was erected, replacing the old rickety timber structure, substantially funded by Lord Gormanston, for whom the stand was re-named. The foundation stone of the Bellewstown stand was laid by Mr Alan McDonogh, the famous owner-trainer-rider. The silver trowel with which he worked the mortar in which the foundation stone was laid had the names engraved of the patrician supporters of Bellewstown at the period when the building was decided on. Following this, the horses ran to the left of the posts, following the English system, whereas before they had run to the right.

In 1872, a steeplechase course was mooted in order to breathe new life into racing at the course, by offering mixed programmes. Due to the determination of organiser, T.H. Simcocks, Henry St. George Osborne of Dardistown Castle was brought on board and also Captain Edward Preston of Silverstream, Gormanstown. A steeplechase with 'water jump' was introduced to Bellewstown, the new course being planned and laid out by the two gentlemen. By 1873, the courses, paddocks, enclosures and stakes had been transformed in Bellewstown, as can be seen below in the excerpt from the *Irish Sportsman*.

July 1873: *The new steeplechase track is about 150 yards more than a mile and contains seven obstacles, constructed on the most approved plan. Directly opposite the stand is what is called a double wattle fence, with a bullfinch or row of bushes in the centre; then after rounding the police turn, comes a brook and hedge- a really charming fence but not quite up to its name, as the supply of water was rather deficient, not to be wondered at in such an elevated position; then after crossing the road is a bank, succeeded by an English hedge, followed by two more banks with a fly to finish over. This course lies outside the flat and had to be altogether put in order with levelling etc. Regarding the flat course, which is too well known to need description, the only change that has been made is making a straight TYC, about four furlongs. The stand and ring remain the same as usual and it need hardly be said are large and convenient, containing weighing room, dressing rooms and accommodation for the press.*
(*Irish Sportsman* 26 July 1873)

1885 saw a sweeping change of stewards, heralding a new dawn for 'old-fashioned Bellewstown'. Changes again took place in 1889 when the course was recast, a strong paling was erected and the site of the stand changed. Having laid out so much money on essential refurbishments, the racecourse now faced financial ruin and there was doubt in 1891 that a meeting would take place at all but this threat was averted by the combined efforts of Thomas Boylan, the local big landlord, Thomas McCann, local miller, and the Mayor of Drogheda. A successful meet of the Tredagh Polo Club was held on the racecourse on Sept 28 1891. An eye-witness described it as a great success 'with a brilliant sun and clear sky, visitors enjoyed the lovely view which is to be had from this elevated spot, close to the Boylan residence.'

Again in 1893, Bellewstown was described as being but a shadow of its former self with not enough prize money to attract runners, while 1894 had a wretchedly small crowd and the racecourse committee faced possible bankruptcy. It was a difficult time for the landed gentry, who were fighting to hold on to their land, they had more to think about than horses and race-meetings. Mr George Gradwell, secretary, brought a great amount of energy to bear on the work of restoring to the gathering some of its old-time prestige around the turn of the century. Things improved in 1899, with Mr Gradwell in charge, who arranged for a special train to carry horses from the Curragh free of charge. A row of loose boxes was erected at the back of the paddock and the apartments utilised for a weighing room and the press-room were enlarged.

Towards the end of the nineteenth century, the code of rules elaborated by the Turf Club became stricter and was more strictly enforced.

At the August meeting of 1887, Bellewstown local stewards were dissatisfied with the conduct of jockey G. McAuliffe in the running of the Meath Plate, when his highly fancied horse *Expectation* came in second. Not satisfied in his riding of the horse, they appealed to the Turf Club to investigate the matter. In a very harsh judgement, the Turf Club subsequently suspended the jockey from riding at all meetings and warned him off all recognised courses for life.

The Opening of the Gormanston Stand: Drogheda Argus 11 July 1868

Heretofore the stand was a rickety-looking skeleton structure of timbers, propped and stayed, but which any day might come down with a run. Its position besides was not that which afforded the best view to be had of the course. Crockafotha Hill excessively competed with it as a view-point. The new stand takes what we may call the natural position for such a structure and crowns Crockafotha. The stand is a solid structure, built of stone faced with cut-stone, the old Hill itself must slip its firm base before this can yield. The view from the stand is truly magnificent. The stand was numerously patronised on both days. Numbers of ladies, well representing the beauty, rank and fashion of Meath and Louth, occupied the space set apart for them. We do not wonder that they left their cars and carriages to enjoy the grand scene which the view from the stand afforded and the occasional exclamations of admiration must have been very gratifying to the gallantry of the gentlemen who originated this great improvement in the course. Before the Tradesmen's Plate was run for on Wednesday, the stand was formally opened. Mr Daly came forward and addressing Lord Gormanston, who presided over the ceremony, spoke as follows:

'My Lord Gormanston, the Committee of the Bellewstown Races have, with the full concurrence of the stewards, placed upon me the high honour and great privilege of asking your lordship to open this Stand, by breaking upon it a bottle of champagne and naming it for all time the Gormanston Stand (cheers). In doing this we feel that under any circumstances, considering the position that the eminent and noble family that you worthily represent hold in this part of the country, we should only be carrying out the wishes of all classes of the people (hear, hear). But there is more to be said on that subject, we feel the revival of those time-honoured sports owe a great deal to your lordship personally (cheers). When some few years since there were great fears that Bellewstown Hill Meeting was in great danger of languishing, your lordship rushed to the front and helped materially, by your powerful interest and generous aid to pull us through. The result is this day a glorious meeting and the establishment, let us hope, for ever of old Bellewstown.' (cheers)

Lord Gormanston in neat and eloquent terms acknowledged the high compliment paid him and made a happy reference to the cordial union of classes, from the peer to the peasant which meetings like Bellewstown did much to cement. He said that that good feeling and better understanding of each other should be fostered and encouraged for the good of our common country and this was his earnest hope. He expressed his readiness on all occasions to use his best exertions to preserve the prestige of the Bellewstown meet. After a few other appropriate observations, his lordship concluded amidst cheers from the assemblage. A bottle of champagne was then broken by his lordship and as the old sod drank up the sparkling tipple, the ceremony of the opening was declared complete.

Law and Order at the Races
Despite the large crowds in attendance at the races during the nineteenth century, there was very little trouble, with the stewards and the police doing their utmost to ensure that all passed off peaceably.

The great order and regularity was observed by the peasantry whose peaceful and unoffending demeanour was gratifying. The Police under the command of Captain Ellis conducted themselves with the strictest propriety and attention...Enough cannot be said for the exertions of our worthy stewards and for their attention to those rules of order and etiquette and which have always been so strongly adhered to by them.
Drogheda Conservative Journal 28 June 1823

Collier the Robber's Beer-Tent at Bellewstown Races
Michael Collier was born around 1785 in Lisdornan, close to Bellewstown. He began in a small way, robbing orchards and stealing hens. By 1807 he was already notorious as a highwayman and had a gang of about twenty-five supporters from the Drogheda, Bellewstown and the Naul areas, with surnames like Arnold, Maguire, Loughrey, Ludlow, Woods, Griffin, Murray and McDaniels. Mail-coaches travelling from Dublin to Drogheda would come through Swords, down along through Ballyboughal and the Naul, on through Lisdornan and on to Drogheda and Dundalk. They came at a set time, every morning, afternoon and night, so it was easy to know when to expect a coach and lie in wait for it to arrive.

Collier's gang regularly robbed the stage-coaches that plied the roads between Dublin, Drogheda and Dundalk and were a scourge to the Post Office, attempting to get the mail through safely from Dublin to Derry by mail-coach. His daring exploits earned him the title of Collier the Robber and he was lauded as a folk-hero. People regarded him as a Robin Hood type person and it was said that he often gave money to poor people to help them out. Bellewstown people were very loyal to Collier and often hid him and his gang from the soldiers who were searching for them. But they also say that Collier was an informer and saved his own life by giving information of importance to the police.

He was eventually caught and given the choice of transportation or joining the army, so he joined the British army and went with the army to South Carolina. Others in the gang were shot, hung or transported for life. Collier was pardoned, after his stint in the army, and made his way back to Drogheda. He bought a pub in Ashbourne and every year set up a beer tent at Bellewstown Races, where he did a roaring trade, capitalising on his unsavoury reputation. For years he lived off the stories that grew up around his exploits. He died of cholera on 13 August 1849 and is buried in an unmarked grave in the Chord cemetery in Drogheda.

STICKMEN MEET THE BILLY SMITHS AT BELLEWSTOWN RACES

The *Drogheda Journal* reported on what could have been a very nasty brawl at Bellewstown Races in June 1835, when two gangs, no doubt fuelled with drink and keen to prolong the excitement of the day's racing, squared up to each other. Disaster was averted by a fine speech by Mr Smith of Annesbrook who managed to persuade the trouble-makers to back off and return home peaceably.

The Stickmen from the County of Louth and the neighbourhood of Drogheda and the part of Meath, north of Bellewstown had arranged to meet their implacable foes, the Billy Smiths from Garristown and the surrounding district, at Bellewstown race-course. However the precautions adopted by the magistrates prevented a conflict which would inevitably have resulted in the loss of life.

Several hundred Stickmen assembled in a body and exhibited a most formidable appearance. They were then addressed by Mr Smith of Annsbrook, who represented in forcible terms the folly and wickedness of their proceedings. The Stickmen received Mr Smith with cheers and said that their object in assembling was to protect their friends from the assaults of the opposing faction, the Billy Smiths. After long speeches from several magistrates and influential gentlemen and also a display of considerable police force, the Stickmen consented to withdraw from the racecourse peaceably. But they remained for some time on Beamont Bridge in order, as they said, to protect the Drogheda people on their return home from the races and to prevent attack on Mr. Joseph McCann's workmen, similar to what had occurred last year when several people were severely beaten. The Billy Smiths remained on the south side of the Hill, detached in small parties, but ready and prepared to unite together at a moment's notice. Had it not been for the extremely judicious and determined conduct of the magistrates in persuading the Stickmen to go home, the collision of the two factions would have been dreadful. Later that evening several persons were beaten in the neighbourhood of Drogheda on their return from the racecourse.

Drogheda Journal 27 July 1835

A huckster at Bellewstown races at the end of the 19th century (Boylan collection)

Pickpockets at Bellewstown Races
(Based on Convict and Transportation Files, 1844-45, National Archives Dublin.)
Dublin chimney-sweep, John Kavanagh, had a bad day at Bellewstown Races on 26 June 1844 and it was nothing to do with the horses. The previous day, he had come down by train on the newly opened railway line to Drogheda and had been unfortunate enough to be arrested by Captain Despard on pick-pocketing charges but had been released due to lack of evidence. Not so, on the 26th, when James Langan Esq. reported that his silk handkerchief had gone missing. Kavanagh was re-arrested and found to have nine silk handkerchiefs of different patterns on his person, one of them being Langan's. He could not give a satisfactory explanation for this and so was hauled before the magistrate in Navan at 7 a.m. on the following morning. The magistrate considered the evidence. James Langan was not aware of his handkerchief being stolen, he just knew that it was missing. He could not identify Kavanagh as the taker of the handkerchief. Indeed, he might have dropped it. However, Kavanagh had nine silk handkerchiefs on his person, so he could even be the leader of a gang of pickpockets, speculated the magistrate, John Plunkett. Police Sub-Inspector John Locke testified that 'a swarm of pickpockets came down to the races' and were closely watched by police. The occupation (chimney-sweep) of the defendant was scrutinised. As the police report of the time stated, 'considering that his trade, that of a sweep, gave him admission into dwelling houses when there were opportunities of stealing valuable property, they transported him.'

John Kavanagh went as a convict to Australia for seven years for stealing a silk pocket-handkerchief at Bellewstown Races in 1844. He was unfortunate in his timing, as a mere nine years later the practice of transportation for petty crime was abolished. In 1844, John Kavanagh was one of fourteen men in Co. Meath to be sentenced to transportation. Transportation was viewed as a means of getting rid of trouble-makers and potential trouble-makers with minimal cost to the state. Of these fourteen men transported from Trim Jail, nine were convicted of larceny, receiving the minimum sentence of seven years, one was convicted of sheep-stealing, receiving a sentence of ten years, and one man was convicted of perjury. The others were probably involved in the agrarian unrest of the time, their crimes being 'arson', 'ribbonism' and 'intent to murder' and therefore received the maximum sentence of transportation for life, as a deterrent to others involved in secret societies.

What happened to John Kavanagh, chimney-sweep and pickpocket? The 1901 census shows that the Kavanaghs were no longer living at 4 Red Cow Lane, Arran Quay, Dublin, their address in 1844. Possibly Maria Kavanagh and her two children joined her husband in Australia, as did many of the convicts' wives. Kavanagh would only have been twenty-six years when his sentence was concluded, Maria only twenty-eight years. Many convicts went on to lead happy and successful lives in Australia.

1865 *On no other occasion does Drogheda give itself up so unreservedly to enjoyment. No one for a moment who can at all get away thinks of remaining at home. Every description of jaunt, barring a hearse or a wheelbarrow, is brought into requisition. Along the route the line of vehicles seems endless. A peculiar feature of the road is the number of rustic equestrians, some well-mounted, who speed past, like estafets to a battle-field; some on huge plough horses, the heavy cavalry in this irregular charge, go ahead at unwonted speed, promoted by cudgel-persuaders; while many, astride steeds of angular build, have to use much circumspection to prevent them from a sudden devotional attitude. The number of low-back cars which used to be so diversifying a feature of the road to the Hill, was not this year so marked as in former ones.*

Bellewstown: Stewards in the Nineteenth century

1805-6 Hamilton Gorges, Esq; Henry Garnett, Esq; Henry M. Ogle Esq; George Tandy, Esq, Treasurer; Henry Chester, Esq; Ralph Smyth, Esq.; Thomas Richards, Duleek, Clerk of the Course.

1811-12 Rt. Hon. Col. Foster, M.P.; Sir Marcus Somerville, M.P.; J.R. Hunter, Esq., Judge

1823 Wm. Meade Smyth, Esq., M.P.; The Mayor of Drogheda; Henry Garnett, Jun., Esq.; James Gernon, Esq.; Philip Elliott, Clerk of the Course; Mr Ball of the Curragh, Judge.

1829 to 1842 Earl of Bective; Lord Langford; Sir M. Somerville, Bart; Sir P. Bellew, Bart.; Mayor of Drogheda; Col. Pratt; Henry Meredith, Esq.; M.E. Corbally, Esq.; James Medlicot, Esq.; James Gernon Jnr., Esq'; Charles Dillon, Esq.; Thomas Blennerhassett-Thompson Esq.; Henry Osborne Esq.; Nicholas Boylan, Esq., Treasurer; Mr Bell, Judge; Philip Elliott, Clerk of the Course; John McGeough, Clerk.

1843 to 1860 Sir William Somerville, Bart., M.P.; The Mayor of Drogheda; The Earl of Clonmel; the Marquis Conyngham; the Hon. E. Bellew; Henry Grattan Esq., M.P.; Matthew E. Corbally, Esq., M.P.; John Preston, Esq.; Captain Armitt; Captain Townley; Captain Williams; J. McCann, Esq.; James Mathews, Esq.; Patrick Casey Esq.; R.M. Bellew, Esq., M.P.; C. Fortescue, Esq., M.P.; Nicholas Boylan, Esq. Treasurer; Patrick Mathews, Esq., Treasurer, R. Langan, Esq., Secretary; Mr McNerney, Judge; Mr Coatsworth, Clerk of the Course and Starter.

1861 to 1869 The Mayor of Drogheda; Most Noble Marquis Conyngham; Rt. Hon. Viscount Gormanstown; the Earl of Charlemont; Viscount Massereene; M.E. Corbally, Esq., M.P.; Hon E. Bellew; Benjamin Whitworth, Esq., M.P.; James Matthew, Esq., J.P.; M. O'Reilly Dease, Esq., M.P.; J. McDonough, Esq.; G.W. Lambert, Esq.; T. Gerrard, Esq.; Colonel Tayleur; Captain White; Captain Townley; Captain Williams; Richard Langan, Esq., Treasurer; T. Owens, Esq., Treasurer; R.B. Daly, Esq., Secretary; E. Markey, Esq., Secretary; Mr Robert J. Hunter, Judge; Mr J.H. Coatsworth, Clerk of the Course and Starter.

1870 to 1880 Mayor of Drogheda, the Most Noble the Marquis Conyngham, Right Hon. Viscount Gormanston, Lord Killeen; Thomas Whitworth Esq., M.P., Benjamin Whitworth Esq., Hon Jenico Preston, Hon E. Preston; J.H. Preston Esq; N. Ennis Esq.

M.P.; M.E. Corbally Esq. M.P., J.J. Preston Esq., J.P., G.W. Lambert, Esq., J.P., James Mathews, Esq., J.P., M. O'Reilly Dease, Esq., M.P., H. St G. Osborne, Esq., R. Percival Maxwell, D.L.; Capt. J.F. Montgomery; Mr W.C.McCausland; P. O'Rafferty, Esq., Agent Hibernian Bank, Drogheda; Thomas Gerrard Esq., Hon Treasurer Thomas Owens, Esq., Hon Treasurer and Secretary; Hon. Sec. R.B. Daly Esq., Hon. Sec. Thomas H Simcocks, Esq. V.S., Drogheda; and Mr R.J. Hunter, Judge; Manager and clerk of the course Mr T.G. Waters C.E; Mt T.G. Watts-Waters, Manager and Clerk of the Course; Starter, Mr Osborne; Starter, Major Williamson; Starter, Mr R.H. Long;

1880-1892 Marquis of Drogheda; Lord Killeen; Right Hon. Viscount Gormanston, Earl of Fingal; Sir Thomas Hesketh, Bart.; Mr P.M.V.Saurin, M. Betagh and John Fox-Goodman; Manager, H. St G. Osborne, Esq., J.J. Preston Esq., J.P., Mr. R.D. Jameson; Hon. E. Preston; Capt W.De Salis Filgate, J.P., M.F.H.; Messrs J. O. Trotter, M.F.H.; B. Woods J.P., R.B.Daly, J.P., Thomas Mathews, J.P., J.F. Gradwell, J.P., A. Tiernan; M Thomas Leonard; P.J. Dunne, J.O. Trotter; M.F.H.; P.Casey Connolly, ex-mayor; Mr T Boylan Esq; Cyril B. Lambart; Hon Treasurer, Mr W.C.McCausland; Hon Treasurer, Mr T.B.Lillis, Munster Bank, Drogheda; Hon Treasurer, Mr A Milne; Judge, Mr R.J. Hunter; Handicapper Mt T.G. Watts-Waters, Manager and Clerk of the Course, Mr T.G. Waters, C.E.; Starter,Major Butler; Manager and Clerk of the Course and Starter, Mr T. Brindley; Clerk of the Scales, Mr L. Hunter.

1893 to 1900 The Mayor of Drogheda; Marquis of Conygham; Sir Thomas Hesketh, Bart.; the High Sheriff of Drogheda; H. Tunstall Moore; Mr P.M.V.Saurin, Thomas Leonard, W. de S. Filgate; Patrick Mathews; P.J. Dunne, E.D. J. N. Pollock; J.O. Trotter; M.F.H.; P.Casey Connolly and Mr T Boylan. Hon Treasurer, Mr A Milne, Starter, Mr F. Ruttledge; Judge, Stakeholder and Clerk of the Scales-Mr Thomas Brindley; Clerk of Course and Handicapper Mr R Waters.

Local Paddy Bellew, who rode a winning horse in Bellewstown in June 1900, enjoying his retirement.

BELLEWSTOWN: THE TWENTIETH CENTURY

Defying the wind and the dust and the cold, setting off in style for Bellewstown in 1907
(Boylan collection)

Racing continued into the twentieth century under the energetic stewardship of Mr George Gradwell. It was now comparatively easy to get to Bellewstown, with the increased use of bicycles, motor-cars and motor-bikes as well as the continuation of carriages, traps and side-cars, alongside public transport like trains and buses. In 1908, people who travelled by motor-car were pitied because of the heat and the blinding dust stirred up by the motor traffic on the road. Increase in the use of motor-cars was leading to parking problems by 1916. Meanwhile those fortunate enough to live in Dublin could get a first class return train ticket for 6s/6d or 3s/6d for a third class ticket. The Great Northern Railway Company also served Ardee, Dunleer, Oldcastle, Kells and Navan, putting on specials from these stations to the races. The *Meath Chronicle* commented on the inventiveness of a Mr Crockett of Ballymagarvey who, in 1919, converted one of his motor-lorries into a 'comfortable charabanc' which held 45 holiday makers. They gladly paid five shillings for the return trip to Bellewstown races and such was the demand for transport that Mr Crockett made two fully-loaded trips to the Thursday races. Hackney cars were charging £1 for a similar return journey. Thompson's Charabancs also ran specials to Bellewstown with a return fare of ten shillings.

Others, who barely knew how to drive, got into the festival spirit by hiring a car and motoring down from Dublin for the races. One such group of race-goers, in the days long before drink-driving regulations back in the early years of the twentieth century, had a good day at the races and then set off for Dublin. Barely yards from the racecourse, the driver lost control on the very steep Hilltown Hill and careered into a group of pedestrians. The car's occupants included Mr P.J. Brophy, the owner of *Final Effort*, who won the Meath Plate at the meeting; Mr Brophy jun., Mr Hurley, Mr John

Thompson, the well-known jockey and the chauffeur, Michael McIlroy. The driver, of course, blamed the car and said the brakes had failed. In order to avoid a collision with the car travelling in front, Mr McIlroy had to pass it on its left side, but as he hurtled down the hill, he came on a large group of pedestrians who scattered in all directions. Unfortunately one of the pedestrians, a nurse named Miss Hynes, got confused and failed to get out of the way of the runaway car. The motor kept going and eventually collided with a gateway with such force that the occupants were thrown out of the car, all except for Thompson, the jockey, who had the presence of mind to jump from the car before the collision and so avoided any serious injury. Miss Hynes and Mr McIlroy were brought to hospital in Dublin. Luckily the others only suffered minor bruising and shock, but the hired car was a write-off.

Heading for the races in an outside car, in the 1920s

DAILY CHAR-A-BANC TRIPS

GLENDALOUGH AND AVOCA

AT 10.30 A.M. FARE 9/-

SEATS Booked and Passengers picked up, Royal Hotel, Bray.

AFTERNOON DRIVES

2.30 P.M. RETURN 5/-

CURRAGH AND POULAPHOUCA TUESDAYS

Starting 11.30 a.m. FARE 8/-

BOYNE VALLEY

THURSDAYS 11.00 a.m. FARE 8/-

KILLARNEY SEVEN DAY TOURS

EVERY WEDNESDAY

BELLEWSTOWN RACES

JULY 1ST AND 2ND

Return Fare, one day 10/-; two days 17/6

THOMPSON'S, BRUNSWICK ST

Phone 2558

While cars gradually increased in popularity, others continued to rely on more traditional means of getting to the races. A court case in 1903 under the Cruelty to Animals Act recalls the days of travelling by carriage to the races. A Mr Vaughey, obviously a keen race-goer, together with his coachman, Mr Tougher, was summoned on the charge that he did '*cruelly ill-treat, over-drive, abuse or torture, or cause or procure such to be done, to a horse of which he was driver.*' It seems that Mr Vaughey attended the July 1903 meeting of the Bellewtown Races, two days running, using the same horse to draw his brougham, containing himself and his coachman, in all a distance of some eighty miles, over the two days. The horse was aged about twelve years and had cost £40.

'On the return journey on the second day when it had nearly accomplished its task, the horse was seen by a policeman to stagger in the streets. When the horse staggered, the coachman struck it a blow under the barrel with the butt of his whip. Mr Vaughey then got out of the brougham and the coachman again struck the animal a couple of times with the butt of the whip. The animal fell on the roadway and the coachman again struck it'. (Irish Times)

The unfortunate horse died the next day. The two men were convicted and both owner and coachman were sentenced to seven days imprisonment with hard labour without the option of a fine.

Watching Bellewstown Races from the comfort of the carriage 1910

A feature, especially of the early years of the twentieth century, was the hospitality. Mr R.D. Jameson and Mrs Jameson of Delvin were especially noted for genially entertaining friends in their marquee in the carriage enclosure at Bellewstown, as was Mr H. Tunstall Moore. Mr Thomas Boylan of Hilltown House always had a large house party during race week. Again the 'fair sex' were praised for making a brave show at the races with 'many sweet faces and pretty dresses to lend colour and add attractiveness to the scene in the enclosure.' (*Irish Field* 9 July 1904)

Improvements to Bellewstown Racecourse in the 20th century

In 1901, the old stand was covered with an iron roof, and the weigh-room, offices etc. situated beneath the venerable structure were all remodelled. The reporter from *The Irish Field* commented in 1904 that the coating of red and blue paint used to freshen up the stands came off on one's clothes and altogether people would have been better pleased if some other means of improving the aspect of the local surroundings had been devised! A new weigh room was installed in 1921 as well as increased stand and luncheon accommodation. However, by 1926, the meagre support given to the long-established fixture by owners and trainers was being decried by the racing correspondent, when only nineteen starters turned out for the entire six races on the card, on the second day. An improvement in rail-road transport for horses helped to attract more runners.

Despite all the major political upheavals of the twentieth century, there was little interference with the races, the rebellion of 1916 and the outbreak of the first World War, having no impact on racing, while the Troubles of 1922 merely caused the postponement of the meeting from July to mid-September. The Second World War seemingly impacted more on those in the racing world, because of petrol rationing and therefore Bellewstown races were cancelled between 1942 and 1945. Although racing used to extend for a full week back in the eighteenth and nineteenth centuries, it was 1974 before the track was raced on for a third day in one season in the twentieth century. Also the first two-year-old race ever held in Bellewstown took place that same year.

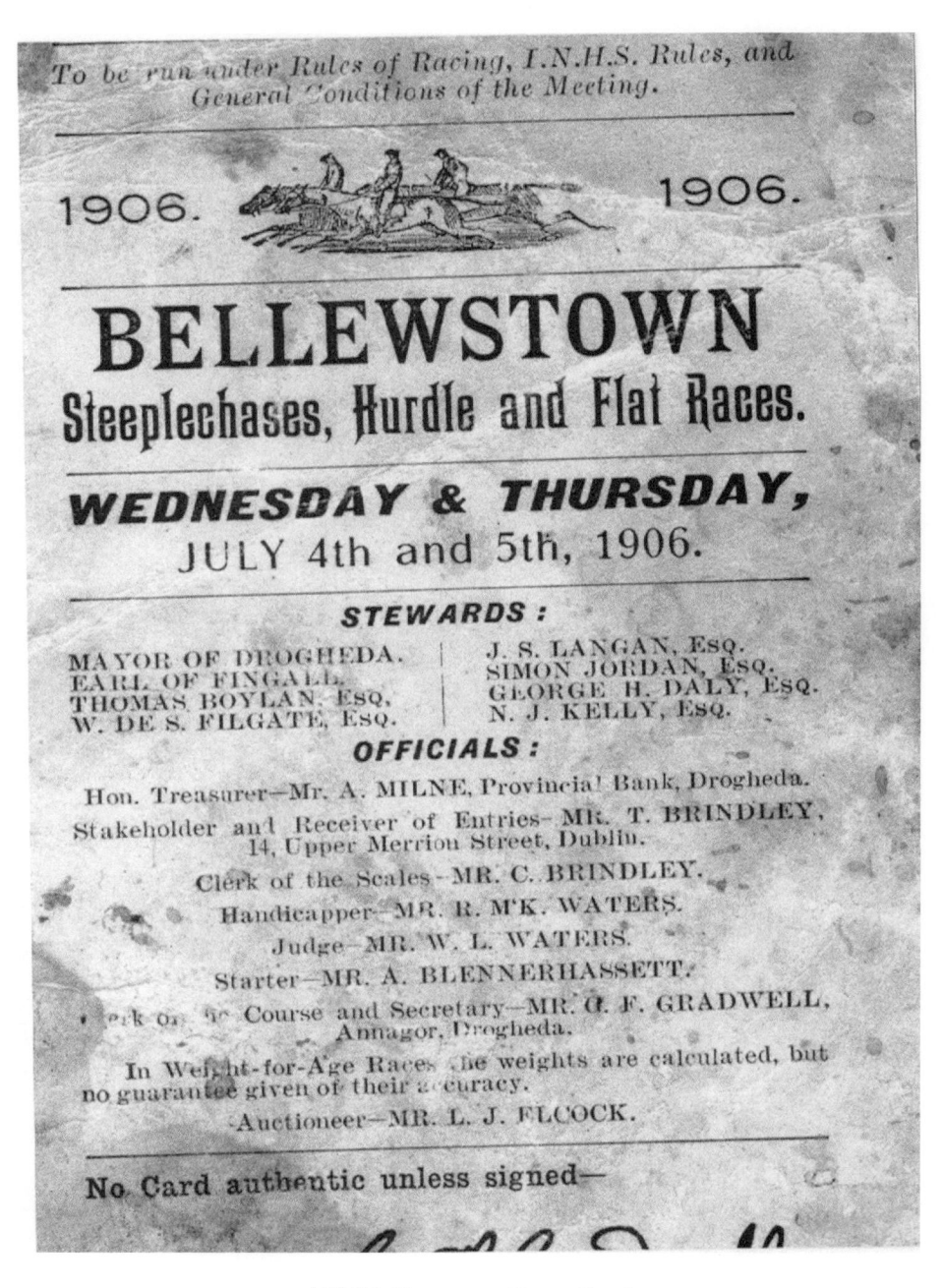

1906 Bellewstown Race Card

**Bellewstown Races were always a big outing for the family.
Mrs Jack Lynch, her sister Dolly Wall, Christo Wall and their children
Thomas, Brendan, Bernadette, James, Colm and John at the races in the 1950s.**

Recalling Bellewstown Races in the 1920s by local resident, Eileen Langan

The long summer holidays and the races, they were the highlights of the year. The tents came months before the races then as horses and carts were their only way of travelling and they came from some other meeting. Those times it was two-day meetings, the first Wednesday and Thursday in July and the taste of Ice Cream from Hughie Commons van would well savour if you didn't get any for another year. The McGinns kept jockeys at the Races. They had a few stables and kept horses. We used look forward to the races. Of course there were no cars except Mr Gradwell's, the boss of the course. He had the first Ford around, all brass and polish. The people came on carts and horses and would be there for weeks putting up the tea and beer tents and at night they lighted big fires along the road to cook the hams and the smell! Mag Neill, she'd collect all the cinders after the races. We used to get coppers from people to mind their bicycles. I often had five shillings after the two days, a small fortune in the twenties. Of course the big thing was that we got ice-cream wafers and we'd suck them to make them last. Then there was Peggy's Leg, another treat, and maybe you'd be lucky, someone passing that won money would give you a couple of bananas or oranges.

They took up the fences after the races each year and we would gather all the bits of birch or thorns (from the fences) and bring them home to wither for fire lighting. We always had salmon and new potatoes on the Friday after the races. It was late then and Mammie and Mrs Crinion and Rosie would have a bottle of Guinness as a treat when the work was all done and discuss how well they had done. Mrs Crinion kept jockeys and fed them, Rosie kept bicycles and Mam always a few horses and a man came every year and left his trap and pony and he gave a guinea. It always was long hot summers those times. We got our summer holidays from school the day after the races. I remember the British Army coming to Bellewstown Races. They frightened everybody, they looked so fierce in tin hats and carrying guns. Next year, 1922, the Black and Tans came, they were worse. They threatened to shoot a man, Darkie Connor, at our railing. They had the tricolour flying on the old library and the Tans took it down and dragged it through the streets of Balbriggan. It was a pouring wet day and everybody went home early, not much money made.

BELLEWSTOWN RACES.
FOR
PROGRAMME
AND
SELECTIONS
See the Current Issue of the
IRISH FIELD
PRICE
=1d.=
OFFICES—11 D'OLIER ST., DUBLIN.
Post free to any address:
Yearly, 6/6; Half-year, 3/3; Quarter, 1/8.

Family party enjoying the races in 1963
Back: Marie Ludlow, Willie Ludlow, Molly Cahill, Alan Ludlow
Front: Brian Ludlow, Colette Ludlow, Jimmy Cahill and Audrey Ludlow

Steve Donoghue writes:

There is a race-course in Ireland, called Bellewstown. It is only a short distance north of Dublin, but it is essentially a country meeting. The course is a sort of rectangle, with four very sharp corners and it is very small. Only the nippiest kind of horse and the most dashing type of jockey has much chance on it.

Years ago, in the days when I was working like a demon to make a name for myself, I had been engaged to ride a very good horse at this meeting. I was rather proud of this distinction, as the horse was a really good one, one of the best in Ireland at the time, and he was normally ridden by Algy Anthony, who used to ride for the King in Ireland and was at that time the Irish champion jockey.

Then just at the last minute, the trainer came to me and told me that he was really sorry but the owner had insisted that Algy should ride him in the race. The horse was carrying a big weight and I only weighed about seven stone at that time, so the trainer said, it had been decided that in preference to my riding and carrying a lot of dead weight, the great Algy should ride the animal. Well, today that would not worry me a bit. But in those days I was trying to build up a name for myself. I was heart-broken.

Just as I came out of the weighing room, which was actually a tent, I ran into a big man called Courtney. He was a well-known gentlemen farmer who owned some fine horses and won a lot of races. He asked 'Are you riding in the King's Plate?'

'No sir,' I replied dismally, 'I was going to ride the favourite but someone else has been put up in my place.'

'Well, will you ride a horse of mine?' he asked me.

Quick ideas for revenge came into my youthful head.

'Is your horse fast?' I asked Mr Courtney.

'Yes, very fast.'

'Does he know the course at all?'

'Sure, damn it, boy, he was born on it. He lives here and so do I.'

I knew what the course was like and I knew that I could make a horse act on it if he was the right sort. This was the sort of little course on which I had ridden all my early races in France, suicidal little courses, all corners and twists.

'Well,' I said to the big farmer, 'if he is fast and knows the course, I think I know how to beat that big horse. I'll be glad of the mount.'

Now immediately it had been known that Algy Anthony, the champion jockey, was going to ride the horse that had brought me down to Bellewstown, the animal became even a hotter favourite. But Mr Courtney had a big following among the local folk, being a local farmer, and so my horse was quite well-backed.

I got away from the gate like a flash and jumped straight into the lead. Once in front I knew I could, if the horse were speedy enough, easily beat the heavily-weighted horse behind me. The horse I was riding was actually very nippy and after I had skimmed him around the first corner, I knew I had the race in my pocket. Once round the corner, I steadied up and let him catch up on me slightly, then round the next corner I flew. The big horse swung wide and I was half-way to the next corner before he had got balanced or was in a position to use his speed again. Once more he caught up on me and once more I popped round the next corner and drew ahead of him. It was an absolute cat-and-mouse or hare-and-tortoise affair. I would draw away round the bends and then let him overhaul me a bit and once more disappear round the next sharp bend. In the end I won as I liked. I was cheered as though I had won the Derby, and poor Algy Anthony had all the eggs, bottles, stones and bad tomatoes thrown at him for getting beaten. He was the villain who had lost on a favourite and I was the hero who won on the local outsider. The horse I had ridden was called *Most Noble* and his nature suited his name. He was a good little animal and after my success with him I rode for Mr. Courtney all over Ireland at the minor meetings and I won him a lot of races.

Taken from *Donoghue Up*. the autobiography of the legendary early twentieth century jockey, Steve Donoghue.

Donoghue up! Perhaps the most perfect picture ever taken to show what is meant by a jockey winning a race with his hands.

Steve Donoghue rides to victory

A Perfect Day's Racing in the 1930s

A group of racegoers at Hilltown House in early 1930s, Mrs Cecilia Boylan standing in the centre.

In 1935, the Boylans of Hilltown House hosted a smart gathering of enthusiastic racegoers before the afternoon's racing. Many were making up a house party, staying at Hilltown for the week. They were joined by several others for luncheon, which was served in a marquee on the lawn. It was a beautiful sunny day, perfect for the races. Among those entertained by Captain Edward Boylan, his wife Eileen and his mother Cecilia were The Earl of Fingall, Elizabeth Countess of Fingall, Lord Hemphill, Lady Lambart, Sir James Nelson, Lady Nugent, Miss Nugent, Lady (Oliver) Nugent, the Hon. Mrs Richard Westenra, the Hon. Gerald and Mrs Wellesley, Major E. Shirley, Major Scott, Colonel Simmonds, Colonel and Mrs McClintock, Capt. And Mrs D. Daly, Captain and Mrs Woods, Miss Ainsworth, Colonel Bramston-Newman, Mrs Lindsay-Fitzpatrick, Colonel and Mrs S.S. Hill-Dillon, Miss G. Cameron, Miss Hughes, Mr and Mrs L. Morrogh-Ryan, Mrs Hamilton of Hamwood, Miss Hamilton, Captain B.A. Boyd-Rochfort, V.C., Colonel and Mrs St G. Smith. Mrs Cairnes, Mr and Mrs St Germans, Captain and Mrs J. Daly, the Misses Laidlaw, Miss Blount, Miss McNeile, Miss Ainsley, Mr and Mrs Nugent Popoff, Surgeon-Lieut. W.A. Ryan, Mr and Mrs Stanley Mathews, Mr and Mrs Harley Bacon, Mrs Osborne, Major H.C. Crozier, Mr Duff Mathews, Miss Mathews, Mrs Page Croft, Mrs Grehan, Mr and Mrs Tullock, Miss Jameson, Mr and Mrs W.J. Hilliard, Mr Woods, Mr David Plunket, Miss J. Ferguson, Mr and Mrs St J. Nolan, Mr F. Tiacke, Miss Gaisford St. Lawrence, Mrs Maynard Linton, Mrs McKeever, Mr H. Ussher, Miss Kellet, Mr and Mrs P. Walker, Miss McArdle, Mr and Mrs B. O'Reilly, Mrs Graham, Mrs Ganley, Miss Loughridge, Captain F. ffrench-Davis, Mr F.W.E. Gradwell, Mrs Iver.

The Hill of Bellewstown (old Bellewstown poem)

I found it today, 'twas hidden away in an attic dark and dim,
'Twas an old racecard, moth-eaten and marred, with the edges far from trim;
Just a single page, black and blurred with age, and the corners turning down;
This treasure find brings my youth to mind: on the Hill of Bellewstown.

It recalls a day in summer array in the month of sweet July;
No clouds to dispel, I remember it well, five and forty years gone by.
'Twas a day I enjoyed, in no way allayed by a single grief or frown;
And the first day for me, at the races to be, on the Hill of Bellewstown.

I was free from care, though my feet were bare, in a new suit spick and span;
I was young and strong and I carolled a song, as across the fields I ran.
In my youthful sense I jingled my pence, amounting to just half a crown;
And I frisked with glee, when I came to see, the Old Hill of Bellewstown.

As these lines I pen, to my mind again the picture comes back to me:
The palings so white, in the dazzling light, the flags all floating free;
The marquees in rows and the penny shows, with dancer, singer and clown.
The booths such a score, with their tempting stare, on the Hill of Bellewstown

Wagonettes and cars, with hampers and jars, in hundreds were surely there.
The lads in their best, lassies well-dressed, smiling, good-humoured and fair;
The bookies on stools, enticing the fools to stake their few shillings down;
With shouting and din, every horse sure must win, on the Hill of Bellewstown

Oh the view from that hill, how it did fill my gay young heart with delight:
The Hilltown demesne, the Royal Meath plains, the sea below on the right;
The heights o'er the Boyne and below in decline Drogheda's historic old town
The Mountains of Mourne and Ulster far borne, from the Hill of Bellewstown.

Oh beautiful hill, you are here with us still, green and breezy as of yore
The view from your brow, as then, it is now; for nature lives ever more:
And though it be strange, time brings a change, as we uphill struggle down;
And racing today ain't quite the old way on the Hill of Bellewstown.

I was easy and free, all laughter and glee, no hurrying, rushing or fuss;
No motor was there, no bike I declare, no charabanc, lorry or bus.
But at races today, these now block the way, with nuts from cities and towns
With special and wire, straight tips they desire, on the Hill of Bellewstown.

Oh dear old racecard since at your face I first stared, many changes took place
And though times have gone, there still lingers on, the Irish love of a race.
So this year once more, as often before, to the Old Hill I'll go down,
To view the fine races and sweet homely faces on the Hill of Bellewstown.

Clerks of the Course and Secretaries at Bellewstown in the 20th Century

Clerk of Course and Secretary

1900 – 1932   Mr G.F. Gradwell

1933 – 1950   Mr T.J. Kelly

1950 – 1973   Mr W.D. Kelly

1974 – 1992   Mr J. Collins

Clerk of Course		**Secretary**	
1993 – 1995	Mr D.P. Martin	1993	John Harvey
1996 – 1999	Mr P.R. McGowran	1994 – 1997	Declan Cumiskey
2000	Mr J.R. Banahan	1998 – Pres.	Kevin Coleman
2001	Mr P.R. McGowran		
2002 – 2003	Mr B. Sheridan		
2004 – 2009	Mr I. Hamilton		
2010	Mr B. Sheridan		
2011 – Pres.	Mr L. Wyer		

Bellewstown: Stewards in the Twentieth Century and up to 2013

1900 – 1941 Mayor of Drogheda; Earl of Fingall; Mr G.J. Ball; Mr Thomas Boylan; Capt. Edward Boylan; Mr George H. Daly; Mr W. De Salis-Filgate; Lord Gormanstown; Mr Simon Jordan; Mr J.S. Langan; Mr N.J. Kelly; Mr T.J. Kelly; Mr J.C. McKeever; Mr T.D. McKeever; Mr F.D. Osborne; Major E. Shirley.

1946 – Present Mayor of Drogheda (1946 – 1983); Earl of Fingall (1946 – 1983); Capt R.A.B. Filgate (1946 – 1968); Mr F.E.W. Gradwell (1946 – 1950); F. Lt. R.S. Langan (1946 – 1975); Mr P.D. Matthews (1946 – 1955); Mr T.D. McKeever (1946 – 1952); Mr C.H. Nicholson (1946 – 1969); Lt. Col. E. Shirley (1946 – 1956); Col. S.S. Hill Dillon (1950 – 1980); Mr R. Kelly (1950 – 1967); Mr E.P.S. Matthews (1959 – 1984); Mr N.W. Waddington (1954 – 1989); Mr C.C. Cameron (1954 – 1982); Major E.A. Boylan (1959 – 1992); Major J.E. Shirley (1965 – 1975); Mr D.F. Boylan (1969 – 1991); Mr R.W. McKeever (1969 – 1996); Mr John Purfield (1972 – present); Mr R.J. Filgate (1967 – present); Major C.W.T. Morshead (1972 – 1984); Brig. A.D.R. Wingfield (1975 – 1994); Judge T.F. Roe (1975 – 2002); Judge D. O'Hagan (1975 – 2000); Mr J.F. Hoey (1975 – 1984); Mr M.McAuley (1985 – 1992); Mr Pat Hoey (1985 – 1991); Mr Thomas Matthews (1985 – 1994); Mr Denis Reddan (1991-1992); Mr P. Whyte (1985 – 1998); Mr James Curran (1980 – 2008); Mr T. Jenkinson, snr. (1986 – 2009); Mr Niall Collier (1993 – present); Mr Alan Delany (1993 – present); Ms Elizabeth Jenkinson (1993 – 2009); Mr Niall Delany (1996 – present); Mr S. Murphy (2000 – present); Mr J. Black (2000 – present); Mr J. Corcoran (2000 – present); Mr A.L. McKeever (2001 – present); Mr G. Mernagh (2001 – 2005); Mr S. Fitzpatrick (2004 – present); Mr M. McGuinness (2004 – present); Mr T. Jenkinson jnr. (2004 – present); Mr G. Duffy (2004 – present); Ms S. Keoghan (2010 – present); Mr P. Kierans (2010 – present); Judge J. O'Hagan (2010 – present).

Studying the form at Bellewstown in the 1930s

There's one born every tick of the clock by Alfred Woods

When I was very young, about 1940, Johnny arrived with his pony and trap, along with a couple of friends. They were on their way to Bellewstown races and his pony needed a new set of shoes. Johnny had plenty of grey hair and had been coming to Bellewstown for forty years or more, not to enjoy racing or back horses, but to earn his living.

He was a 'three-card-trick' man and his two companions were his assistants. They were Dublin men, with pronounced Dublin accents, and were proud of their ability with the cards and how they could melt into the crowd when the 'peelers', as they called the guards, came along. The man with the loose gabardine coat would place a little collapsible card table on the ground, while another placed the three cards on it and the third man held the money and played 'Find the Lady and you'll find me.' One of his pals would place a bet, a ten-shilling note perhaps, on a card and he would win, just to start proceedings.

Then an onlooker might sneak a look, to see if the one he thought was the Queen was in fact Her Majesty and he would place a bet. But when the card was turned by the trick man, sure it might be the ten of clubs and the money was lost. This would continue until the crowd around the table got big enough to attract a couple of guards and this was when 'Fingers' the card man pocketed the money on the table, the second man pocketed the cards and the man with the loose-fitting gabardine coat folded the table and slipped it out of sight under his coat in one easy movement. All three would disappear into the crowd in different directions, to reconvene at a different site, which was free of guards, and the whole procedure began again.

In the forge, while the pony was being shod, with four new shoes being made and fitted for twelve shillings, my father said, 'Johnny, isn't it extraordinary that in this day and age, people would lose their money on the turn of a card?' Johnny, in his best Dublin accent, answered 'Don't be talking rubbish, man, sure there's wan born every Dic of the Glock.' It's over seventy years now since I heard Johnny, the three-card-trick man, say this, but I've heard it many a time since and I think it may well be as true today, as it was then. Johnny added as an afterthought, 'Bellewstown never was any good for our line of work. I lives for Galway, Galway Week keeps me going for the rest of the year.' I am sure Johnny and his companions have long gone to their reward and ponies and traps and three-card-trick men are rarely seen at Bellewstown Races these days.

KAY CROZIER LOOKS BACK FONDLY AT RACES IN HER YOUTH

When I was a child, me and my pal Rita Brannigan were inseparable and we were two divils. We looked forward to the races for weeks beforehand. When the races came along, the grooms and the horses were left here. The horses weren't taken away like they are nowadays in horse boxes. McGinns down here used to keep the horses, they had stables and Arnolds had stables and they used to keep the horses too. The grooms would sleep with the horses because there was nowhere else for them. Rita and myself were two villains and we were watching the jockeys, more than the horses and the grooms. They used to get the water from the well here in the wood. We'd get up early the morning of the races, well I would particularly and Rita would be over to me at cockcrow and we'd have to see the grooms with the horses and the water and the buckets and we'd have great craic with them. And the same the next morning until the races were over. And then the horse boxes would come and take them all away and then we'd cry for a week, because we loved the races and the craic.

Everybody cleaned up for the races with whitewash and tar. Once Bellewstown Races were coming, everybody would be out cutting hedges and whitewashing and putting tar places. The walls would be as white as snow and the doors and the gates were perfectly black. It was a great occasion and we loved it. And you'd get a new dress, whatever we could afford and the weather was so warm, you didn't need a coat. Everyone came to Bellewstown Races on their bicycles. Our gate was always open and we might have twenty, thirty or forty bicycles, all thrown along the hedge and they'd bring in their bicycle pumps, maybe a lamp or their coat if it was really fine and mother would have them all up in the bedroom. And we'd have to be home on time after the races, to open up and give them back their coats and so on. Most of the men, if they saw a child out there, they'd say 'Here's thruppence for you.' If we got a couple of thruppences we were right for the next day at the races. It used to be a great family occasion. Bellewstown Races were for everyone, fathers would come with a child on the bicycle, they came from as far away as Navan. The twinnies came every year, they cycled from Navan and left their bicycles in here, the Twinnie Byrnes.

We didn't have the money to back horses. We might have a shilling or two shillings and we'd be asking the grooms to give us a winner. But they didn't know and even if they gave us some information, sure we didn't have the money anyway. It was a matter of going up and looking at them. We used to run down, there was a jump called the Regulation, there was Sherry's Jump, the Regulation, McGinns Jump, Martin's Jump, the Post-Office Jump and the Standhouse Jump or Tallons Jump. And we'd go down to the Regulation to see them jumping over it because it was the biggest jump and we'd run from that straight back up to see who was winning, because we were that fast at running back then. My mother and Mrs Ludlow would stand along the railings and we'd be sent to get the ice-cream and we'd be mixing around to see the boys and what have you. Then we'd have to come back down with the ice-cream and they'd be saying 'What kep ya? We thought you'd never come back.' But we'd be up having the bit of fun. And the days were so fine you could sit or lie on the grass with your ice-cream. After the races we'd come home and have our tea, because they were day races and then we'd go back over to the standhouse and put our arms up on the railings and watch them all coming out of the pub. We were never allowed into the pub.

And the swinging boats, Rita never liked them because she got light-headed but as for me, I'd go up that far, I could see down my mother's chimney! And of course the lads would be there and they'd be cheering us on and then we'd go on the bumping cars.

Whatever was on the go, we'd have a go at it. We didn't have the big roundabouts they have now, just the swinging boats and the bumping cars and a few little things like chairoplanes and so on. Then when the night came, we were away down to Arnolds for the dance. We were allowed go down there with warnings, 'Mind yourself coming home' and this, that and the other and the crack was ninety.

Thimble Rigger by Alfred Woods

Many years ago, Mr Walsh lived in one of the Annesbrook lodges, near my home. He was the land steward on the Annesbrook estate and he always wore a rather peculiar hat, much like the one worn by Baden Powell, in his photographs as founder of the Boy Scouts, so he enjoyed the nickname of 'Baden', not openly, of course, just by a few of us locals. When his son, William, a boy of around twelve or fourteen, decided he would go to the races in Bellewstown, his father gave him a ten-shilling note and lots of good advice on how to mind it.

William walked the four miles to the races and enjoyed all the sights and sounds of the funfair on the Hill. Then he spotted a Thimble Rigger in action, shuffling his three thimbles over and back across the little table-top, openly displaying the little black pea and which thimble it was hiding under. Having observed for some time, William was sure which thimble the pea was under, so he took the ten bob from his pocket and placed the note on the thimble covering the pea. Horror of horrors! The pea wasn't there and all his races money was gone in an instant! The rest of the day passed very slowly and William felt very sorry for himself, when he recounted the story that night to his parents.

Baden decided to go to the races next day. Arrived on the Hill, he studied Thimble Man for some time, then approached and laid down a ten-shilling note on the thimble of his choice. He won! 'Double or quits,' said Thimble Man. Baden agreed to try again and surprise, surprise, again found the thimble. He collected his two pounds and stepped away from the table, carefully placing the money in an inside pocket. Then came the shout 'Peelers! Peelers!' and the table disappeared under a long coat. Thimbles, money and men were gone in a flash, vanished.

Later, Thimble Man met up with Baden and asked 'How the devil did you do that?' Baden explained about his son William being tricked out of his ten-shilling note the previous day. 'You took mean advantage of a young boy and took all of his races money. I came to get it back and I thought it only fair that you should pay me for my time and trouble, so I took the second pound for that.' 'Fair enough,' said the Thimble Rigger, 'but how did you find the pea? That really puzzles me.' Baden smiled and held up his hand and there, under the nail of his middle finger, was a little black pea. 'I always carry my own pea,' he said, smiling sweetly.

My father had this old myth and it lives with me to this day, 'the first horse you see in Bellewstown, you back it'… JIM CURLEY remembers tips for betting in his younger days.

I'll always remember my first communion suit, it was navy blue, and this would only be put on me for a Sunday for mass and that, but Bellewstown was a special day and my aunt took me to Bellewstown that year. Jimmy Woods was the local hackney driver and he ferried people around the village, here, there and everywhere. My aunt had a particular association with him, he used to bring us into Drogheda for shopping and so on. But this day, I was particularly lucky, I was allowed put on the suit and the tie, this would be in the early fifties and my aunt Maryanne would always treat me to something special. At the time there were tents with catering facilities in them and they supplied teas and minerals and you name it, they had absolutely everything. And the ladies who were in charge of the tents, they all had Dublin accents, I remember. And I remember when we arrived at the course, the first place we made for was one of the tents and I was treated to a bottle of orange, and the old familiar ham and egg bun, a big pink and yellow square of bun which we called ham and egg. But that particular day, though it was July, I'll always remember the hailstones, so we had to spend an extra long time in the tent, because the hailstones were falling, so I was very lucky, I got a second round, I got another ham and egg bun and another bottle of orange to pass the time. Everybody was sheltering in the tent. And I remember when we came out, the ground was absolutely white with hailstones. The aunt liked to have a little bet and she often put on a bet with the local bookies in Duleek and I would often bring it over for her to the bookies. It was shillings at the time. And I remember she had a horse picked out. Anyway the races had been postponed for a while because of the hail and she took me by the hand up to the bookie outside the enclosure. And she said 'I'm putting a half crown on for me and there's a shilling going on for you.' Believe it or not, the horse DID win. I'll always remember, it was six to one and sure it made my day, she gave me the two shillings. I think it was our only bet for the day, actually.

Picking a winner: Ita Ludlow, Mary Power, Molly Townley and Margaret Ludlow, with baby Colette Ludlow observing from the pram

I would have travelled up and down for maybe two years in the hackney car and then eventually, when we got our first bike, our father would cycle up to Bellewstown with us. My father had a good friendship with a Mrs Martin, who lived where we came in from the Carnes Road, he knew her quite well and we were allowed leave the bike in there. And then we'd proceed up the course with my father. Of course he'd know a lot of people and be talking to them. The first one my father would go to, when we were coming up the course, would be to Bobby Power. And he'd say, 'Bobby has a winner'. And Bobby, he must have been the greatest ambassador Bellewstown ever had, he'd have a good word and a friendly word for everyone and he'd always have a horse to tell my father and nine times out of ten, we'd all back it and it would win. The horse boxes were parked along the road, down in front of the school, all along that area and we'd watch the horses coming out of the boxes. My father had this old myth and it lives with me to this day and that was 'the first horse you see in Bellewstown, you back it.' The horses would walk up the course, they'd be led up the course and they would go in then into the enclosure for saddling and that. And we'd be watching the horses to spot the first one we had seen, to see what number it was and my father's old theory had to be tried out, that we'd put a bet on that horse. It must have been handed down to him at some stage, long before my time and it worked! And even about two years ago, we were in the enclosure, looking at the parade ring and I remember saying to the lads, my brother included, about my father's old saying and this horse came into the enclosure, number two, trained by J T Gorman and we backed the horse. It won at nine to two, so it still works.

As we got a bit older we'd have our own bikes. And actually we walked up to Bellewstown on a few occasions. We would have been around twelve or fourteen at the time. We would have walked up across the fields. And one lad that was in the group, Paig we always called him, Patsy Sullivan and Patsy always knew the shortest way across the field and when we would come to back the horse, Paig was the expert. He'd have to pick out. Now we'd only have a few shillings at that time, maybe about five shillings at the most and the thing was that we would all give Paig a shilling each to back the horse for us and ninety nine times out of a hundred he was successful. And at the pay-out time we'd be standing around him in a ring and he'd be giving us all our share of the winnings.

Bellewstown Races were a wonderful treat for boys in the 1960s

Padlocks and chains

Then we moved up in the world a bit more, my brother was working in John Collins in Shop Street at the time and we managed to get a big chain, we bought the chain between us and one of the lads would carry it on the bike and the chain was long enough to go round the nine or ten bikes, through the crossbar and we even had a lock that we would lock it. But one very funny incident that sticks out in my mind, was that we had a couple of extra bikes with us one day and the chain just wasn't long enough to go round all the bars of the bikes. At that time we actually wore long stockings up to our knees, we would have been in short trousers up to fourteen. We used to find the thickest thorn or whin bush and tie the chain to it but on this particular day the chain wouldn't go round because of the two extra bikes. And I remember this particular lad having the brilliant idea of taking off his stocking and tying it with a big knot to the chain to get the extra length. But when we came back after the races, we couldn't get the knot open, we could get the padlock open but we couldn't get the knot open. One of the lads had a penknife and the penknife was used, with the consent of the owner of the stocking, to cut the top off it and get the situation sorted and get the chain free. But I remember the next day when he came out, he had the stockings turned down and the boys were having a bit of craic with him and he laughed 'I didn't want me mother to see that I had one and three-quarter stockings on me.'

Picnic

We'd come up to Bellewstown on a regular basis to the races after this. And I remember one particular character, Johnny, he used to get a lift on the bar of the bike. We'd often be robbing orchards and that, even though we had apples ourselves, we'd have to see what other apples tasted like. And this particular guy, Johnny, had a jacket with massive big pockets in it, he'd always have the most apples when we'd come out of an orchard. I remember this particular day, when a horse broke loose in the parade ring and it came right through the fence, right through the metal fence. At that time the hawkers would be shouting out 'Chocolate, oranges, apples', not Cadbury chocolate but Carbury Chocolate. Anyway the horse broke loose and there was a scattering match, with everyone running to get away from the horse. The women used to use an old bread-board for the stalls and everything would be built up on the bread-board with maybe a couple of crates to keep it steady. Anyway, Johnny was looking behind him and he ran straight into this stall and knocked everything and there he was, lying on his back in the middle of the mayhem and we running like hell through the crowd to get away from the horse. We looked back to see where Johnny was and Johnny was coming running, holding the two pockets. 'Come on,' he said and we went down to the back of the course and Johnny had, you name it, apples and oranges and bars of chocolates. I know there wasn't enough apples to go round, but the famous penknife that cut the stocking was produced and the apples and oranges were cut into quarters and we had them with a few squares of chocolate each, a great picnic and a very funny memory.

Yellow Sam

And I remember the Yellow Sam incident, I'll always remember it. The boys used to call me Sam, after a famous American golfer, Slamming Sammy. At that time we had our own style of pitch and putt and we'd be hitting the golf balls into the holes. The old tennis courts in Duleek had a putting green and I kind of fancied myself as a good golfer. I used to say I was Slamming Sammy in action when I'd be hitting the ball, so the boys all called me Sam and I still get called by that sometimes today. So a group of us that was involved in the angling at the time, we were looking down through the race-card that particular day and we spotted Yellow Sam and the boys were saying 'You'll have to back that one.' I looked at it and it had a load of noughts in front of it and I said 'Ah no, sure it wouldn't have a hope.' And they were saying 'Ah go on, put a few bob on it anyway' but I declined. Then when it won, I got a terrible doing from the boys. So that was the famous Yellow Sam. And when the documentaries appeared about it, I remembered well that I hadn't put the money on it. But, I would have to say, of all the race-courses I attend, Fairyhouse, Navan, Dundalk, Bellewstown is my lucky racecourse.

Journalist Deirdre Purcell attended Bellewstown Races in the eighties

Wednesday evening and it's back. Bellewstown in Co Meath, where they're having an evening race meeting on top of a hill, is awash with the colours and the scents of it. On the way up, the heady scent of silage sharpens up the hay and hedgerow smells; on the course itself horse smells, dung and sweat, compete with beer and sweet grass. To the uninitiated, the bookies shout unadulterated gobbledy-gook. Even the race-card has its mysteries. What for instance is an upside down handicap? Enquiries of knowledgeable-looking gents with cigarette ash on their shirt fronts prove fruitless, they suspect a trick question. In the end, it turns out that it is a handicapping system in reverse, starting with the worst horse, in other words, the Upside-Down-Handicap race is for duds.

The money you can win on duds is as good as the money you can win on anything else, of course, and the bookies don't abate their efforts. The idea is that you hang around in a big crush with the rest of the punters, staring at the prices until a sweating fat man with a hat arrives and whispers something to the bookie. The bookie then changes the figures on the board and everybody rushes forward with rolls of twenty pound notes. A man staggers purposefully out of the saddling enclosure, clutching his own personal wodge of tenners. Twice he aims at the back of a horse, in an effort to stuff the money under the saddle. Twice he misses, as the horse is led towards the parade ring. Disappointed, he wanders off erratically mumbling.

The beer hall (you couldn't call it a bar, although they do sell spirits) operates a sort of unofficial apartheid. The money, as in flowers-in-the-buttonhole and gins-and-tonics, stands around at one end, being studiously ignored by the bar staff, there is even a shooting stick on show, and Pat Quinn in his white jacket. He doesn't gamble any more, he's there with a friend. He's still wearing the silk shirts, rosy cheeks and little-boy smile, things are going well. At the other end is the bottles-of-Harp-and-Smithwicks set, by the neck, no glasses, great gas.

The course commentator is so laid back, that sometimes you miss the 'Off', you're so wrapped up in watching the apprentice jockey spitting out a worm he's discovered in his peach. So laid-back, in fact, that there's no great rush to the rails to watch the races. The thing to do is pretend you don't care, and keep chatting to your friends, or if you're pushed to it, to raise your binoculars casually to your eyes. Everyone knows everyone else in the sunshine, there are some Anglo accents with houseguests, and there's a horse, Welshwood, who, they say, is owned collectively by 25 fellows from Navan, and once it won last year and all 25 fellows went into the winners' enclosure…

There are swingboats, and apples, plums and peaches from Dublin (with or without worms) and the course dips here and there so even the commentator can't see the horses and there's a suspenseful silence until they come into view again… It's a wonderful evening blessed by the summer, and one of the events to remember for your old age, when all the summer evenings have been like this.

The Sport of Kings by Tom Winters

When I was a young fella, I was often sent to Johnny Brennan's old galvanised betting office on the Chord Road in Drogheda, with bets from customers in my father's old thatched pub. Since then, horse-racing has fascinated me, because this was a grounding in the ways of the Turf, afforded to few twelve-year-olds. Sixpence three-cross-doubles; shilling doubles; trebles; accumulators, all of which seldom led to a fortune in winnings. There was talk of Gordon Richards, Willie Nevitt, E. and D. Smith, M. Beary, Charlie Smirke, Harry Wragg, known as the head-waiter and other great jockeys like Edgar Britt, who usually had a winner or two every week and Joe Sime, a surname I have never heard of since then. Some of the writing on those dockets I took to Johnny Brennan's betting office was unreadable, especially those of a great character called Web Woods, who loved to bet, but whose scrawl would take all the ingenuity of the boffins of Bletchley Park, that famous decoding centre of World War Two fame. Johnny never seemed to have any trouble interpreting them and he seldom had to pay out on them.

All of the action seemed to take place on Saturday afternoons and the Saturday Herald was eagerly awaited for early results, as there was no television in those days. Great racehorse trainers of the era, like Walter Nightingale and Harvey Leader and Noel Murless were great favourites with the punters. Old-timers would occasionally mention Fred Darling, Frank Butters, Steve Donahue and the great tragic jockey, Fred Archer. As well as the famous English tracks like Epsom, Newmarket, Ascot and Aintree, Irish tracks like Baldoyle, the Curragh, Fairyhouse and Punchestown were often recalled, as well as the local track, Bellewstown. Bellewstown would feature when a great old character called Harry Banks would recall, over a few bottles of Guinness, his riding days there, when he was known as Buckskin Banks, a fearless rider without equal. I would listen with great interest, as he doffed his cap and related how Lady Nugent of blessed memory told him 'Well-done, Buckskin!', as he got home by a short head, in a thrilling finish with Michael Beary. I heard later that Harry's tales were fibs and I never recall him having a bet, but he was certainly one of the best story-tellers I've ever heard.

Two of the most exciting days I remember were the day that Cottage Rake, trained by the great Irish trainer Vincent O'Brien, won the first of three Gold Cups at Cheltenham, at big odds, in 1948. Practically the whole town had a few shillings on him. Johnny Brennan was cleaned out and was in very bad humour for weeks. Vincent O'Brien went on to win three Grand Nationals in the early fifties with Early Mist, Royal Tan and Quare Times, all of them well-backed by the customers in the pub. What lover of the Sport of Kings can ever forget those great commentators, Michael O'Hehir and the plum-voiced Peter O'Sullivan, thankfully still race-going into his nineties.

Another great race I will never forget was the 1949 Epsom Derby and the blanket finish between the Nimbus, ridden by Charlie Elliott, Amour Drake, the mount of that great Australian jockey, Rae Johnstone II and Swallow Tale, ridden by D. Smith, one of the most prolific riders of winners during that period. If memory serves me, I backed Swallow Tale. What lover of the Turf can ever forget the great characters of those days, like Prince Monolulo and his cry of 'I've got an orse', as he waved his lucky wand, or the

Aga Khan, who got his weight in gold every year from his loyal followers in Africa. He caused a sensation, when he visited Laytown Races with his wife, the Begum Aga Khan, in 1950.

Father loved horse racing and one of the things I will always remember was him putting a few Baby Powers in his pocket and taking a wad of notes out of the till and then heading off to the races, with a few cronies, to Baldoyle or Leopardstown, as they discussed the chances of Morny Wing or Paddy Prendergast. Needless to say, the only thing he took home was a few empty bottles. Nobody was surprised, when he died a few years later, that he had not enough money to pay for his funeral.

Some of the happiest days of my life were spent at race meetings, with great friends like Tom Mooney, Mattie Keeley and Sean Kierans, men who loved the Sport of Kings. Having a few pints and beef sandwiches after the races in our local pub in Drogheda, was as good, if not better, than having a bottle of Bollinger Champagne in the Royal Enclosure at Royal Ascot, as we held post-mortems on the day's racing. The most memorable day in my racing life was the only time I attended the Grand National in Liverpool in 1956, when the Queen's horse, Devon Loch, slipped up yards from the winning post, enabling E.S.B. to take the prize. My greatest memory of that day was having a pound each-way on a horse called Blessing, at odds of 20/1. Blessing was ridden by the great D. Smith, winner of the six-furlong race, held before the National in those days. Truly a blessing, like all the marvellous days spent attending the Sport of Kings. But my best win ever was at Bellewstown, when I got almost 700 euro from a winning forecast, just a few years ago.

Michael Collins on John Joe Collin's donkey at the tote in the 1960s

250th Anniversary of Bellewstown Racecourse in 1976

On 13 June 1976 Bellewstown Racecourse Committee celebrated the 250th anniversary of Bellewstown Races by officially opening a new grandstand and bar at a function attended by leading racing personalities. The bars and dining-rooms were refurbished and the track greatly improved. The new stand replaced the old Owners and Trainers Stand and has a capacity for 600 race-goers. Speaking at the official opening, the chairman of the racecourse committee, Mr. Nesbitt Waddington warned that Bellewstown would have to keep abreast of modern developments in racing, in order to compete with other racecourses. 'Unless a good cover of grass can be provided on the track, trainers will become increasingly reluctant to run valuable thoroughbreds on a course where they run the risk of injury.' On a more optimistic note, Mr Waddington continued:

'We hope however that the improvements we have been introducing gradually in the past few years will go some way to ensuring that Bellewstown survives as a viable proposition for many years to come. Bellewstown is a non-profit-making organisation. All the profits are ploughed back into the maintenance of the racecourse. Thus we have been able to complete major alterations at each end of the track in 1970 by cambering the bends. A large part of the Committee's funds has gone into the erection of the new stand and bar, but all construction has been carried out by local contractors, providing local employment.'

In June 1977 night racing began. A three-day meeting was held in June 1978 but it was not a success, bad weather, a glut of racing during Ascot week, no steeplechases and the World Cup were all contributory factors. The 1980s saw great improvements to the racetrack, under the management of Joe Collins. The flat course was now railed on both sides in the straight, switched to the inside and the hurdle course moved to the stand side. In addition to safety the change permitted the Bellewstown Committee to mix flat and hurdle races through their programme without the cost and worry of moving hurdles.

Bellewstown, You're a Beauty

Tony McClafferty gives top marks in his report on Bellewstown Racecourse under the capable management of Joe Collins in the mid-eighties.

The second evening of the Festival meeting – Ladies Night – was held under showery conditions but still attracted an attendance of over 4000. The ample well-regulated car-park adjoining the course was not unduly taxed and despite the light showers, grass surfaces and lead-roads were bone-hard making underfoot conditions quite firm. Parking cost £1 and admission to the course £4. Racecards were 50p.

Catering arrangements were in the capable hands of the Peter O'Brien Organisation, Maynooth, who had a staff of 42 employed to cover the self-service snack bar, two public bars and several sponsors' marquees. In order to provide additional accommodation in the snack bar, the liquor section that was housed in this building has now been moved to an adjoining tent-site. The additional dining facilities are most welcome.

The snack bar itself is well laid out to facilitate a steady flow of customers. As kitchen facilities are extremely limited, only three hot items appeared on the menu, soup (£1), steak and kidney pie (£1), and sausage rolls (60p), although hot beef rolls were available from a special oven-unit in the tent bar at £2.50. Other items available included Salmon Mayonnaise (£6); Cold Meat Salad (£3.75); Various Sandwiches (95p); Tea/Coffee (50p); Fresh Strawberries and Cream (90p).

Counter service was speedy and efficient as was the clearing and cleaning of the high tables. Spread throughout the complex were a number of stalls and vehicles dispensing such goodies as ice-cream, baked potatoes, burgers, hot-dogs, chips etc. These were very popular with the young folk. As already mentioned, the kitchen facilities are very limited but the caterers had their own cold room van parked just outside the kitchen door. This was equipped with spotless stainless-steel shelving on which all foodstuff was neatly stored until required.

The two public bars, the long bar and the tented bar, carried a full range of popular drinks, including draught lager and stout. Both bars were fully manned by experienced, courteous staff, but more bus boys on the floor would have helped to clear an accumulation of empty glasses, discarded bottles and full ashtrays. As is to be expected at a festival meeting, the bars generally were uncomfortably over-crowded. Service however was quite good, if and when one managed to reach the counter. Price lists were prominently displayed and included the following: Murphy's Stout (£1.50 per pint); Heineken Lager (£1.70 per pint); Bottled Ale and Stout (£1.04); Whiskey/Gin/Vodka (£1.30); Glass of Wine (£1.20); Minerals (72p).

We are reluctantly compelled to again refer to the unpleasant practice that has become all too prevalent on Irish racecourses, the habit of drinking around the enclosures. It is now quite common to see ladies and gents *with glass in hand* queueing up outside a Tote window or watching a race from the stand. Perhaps we are too old-fashioned in our outlook, but we still feel that drinking should be done in the place where it belongs – in the bars. Apart from considerations of deportment, there is nothing more unsightly than to see empty glasses, bottles, coke-tins etc strewn all over the place. Not only does it look unsightly but broken glass can be a serious hazard for the unwary. We suggest that large notices should be displayed at all bar exits, urging patrons to drink up before leaving. This should be done immediately before the present situation gets out of hand.

We were pleased to find the Gents' toilet fresh and clean with ample supplies of soap, paper, hand-towelling, toilet-rolls etc. A full-time attendant on duty kept the facility well-maintained during the course of the evening. We heard glowing reports about the Ladies room, where once again a full-time attendant was on duty.

Under favourable weather conditions the two small uncovered stands provide pleasant viewing of the racetrack, although they both become very congested during a race. We were delighted to find numerous garden seats on the lawn behind the parade ring. These were greatly appreciated, especially by elderly patrons, who find the standing around over a prolonged period somewhat trying.

Arriving at the racecourse in the late afternoon, we found the whole complex spic and span. A team of local cleaners had moved in that morning and so well did they do their job that little evidence remained to show that racing had taken place the previous evening. Litter bins were apparent everywhere. Unfortunately, these served little purpose with hundreds of litter louts prancing around. During a brief chat with busy, energetic manager, Joe Collins, we learned that over the last five years attendances at Bellewstown have increased by 50%.

Racecards: provided basic information with previous form of runners; useful map of racecourse facilities.
Runners Riders Info: No undue delays in completing list.
Betting facilities: Bookmakers and Tote (uncovered) readily accessible. Betting show displayed above Tote Credit building.
Race Commentaries: Articulate, accurate, exciting.
Closed-circuit TV: Excellent coverage in bars and snack bars. Constant stream of information on betting shows and results.
Communications: Four instrument mobile digital telephone unit centrally located.
First Aid: Single bed ambulance room manned by Order of Malta. 3 doctors and 18 personnel on duty. 2 ambulances on site.
Signposting: Good visual guides to all internal racecourse facilities.

Ladies Day at Bellewstown
The introduction of Ladies Day has transformed racing at Bellewstown in recent years. Fashion and glamour have come back to the race-track, bringing a fun atmosphere to the evening's proceedings. In the 1980s, a prize for the Most Appropriately-Dressed Lady attracted enormous crowds, while the women dressed in anything from sensible dungarees to matching-dress-bag-hat-shoes-gloves outfits. As a sports reporter commented 'The title "Most Appropriately Dressed" can cover a lot of things and on Wednesday evening the only thing it ruled out was a wet-suit.' Some women indulged in cool, strapless off-the-shoulder numbers, but most women wore simple straight-forward chic outfits, suitable for traipsing around the racecourse.

Noreen Wiseman (1994 Runner-Up) and Aidan Cunningham

Best-Dressed Ladies Competition, a winner recalls the excitement

Noreen Wiseman was working in Coca-Cola in 1994, when she decided that she was going to win a holiday in the Best Dressed Ladies Competition at Bellewstown Races that year. 'I made it a project that I was going to win a holiday and threw myself into it for the week before the races' she recalled. 'I used to do quite a bit of dress-making at that time, so I bought the fabric and the pattern in Tully's in Drogheda. It took two or three days to finish it. I made the collar as well, exactly like the pattern and used a bit of left-over material to make the matching spotty bows for the shoes. I pushed those bows in over the original bows that were on the shoes. I hired the hat from a shop in West Street in Drogheda especially for the competition and got my partner Aidan to dress up too'.

Noreen's mother, Nora Crinion, grew up in Bellewstown and Crinions lived there for generations. Aidan also is from Bellewstown and his grandfather, Christopher Cunningham, was the coachman at Hilltown, living in the White Cottage for many years.

Despite the close associations with The Hill, when Noreen entered the competition it was her first time in the enclosure. 'You had to be in the enclosure to be in the competition', she explained, 'usually we'd watch the races from outside. You just walked around in the enclosure. It started to rain. I had to run and find shelter somewhere, because of the hired hat, I was afraid they mightn't take it back if it got ruined with the rain. So I was delighted to be spotted by the judges and we all had our photographs in the newspaper afterwards.'

'I came second in the competition. The winner was Theresa McCann from Dunleer.' Even now, you can still hear the regret in her voice, that she wasn't the outright winner. 'I knew I had won a holiday and was quite excited when the big white envelope came about a week later with my prize in it. Can you imagine how I felt when I realised that I had won a prize of a week in Mosney, a voucher for £250! Mosney is only down the road from me, a stone's throw from where I live.'

So did she spend a week in Mosney Holiday Camp? 'I did not! I sold it in *Buy and Sell* to a woman from Kilkenny and she came up and had a week's holiday with all her family and enjoyed it. I got £200 for the voucher and I spent it on a weekend in Paris. We had a great time there, so it actually worked out very well.'

BELLEWSTOWN: MANAGING THE RACECOURSE

AND REMINISCENCES

John Kirwan interviewed Jim Corcoran, Chairman of the Races Committee, in the historic weighroom of Bellewstown Race-course

I came with my grandfather as a little lad, by the hand. He was from the far side of Bellewstown, Bellewstown House. And he had a great interest in Bellewstown races. As a matter of fact, he used to say, once Christmas was over 'all we have to look forward to now, is Bellewstown Races.' He never missed the races and he also had some great stories. Now you must remember this would be in the late forties, so I was only a little lad, but like everyone else, I heard the stories. In those times, a lot of the horses would be stabled in the houses around Bellewstown. And at that time McKeevers were the people who owned Bellewstown House, they were horsey people. So the horses would be stabled in Bellewstown House and I used to hear them talking, 'Oh that's a lucky box or that's a lucky shed.' My grandfather absolutely loved Bellewstown, he loved the races and at that time Bellewstown was one of the great events of the year. I remember being brought by the hand and walking up past where the Cosy Bar used to be and walking up past the Hurdy Gurdies, the three-card-trick men, the usual. It had a great atmosphere, still has. We'd be mainly outside, that's where the locals congregated and all were there. As far as I know, Bellewstown is one of only three racecourses with an outside, in other words, you don't pay, you can watch the races from there. And the hurdy-gurdies are bigger than anywhere else. I always make sure, even today, that I walk down along once or twice per day, to see what it's like, because you get a great atmosphere. The atmosphere in Bellewstown is, in my opinion, superior to that of any racecourse in the world.

Then I came with my father and my mother and my aunts. It was a great meeting place, they all met people they hadn't met for six or seven months and they'd all meet at Bellewstown racecourse. I have an aunt who still lives in Bellewstown but back then we would all go back to her place and she would give us high tea and that was part of the races as well.

I remember horses getting loose and running and they'd be found at the bottom of the Carnes Hill. And I think it was 1958 that I remember well a horse bolting in the parade ring, it came out through the fence that was there, took four bars out of the fence and down through the crowd. I remember someone was quite severely injured at the time, but I was there with a couple of my mates and sure this was adding to the excitement of the races. My mate, who couldn't stand the sight of blood, had to go over and look, whereupon he fainted and everybody was coming over asking was he hit by the horse. There were a number of people seriously injured that day. It also was the start of drug-testing on Irish race-courses. They reckoned the horse was doped before the race. From that on, horses were always tested.

Steeple chasing was great but there was a problem because entries were bad. Bellewstown races were held in the first week of July, the ground would be as hard as the hobs of hell. Watering was unheard of. As a result of that any good steeple-chasers would be kept out and entries were falling back all the time, you might have three or four horses in a race, or less. I think '77 was the last year for steeple-chasing. Also the course wasn't fenced, so when a horse fell, which was more likely with steeple-chasing, he could go any place. So that was the end of the steeple-chasing, but I have an ambition, before I finish as chairman of the racecourse committee, that I would have steeple-chasing back in Bellewstown. We have the most modern watering system in the country, we can now give you any ground that you want in a dry summer, it's very good and it's very efficient. We have applied for steeple-chasing to be brought back and I hope it will be.

I joined the committee in the late nineties, I was asked by the then chairman, John Purfield. I remember coming up to my first meeting in the weighroom and I looked around the table and I saw a lot of old men that I knew. But I would have been one of the youngest, myself and Elizabeth Jenkinson were the two youngest on the committee and we weren't young either. But I always like to see young people on the committee, because they are the ones with the ideas and they are able to do a lot of the work. Most of the work that is done in Bellewstown is voluntary, the committee work is all voluntary. And we are very, very lucky that we have a good staff and they keep the place in excellent condition and it's always kept very well. Several people on the committee have died since I started: two Jenkinsons, Elizabeth and her father Tom, George Mernagh and Judge Frank Roe. I try to keep the committee to people who are interested in racing and to locals. In years gone by most of the people on the committee were from outside the area and didn't have much affiliation with the area. But I would try to keep it local. The committee are entirely voluntary, they meet on a very regular basis and coming up to racing, would be meeting almost on a daily basis. Through the winter, we would meet about once a month. And there's a lot of work to be arranged, a lot of planning to be done. When you come to Bellewstown, you think there is a lot of infrastructure but in actual fact when you come a few days after racing, you would realise that we have two stands, a weighroom, an ambulance room, two bars and that's it. Everything else is temporary, the stables, the extensions to the bars, the catering facilities, they are all temporary. Now we have improved on things over the years, this year we put on two new roofs. But we have to keep everything as it is. We race for five days of the year and then basically we would like to see it used a bit more. We do have a dog show, the caravan club use it as well and the bicycle club, but we would be interested in letting anyone who had a local function use the premises, we want to keep the place aired.

My biggest concern nowadays is health and safety e.g. on race days we have to have three ambulances, a full para-ambulance service, and it's a big headache to make sure that everything goes safely because safety is the main thing. We don't want any horses injured, we don't want any people injured. And since we put the watering system in, the injuries have gone away down, we are able to control that. This year, of course, (2012) we didn't use the watering system because it rained and rained. On the Friday of this year's July meeting, we were the only racecourse able to run a meeting in the British Isles. All the rest had to cancel, so it shows you how high we are, how well-drained the course is. And every year we spend money on drainage and keeping the place right. The two bends have been widened, it's not fully completed yet, we'd like to see them a bit better, the drainage has been improved and the watering system, which goes right round the course, has been put in. In the spring of this year we had all the racecourse people here to see that watering system in action and they were all very impressed. Unfortunately for them we were able to do it with local labour and with local help and we were able to do it at a certain price. The machine itself was not that expensive, about 40,000 sterling, but putting in the mains and pumps all around has been very, very expensive. But we have it paid for and it's a fantastic system. One man can operate the whole thing. We have the capability of pumping twenty thousand gallons an hour, we have storage for about 30,000 gallons. It is right round, every furlong has a hydrant and if we ever had to, it could be used in a fire situation, hopefully we will never have to use it for that.

I think the future for Bellewstown is very bright. It is well-known, it is getting the crowds even in the bad weather. It is the place to be in July, it is the social event of the Drogheda area, the July meeting in particular. The August meeting will always be a bit behind, but we have the Best-Dressed Lady's Competition at both meetings and this brings in a lot of people who wouldn't normally go racing. There is the social element to it, but as far as I am concerned I would like to keep Bellewstown the way it is, but we'd like to modernise the stands. One of the stands was funded by Lord Gormanston in the 1880s so we have to do a bit of refurbishment on that to keep it right. The facilities are very good, so hopefully the future is bright, hopefully we can get a couple of graded races, hopefully we can get steeple-chasing back. And I think when we get the steeple-chasing again, I can step down and let somebody younger take over as chairman.

Paul Ludlow, a Bellewstown institution, worked as assistant to James Black on the grounds.

Bellewstown Memories and Management: Kevin Coleman, Secretary/Manager Bellewstown Racecourse

I can always recall the first time I stood on the Hill of Crockafotha. As a youngster I would spend most school holidays in my grandmother's in nearby Duleek. My late mother and father were both born and raised in 'sweet Duleek in the hollow ground' so it was not unusual to be drawn to the country even though we lived beside the sea in Laytown. Of course my uncle, John Potter, who worked for Meath County Council in the Courthouse, still lived in the old family home and he was the one with the motor car and the television set, both of which were few and far between in those days. Uncle John was the lifeline for transporting our family to visit our relations in places like Hayestown, Glasnevin and Avoca in Wicklow. There were also day trips to the Botanic Gardens and the Dublin Horse Show. He also regularly brought us to the annual Hilltown Horse Trials and I can well remember coming over the hill and seeing the Steeplechase fences which were a permanent fixture in those days.

Kevin Coleman as a young boyscout on Bellewstown Racecourse

The annual races were originally held on Wednesday and Thursday and, as Wednesday was the traditional half-day in Drogheda, my late father, also Kevin Coleman, would bring me to the races, often getting a lift from his boss Willie Wall, who owned a butchers shop in Drogheda. It was a really exciting time and, at one stage, I thought that *Tax Law* won the Duleek Handicap Steeplechase every year. I would stand along the railings on the 'outside' at the fence adjacent to the winning post watching the horses stream by and then climb up on the railings to see the finish on the final circuit. I was also a fan of jockey Joe Larkin and I can remember well the day he won on *Tic Tac* for Sir Hugh Nugent. My father became engaged in deep conversation with one of his pals and I couldn't get his attention to bet a shilling each way for me.

One day, at the races, I was approached by the late Paddy Whyte who asked me if I would give them a hand with some figures and paperwork. Gradually, I became involved in other aspects of organising the races and in 1997 I was appointed as Racecourse Manager. It was now a three day meeting with Friday having been added to the traditional Wednesday and Thursday. At the end of the third day I would reverse my car down the slope to the Secretary's office and fill the boot with all the stationery, the Fax machine, walkie-talkies, unsold race cards, lost and found items and the odd trophy that some winning connections had forgotten to collect after they had celebrated their big win in the Tent. By late evening, the water would be turned off and the electric disconnected and the whole place would close down until the following year. The following day, Saturday, I would drive over to Bellewstown to pay the staff, who by lunchtime, would have dismantled all the railings and secured the road crossings.

During the next few years there were rapid changes in the racing industry. Health and Safety became the buzz words and greater emphasis was placed on facilities for the racing fraternity and the general public alike. John Purfield, who had presided for many years, was still Chairman and the first major job undertaken was the dismantling and replacement of the old Judges box. This gave more space, and safety, to the judge, the photo-finish operators, the camera man and the commentator. The work had finished just in time for the race meeting but had resulted in the ground becoming a mess, due to the inclement weather, and it was only natural that soon a lot of the grassy areas were replaced with tarmacadam to the great delight of the delivery vehicles and the ladies in their stiletto heels. Following that, the steps of the small Grandstand were re-pointed and the Parade ring extended with a horse walkway providing direct access to the stable yard area, thereby obviating the need for animals to be led up the track and allowing for complete segregation from the general public.

The horse box area was still in grass but 2002 was the last straw when George Mullins' horse transport lorry became embedded and was eventually hauled out after midnight thanks to the intervention of locals Seamus Fitzpatrick and Tom Jenkinson, who were later to become members of the organising Committee. That lorry contained the winner of the bumper in *Liberman*, ridden by Mr Keith Mercer, for trainer Paddy Mullins. The following year *Liberman* won the Champion Bumper at the Cheltenham festival when trained by Martin Pipe and providing A P McCoy with his only winner at that year's festival.

John Purfield retired after being in the Chair for over 40 years and was replaced by Jim Corcoran, the current Chairman. More improvements were made and, mainly thanks to funding through the HRI Racecourse Improvement Scheme, these included complete new railings around the enclosure and a brand new watering system. The watering system, in particular, is important in the preparation and maintenance of a track. Obviously, if the weather is bad, as it has been in the past couple of seasons, watering is not necessary, but if it turns warm and dry, which is always anticipated, then watering can be vital.

For many years, the ambulance track consisted of dirt and grass. When the weather was dry the dirt created a great deal of dust which was a hazard in itself. Alternatively, when the weather was wet the grass parts were difficult to access. The only solution was to put down a permanent tarmac surface and this has been a great addition and well received by everyone. Indeed, this track has also served the local community as it provides an ideal facility for fitness fanatics, families with young children or people just wishing to stretch their legs and take in the fresh air.

As a manager, there is a great deal of reliance on the people around you. This is particularly true in the case of Bellewstown, where the locals step in twice a year to provide invaluable assistance as fence stewards, manning the road crossings, footing in, or as general help to our grounds-man. Back in 1997 some of these individuals, particularly the course staff, were affectionately known as 'Shuiler's' men, a fitting tribute, perhaps, to Sean 'Shuiler' Black who was head grounds-man for many years. A race was subsequently named in his honour, to commemorate the many years of service he gave to Bellewstown.

When Shuiler retired his natural successor was John Kirwan. A local man, John must know every blade of grass and is easy to find particularly during the months of May, June, July and August. If he's not out on the course on his tractor, cutting grass, he's strimming around the enclosure or checking the going at the 5 furlongs. He's also probably the first man on course during Race week and the last man to leave every evening. There is hardly a year goes by that we don't receive a kind letter from the Trainers Association complimenting the way in which the course is continually presented, a fitting tribute to John Kirwan and his regular assistants, Pat Brannigan and Terry Kearns. Of course nothing can run completely smooth without some officialdom. As part of our Racecourse Licence, issued annually by the Turf Club, it is necessary to list everyone who is involved, including their length of service and their experience. To this end we are blessed to have Vincent Eivers as our Course Foreman. He comes from Trim and is employed on a full time basis, in a similar role, at Navan racecourse. Vincent's role is to ensure the complete safety of the track for all participants. Under the guidance of the Clerk of the Course, he also plans the track for each days racing. This usually involves the movement of rails on at least 2 or 3 occasions during the course of both the July and August festivals. He also supplies the yardage markers near the finish line and the orange warning flags and markers should anything go wrong during the running of a race.

He follows each race in his jeep and is on the lookout for a fallen jockey, a loose horse, or a damaged hurdle or section of rail. A couple of years ago, so that I could see for myself exactly what was going on, I took a spin round with Vincent, following a race. I can say, with hand on my heart, that the whole field were finished and unsaddled, 'home and hosed' as they say, before we returned to the enclosure. So much for thinking we'd be chasing behind the field at high speed like the race camera filming the excitement of the Grand National. It was the same Vincent who, many years ago when I was asking the names of the local staff, told me not to worry because they'd turn up no matter. And every year he's been right.

The overall responsibility for the track is vested in the Turf Club and their assigned officials. When I started first in 1997 our Clerk of the Course was Peter McGouran and then Brendan Sheridan. In more recent years it has been Ion Hamilton, a man who has endeared himself to the Committee with his advice, practical help and friendship. A couple of years ago, in a Turf Club reshuffle, Ion was replaced by our current Clerk, Lorcan Wyer. He has carried on in the same vein as Ion and is of huge help each year in preparing the venue. Lorcan was a top jockey some years ago and in 1999 led over the last in the Aintree Grand National, on *Blue Charm*, only to have his dreams of success dashed near the finish line by the flying Irishman Paul Carberry on his father's *Bobbyjo*. The rest of our local team is organised by John Ludlow and Ann Collins who make sure that everywhere is spick and span for each days racing and for the comfort of our customers.

The Secretary's office is usually a hub of activity each year. The office is managed by Rita Eivers, Vincent's wife, who deals with all the race-day queries in a calm and informative way. Rita also checks all the staff in and out and makes sure that everyone knows their respective duties. In 2002 we engaged Cash Keeping Services, and their principal Paula Connelly, to look after all the Gate men, race-card sellers, etc. Paula also provides all our race-day statistics and, by the end of each day, she can tell us if our attendance is up or down on the previous year and whether we've got it (nearly) right in the amount of race-cards ordered and sold.

The final preparations for race week start in earnest a week or so before the appointed date. At this stage, I am full time on site to supervise the arrival and setting up of the marquees and the temporary stables. The telephone lines and the broadband have to be checked and there is a myriad of tasks involving the electrician and plumber. Usually the general maintenance is completed by then but provision has always to be made for any unforeseen last minute items that need to be addressed. The question of watering is always a major issue. Sometimes, if there is a lot of rain about, decisions are easily made and mother nature takes care of everything. Alternatively, if there is a doubt, it is necessary to keep informed of the weather forecasts to arrive at a calculated decision whether to water or not. The final decision is made in conjunction with the clerk of the course, and the horse racing industry is kept informed of developments and, ultimately, the state of, or the projected state of, the going. Going reports are critical for trainers in helping to decide whether to run their horses, or not.

Sometimes I attempt to complete other tasks such as paperwork, checking and answering mail, etc. This often proves impossible because your mind is on the racing and the 'buzz' is really beginning to take a hold. Race week itself can be manic. Usually, I would transfer the course phone to my mobile which means that the course is contactable at all times. The downside is that as soon as the mobile is switched on, in the morning, the calls are relentless. So it is important to get up early, have a shower, then breakfast. The first call, around 7.45am is to our groundsman, John Kirwan, to get an overnight going and weather update. Then it's often a call to John Ludlow for a rainfall count before I contact Lorcan, the clerk of the course. Cliff Noone is the Turf Club press officer and his job is to get a going report as early as possible, together with a forecast of the weather and whether or not watering has taken place or will continue, whatever the case may be. Cliff is always helpful in deciding the exact wording and description of the going report, which has to be communicated to Horse Racing Ireland. This should be done, ideally, by 8.15am to give the trainers time to weigh up their options before declarations close at 10am.

Then it's off to Bellewstown where, on arrival, you can be sure of a plethora of things to be sorted and a queue of people with questions and requests. At this stage, I often resort to my 'Things to do List' and attempt to sort out some paperwork such as staff schedules or list of accounts to be paid, etc. It's amazing, that despite all the information having earlier been given to the relevant authorities, the number of calls that come in from owners and trainers looking for going updates and whether we're having the same weather as 'it's lashing here in Tipperary'. The same format follows each day and slowly but surely everything begins to slot into place. Tom Holden is our Health and Safety advisor, and he will completely survey the enclosure to make sure that everything is properly secured and, for example, there are no hazards exposed which could cause us problems over the following few days.

When Race day arrives there is certainly a change both in atmosphere and anticipation. The service vehicles arrive early and move into position and the PA system springs into life with 'testing one two…..one, two three, four, five….testing one two'. By the scheduled time of the first race, the turnstiles are clicking away and there's an air of excitement coming from the bars and around the parade ring. The racing itself can be somewhat of a blur as everything moves so quickly. I am usually in and out of the Secretary's office checking how things are going and I will have regular contact with the clerk of the course throughout the day. I also seek out the course Vet just to be assured that everything is going according to plan and there are no incidents to report. At the end of racing, we can wrap up for the evening. Before that I get the statistics for the day and I usually check in with the Chairman and we do a quick final check before leaving everything in the capable hands of the course Security personnel. Then it is home for a well-earned rest, to awake fresh the following morning to do it all again.

One of the other tasks to be carried out prior to racing is to finalise the panel of Stewards who officiate on each day. This is done in conjunction with the Chairman of the Stewards and involves working from a draft list prepared by him and then confirming by phone that everyone is available as selected. Stewards usually are people who have been previously involved in racing itself and who complete a course organised by the Turf Club and who then volunteer to go on a Panel which is allocated to each racecourse. Their job is to ascertain that the Rules of Racing are adhered to, hold enquiries, and report to the relevant authority, the Turf Club.

When there is a public address announcement such as 'Would Kevin Coleman, Manager, please go to the weigh-room', you know that something is wrong. This happened to me on one occasion when we had an earlier start to the original scheduled one, as a result of a race divide, and we only had one ambulance on track instead of the necessary two and racing became delayed. In any event, I became the subject of the Stewards Inquiry but was able to answer any questions asked. This is the real secret of success as a manager. You simply need to know, and should know, everything that is going on round you relevant to running a successful race meeting. I was honoured to serve on the board of Directors of the AIR, the Association of Irish Racecourses, for three years from 2007 to 2010. The future of Bellewstown races is looking bright and there are many plans in mind to make it bigger and better for future generations who, like their predecessors, will look forward to the first week in July each year for their annual pilgrimage to the Hill of Crockafotha.

Joe Collins, former secretary manager, on managing Bellewstown Racecourse 1974 – 1992

I was manager of the racecourse during the period from 1974 until 1992. When I started in Bellewstown, it was a two-day meeting, with two afternoons in June. It used to be held on the first Wednesday and Thursday in July, but it had been allowed to slip down into the middle of June and it clashed with Royal Ascot. The attendances were dropping and funds were getting low. At that time I was working for the Turf Club and I was asked to go forward as manager. The manager before me was a man called Billy Kelly and he had been manager there since the late forties and before that his father, Tommy Kelly, was manager. The Kelly's lived in Rathmullen, in Drogheda, and they had a farm where LMFM is at the moment. Billy was Clerk of the Course in places like Galway, Leopardstown, Curragh, Naas, Dundalk, and Navan. I was Billy's understudy at the Turf Club. I had been with the Turf Club since 1968 and Bellewstown was a big challenge for me at that time.

When I went up to Bellewstown for the first time as manager, I walked the track with the chairman Nesbit Waddington, and James Black. There were so many holes in the railings around the enclosure that people could walk in freely and the only solution, as they hadn't the money to buy iron railings, was to buy rolls of chain-link wire and roll it out along the rails to block the holes. I can still remember the price of the wire, it was £39, and the question was, could we afford to spend £39? Times were that bad. A few years later Leopardstown gave Bellewstown some old iron railings they no longer required and the Committee were able to secure the enclosure.

There was no electricity in the enclosure. There was electricity going into the pump for the water and that was all. For the afternoon meetings, you didn't need electric light. The caterers used gas for cooking and the tote used their own generator. The only reason why we got electricity in the place was because Father Tully, the parish priest at the time, asked for permission to use the weigh-room as a schoolroom. He wanted to do alterations to the school, and he asked the Committee if he could use the weigh room. The

Committee told him he could use the weigh-room but that there was no electricity. So he said 'I'll put electricity in'. And he did, and that is how we got electricity into Bellewstown racecourse. Father Tully put it in.

In the seventies, evening meetings had become very popular and were the way forward. In the Committee there was a lot of opposition to evening meetings because people used to have lunch parties before the races and if we changed to evenings the guests would have to be entertained for too long. Eventually, I convinced Nesbit Waddington that we would have to change, or that Bellewstown would go broke. Attendances improved dramatically when we got evening meetings. But the biggest change was convincing the Turf Club and the Racing Board to let us have our proper dates in the first week of July. I did a study at the time showing them that the Bellewstown dates were always the first Wednesday and Thursday in July, and I was able to get the Racing Calendars going back years and show that Bellewstown always had those dates. Bellewstown had been allowed to slip back into June and the Curragh had taken one of its dates, and Tipperary had taken the other. The Committee was able to convince the Turf Club and the Racing Board what their correct dates were. At that time Cahir O'Sullivan was the Chief Executive of the Turf Club and Pat Walsh was the Chief Executive of the Racing Board and they said 'Ok, we'll give you back your dates' and we got them back. When the Committee got their correct dates in early July they had no competition from other fixtures and this helped improve attendances more.

When I went to Bellewstown first, the racecourse wasn't enclosed, it was commonage and cattle belonging to the locals grazed it. There was no grass on the track because the cattle would have eaten it all. On the morning of the races, the local people who owned the cattle would have to take their stock off the track and then the track would have to be cleared of all the cowpats. Rain on the cowpats is a lethal cocktail because it makes them very slippy and the riders would be very anxious if they saw a hint of rain. Gerry Marry was a local councillor, an auctioneer and a rate collector. I went to Gerry and explained that something would have to be done about the cattle, that the Committee could not run a race meeting with cattle grazing on the track up to the day of the races. The solution was, the Committee rented a field from Boylans. The cattle were put into this field for the three weeks before the races and this helped improve the track.

In 1979 a horse named *Beau Chaval* ran out after the last bend and ran towards the horseboxes that were parked along the road on the outside of the track. *Beau Chaval* ran into a groom who was leading a horse named *Cradle Days*. The groom, Christy Cole, was seriously injured and *Cradle Days* got loose. *Cradle Days* ran wild around the track doing untold damage to cars, luckily nobody else was injured. In those days the horseboxes were parked opposite the school, on the green, above where the hurdy-gurdies are now. Shortly afterwards the horseboxes were moved to where they are today.

After the races in 1955 and before litter management of the racecourse
Tony Ludlow, Biddy Martin, Tommy Reilly, with Rita Brannigan at back

When I went to Bellewstown first there was a chase course. There were two chases run each year, one on each day. The Committee used to have to maintain this track along with seven fences for these chases. The chases were attracting very small numbers of runners and when one of these runners fell and got loose you never knew where they would end up, but it was usually galloping on the road. In 1977 the Committee decided to stop having chases in Bellewstown because of the lack of runners and also due to the cost of maintaining the fences. So because of the cattle grazing the track and also because of the loose horses the committee realized that would have to try and enclose the track to make Bellewstown a safer place. The committee had a responsibility to the riders, owners, trainers, customers, the road users and the horses to make Bellewstown safe. The cost of enclosing the track was going to cost 10,000 pounds and the Racing Board could not find that amount of money to give to the Committee. I suggested to the Committee that we do what we could afford each year. James Black was the person who looked after all the work on the track for the committee, as his father Michael had done before him. The committee purchased two furlongs of pressurised creosoted posts and rails and James put it up on the outside of the track from the mile-start to the road. Nesbit Waddington and the Committee were happy with the job and each year we purchased more fencing and in a few years the track was enclosed thanks to the help of James Black. The Racing Board grant-aided the Committee to do this work as they did with all of the major projects that the Committee did. Bellewstown would never have been enclosed without the co-operation of all the people from Bellewstown, because if the Committee did not have their trust it would never have happened.

One of the first things that happened at Bellewstown when I started was the building of the stand to the east of the enclosure. In the eighties the Committee purchased cladding from Leopardstown which had demolished a stand and Bellewstown used this cladding to cover the two stands. The cladding cost 500 pounds and was stored in Jimmy Curran's farmyard for a number of years until the Committee got a contractor to do the work at a reasonable price. The two stands were covered for about 10,000 pounds each. I recall that the committee got a quotation amounting to £250,000 to cover one of the stands.

Major Boylan was instrumental in correcting the bends on the track. They were cambered and made longer. When I arrived in Bellewstown one person who was very dynamic on the Committee was John Purfield. He was a farmer and he owned a farm beside the track, and he gave a lot in terms of his machinery, his time, and his staff to the racecourse. Bellewstown didn't own any machinery and he used to get his staff to mow and roll the track. There was another farmer down the road called Jimmy Curran who helped in many ways as well. Denis Reddan made a big contribution to Bellewstown, both in sponsorship and in the maintenance of the track. When these men came on to the committee they were very active in helping to run the racecourse. John Purfield succeeded Nesbit Waddington as chairman and he came up with the idea of watering the track. He got one of those tankers with a spray gun on it and before Bellewstown got its own water-system, they used to drag the water up the hill from the Nanny River.

Another unique feature that Bellewstown has is its free outside enclosure. Race goers can savour all the thrills of racing at no cost in the outside enclosure. They have bookies, tote, food stalls, bar and a carnival all for nothing. This is the place where many will experience their first taste of racing and hopefully they will become the fans of the future. Bellewstown in now a good track and they always have it in great condition and the racing surface in Bellewstown is second to none. There's not a weed in it, it's cared for and attended to with absolute care and devotion by John Kirwan. The watering system they have is second to none. There are bigger racecourses that haven't got anything as sophisticated! Jim Corcoran is the chairman now and he is leading the committee to bigger and better things. Bellewstown has widened both bends, constructed an ambulance road, installed an excellent watering system, increased the size of the parade ring and the enclosure, and built an extension to the weigh room. The list is endless. Bellewstown is now considered one of the festivals of racing. The Committee is a non- profit sharing Committee and all the profits are ploughed back into the track and enclosure. The success of Bellewstown can be attributed in no small way to the pride that the local people have in the races and the great local spirit that can be seen among young and old in preparing the track and enclosure for the races. I am delighted to see Bellewstown going from strength to strength and I wish the Committee continued success in the years ahead.

John Purfield, Honorary President and Former Chairman of Bellewstown Race Committee by Kevin Coleman

John Purfield has been involved with Bellewstown for over 40 years. This all began when he became a Committee member in the early 1970's, then as Chairman, from the early 1980's to 2007 and now as Honorary President. He has worked with many Turf Club officials down through the years including Richard Teevan, Michael O'Donoghue, and Peter Matthews. One of the longest serving stewards, still officiating today, is Richard Filgate. He took over the chair from the late Nesbitt Waddington and received great support at that time from his good friend the late and legendary Judge Thomas Francis Roe, who was always known and, will always be remembered as simply Frank

Roe, a great supporter of racing during his lifetime as a Turf Club official, owner of some regard, and amateur jockey.

It was with the late Paddy Whyte, who was his vice chairman until his untimely death in 1999, that the future of Bellewstown Races, in the more modern era, began to take shape. One of the biggest decisions back then was to dispense with steeplechasing and the last of these races took place in 1977. When a horse got loose in those days it might take 'til night to find him in faraway places like Ardcath or Garristown. The advice was given to do away with the fences, which were a permanent fixture on the track, due to upkeep and vandalism. In those early days the track preparation was very different than it is today. At that time, cattle grazed on the track and these had to be removed a few days before racing, together with their droppings, to allow for rolling and harrowing of the ground with 'some small cutting of grass.' In fact, in 1975 there was a grave doubt about the running of the races because of the cattle and the effect to the racing surface.

The running rails were borrowed from Fairyhouse and a water tanker was purchased between Navan, Fairyhouse and Bellewstown, the water being brought up from the Nanny River, before Bellewstown ultimately sunk its own well, which is used today. The ground condition was almost always 'hard' as there were very few summer floods of rain and it was 'always good weather'. The official going report could be given as Good to Firm even though Firm might have been more appropriate. This is a far cry from today when going reports, rainfall measurements, and weather forecasts are part of a manager's duties and which the racing fraternity and public alike rely upon. Trainers would always come and examine the ground and agree that 'there was nothing better anywhere else'. If fact, many horses came back year after year for the fast ground that they waited for all year. These 'summer ground' horses probably sparked that well known racing term 'horses for courses'. However, the number of steeplechasers got fewer and fewer probably due to these ground conditions and the fact that other full-time courses were improving at a faster rate, and it was only a long time afterwards that things at Bellewstown began to improve due to grant money from the Racing Board.

One of the main problems on the track was the home bend as horses scrimmaged for position turning into the straight. This brought about huge improvements when a new bend was put in place in 1970. The steeplechase fences were made from birch which was sourced in Co Westmeath and dressed from furze which grew in abundance in Bellewstown. The main contractors were the Black family and they have been associated with the races for many many years. The leading trainers then were Dermot Weld, Kevin Prendergast, and his late father P J (Darkie) Prendergast. There were also plenty of runners from Northern Ireland from the likes of Willie Rooney, Leslie Crawford, and Frank Fitzsimons, whose sons Brian and Frankie Fitzsimons continue to act as stewards to the present day. The late Tom Dreaper had 32 winners on the 'Hill' and amongst them were *Fortria, Arkloin, Black Secret* and *The Big Hindu*.

Horses were often stabled overnight in Arnolds or Langans and would be led up the road on race day to the Enclosure. In the early days, horse boxes would park on the outside of the track near the local primary school and would form a natural barrier. One day a horse ran wide off the last bend and crashed into a horse being prepared for a later race. After that the entire course was railed in. This was during the tenure of NW Waddington as chairman. Another day a horse called *Fledgling* won first time out at odds of 20/1. The race was run in a hail storm and only the stewards out the track saw any of the race. *Fledgling* was ridden by Tommy Murphy and trained by Clem Magnier, whose son Colin Magnier is a present day steward at Bellewstown and who won the 1982 Champion Hurdle on *For Auction* for local trainer Michael Cunningham. There was also another time when a crowd of up to 30 people converged on the weighroom maintaining that their horse had won in a photo finish. Even after they had been shown the photo they still almost wouldn't believe that their horse had actually been beaten by a short head. Often there would be no ambulance, or at least not more than one, in attendance and injured jockeys were often taken to hospital in the chairman's own vehicle. One of the late great trainers to have runners at Bellewstown was Paddy Mullins. He often rang enquiring about the state of the ground. The Chairman's answer was often 'As good as it will ever be' and Mr Mullins reply would be 'Well, it's always good at Bellewstown'.

Chrissie Arnold, Josephine Townley and Mary Sherry at the racecourse in the 1940s.

Interview with Roy Craigie, who was Chairman of Stewards at Bellewstown Races for many years

Genial Roy Craigie and his lovely wife, Pat, called to Bellewstown on the first day of May 2013 to reminisce with us about racing in Bellewstown. He recalled that in the old days in his father's time, Merville Dairy, which was owned by the Craigie family, used to sell ice-cream at Bellewstown Races. Merville Dairies at that time was one of two big companies in Ireland making ice-cream. The dairy was in Finglas and the ice-cream would be hand-wrapped in paper and placed in brine containers, boxes containing salt water, frozen and then packed into the insulated boxes that were attached to the front of carrier bikes. The men would travel by train to Drogheda, with their bikes and then cycle out to the hill of Bellewstown. Afterwards, Roy recounted, the takings would be all in coppers, halfpennies and pennies stuck together and the lads would be 'half-scuttered' arriving back at the dairy after their big day out at the races.

Roy's association with The Hill goes back to the mid-forties when he can distinctly remember, as a young boy, travelling down, from Finglas to Bellewstown in the pony and trap with his parents, in the days after the war when petrol rationing still applied. Since then he has been a regular at Bellewstown, in varying capacities from rider to owner to steward to chairperson of the Stewards Committee. Looking back, it seemed as if racing at Bellewstown always took place in sunshine, right at the middle or end of the hay-making season. The course was more dangerous back then and he shuddered as he recalled a particular stretch where the ground was cambered away to the left and 'you'd find yourself heading towards Drogheda if you weren't careful.' Dry or wet, that section was always slippery and required particular skill.

Roy recalled riding in a hurdle race and being at the second last hurdle. He could hear T.P. Burns roaring at him to get out of his way. He must have obeyed, as T.P. won the race and Roy came in second. They remained good pals despite this. A little mare, called *Clonrosse*, bought from Barry Geraghty's grandfather in Drumree, partnered Roy to victory at Bellewstown one year. She was not a great horse but she did the business. Roy does not recall many victories at Bellewstown, as there were only two races for amateur jockeys in his day. He remembered a horse getting loose in the enclosure after falling during a race. His sister-in-law, Tina, who rarely attended race meetings, was walloped by the horse and 'had to be carted off to hospital', although she was not badly injured. Health and safety issues were not as prominent then as they are nowadays. Trainers were forever complaining about the ground back then, watering was always a problem, not alone at Bellewstown but at all the racecourses

Roy Craigie also looked back fondly on point-to-point racing at Beamore, down the road from Bellewstown and recalled one race in particular when he was riding for Georgie Wells, as was Bunny Cox who was expected to win on *Tear Glory*. At the last fence, Bunny Cox's horse's legs went down and 'I ended up beating him'. That night Roy visited Georgie Wells, who was sick in bed at the time. 'Well, we won' he said and George Wells couldn't believe that he had beaten Bunny Cox.

Roy has good memories of hunting with the Ward Union in Bellewstown. They would meet at the pub at the start and finish the day in the pub too. He recalled a winter evening when the 'boys' all gathered in the pub, among them Paddy Hendron who hunted with the Wards. As the drink and talk flowed, someone proposed riding over a couple of the jumps that had been left standing on the racecourse since the summer meeting. Money was wagered and the upshot was that Paddy Hendron mounted his hunter in almost pitch black conditions and went at the fences. He won a good few quid from everyone in the pub, recalled Roy, with a chuckle.

Roy Craigie was appointed as a steward by the Turf Club, serving first as a steward and then chairman of the Stewards Committee for about twenty years. He resigned, reluctantly, on his seventy-fifth birthday and misses the buzz and excitement of those days. He fondly remembers many race meetings in Bellewstown, recalling especially the generous hospitality of John Purfield and how well he looked after the stewards. His wife recalled the swallows flying in and out while they were taking tea, the swallows fearful for their nestlings tucked into nests under the stands.

Peadar Flanagan: Legends at Bellewstown
A couple of years ago some wise person came up with the idea of a legends race at Bellewstown. What a wonderful spectacle it turned out to be and a reminder to us all of the amazing skills and horsemanship of the likes of Norman Williamson, Adrian Maguire, Charlie Swan and Conor O'Dwyer, some of the riders who took part. This was to have been a bit of crack, one supposes. But the guys out there on horseback saw things much differently. If we had forgotten, and I almost had, how good they were, they sure as hell were about to remind us. It was riveting to watch the race unfold, close to trackside. This is one of the joys of going racing on the hill at Crockafotha. The action never seems as far away as at many other tracks.

Here was a determined Adrian blazing the trail on *Teak*, reminiscent of the days when he and the Duke, God rest him, cleaned up throughout Britain. For a long time it appeared that Adrian had stolen the race on the long leader. But eventually *Teak's* stride shortened and along came Norman polished as always and looking like the winner on *Priors Gold*. But it was not to be. Conor had the last word as he stylishly unleashed the favourite, *Bullock Harbour*, for what proved to be a facile victory. Gold Cup winning riders, Conor O'Dwyer, Norman Williamson and Adrian Maguire first, second and third respectively. An unexpected treat of a race from a bunch of great riders, courtesy of Bellewstown.

Those who were lucky enough to be present on this magical occasion will have shared the delight one experienced. But I shouldn't have been surprised. Bellewstown has been regaling me since I first set foot in the place in my youth. On first discovering that there was racing there, the big task was to find the place, which, in the days when motorways were non-existent, was a task in itself. But once there, high up on the hill with horses and the crowds about and a buzz which is hard to match even in far flung exotic places, I was hooked. The close proximity of both the exciting racing and the facilities and also the feeling that here in this place in the countryside there was a certain tranquility and good old fashioned Irish friendliness were captivating forces. With form sheets almost non-existent, finding winners was a real test. Success however was achievable by keeping your ears open and by watching out for the canny trainers who year after year would lay their horses out for the meeting. There was a chap in particular called Walls who was very good at that. Once there was a move for one of his runners, the bookmakers' panic became all too evident. The rain suddenly came pelting down, I recall, when a gamble had just commenced on one of his runners. It was hilarious to watch punters caught between the two stools of running for cover and trying to make a path through the hordes in the ring to get on. Of course the big stables sent runners to Bellewstown then as they do to this day. But even mighty forces of other tracks are sometimes brought to their knees here by smaller handlers like Mr Walls. Over the years it has been noticeable how the lesser known names in racing can strike out of the blue. To take a fairly recent example, in 2000 my good friend Alfie Evans sent a horse called *Illusions Tom,* for Seamus Kirwan, here from his Delgany base and it won at 33-1. The same horse failed to follow up in a number of subsequent races until coming back to Bellewstown the following year and winning at 20-1. Never mind that *Illusions Tom* failed to complete the hat-trick in 2002. He paid Alfie and Seamus for the expenses by finishing third. Wayne Smith who rode *Illusions Tom* in all three races later became a champion jockey in both Dubai and Macau.

Everyone has a chance, it seems, at this most democratic and non-pretentious place. Bellewstown never strives to be anything more than it is. A good old-fashioned Irish race meeting, where even the stony-faced smile. Some years ago, a dear old uncle of mine who would soon be called home by his Maker, came up with this strange request. He asked his non-racing son to drive him to Bellewstown. Too unwell to enter the track, he was happy just to sit outside in the car. Evidently that good man's life had been enriched, as ours has been, by Bellewstown races.

Memories of a By-Gone Age by Tony Redmond, ex-jockey and trainer

My father was a blacksmith, so I suppose I was used to horses but there was no history of horse-racing in my family. However from an early age, the only ambition I had was to be a jockey. I started in Tipperary working with Jimmy McClintock, then moved to Vincent O'Brien and then on to Paddy Norris who trained at Castleknock Park gate. It was from there that I took my first trip to Bellewstown and I rode a couple of winners at the Hill before I started training horses myself.

One race I remember particularly well was the day I rode *Fairy Pack*. She had a bandage on her leg and with a circuit to go the bandage began to unravel and stream out behind her. I didn't know anything about this so I was totally unconcerned and fully concentrated on winning the race. Up on the stand, of course, it was a different story, they were worried that the horse would be tripped up by the bandage. But they needn't have had any worries, I went on to win that race anyway.

It was some track, before they cambered Bellewstown, you'd nearly say an act of contrition before your race, I can tell you! In those days you adjusted your race to the track, nowadays it's the track that has to be adjusted to the jockeys. It's a shame the chases were done away with, the last one in Bellewstown was in 1977. But the chase fields were getting very small. The chase track ran right in along the wall, you knew where the problems were, so you rode to suit those problems. We were always told, 'Take your time or else you won't finish.' The bend at the top was tricky and the one coming out at the back. If you didn't handle it properly, you'd be out on top of the hurdy-gurdys.

I knew all the jockeys of course in those days, Frankie Shortt, Francis Carroll, Pat Taaffe, Paddy Woods, Liam McLoughlin and before their time, Eddie Newman. I remember my first winner, I beat Eddie Newman in Galway. Of course like every jockey, I had falls but I was lucky. I never broke my collar-bone. One fall I remember was in Navan, it wasn't the fall, because you learn to fall as best as you can and a horse won't run over you if he can possibly avoid it, but that day I got a kick in the face from a horse, that's one I won't forget! I rode a lot of schooling grounds over a six-year period at the Curragh and never had a fall in all that time. I remember getting kicked by a horse and my arm being broken in three places. Nowadays there are back protectors and chest protectors and better helmets but jockeys still get injuries, sometimes from the simplest of falls. Some jockeys won't turn out for certain racecourses but everyone turned out for Bellewstown. There are horses for courses. People are more protective of their horses nowadays. I remember *Arkloin* won a bumper in either Clonmel or Tramore and his maiden hurdle in one of those two. He won chases at Bellewstown at 12st7 lb. Nowadays you wouldn't bring a Cheltenham winner to Bellewstown. But Kevin Prendergast, Seamus McGrath and Dermot Weld too all run in Bellewstown and even at Laytown, where you might consider it to be beneath their dignity.

I retired from riding in December 1968 and started training at Mountjoy Lodge, at the Curragh. The stables there had been owned by Joe Canty and Phillip Behan, and John Oxx was there for a time. Steve Donoghue worked there also, back in the day. I bought the stables from Stephen and Martin Quirke. I've given up training nowadays and nobody uses the place any more, it's gone derelict. Back in the sixties, horses used to travel by train, you'd get on at Kingsbridge. Horses walked to Fairyhouse from Ratoath. I still enjoy a race meeting. With Bellewstown, it's like the call of the wild, you feel you have to go. Like a family going to the seaside when the weather took up, you couldn't wait to get there. Back in the day, it was a once a year job. It was a place that was easy to get to from Castleknock, where I was working. It was a social occasion for an awful lot of people within a fifty-mile radius of Bellewstown. But racing has changed, the numbers attending race-meetings are really down, if it wasn't for the SIS money, a lot of race-meetings wouldn't be held at all. It's just so expensive for a family, getting in at the turnstile is the cheapest part. In the old days, people could watch the races from the outside, Punchestown and Tramore would have a rake of people on the outside, nowadays I think that only happens at Bellewstown. There's such an emphasis on Health and Safety nowadays.

For my money, Lester Piggott was the best jockey on the flat, Richard Dunwoody on the jumps. Matt Moloney used to be put on a pedestal by the old-timers, any one of them would hold their own still today. I love racing, different lies told every day, the same product, the horse, but a different canvas. I've been a devotee of racing all my life and even on holidays I keep an eye on my constituents. Bellewstown holds an important place in the racing calendar and fulfils a useful need. There should be more racing there.

Racing at Bellewstown in the 1960s (Photo courtesy Jim Curley)

James Black, Former Course Foreman, on the Preparation of the Racecourse

Preparing for Bellewstown Races was really a major job. There was actually nothing on the commons then, only grass. Everything used to have to be taken out and put up. We started early, maybe early March taking out the railing, and then we'd keep going with that until the first build of the fences. It was really a three-month job. All the gear was stored in the old wooden stables that used to be down along the main road where the open bar is now. At that time most the horses used to come by train to Drogheda. Then some of them used to walk from Drogheda out to the course. There were only saddling stalls at that time, and the horse boxes were normally parked opposite to where the school is, where the old post office used to be back then.

The most famous stables around here were Michael Arnold's, which were beside where the mile-start was. Tom Dreaper used to use Arnolds stables. On a beautiful summer's day you could not find a nicer place for horses. Tom Dreaper brought some of the best horses he had, to run in Bellewstown. The other main stabling areas were Hilltown estate and Kilsharvan and they'd walk them up from these yards. At that time horses could run more than once on the same day and they often did at Bellewstown. There was one particular horse that used to run every year and one year he won twice, he was called *Little Champ* trained by George Dunwoody. George Dunwoody was a great supporter of Bellewstown and he loved running his horses on the hill.

Back then, the course was a lot different. There were no permanent railings and ropes were used to control the crowds. The only railing that we had was along the flat track, which was desperate at that time because the bends were so bad. There were no railings at the outside of the track at all. They were brave men that rode around the track in those days. The chase track was a separate track that used to go further around. There were no railings there at all, except at Slevins, where there were one or two guides for the fences. At the finish we'd control the crowds by using ropes. These ropes were held by what was called the Drogheda staff. For the hurdle races there was always a hurdle at the winning post. In a two-mile hurdle race when they would jump it once, we'd take the hurdle down before they'd come around to finish.

The other big spectacle at the time was the fence in front of the stand. To see the horses jump and stretch across that fence was something else. That was really part of Bellewstown. There was a winning post there at the time and on a really foggy day you couldn't see the disc on top of it. That's how high it was. People could walk around anywhere they wanted; there was absolutely no crowd control. People were everywhere, even on top of the fences and hurdles! At that particular time, we used to tar the wing of the fence in front of the stands to try and stop people from climbing up on it, even though they got their clothes destroyed!

There were always problems with loose horses. There was one terrible incident of a horse that fell in a chase, a horse of Jimmy Brogan's, called *Paddy Field* got loose, and Kevin Kerr, who was a brother of Bertie Kerr's was up saddling a horse for the next race, up along where the school is now. While he was walking back up the track, having saddled the horse he was knocked down by *Paddy Field* and he was very seriously injured. The other incident was a horse of Mick Hurley's named *Bearna Na Saileach* that went bizarre in the parade ring. While *Bearna Na Saileach*, was being mounted he went bizarre and galloped through the parade ring, he continued through the bookmakers ring and then he went through the iron railings to the outside enclosure and caused havoc with the bookies again. During the excitement they say one bookie had his moneybag snatched never to be seen again. There were other horses that got loose and did damage to cars. At that time we had a lot of horse fatalities. There was a local lad who used to take the dead animals away, Johnson. He'd be there sort of hoping that one would go down.

There were very well known people that frequented Bellewstown. A day that always stuck out in my mind was in 1958 when Sir Gordon Richards set foot in Bellewstown. He stayed with Brigadier Boylan, the owner of Hilltown, who took him up to the races and unfortunately it was the foggiest day there ever was. You could hardly see anything. It was great that Gordon Richard stood there on the old steward's stand and that I saw him.

In relation to the buildings in the enclosure, there was the stand, the stables, the weigh-room, and the old toilets. When they erected new toilets they renovated the stand. The Owners and Trainers Stand was wooden and it was erected every year. Gradually, down through the years, there were improvements. Collen Brothers built new toilets and renovated the stand and then they built the totes. Before that there were only wooden totes. My father used to bring them from Leopardstown where they were stored. I can't believe how much Bellewstown has grown in my time. In those days a particular family looked after each fence. This was a great tradition of the races. Most of the fences had names. The post office was one fence, Larkin's was the last fence, the Lodge was another fence, and Maginn's was one and it was where the old Barracks was in the woods. I heard about Maginn's through a local man called Joe Sherry. He knew about the races going back years before me. Joe lived in what was the Barracks, which is the yellow house directly opposite the horse gate. Joe could name horses that had been running at Bellewstown for years. At the end of May each year, Joe could tell me the entries for the races. Joe used to work in Hilltown, which belonged to Brigadier Boylan who was the chief executive of the Turf Club (Keeper of the Match Book). In Hilltown Joe was able to see the Racing Calendar, which contained the entries.

The fences were built by two fellows, one was Hughie Farrell and the other John Black, who was nicknamed Carvin. The fences were taken down in 1977 and that was the end of steeplechasing in Bellewstown. It was a sad day when steeplechasing finished in Bellewstown. T.J.Kelly was the manager until around 1947 and then his son Billy succeeded him. Billy Kelly was an out and out gentleman. He wanted to save money rather than spend it, but the money wasn't there at the time. He was such a gentleman. He groomed Joe Collins, but Joe Collins wasn't afraid to spend. Joe, however, was the start of good things in Bellewstown and I must say that they're continuing and they're getting better and better. The bends were restructured in the seventies and they began to rail off the course, thanks to Joe Collins. Bellewstown was known for the desperate elbow bend it had, three furlongs from the finish. I said to Joe we could straighten that and Joe said 'We'll do it'. I said 'What about railing?' to Joe and he said 'I'll get stud railing' and fair play to Joe, he did. We got the stud railing, we got it all done and levelled out and then called the chairman Nesbit Waddington to come and inspect our work. Mr Waddington was shocked initially but then he realized what an improvement it was. I am trying to say that Joe Collins helped to make Bellewstown what it is today. He was a major influence in Bellewstown. Even when Joe left Bellewstown, it has continued to improve. They have got more meetings and I hope to see them bring back chasing.

I reckon the best chaser that ever ran in Bellewstown was *Fortria*. Funnily he didn't run in a chase. He ran in 1960 and was ridden by Pat Taaffe and he carried 10st 7lb in a flat handicap. He ran an absolute blinder and was only beaten by a horse of Bunny Cox's, a horse called *Snow Trix* ridden by Mick Kennedy. That was one of Tom Dreaper's great runners. Another great chaser was *Arkloin* that came to the hill, where he won two years in a row 1965 and 66, having won at Cheltenham in the same years. Tom Dreaper ran other great horses on the hill, Mark Hely Hutchinson's *Digby Diver* and *The Big Hindu*. *The Big Hindu* was one of the horses that won in a fog. We only saw him going out the horse gate and coming back in. In the fifties and the sixties, Pat Taaffe was a wonderful rider around Bellewstown over jumps and in the same era Johnny Roe was his equal on the flat. Paddy Sleator was another trainer who supported Bellewstown. He used to bring some great runners to run in Bellewstown before they went on to Galway. Paddy Sleator brought the winner of the Galway Plate, *Sparkling Flame,* to run in Bellewstown. Another great man to ride around Bellewstown was Tommy Carberry, Paul's father.

I'll always remember Billy Kelly and I walking down the track, as usual Billy was smoking his pipe and we heard some people saying 'Some desperate horses run here in Bellewstown' and Billy, after pulling on his pipe said to the fellow, 'I can tell you something for nothing, the winner of the Leger, *Allangrange,* ran here last year, and he wasn't good enough, he could only finish fourth', and that shut your man up.

The hill is reckoned to be one of the fastest tracks in Ireland. I remember Des Lake who was an Australian rider riding here. Nobody rode the track better than Wally Swinburn. He would go around those bends without any fear. Kevin Prendergast was another, who was like dynamite. One year Swinburn had four wins in Bellewstown, it was his favourite track. Francis Short would stop at nothing. He was afraid of nothing. Frankie Carroll was another good jockey. Bobby Beasley was class. Now we have Paul Carberry, there's so many of them now.

Bellewstown to me now is getting better and better. There are more facilities now inside the hospitality, the big television screen where you can see every part of the race. The only thing I have to say is, there's so many of the good people who made it happen have gone, if only those people could come back and see what Bellewstown has become today, they wouldn't believe it.

Bellewstown locals Willie Ludlow, Tommy Arnold, Nora Crinion and Jackie Tallon look back on the excitement in the old days during Bellewstown Race Week

Willie Ludlow

My earliest memories of the races are from the late forties, early fifties, ever since I started school. I think years ago, when I was young, it was always good weather, always warm. Getting the course ready, that's what I remember. You'd have Mickey Black, James's father, he would look after the course and for three weeks or a month beforehand the steeplechase jumps would have to be got ready. That was a big job, they built the jumps with birch and after they were built they would have to be clipped. John Black looked after the clipping, that's Cathy's father, a big quiet man. The birch came from one of the bogs, maybe the Bog of Allen, branches about six foot tall and they were pushed into the fences and then they had to be clipped. That took a long time to do, John did all the clipping. He had a small black car, and if you saw it at a jump you'd know he was there, so after school you'd head down there. There were seven jumps, you'd start off with the Tholsel, that was at the top of Hilltown, then you had the Regulation, it was faced the opposite way and then there was Maginns jump. And then you came round where we lived and Slevins and Briens, right around the very outside of the track and up above that you had Martin's jump and after that the Post Office jump and then one here at the Cosy Bar, Larkin's jump and then one at the Standhouse. And I can always remember the day before the races, a red and white flag went up on the wing of each jump and you knew the races had arrived when you saw those jumps, every jump had a red and white flag on each side. And the hurdles would be put up the day before too.

There wouldn't have been as much work put into the ground as there is now. People with horses now, they wouldn't have run them the way the course was back then, it was very uneven, but it has come on a lot since then. And then the palings had to be white-washed, that was another way of knowing that the races were on the way. I can remember Mick Whearty doing it one year. There would be a barrel of lime and water in the stand-house. You'd take out a shovel or two of that into a bucket and start mixing it with water. If you got that in the eye, you had a sore eye I can tell you, or even if it went on your skin. You'd have to do the palings.

Jackie Tallon

My father had the pub and it was a very busy time for us. I remember going around the houses in the weeks coming up to the races, collecting bottles. Bottles were very scarce after the war. The bottles would have to be washed, there'd be a man there with a brush washing them. The jockeys would come down the week before the races, they'd sleep on the racecourse. A lot of Dublin people came. We'd all have to help out in the pub, I hardly saw the races at all.

Tommy Arnold

Well, I lived right on the racecourse when I was growing up. My father used to work with horses. People used to bring horses to the racecourse and they would stay, we had stables then, there were ten or twelve stables there, they are still there in fact. The trainers used to bring them in horse-boxes, C.I.E. used to bring them, they used to come by train and then CIE would bring them. And they'd stay until the Friday after the races. And the grooms would stay over too. Apart from that the stables weren't used during the year, unless my father had calves in them or something. There were stables at Langans too. The same trainers would come year after year, Dreapers used to stable their horses with us. The horses might arrive the day before or the morning of the races and then they would be walked down to the course.

There would be great excitement but there was nothing like they have nowadays, just a few tents and stalls. There used to be the three-card-trick men, but I don't see them any more. There would be three cards face down and you'd have to find the queen. One of their own lads would come in and bet on it and win. Then they would move around the cards and another of their lads would pick and win. You'd think it was simple then to find the queen and you'd put down some money. I don't know if they would catch anyone nowadays, I haven't seen them around Bellewstown lately.

Stall-holder who came for years to sell Lucky Dip Favours at Bellewstown Races.

Willie Ludlow

The school would close the days of the races but you had to go in the following day for a half-day. You got your holidays the Friday after the races and woe betide if you didn't appear that day, you got a hammering the next September. From the age of eleven I would be working around the race-course, maybe collecting glasses for Tallons and it would always be remembered in September. You'd be looking forward to the races. At that time a lot of people came home from England for the races and from Dublin and different places, it was like a meeting place, a gathering. Fellows would go off to work in Dublin and the only time they would come back maybe would be for the races. I had uncles used to come every year for the races, one from Howth, another from Kildare, another from Wicklow, they'd always make it home, my mother's brothers. They'd stay around either with my mother or with John Kirwan's people, so there would be a few late nights, mostly in people's homes. There would be people there now that wouldn't have any interest in backing a horse, they'd be more interested in chatting to people that they mightn't have seen in maybe a year or two years. It was a way for people to meet. I remember the night before the races, on the Tuesday night, there might be ten fellows standing around talking in a group and you'd go another bit and there'd be another group, people just standing around.

Them times, there would be a bigger crowd outside, most of the locals stayed outside, there were always a few bookies and stalls there. At that time they had a rope. The crowd used to go out across the paling and up along the track up to the winning post. There used to be a few 'hard boys' from Drogheda and they'd hold the rope to keep the crowd back. There were no health and safety regulations back then. You had three tents in front of The Loft. They'd be serving sandwiches and marble cake and fruit slab and the tea, the smell of the tea. She had a huge big teapot, lovely tea. A woman by the name of Agnes Walsh used to run it, she was a Moore Street trader. She'd come down for the two days.

Bellewstown's Best studying the form outside Bellewstown Race-course Weigh-Room. The line-up includes L to R: this book's author John Kirwan, Willie Ludlow, Paul Black, Mick Collins, Gerard Townley, Pat Brannigan, John Ludlow, John Bellew and Tommy Arnold. (Taken 2013)

RACING ROUND-UP: AN ACCOUNT OF MEETINGS AT BELLEWSTOWN 1900 TO 1999 COMPILED BY JOHN KIRWAN

In Bellewstown, from 1900 to 1905, for professional jockeys on the flat there were three sprint races, one over one mile, and the King or Queen's Plate over 2¼ miles. On the steeplechase course, four races over varying distances were run, and there were two flat races for qualified riders, generally over 2 miles. From 1906 until 1909, the three sprint races were discontinued and were replaced by two hurdle races and an extra chase, leaving just three races for the flat jockeys.

In **1900** Mr. H. Tunstall Moore, who resided at Stedalt House, Stamullen, owned *Benoni*, the winner of the Crockafotha Handicap at Bellewstown, over one mile, for jockey Peter Hughes. The mare *Rose O'Neill* won the first of her successive wins in the Drogheda Tradesmen's Chase, for trainer Captain Dewhurst, and Drogheda native Paddy Cowley was in the saddle on both occasions. Another local owner Mr. Nicholas Markey from nearby Rockbellew, Julianstown, owned *Juno* who won different chases in both of the opening years of the century. In 1900 he was ridden by Paddy Bellew, who in 1903 came to live in Bellewstown, and worked in the local stables of Richard Courtney, Carnes Road, for whom he rode a good number of winners. The following year Mr. G.J. Ball of Wintergrass, Bellewstown rode *Juno* to victory. It is interesting to record that, as the riders were mounting in the parade ring for the Queen's Plate, the locally owned Leggan Hall reared up and turned over, giving his jockey F. Mason a terrible fall. Unable to ride as a result, Thomas Horton was hastily substituted for him and finished second.

1901. The main feature of this year's racing was the successes of both *Leggan Hall* and *Night Time* on both days of the meeting. Leggan Hall may have caused a bit of trouble in the parade ring the previous year, but reverting back to sprint distances, he had no trouble winning the 5 furlong Hilltown Flat race on the opening day and followed up the next day in the Bellewstown Plate over 6 furlongs and 80 yards. Leggan Hall, an entire horse, was owned by Mr. J.S. Langan of Bellewstown House and went on to stand as a stallion at his owner's stud nearby at Leggan Hall. The durable *Night Time* won the Tally Ho flat Handicap for hunters on the Wednesday for amateur Mr. W. P. Cullen and the following day won the Grand Stand Chase in the hands of Paddy Cowley. *Night Time* was owned by Mr.W.H. West, and was trained by Capt. Dewhurst. Count Stolberg, a German nobleman, was a frequent visitor to the country and kept a stable of racehorses and hunters for his pleasure at Dunshaughlin. He rode his own horse *Armine*, repeating his success of the previous year's Meath Plate and the combination went on to win the same race in 1905.

1902 Jockey John Thompson rode three winners at this year's meeting including winning on *Ferriera* on both days for owner Mrs. Sadleir Jackson. The Delany family from Corballis, Laytown had a long association with the course and they were on the mark with *Aesculapius* in the Tally Ho Hunters Flat Handicap, ridden by Mr. H. Nuttall. In the race itself *Aesculapius*, finished second to *Wintergrass* owned and ridden by Mr. G.J. Ball, but following an objection, *Wintergrass* was disqualified, and Mr. Delany's charge promoted to first.

1903. For some reason this year the racing took place on Tuesday and Wednesday. The weather was perfect on both days and with the going riding good, fields were satisfactory throughout. Jumps Jockey Paddy Cowley was the man in form, winning all four chases over the two days, including winning the featured Drogheda Tradesmen's Chase on *Mysterious Lady* for owner Mr. O.J. Williams and trainer Capt. Dewhurst. The Delany family continued on their winning way when *St. Corinne*, none the worse for finishing second on the opening day, won the Annagor Plate for rider Mr. M. Hayes. The following year *St. Corrine* went on to win the prestigious Conyngham Cup at the Punchestown festival.

1904. Rain fell heavily at times on the opening day at this year's meet, which was back in its usual Wednesday and Thursday slot. Mr. Richard Crokers's *American Boy* won sprints on both days with leading jockey John Thompson in the saddle. The most controversial race of the meeting came in the Crockafotha Flat Handicap where the hot favourite *Bayleaf* passed the post first. The owner of the second horse *Most Noble* lodged an objection on the grounds that F. Morgan, rider of *Bayleaf*, had lost a stirrup before reaching the winning post, and that an onlooker had handed him the stirrup after the race. The stewards upheld the objection and awarded *Most Noble* the race. *Most Noble* was owned and trained by Richard Courtney, who trained his own horses at Carnes West, Bellewstown with a fair degree of success, and was ridden by apprentice Nicholas Walsh. *Duckey*, who won the concluding Corporation Chase was winning at the course for the third successive year for the Captain Dewhurst/Maxie Arnott combination.

1905. This year the going was as hard as iron, but contrary to expectation, this drawback did not militate against the strength of the fields as much as anticipated. This was the last year that sprints were run at the track in this era, with two races being run over the 6 furlong 80yd track on the first day. In the first of these the locally owned *Signora* sprang a bit of a shock for Mr. J.R. Markey, trainer Michael Dawson and jockey Henry Buxton. The second sprint was won by Mr. Richard Croker's *Herbert Vincent*, and was ridden by champion jockey John Thompson. Another local owner Mr. Ned Delany had a winner on each day with *Nenemoo'sha* winning the Corporation Chase, ridden by Capt. Stacpoole and the Laytown owner/trainer won the concluding event of the meeting with *Shallon* winning the Stewards Handicap Chase for top amateur Mr. Reggie Walker, who was completing a riding double, having earlier won the Grand Stand Chase on *Rose Craft*, trained by his father.

1906. The opening lines in the Irish Field report of the meeting July 4th/5th this year merit repeating here "The regular division who foregathered in fair force at old-fashioned Bellewstown on Wednesday and Thursday last were able to appreciate the comparative ease and quietness associated with racing on the Hill of Crockafotha. It was a charming afternoon, for the heat was not too oppressive, and the atmospheric conditions were exhilarating to a degree of eminence which some anonymous poet has eulogised in the following lines:

> 'Arrived at the summit, the view that you come at,
> From etherealised Mourne to where Tara ascends,

> There's no scene in our sireland, clear Ireland, old Ireland
> To which nature more exquisite loveliness lends.'

The ground rode quite well this year but the meeting opened with a hurdle race which turned into a fiasco. The well-backed favourite *Sin* bolted after a couple of furlongs and ran out, and the new leader *Grey Face* went the wrong course, taking a short cut which must have saved her nearly a quarter of a mile. Naturally *Grey Face* finished first past the post, but in the subsequent enquiry she was disqualified and the race awarded to Mr. E. Mooney's *Ardee*, ridden by John Lynn. Lynn completed a double in the featured Drogheda Tradesmen's Chase on *Bitter Still* owned by Mr. B.W. Parr. *Signora* for local owner Mr. J.R. Markey, repeated her course success of the previous year, this time winning the one mile Hilltown Handicap under Algy Anthony.

On the second day there were successes for leading jockeys John Thompson and Paddy Cowley, while in the concluding Stewards Handicap, amateur rider Mr. Reggie Walker got the favourite *Flight* home in front.

1907. July 3rd/4th. "The Hill of Crockafothe in disagreeable weather is not a particularly enticing rendezvous, and Wednesday was one of those occasions upon which one would wish to be anywhere else for choice. However, though there was thunder and lightning galore, and one of the two extraordinary heavy showers which fell was accompanied by hail, as if to impart extra variety to the climatic samples of the moment, we escaped better than might have been expected. In the intervals it was pleasantly warm, but the unsettled conditions interfered badly with the strength of the company, and the overnight deluge had the effect of keeping many of the metropolitan contingent away" - so did the Irish Field reporter record the climatic conditions.

Not surprisingly the ground rode deep, and while fields were satisfactory on the opening day, they cut up on the closing day. Amateur jockey Mr. Reggie Walker was the man in form riding a double on both days, including winning on Mr. Silver's mare *Rustic Queen* on both Wednesday and Thursday. He also rode Col. Kirkwood's *Apollo Belvedere* to win the featured Drogheda Tradesmen's Chase, who in his next outing won the Galway Plate for trainer John Currid.

On the second day Steve Donoghue, who was riding in Ireland at that time, mainly for Philip Behan, recorded two wins. The second of his wins came on the veteran course specialist *Most Noble* for local trainer Richard Courtney, in the Crockafotha Handicap, a race he describes in his autobiography. Steve Donoghue, reckoned by many good judges to be the best jockey of the 20th century, was champion jockey in England many times.

1908 1st/2nd July. Sweltering heat on both days greeted patrons who made the annual trek to the Hill of Crockafotha this year. Although the ground rode very firm, the size of the fields held up, resulting in some interesting racing. A new race, the Conyngham Club Cup, subscribed by members of the ring, and consisting of an imposing trophy, was competed for on the opening day. Mr. George Tunstall Moore who lived locally at Stedalt, Stamullen became the first winner of the trophy when his *Sheepstown* obliged in the hands of Mr. C. Brabazon, who was presented with a gold-mounted whip. *Dublin Fusilier,* who won the opening Hill Handicap Hurdle for amateur rider Mr. T. Price, also won on the second day. He was successful in the Crockafotha Flat Handicap, this time ridden by John Doyle. On the second day, Mr. Percy Maynard, Master of the Ward Union Hunt, owned *Guy,* winner of the Stewards Handicap Chase in the hands of Thomas Dowdall.

1909. July 7th/8th The winner of the opening race at this year's meeting was *Hampton Lad,* owned by Mr. H. Matthews and ridden by Mr. T. Price in the Hill Hurdle, and he doubled up the next day by winning the Crockafotha Handicap on the flat, this time ridden by Alfred Sharples. The legendary Steve Donoghue rode another winner at the course, this time on Mr. N.J. Kelly's *Finner* in the Hilltown Handicap. The race for the Conyngham Club Cup had to be declared void, after the only horse to finish, *Oniche,* was deemed ineligible to run and was disqualified. *Oniche* went on to win the following year's Irish National.

On the second day Mr. W. Baileys *Georgetown* replicated his success of the previous year in His Majesty's Plate from trainer J.J. Parkinson and jockey John Thompson. The Grandstand Chase was won by *Red Orchid* from the Clonsilla stable of Maxie Arnott who was recording his fourth win at this year's meeting. *Red Orchid* was ridden to success by Drogheda native Paddy Cowley, who was winning his final race at the course. Paddy Cowley was apprenticed to Capt. Dewhurst at the Clonsilla establishment, and Arnott took over as the trainer there when Capt. Dewhurst moved to Newmarket to train there in 1904. Paddy Cowley moved to England to join him and was champion jumps jockey in Britain in 1908. In August 1911 he died from injuries received in a fall at Hooton Park, Cheshire.

1910. July 6th/7th. The ground rode good this year, following deluges of rain in the week before racing. In the opening Hilltown Plate, Mr. John Maher's *Balscadden* overturned the hot favourite in a match, and was ridden by Chris Symes. Jockey John Lynn rode three winners over the two days, while amateur rider Mr. Reggie Walker recorded two wins, which included winning the 3-mile Demesne Handicap Chase on *Small Polly*. Among the opposition in this race was Mr. Nicholas Markey's stalwart chaser *Little Hack II* who won the Irish Grand National twice (in 1909 and 1913) when she was 14 years old, ridden by Stephen Matthews. A peculiar and unfortunate incident took place in the Nanny Steeplechase. Mr. Ned Delany's filly called *Nanny* (ridden by John Tiernan) fell during the race and had to be put down – a coincidence that she was killed in a race called the Nanny Plate. Navan owner Mr. Albert Lowry won the concluding Tally Ho Corinthian Plate with *Thimblerigger* ridden by Mr. Patrick Nugent and trained by Larry Hope, one of 4 winners the Clongiffan trainer had at the meeting.

1911. July 5th/6th Delightful weather led to a capital attendance at this year's fixture and while runners were satisfactory on the opening day, they cut up somewhat on the Thursday. Young jockey Robert Trudgill was the star of the show at this year's meeting riding three winners over the two days, including a winner each day on *Tory Hill II* for trainer Atty Persse. The feature Drogheda Tradesmen's Chase on Wednesday was won by *Piccaninny II* trained by Larry Hope and ridden by Ben Ellis. Amateur jockey Mr. Reggie Walker also rode a winner on both days, including winning the 3 mile handicap chase for the third year running on *Small Polly*, who went on to win the Irish National at Fairyhouse the following year.

1912. July 3rd/4th The weather was very pleasant on both days and the number of runners was much more plentiful than in recent years, particularly on the first day. Among those present were Mr. La Touche, the senior steward of the Turf Club, Lord Enniskillen and Mr. William Dunne, not often seen at gatherings of the country variety.

The opening Hilltown Handicap was won by Ratoath owner Mr. P. Roger's *Never Again* ridden by John Thompson. Unfortunately for John Thompson he never again rode another winner at Bellewstown, as in the spring of 1913, he had a bad accident schooling a horse over hurdles, and tragically died a couple of weeks later. John Thompson was champion jockey ten times between 1901 and 1912 and became the number one at J.J. Parkinson's Maddenstown stable.

The featured Drogheda Tradesmen's Chase went the way of *Cooldreen,* owned and trained by Mr. P. McLoughlin at Stone Hall, Multyfarnham and ridden by capable amateur Mr. J. Manley. Jockey John Doyle rode two flat winners for owner Mr. Paddy Cullinan, while dual purpose jockey Thomas Sheridan rode two chase winners for Maxie Arnott. Mr. J. Barron from the North of Ireland owned, trained and rode *Mallusk* to victory in the concluding Stewards Chase, landing some tidy wagers in the process.

1913. July 5th/6th Although the ground was firm enough there were plenty of runners on the opening day, particularly in the chases. The opening Hilltown Plate, a one mile flat Handicap, was won by *Faria* who had run in the Irish Derby the previous week. *Faria* was trained by Mr. R. Harrison and ridden by John Doyle, both of whom combined for a first day double with *Rosey Ina* winning the Meath Plate. A good field of eleven turned out for the Drogheda Tradesmen's Chase, and the honours went to Mr. W. Jackson's *Cathal*, who was ridden by Edward Houlihan. Very often a horse wins on both days of the meeting, and this year Mr. N.J. Kelly's *Dysie* achieved this feat, winning a flat race on the opening day, and the Grandstand Chase the next day, both times ridden by crack amateur, Mr. Reggie Walker, who had also won on his own horse *Merry Point* in the Conyngham Club Cup on the first day. English Jockey George Duller, paid a winning visit to the course, by winning the Bellewstown Plate on Hubert Hartigan's *Persian Chief,* completing a double for the owner trainer, who had earlier scored with *Bruce* in the Leggan Hall Chase for rider Mr. B.H. Nicholson.

1914. 1st/2nd July A prolonged dry spell led to reduced fields at this year's reunion at which Colin Barrett and William Lynn were the only jockeys to ride two winners. Local trainer Richard Courtney got the meeting off to a great start, when the outsider of the three runners, *Enchanted Prince* won the Hilltown Plate under Peter Hughes. William Lynn rode both chase winners on the opening day, *Turkish Maiden* in the Hill Chase and

Alice Rockthorn for Major Honner in the Conyngham Club Cup. Colin Barrett's double consisted of winning the Meath Plate on *Rathleague*, another winner for Ratoath owner Mr. P Rogers, and dead heating on *Double Ditch* in Thursday's opener. The concluding Steward's Plate saw Wednesday's winner *Alice Rockthorn* first past the post, but an objection to her for carrying the wrong weight was upheld and the race was awarded to Mr. T. Nolan's *Never Fear*, ridden by Frank Morgan. Compensation awaited *Alice Rockthorn* when she won the Galway Plate on her next outing.

Local jockey, Paddy Bellew in action on Fond Lucy at Bellewstown Races in 1914

1915. 7th/8th July On Wednesday rain fell continuously from the beginning to the end of proceedings, resulting in unusually soft ground for this venue. Those who made the journey in open carriages had a far from pleasant experience. The featured Drogheda Tradesmen's Chase went to one of the outsiders, Lady Ainsworth's *Turkish Price* in the hands of claiming jockey Murt Farragher. An unusual occurrence took place for the Conyngham Club Cup. When the Laytown trainer Ned Delaney realised that no horses were declared to run for the above race, he despatched a man to fetch his own horse *German*, who was entered for the race. He arrived back with the horse with minutes to spare before declaration time for the race and consequently walked over to claim the prize.

In contrast to the opening day the weather was most pleasant on the second day. In the opening Crockafotha Handicap Mr. W. Watson's filly *N.E.* was first past the post. An objection to *N.E.*, on the grounds of wrong description was overruled, but on appeal to the stewards of the Turf Club, this decision was reversed and the race awarded to Mr. J. O'Callaghan's *Raw Material*. Amateur jockey Mr. Leslie Brabazon recorded a double on the second day, winning the Grandstand Plate for Harry Ussher on *Crovederg* and the

109

Corporation Plate on *Cello* for Maxie Arnott. Last years Galway Plate Winner, *Alice Rockthorn,* started at odds of 7/1, the outsider of the three runners in the Stewards Handicap Chase, but belying those odds she recorded a good win in the hands of Mr. Pat Nugent for trainer Algy Anthony.

Mr H.M. Hartigan was home on short leave from the war-front and in order to have a ride, he matched his horse *Laveco* to run against *Night Out* in a special match race during the races.

1916. 5th/6th July "Bellewstown is one of the oldest meetings in Ireland, and the antiquated stone stand lends a touch of quaintness to the surroundings, which in a way is a pleasant variety in this age of red brick and mortar". This was how the Irish Field reporter started his report on this year's meet. Well some things never change as this stand is still with us, albeit with some modifications. At least two very good horses won at the meeting this year. Mr. Frank Barbour's *Shaun Spadah* won the Drogheda Tradesmen's Chase for amateur rider Mr. Stanley Harrison and was trained at this time by Reggie Walker. He repeated his victory in this race the following year and went on to earn eternal fame by winning the Aintree Grand National in 1921, when he was the only horse to jump a clear round. The other good horse to win at this year's meet was *Golden Fleece*. A very versatile horse, *Golden Fleece* won his first ever race for his then owner/rider Mr. L.S. Ward, at Bellewstown this year, in the Hill Chase and followed up the next day by winning the 3-mile Stewards Handicap chase. Sold to leading owner William Parish in 1918 he won that year's Galway Plate, when trained by J.T. Rogers. *Golden Fleece* was speedy enough to win several handicaps at the Curragh over 6 furlongs, and later, when sold on to race in Britain, he won numerous chases. In all he won a total of 32 races, his last win coming at Newport in June 1925.

Laytown trainer, Ned Delany had his name etched on the Conyngham Club Cup for the second year in succession when *Genus* got the better of local favourite *Fond Lucy,* for rider Bernard Twombley. The second day was run in miserable wet conditions, during which trainer Jim Parkinson recorded a double. He trained Mr. Lowry's *Batchelor's Trick* to win the Crockafotha Handicap for rider Jos. Harty, and won the Corporation Plate with *Henriette*, ridden by his son Mr. W.J. Parkinson.

1917. 4th/5th July The Hill of Crockafotha was bathed in sunshine on the opening day of this year's reunion, which saw subsequent Aintree Grand National hero *Shaun Spadah* repeat last year's success in the Drogheda Tradesmen's Chase, this time trained by Bob Fetherstonhaugh and ridden by Charles Hawkins. Despite winning the race the previous year, *Shaun Spadah* started at the remunerative odds of 8/1, for which the prolific *Golden Fleece* started favourite. Leading trainer J.J. Parkinson saddled three winners over the two days, while, on the second day, owner Mr. D.M. Gant, trainer William Rankin and jockey James Clarke combined for a double, which included *Palley* the complete outsider of the field, winning His Majesty's Plate. The meeting concluded with the Stewards Handicap Chase, which was won by Major McCalmont's consistent chaser *Privit*, trained by Maxie Arnott and ridden by Frank Morgan. *Privit* won the Galway Plate a month later at the nice price of 20/1.

1918. 3rd/4th July The ground was not as hard as expected after a prolonged dry spell, with the result that trainers were not afraid to run their horses, resulting in more than satisfactory fields. The Rathvale Stable, which was carried on so successfully by Mr. Stanley Harrison in the absence on active service of Mr. R.H. Walker, accounted for the lion's share of the spoils, winning three races on the opening day, and bagging a brace on the second day. In addition, Mr. Harrison rode three of the winners with Michael Dowdall and William Barrett on the other two. Jockey Frank Morgan, who was champion jockey in 1917 and 1918, rode a winner on both days, including repeating last years win on *Privit* in the Stewards Chase.

Again, favoured by the weather, the second day's racing brought a capital crowd to the old course, and with seven races down for decision, and an additional one thrown in through the running off of a dead-heat, punters got great value for their money. The dead heat occurred in the opening Crockafotha Plate, a flat race over one mile and three furlongs. In the run off, *Gemsbok* ridden by Dinny Ward, comfortably beat *Jilltrim* with James Dines in the saddle. Harry Ussher, still training in Co. Galway, made the journey worthwhile by saddling *Gerard* to win the Grandstand Chase with James Hogan in the plate. The meeting concluded with *Good Health* winning his second race of the meeting in the Summer Flat Plate for Mr. Stanley Harrison.

1919. 7th/8th July While fields were very satisfactory on the first day, they cut up somewhat on the Thursday, due to the firm ground. The featured race on the opening day, the Drogheda Tradesmen's Chase provided a thrilling race for the large crowd. A field of ten faced the starter, and at the finish the judge could not separate *Ben Cruchan* trained by Reggie Walker and ridden by William Smith, and the course specialist *Privit*, ridden by Henry Harty for Maxie Arnott. Hubert Hartigan owned and trained *Mayhap*, and was the winner of the Bellewstown Plate, in which *En Avant*, owned locally by Capt. Thomas Boylan of Hilltown House, finished second on his racecourse debut.

Another locally-owned horse, *Saxham Price*, in Mr. T.D. McKeever's colours, won the opening race on the second day – another winner for trainer Reggie Walker. The outsider of the four runners in His Majesty Plate, Mrs. M. Scott's *Cellar Glen* sprang a big surprise to win for trainer Cecil Brabazon and jockey John Patman. The Delany family had another winner at the course when *St. Pam* upset some better backed rivals to win the Stewards 3-mile Handicap Chase in the hands of Dan Colbert.

1920. 7th/8th July This year saw the introduction of Hurdle races at the course on a permanent basis – hurdle races took place occasionally before this. With 2 hurdle races, 6 steeplechases and one flat race in which both qualified riders and professional flat jockeys could take part, there were not many opportunities for the latter category at the course in this era. The weather was very favourable on the opening day, but on the second day heavy rain rather spoiled proceedings.

There were two 20/1 winners on the opening day, firstly Mr. C. Hope's *Ballyfore* won the Hilltown Flat Handicap for rider Clyde Aylin, and in the Hill Chase, Mr H. Loughran's *Dowdstown* kept bookmakers happy, winning for trainer Leslie Brabazon and jockey Nicholas Hayes. The featured Drogheda Tradesmen's Chase went to the Co. Limerick trainer R. Moss, whose *Hawker* obliged for Jack Moylan, and that combination had another good winner on the second day when *Aegean* won the Stewards Chase. Other jockeys to have two winners at the meeting were Joe Canty and Clyde Aylin. In the concluding Grand Stand Chase, Ned Delany's *Pam Nut*, none the worst for finishing second on the first day, obliged for Clyde Aylin.

1921. July 6th/7th The hard ground this week kept fields on the small side, but at the same time, the sport was thoroughly enjoyable. Since last year, some much needed improvements had been effected. A new weigh room was built as well as increased stand and luncheon room facilities. The opening Meath Hurdle was won by *The Trade*, owned by Co. Longford breeder Mr. L.H. Reynolds, and trained and ridden by John Banahan. The following Hilltown Plate saw *Enchanted Duke* provide local owner / trainer Richard Courtney with his final win at his local course, where he had so many special occasions over the years. Reggie Walker and his jockey Clyde Aylin had a winner in the feature event on both days. In Wednesday's Drogheda Tradesman Chase, *Zenon* proved an easy winner, while Mr. Frank Barbour's *Ben Cruchan*, likewise shrugged away the opposition in Thursday's Stewards Handicap Chase. Mr. J.L. Mc Glew owned and trained *Quai D'Orsai,* which came to the relief of the layers, by springing a major shock in winning the Bellewstown Plate under Fred Hunter.

The main honours of the second day went to Michael Dawson who recorded a mixed training double. He won the opening Crockafotha Handicap Hurdle when *The Tatler* won for John Hogan Jnr., and doubled up in His Majesty's Plate when *Tiermourne* turned over the favourite *Southern Gleam*. *Tiermourne* was ridden by Henry Jameson.

1922. 1 September The traditional festival which was generally held during the first week in July had to be abandoned this year due to the Civil War, but fortunately a one day meeting was allocated for Friday 1st September with seven races down for decision.

It proved a very rewarding day for the Reggie Walker/Clyde Aylin combination, who won three of the races. The treble was initiated by Mr. T.D. McKeever's *Merry Miner* in the Hilltown Flat Handicap, following which *Zenon* repeated his win of last year in the Drogheda Tradesmen's Chase. The treble was completed when *Crock Hill* made short work of his rivals in His Majesty's Plate. The meeting had opened with a shock win for Co. Westmeath trainer Dick Cleary, when *Graystown* won the Crockafotha Handicap Hurdle in the hands of John McCarthy. There was a dramatic conclusion to the meeting in the Hill Steeplechase. *Helmet* and the favourite *Start Again* came to the final fence on level terms, and both of them fell. With admirable resourcefulness Paddy Powell, rider of *Helmet* recaptured his horse, remounted and had the satisfaction of getting him home from *Kinegar,* who was tailed off coming to the last fence.

1923. 4th/5th July The main feature of this year's meeting was the domination by the large stables of the era. Reggie Walker had a treble on the second day, while Max Arnott secured a double on both days. In addition Hubert Hartigan won both hurdle races with *Trayeen Trisough*. On the jockey front Anthony Escott, Dinny Ward and Thomas Kelly Jnr. all had doubles on the second day.

In the first day's feature, the Drogheda Tradesmen's Chase, *Helmet* who had scored in dramatic circumstances at the previous year's meet, was a comfortable winner. Now in the care of Cecil Brabazon, he was ridden by Bill Horan. Harry Ussher, now located at Brackenstown near Swords, had the first of his many triumphs at Bellewstown from that establishment, when *Sunny Bird* won the Hilltown Plate, ridden by Henry H. Beasley.

The Stewards Handicap Chase, the second day's feature was won by *Brendan's Glory*, the middle part of Reggie Walker's treble, and was partnered by Anthony Escott. Ratoath owner Mr. P. Rogers had a winner on both days and included *Double First*, trained by Max Arnott and ridden by Dinny Ward in His Majesty's Plate.

1924. 2nd/3rd July Harry Ussher dominated this year's meeting, winning six of the twelve races on offer, while Clonsilla trainer Max Arnott had three winners. Jockey John Hogan Jnr. had five rides at the meeting and won on all five, and all were trained by Ussher.

On the opening day Harry Ussher saddled four winners, the first two of which were owned by Col. Croft. They won the opening Meath Hurdle with *Happy Release* and followed up, when *Sunny Bird* replicated his success of the previous year in the Hilltown Flat Handicap, this time ridden by Tom Morgan. The third Ussher winner carried the colours of Mrs. Croft when *Goffee* won the Drogheda Tradesmen's Chase, and *Menelaus* completed the four-timer by winning the Hill Chase. Interestingly, none of the four winners were favourites and the cumulative odds were 480/1.

The second day's racing took place in continuous rain, making it very unpleasant for all concerned. Joe Canty steered *Knight Templar* to a narrow success in the opening Crockafotha Hurdle for owner/trainer Hubert Hartigan. Mrs. Croft owned another two winners with *Golden Street* winning the Stewards Chase and *Glass Island* the Grand Stand Chase, thus completing Harry Ussher's six winners, and John Hogan Jnr's five winners.

1925. 1st/2nd July The ground was very hard at the course this year which resulted in a dearth of runners, including a walk-over on each day. Maxie Arnott was the trainer in form with a treble on the second day, two of which were ridden by Dinny Ward, who also had a winner on the first day. The Brackenstown trainer Harry Ussher and his jockey J. Hogan Jnr. had a winner on each day which included *Goffee* in the featured Drogheda Tradesmen's Chase. However, the best horse to win at the meeting was Mr. Frank Barbours' *Blancona* which won the Hill Novice Chase and went on to win the Galway Plate later in the month, as well as winning the Galway Hurdle the following year. He was trained by Cecil Brabazon and ridden by Charlie Donnelly.

1926. 7th/8th July Another prolonged dry spell led to very small fields again at this year's meeting, particularly on the second day. Trainer J.J. Parkinson and his jockey Martin Quirke combined for a flat win on both days and Parkinson supplemented his tally, by also winning the Meath Hurdle on the opening day with *Grosvenor's Reward* ridden by Jack Morgan. He also rode a winner on the second day with *Stage Management* in the 3-mile Chase for owner/trainer Paddy Dunne Cullinan. The firm ground didn't prevent the Tom Taaffe-trained *Anillab* turning out and winning on both days for jockey J. Hogan Jnr. Local trainer Ned Delany won the featured Drogheda Tradesmen's Chase with *Burgomaster* ridden by Martin Hynes. Another local trainer Tom McKeever owned and trained *Irish Destiny* which walked over for the Bellewstown Plate.

1927. 6th/7th July Poor weather on the opening day, and another year with very small fields, resulted in a somewhat subdued meeting this year. However, there was a dramatic start to the meeting in the three-runner Meath Hurdle. All three horses fell during the race, but Mr. Tom McKeever's *Buster* was the only one to remount and finished alone in the hands of Mr. Eric McKeever. Interestingly, one of the other fallers in the race *Tenrob* turned out later in the day and fell again. The main honours of the meeting went to trainer Reggie Walker who saddled three winners over the two days and jockey Jack Moylan, while doubles were recorded by trainer Harry Ussher and jockeys Jack McNeill and amateur Mr. Tim Brady Cullinan.

1928. 4th/5th July Runners were a bit more plentiful this year, with the first day's activities being compromised by a very wet day. Trainer William Ashe and Tim Brady Cullinan, now riding as a professional, combined for a double on the first day with *Tiranogue* in the Meath Hurdle, and *Coarlovia* in the featured Drogheda Tradesmen's Chase. The very durable *Orby's Beau*, owned and trained by Tom O'Rourke, won the Conyngham Cup Chase, the last race on the first day, He turned out the following day and won the opening Crockafotha Handicap Hurdle. Jack McNeill was in the saddle on both occasions. The two flat races on the second day supplied a double for trainer Harry Ussher and jockey Jack Moylan. Amateur rider Mr. Tom Nugent rode a winner on each day. He rode *Lloydie* to win the Hill Chase on Wednesday for Max Arnott, and he won the concluding Shallon flat Handicap on the John Turner-trained *Bathoi*.

1929. 3rd/4th July Trainer Maxie Arnott dominated the racing at this year's meeting by saddling six winners over the two days, including a four-timer on Wednesday. Among his winners were *Liscarroll Castle*, who won the opening Meath Hurdle and doubled up by winning the concluding Shallon Handicap on the second day. Two of his winners were ridden by amateur Mr. Tom Nugent, while the other four were all partnered by his long serving stable jockey Dinny Ward. Unfortunately this was the last time Dinny Ward rode at Bellewstown, as in May of the following year he died of injuries received from a fall at Limerick Junction. *Orby's Beau* won the Conyngham Club Cup for the third year running, thus enabling his owner Mr. Tom O'Roarke to keep the Cup outright.

1930. 2nd/3rd July Although runners were scarce enough at this years meeting, the racing provided several interesting moments. Maxie Arnott continued on his winning spree at the course, saddling four winners this year. Crack amateur rider Mr. Eric McKeever equalled Arnott's tally by riding four winners, including a treble on the final day. Two of McKeevers winners were for owner/trainer Major Beamish on the second day. His genuine stayer *South Louth* won the Stewards Handicap Chase for the second year running, beating the year's Irish National Winner *Fanmond* in the process, and the highly talented *Knuckleduster* won the Shallon Amateur Handicap. *Knuckleduster* went on to win the Galway Hurdle twice in 1932 and 1933, both times with Eric McKeever in the saddle. In the Leggan Hall Chase, the 100/1 outsider *Partisian*, benefited from his four rivals falling and went on to win for owner/trainer Mr. J.D. Wilkinson and jockey Mr. Ian Alder. Jockeys Mr. Tom Nugent on the first day and Martin Quirke on the second day both rode doubles at the meeting.

1931. 1st/2nd July The size of the fields held up well resulting in competitive racing over the two days. The talented *Knuckleduster* won the final race at the previous year's meeting, and Major Beamish's gelding got the favourite backers off to a good start by winning the opening Meath Hurdle, once again ridden by Mr. Eric McKeever. The brilliant amateur completed a double on the first day when steering *Thomond II* to a facile success for Reggie Walker and colourful owner, the Duke of Stacpoole. *Thomond II* won five races in a row this year, after which he was sold to wealthy American owner Jock Whitney to race in Britain. Here he developed into a top class chaser and became the chief rival to the immortal *Golden Miller*, being placed second to him in the Cheltenhem Gold Cups of 1934 and 1935 and, also, ran third to the '*Miller*' in the 1935 Aintree Grand National. Another highlight of the first day was a double for leading owner Mrs. Bee Webster and her trainer Charlie Rogers, whose *Essexhall* won the bumper for Mr. Bill Hilliard, and *Old Bachelor* won the featured Drogheda Tradesman's Chase for Sean Magee.

The highlight of the second day was a treble for trainer Maxie Arnott and his jockey Mr. Tom Nugent, while Martin Quirke won the King's Plate on *Nice Token* for owner/trainer Mr. J.T. Rogers.

1932. 6th/7th July This year's meet opened with a shock win for local trainer Ned Delany, who saddled *One More* to score at 33/1 in the hands of Stephen Regan, older brother of the more famous Timmy Regan. Amateur rider Mr. Ian Alder recorded a double on the first day, winning the Bumper on Mr. B.L. Coleman's *Biddles* trained by Harry Ussher, and on the Mr. J.M. Ennis owned and trained *Ballymoe* in the Duleek Chase. The featured Drogheda Tradesmen's Chase was won by *Sherdoon*, trained by James Dawson and ridden by James Costello.

The second day featured doubles from trainer J.A. Mangan and jockey Tommy "Scotchman" Burns. Mangan's double was initiated by *Rada,* who walked over for the Kings Plate, and in the concluding race of the meeting he rode his own horse *Modest Study* to victory in the Shallon Handicap. The versatile Tommy Burns had a mixed double, winning the opening Crockafotha Handicap Hurdle on Lady Helen McCalmont's

Lady Frivol, trained by Hubert Hartigan and the Corporation Maiden on Mr. R.S. Croker's *Chieftan* trained by Cecil Brabazon.

1933. 5th/6th July The aggregate of runners at this year's meet fell short of expectations, and this was attributable to the hard state of the ground, not only at the course, but at many training quarters. The meeting opened with a heart warming success for Major Beamish's old favourite *South Louth* in the opening Meath Hurdle for Mr. Eric McKeever, who completed a double on Lady Nugent's *Lacatoi* trained by Reggie Walker. *Lacatoi* subsequently won the 1935 Welsh Grand National for leading owner Mr. J.V. Rank, when trained in Britain by Gwyn Evans. Mr. D. Murray's *Lady Breemen*, who had won a novice chase at the course the previous year, won the featured Drogheda Tradesmen's Chase, this time for rider P.J. Murray.

There was a sensational start to racing on the second day when the three runners in the Crockafotha Hurdle took the wrong course. The stewards ordered that the race be re-run, but *Cold Bird* declined that offer. In the re-run Mr. R. Collen's *Silver Work* ridden by William Gilmore beat *Cygalice* into second plate. Owner Sir James Nelson, trainer Jack Ruttle and jockey Martin Quirke combined to win the Corporation Maiden with *If You Please,* and the Kings Plate with *Santaria*. Local trainer Tom McKeever recorded a training and riding double. In the Ardcath Chase over 3 miles Mr. J.S. Leonard's *Lerida* and Mr. J.J. Ennis's *Ballymoe* were the only starters. When the latter fell early in the race, Lerida only had to jump a round clear, but he fell at the second-last fence. Luckily Mr. McKeever caught her, remounted and jumped the last fence to claim the prize. The double was completed on the aptly named *Crockafotha*, winning the Leggan Hall Chase from *Old Spinster*.

The night before the races in the 1960s

1933 Mr J.S. Leonard's Lerida, ridden by Tom McKeever, wins the Ardcath Plate.

1934. 4th/5th July The ground rode very firm for this year's renewal, leaving fields again on the small side. However, it didn't stop the year's Irish National Winner *Poolgowran* making an appearance, and he duly won the featured Drogheda Tradesmen's Chase for owner Sir James Nelson, trainer Jack Ruttle and his Australian born jockey Bob Everett, who was killed in action in World War II. Eric Mc Keever, now turned professional had a double on the first day, which included a dead-heat in the opening race. Both of his winners were trained by Reggie Walker. They shared that prize with Ned Delany's *Magnum II*, ridden by Timmy Regan, and completed the double on *Mollison* in the following Duleek Chase.

On the second day the fortunes of Harry Ussher's Brackenstown stable were in the ascendant with three winners, one of which was a dead-heat. Jockeys Jack Morgan, Mr. J.H. DeBromhead and Willy O'Grady each rode a winner for him. O'Grady completed a double on Maxi Arnott's *Cottage Owl* in the Stewards Handicap Chase. Laytown trainer Ned Delany and his jockey Timmy Regan completed a brace for the meeting when *Slanthe* won the Crockafotha Handicap Hurdle.

1935 3rd /4th July The delightful weather ensured good crowds on both days, and with a reasonable supply of runners, the patrons witnessed some exciting action. The opening race saw *Yellow Furze*, owned by long time steward at the course Lt. Col. S.S. Hill-Dillon triumph for trainer Bob Fetherstonhaugh and jockey Timmy Regan. Reggie Walker and his jockey Eric McKeever combined for a double with *Mollison* who repeated the previous year's success in the Duleek Chase, and with *Markington* in the featured Drogheda Tradesmen's Chase.

Harry Ussher and jockey Willy O'Grady combined for a winner on both days, and O'Grady went on to record a third win on *Water Gipsy* in the Stewards Handicap Chase. A flat race double was recorded on the second day by trainer H.G. (Ginger) Wellesley and jockey Peter Maher, with *Delightful* in the Kings' Plate and *Miss Honour* in the Corporation Maiden. Mr. T. Plunkett's *Little Ant*, who had finished third in a chase on the opening day, showed no ill effects, by winning the 3-mile Stewards Handicap Chase for young John McCarthy.

1936 1st/2nd July Local trainers Tom McKeever and Ned Delany both recorded doubles on the opening day of this year's meet, and Delany saddled another winner on the second day. Mr. Clifford Nicholson's *Bard of Meath* was McKeevers opening success in the Meath Hurdle, and *Mountain Breeze* owned by Captain J.A. Hornsby, completed the double for enthusiastic amateur rider Mr. M.J. McArdle, in the Bumper. Mr. Delany's two winners, both of which were ridden by Timmy Regan, were *Speakeasy II* in the Duleek Chase and *Magnum II* in the Drogheda Tradesmen's Chase. Dundalk trainer John Cox saddled his first winner at the track when *Little Thrill* won the Hill Chase in the hands of 'Red' Mick Prendergast.

On the second day of the meeting torrential rain poured down incessantly, to the great discomfort of everybody. Eric McKeever, who rode *Bard of Meath* to win the first day's opener, recorded a double on Thursday, with *Embattle* for Reggie Walker in the Crockafotha Hurdle, and on Maxie Arnott's *Southern Era* in the Leggan Hall Chase. *Water Gipsy* repeated his win in the Stewards Handicap Chase for rider Willy O'Grady and Maxie Arnott, thus completing three winners at the meeting for the Clonsilla trainer. Ned Delany's third winner came when *Clatterbox* won the Shallon Handicap with Mr. Paddy Sleator in the saddle.

Timmy Regan, who had a double on the first day, and his elder brother Stephen, were an integral part of the Delany stable at Corbalis, Laytown. In 1936 he shared the Jockey's title with Willy O'Grady and the following year he was involved in a close battle for the title with Eric McKeever. In May of that year, Timmy Regan fell ill to pneumonia, and sadly died at the age of 26. Among Tim's big race victories were *Seaview* in the 1932 Galway Plate, two Galway Hurdle wins in 1934 and 1935 and the 1935 Irish National on Mr. J.P. Markey's *Rathfriland,* trained by Tom McKeever.

1937 30 June/1 July The opening race of this year's festival, the Meath Hurdle, went to the Mr. J.V. Rank owned *Opticien II*, trained by Bob Fetherstonhaugh. He was ridden by Paddy Murray, for whom this was a first racecourse success. The following Duleek Chase was won by *Mar-Din* for the Turner stable from the North, and they both completed a successful trip by winning the Leggan Hall Chase on the second day. He was ridden on both occasions by Mick Prendergast. The Brackenstown trainer Harry Ussher and his jockey Jack Moylan also had a winner on both days – *Golden Toff* won the Hilltown Flat Handicap on Wednesday and *Foxie* completed the brace in Thursday's feature, His Majesty's Plate. Local owner Miss H. Ball's colours had a successful airing in the Bellewstown Plate for trainer Joe Osborne and amateur Mr. Paddy Sleator.

Eric McKeever, who rode the winner of the first day's feature the Drogheda Tradesmen's Plate on *Vesuvian* for Maxie Arnott went on to ride a double on the second day, both for Reggie Walker. Mr. Bert Kerr's red and black silks were to become famous over the years, and they had their first Bellewstown success, when *Currock* won the Shallon Flat Handicap under Mr. P.J. Lenehan, who also trained him. Mr. J.J. Parkinson's *Hammock* sent punters home happy, winning the concluding Corporation Plate for leading flat rider Morny Wing.

1938 6/7 July This year's meeting was well patronised, even though the weather on the second day was particularly damp. Jockey Willie O'Grady was the star turn on the first day, riding a treble, the first two of which were trained by Ned Delany. He started off by winning the Meath Hurdle on *Serpolette*, and this horse went on to win the Galway Hurdle later in the month from Thursday's hurdle winner *Savota*. O'Grady and Delany also won the second race, this time with Mr. Joseph Leech's *Golden Fizz* in the Duleek Chase, and O'Grady completed his hat-trick in the featured Drogheda Tradesmen's Chase on Mrs. Croft's *Golden Toff*, trained by Harry Ussher. Curragh trainer Bryan Rogers enjoyed a good meeting, including a winner for both Major E. Shirley and his wife – the Shirley family long being associated with Bellewstown as stewards at the course. He saddled *African Queen* for Mrs. Shirley to win the Hilltown Handicap, ridden by Herbert Holmes on the opening day and *Painters Song* won the Corporation Maiden for Major Shirley, ridden by Harry H. Beasley. Rogers and Beasley both completed doubles on the second day, when *Bulletin* won His Majesty's Plate. Tom McKeever saddled *Savota* to win Thursday's opener for local rider James (Midge) Tiernan from nearby Laytown.

The evergreen *Little Ant*, repeated her course win of three years previously (1935) in winning the 3 mile chase, despite having fallen the previous day. Eric McKeever rode two winners on the second day – firstly on *Senville* for Tom McKeever in the Shallon Handicap and finally on *West Point* for Maxie Arnott in the Leggan Hall Chase. Sadly, this was the last winner Eric McKeever rode at Bellewstown as later in the year he was tragically killed in a motor accident.

1939 5th/6th July The ground rode good enough this year, resulting in reasonably sized fields in most of the races. Trainer Maxie Arnott and jockey Jimmy Brogan recorded doubles on both days. Three of the winners were shared. Also, veteran trainer J.J. Parkinson had a double on the first day.

In the featured Drogheda Tradesmen's Chase, only three faced the starter, however these were the previous three winners of the race, *Golden Toff* in 1938, *Vesuvian* in 1937 and *Magnum* in 1936. In a very exciting race the top weight *Golden Toff*, ridden by Willie O'Grady for Harry Ussher and *Vesuvian*, ridden by Jimmy Brogan for Maxie Arnott could not be separated by the judge and a dead-heat resulted with the gallant *Magnum II* only 1½ lengths behind. Brogan had got the day off to a good start by winning the opening Hill Chase on *Brittas* for Jack Ruttle, and completed his hat-trick on *Arnott's Bistro* in the Duleek Chase. Senator Parkinson's two winners came courtesy of *Fortunes Favourite* for Morny Wing in the Hilltown Flat Handicap, and, fittingly, his final winner at the course, was *Young Queen*, ridden by his son Emmanuel in the Bellewstown Plate. The other race of the day, the Crockafotha Handicap hurdle was won by the outsider *Shanagarry* for owner trainer S.J. Duffy and jockey Thomas McNeill.

Unusually this year the Meath Hurdle opened the second days racing and resulted in a win for Mr. R.F. Coonan's *Hearty Welcome*, trained by J. Burke and ridden by Farnham W. Maxwell, who went on to forge a successful training career for himself in Britain. The following race, His Majesty's Plate, resulted in another course win for Major Shirley, with *Fisherman's Prayer*, trained by Bryan Rogers and ridden by Herbert Holmes. *My Branch* won the Wintergrass Chase for Tom Dreaper, and in doing so, provided the Greenogue master with his first win at the course. Maxie Arnott's training double on the second day was initiated by *Bridgewater* in the Shallon Flat Handicap under Mr Paddy Sleator, and *St. James's Gate* in the Leggan Hall Chase completed the double with Jimmy Brogan in the plate. The concluding Corporation Plate went to the Harry Ussher trained *Bonnie Blue*, with Jack Moylan riding.

1940. July 3rd/4th Although the ground rode very firm, most of the races were well contested, save for a match on either day. The main honours went to owner Ms. Dorothy Paget and her trainer Charlie Rogers, who had a first day double, as also had jockey Dan Moore. Amateur 'Bunny' Cox rode a double on the second day, while course specialist Maxie Arnott and his young jockey Vince Mooney had a winner on both days.

Arnott and Mooney started the meeting well when the outsider *Minstrel Boy* bolted up in the Hill Handicap Chase for owner Ms M. Gaisford St. Lawrence, whose family have had a long association with the course. Ms. Paget and her trainer's double was initiated when *Atco* won the Drogheda Tradesmen's Chase for the recently-turned professional Tim Moloney, and *Knight of the Border* had an easy task in the two runner Duleek Chase for Dan Moore. Moore's first winner had come in the Crockafotha Handicap Hurdle on Reggie Walker's *Smerwick's Nephew*. The Hilltown Flat Handicap was won by the Mr. D. Malone, owned and trained, *Dandy Boy*, ridden by Thomas Whitehead. In a stewards' enquiry following this race, the riding of John Doyle was referred to the stewards of the Turf Club, who subsequently withdrew his licence. Locals might be interested to know that Mr. A. Jeserich, who came to reside in Bellewstown after the outbreak of World War II, had a runner, *Hunthill*, in this race.

The second day opener saw Bunny Cox ride the first of his two winners when *Littlestep* won the Meath Hurdle for his father, and he completed the double on the N. Kelly-trained *Swing Fro* for veteran owner Mr. J.H. Nicholls in the Shallon Handicap. Max Arnott and Vince Mooney's second winner of the meeting came with *Brown Admiral* winning the Leggan Hall Chase for owner Mr. A.D. Comyn. The meeting concluded with the Mrs. T.

Horses jumping the hurdle at the winning post in the Joseph Bellew Handicap Hurdle. The winner was the grey horse Killykeen Star ridden by Francis Shortt, 1962

Marie Collins holding Veni Vici, Tom Dreaper's last winner at the Hill, at Mag Arnold's Stables, 1971

Kathleen Martin and May Brannigan with baby Paul at the races, 1975

A HISTORY OF THE RACECOURSE   1726 - 2013

Famous commentator Michael O'Hehir studies form with top Irish jockey Tommy Murphy, 1976

Michael Kinane coming into the winners enclosure after winning on Muscari, 1980

'Lark' Brien at the Races in the 1980's

300 years of *Racing* at BELLEWSTOWN

Sean Graham Amateur Handicap Hurdle Winner Half Shot, owner James Curran, trainer Pat Rooney, jockey Tom McCourt, 7/7/1982

Seamus Mulvaney Hurdle Winner Winning Nora, owner D.J. Reddan, trainer M. Hourigan, jockey K.F. O'Brien, 2/7/1986

Winning Nora's connections with Mrs Denise Reddan holding the horse

A HISTORY OF THE RACECOURSE   1726 - 2013

Bellewstown Mares Maiden Hurdle Div. II Winner Ella Rosa, owner Mrs E. Hackett, trainer Thomas Carberry, jockey David Geraghty, 3/7/1986

A snapshot of the outside enclosure in the 1980's

Locals John and Bernie Moore enjoy the races, along with Alma Gogan

300 years of *Racing* at BELLEWSTOWN

Tom McCourt on Saintfield winning the Michael Moore Car Sales Maiden Hurdle, July 1987

Bellewstown Races Committee. Back L-R: Tom Jenkinson, Pat Hoey, Eamonn Delany, Joe Collins. Sitting Middle L-R: Jimmy Curran and Brigadier A.D.R. Wingfield. Front L-R: John Purfield and Desmond O'Hagan, taken in the 1980's

A HISTORY OF THE RACECOURSE   1726 - 2013

Murphy Sand and Gravel Handicap Division I Winner Mr Mystery, owner S.J. Murphy, trainer Pat Martin, jockey Pat Gilson, 5/7/1988

Michael Kauntze with Mrs Gaisford St. Lawrence and jockey Warren O'Connor receiving a prize from Heineken after winning the Heineken Handicap, 1990

300 years of *Racing* at BELLEWSTOWN

Niall Byrne on Corporate Raider clears the last hurdle before going to win the Bernard Barry Crockafotha Handicap Hurdle

The East Meath Racing Club celebrate the victor of Corporate Raider in the Bernard Barry Crockafotha Handicap Hurdle, 1989. Pictured are John Gogarty, Brendan Whyte, James Gogarty and Martin Curran (far right)

Tymoole and Harry Rogers jumping the last hurdle before going on to win, 1992

A HISTORY OF THE RACECOURSE   1726 - 2013

Kilsharvan 2 year-old EBF Maiden Winner Almaty, owner Peter Savill, trainer Con Collins, jockey P.V. Gilson, 4/7/1995

Vincent Keating INH Flat Race Winner Jackpot Johnny, owner T. Farrell, trainer / jockey Mr Ger. Farrell, 3/7/1997

300 years of *Racing* at BELLEWSTOWN

Charlie Swan and Norman Williamson, with Duleek man, Mick Heaney and his grandson, 1997

Bellewstown schoolchildren on the Gormanstown Stand with Charlie Swan and Norman Williamson, 1997. Includes schoolboy Mark Callaghan, now working with Jim Bolger

A HISTORY OF THE RACECOURSE   1726 - 2013

Robbie and Ann Gogan and son, with trainer Noel Meade and winner Tymoole, 1992

Kevin Prendergast receiving his trophy from Seamus and Rory Murphy after Night Scout won the Murphy Sand and Gravel Maiden, 1998

300 years of *Racing* at BELLEWSTOWN

John Purfield presents Paddy and Maura Mullins with a trophy after No Avail won the Derek Plant Handicap, 1998

Bambury Bookmakers Handicap Winner Society Queen, with Francis, Peter and Oliver Casey (jockey), 1/7/1999

A HISTORY OF THE RACECOURSE   1726 - 2013

Tattersall's Ireland 2 year-old Maiden Winner Sir Azzaro, owner Cameron Express Inc., trainer F. Mourier (USA), jockey Eddie Ahern, 5/7/2001

Sam Dennigan Maiden Hurdle Winner Mac's Valley, owner Mrs M. McManus, trainer Willie Mullins, jockey Ruby Walsh, 5/7/2002

300 years of *Racing* at BELLEWSTOWN

Jockeys, led by Jim Keeling leaving the Weigh-room, July 2003

The Shuler Black Hilltown Handicap, Kevin Coleman, Eamonn Delany, members of the winning syndicate, Sean 'Shuler' Black, Tom Jenkinson, Andrew McKeever, Jim Corcoran and John Purfield, 2003

A HISTORY OF THE RACECOURSE 1726 - 2013

Sean McManus Tyres Novice Hurdle Winner Grand Lili, owner P. Gilsenan, trainer John McConnell, jockey Brian Byrnes, 30/6/2005

Best Dressed finalists, 2007

300 years of *Racing* at BELLEWSTOWN

Local man 'Chap' Black who came home every year from England for the races with his daughter Janice, 2008

Padraig Beggy, in blue, and Fran Berry, 2008

A HISTORY OF THE RACECOURSE   1726 - 2013

July 2009

Mairead McGuinness, David Beggy, Barney Rock, Bernard Jackman and Shane Horgan with the Heineken Cup won by Leinster, 2009

300 years of *Racing* at BELLEWSTOWN

Alan Delany, Jim Corcoran and Gavin Duffy with model Caprice, 2010

July 2010

A HISTORY OF THE RACECOURSE 1726 - 2013

The Briggs Watering System in action on the track

Local winner, Hamalka, ridden by Paul Carberry, with members of the Click Syndicate, 2010

300 years of *Racing* at BELLEWSTOWN

Sam Dennigan and Co. Hurdle Winner Bacher Boy, owner Sean F. Gallagher, trainer Gordon Elliott, jockey Paul Carberry, 3/7/2010

The line up of 'Hunt' jockeys for The Ward Union Rehab Bellewstown Charity Race, raising over €7,000 for charity, July 2011

A HISTORY OF THE RACECOURSE   1726 - 2013

Rose McCullen and Geraldine Maguire, 2011

John Purfield presenting a trophy to Donal Kinsella Dunleer

Lester Piggott with Conor O'Dwyer who won the Arkle Memorial, August 2011

300 years of *Racing* at BELLEWSTOWN

Mt Weather and Declan McDonogh win in a thrilling photo finish from Big Bad Lily, Sovereign Secure and Queen Gracie for trainer Dick Donoghoe, 2011

Off and running in The Indaver Ireland Novice Hurdle won by High Importance under Ruby Walsh, July 2011

A HISTORY OF THE RACECOURSE   1726 - 2013

The jockeys who took part in the Arkle's Legends race at Bellewstown. From left: Conor O'Dwyer, Ger Dowd, Charlie Swan, Jason Titley, Norman Williamson Dermot McLaughlin, Joe Byrne, Robbie Hennessy, Arthur Moore and Adrian Maguire, 18 August 2011

Jacksonslady and Barry Geraghty (right) wing the final hurdle before beating Inspector Clouseau (left) by a short head for trainer Philip Dempsey, 2011

300 years of *Racing* at BELLEWSTOWN

John Ludlow, Head Supervisor of the Clean-Up Team in action in 2011

Locals Eugene, Josie and Marina Cassidy at the Races in 2012

Louth Hounds Meeting at Bellewstown Racecourse in Nov. 2012. Huntsman Alan Reilly, flanked by whippers-in Christopher Rogers and Alan Tighe

Ruby Walsh on Rossvoss in the Parade Ring wearing Dermot Desmond's colours in 2012

A HISTORY OF THE RACECOURSE 1726 - 2013

Beltany Gent, jockey Dean O'Hagan and groom Mick Brannigan before the Liz Jenkinson Memorial Cup Race (Ward Union Rehab Charity Race), 8/7/2012

Glebe House Nursery Winner All Ablaze, trainer D.J. English, jockey Rory Cleary, 22/8/2012

300 years of *Racing* at BELLEWSTOWN

McCairns owned *Diamond Line* winning the Corporation Plate for Jack Ruttle and jockey Bill Howard.

1941. 2nd/3rd July "Somehow or other the notion prevails that in time of drought galloping is hard on the Hill of Crockafotha, but in fact the going is never hard there – hard in the sense of the surface being unmarkable - for the subsoil is shingle, not heavy clay, hence it does not become baked" The above comments were part of the Irish field report from this year's meet. Two horses *Silver Fizz* and *Crafty Prince* won on both days at this year's reunion, while jockey Jimmy Brogan recorded three wins, including a double on the first day. Mr. Joe Leech's *Silver Fizz* won the Crockafotha Hurdle on the opening day, and followed up in the Leggan Hall Chase on Thursday – trained by Ned Delany, he was ridden on both occasions by Thomas McNeill. Mr. A.D. Cooke owned and trained *Crafty Prince* which won the bumper on the first day, when ridden by Mr George Malcolmson, and Jimmy Lenehan was in the saddle when he won Thursday's opening Meath Hurdle. Jimmy Brogan and Maxie Arnott combined for a double on the opening day with *Charon* in The Hill Handicap Chase, and with *Brown Admiral* (repeating the previous year's course win) in the Drogheda Tradesman Chase. Brogan's third winner of the meeting came courtesy of Mr. P.J. O'Hagan's *Golden Ivy* which won the Wintergrass Chase for trainer Frank Ward. The meeting concluded with the Corporation Plate, which was won by the Mr. J.A. Farrell owned and trained *Hazel Fair*, ridden by George Wells. This was the last meeting to be held here due to the deprivations arising from World War II, until racing resumed in 1946.

1946 Racing resumed at Bellewstown in 1946 after a four-year gap due to World War Two. The opening paragraph of the Irish Field's report stated 'When the regulars revisited Bellewstown this week they found little or no change in the old place and it is doubtful if they would have preferred it otherwise. Bellewstown is as full of charm as ever and the only suggestion of modernisation was the presence of the public address system in the enclosure.'

Trainers who saddled winners at the meeting in 1946 were M.J.Webster, John Kirwan, Harry Ussher, Maxie Arnott, Reggie Walker, Barney Nugent, Dick O'Connell (2), Seamus McGrath, R.J.McCormick, Tom Dreaper, Charlie Rogers and P.J.Prendergast. Jockeys who rode winners were D.McCann, Mr Pat (P.P.) Hogan, Mickey Gordon, Aubrey Brabazon, Tommy Burns, Commdt. Dan Corry, J. Walshe, Georgie Wells (2), Eddie Newman, Mr J.R. Cox Jnr. and Martin Molony.

Whatever about the lack of improvements at the course since the previous racing in 1941, there was no argument about the quality of some of the winners on display. Pride of place must go to *Hatton's Grace*, who later won three Champion Hurdles at the Cheltenham Festival in 1949, 1950 and 1951 for Vincent O'Brien and won his first ever race at Bellewstown in the Bellewstown Plate. He was owned at that time by Commdt. Dan Corry, who also rode him and was a regular competitor for Ireland at show-jumping. *Hatton's Grace* was trained by Dick O'Connell, who held the training license for Dan Moore, as he was still riding. The other flat race for amateur riders at the meeting also resulted in a win for a horse that went on to much better things. This was *Freebooter* who won the 1950 Grand National at Aintree for Bobby Renton. Owned then by Mr J. Johnson, he won the Shallon Plate and was also trained by Dick O'Connell and ridden by Mr J.R. (Bunny) Cox.

Another high profile winner at the 1946 meeting was *Senria*, who won the 3-mile Wintergrass Handicap Chase for the Craigie family and Tom Dreaper, ridden by Eddie Newman. *Senria* is probably better known as the dam of *Fortria*, whose numerous wins included the 2-mile Champion Chase at the Cheltenham Festival, the Mackeson Gold Cup (twice) and the Irish Grand National. *Senria* also bred a second Irish National winner, when *Last Link* won it in 1963 for Paddy Woods. *Last Link* gained further fame when one of her progeny, *Last Suspect*, produced a storming finish to win the 1985 English Grand National.

The Meath Hurdle opened proceedings on the first day and it provided an initial training success for M.J. Webster, when Danny McCann steered *Penny Plain* to victory. In the next race, the only southern-trained runner at the meeting, *Indecision*, won the Amateur Hurdle for Kilkenny trainer, John Kirwan, and his illustrious pilot, Mr P.P.Hogan. The featured Drogheda Tradesmen's Chase went to the Maxie Arnott trained *Smiling Marcus*, piloted by Mickey Gordon. The other chase on the card was won by the Reggie Walker owned and trained *Colehill*, ridden by Aubrey Brabazon. The best finish of the day came when *Wrong Note*, owned by Dick McIlhagga and trained by Barney Nugent, prevailed by a short head for veteran jockey, Tommy Burns.

The Crockafotha Hurdle opened proceedings as usual on the second day and it was won by the Seamus McGrath-trained *Sweet Haven*, ridden by James Walshe. Seamus went on to record many victories on the flat and another leading flat trainer to have a jumping success at the meeting was the legendary Paddy Prendergast, whose *Clare Man* won the Legganhall Chase, ridden by Martin Molony. The only jockey to record two wins at the meeting was Georgie Wells, who won both flat races on the second day. His first win was on *Lady Antoinette* for Dick McCormick in His Majesty's Plate and he won the final race of the meeting on the Charlie Rogers-trained *Conkers,* in the Corporation Plate.

1947 July 2 The opening day of the 1947 meeting brought plenty of runners and an extremely good day's racing was had. Honours for the day went to trainer Barney Nugent, who supplied two winners. In the opening race, his *Drumbuoy* justified plenty of support under Martin Molony, to win the Meath Hurdle. In the Hilltown Plate, William Howard steered *Northern Dandy* to a narrow success. The main event of the day, the Drogheda Tradesmen's Chase, saw *New Pyjamas*, from the Harry Ussher yard, ridden by Aubrey Brabazon, gain a narrow success over the locally trained *Athlone Calling,* from the George Barry stable. In the Amateur Hurdle, *Wervina,* trained and ridden by Mr J.A. Osborne for Mr J. Jeffers, was successful. In the Bumper, M.J. Webster supplemented his initial training success of the previous year, when *Grey Point* won, ridden by promising young amateur, Mr Anthony Scannell. The final race of the first day, the

Duleek Chase, went to the Tom Dreaper-trained *My Twig*, for the Baker family. She was ridden by Timmy Hyde.

July 3 The second day opened with a win for *Sir Gabriel*, owned and trained by Patrick J. Ryan, with Mickey Browne in the saddle. The time-honoured King's Plate went to the John Power-ridden *Lorimer* for trainer Dick McCormick and owner Mr A.P.Reynolds. In the three mile chase, Danny Morgan piloted Dick McIlhagga's *Cadamstown*, to win for trainer P.Nugent. Prolific trainer, J.J.Parkinson owned and trained *Come and Go* to win the Shallon Plate under Mr Waring Willis. The outstanding feature of the second day's sport was the tremendous finish for the Legganhall Chase, which resulted in a dead-heat between Reggie Walker's *His Eminence* and Tom Dreaper's *Confucius*. Their respective jockeys, Jimmy Brogan and Eddie Newman, deserved full marks for some fine riding. The final race of the meeting, the Corporation Maiden Plate, resulted in a win for H.H. the Aga Khan's filly, *Teretania,* for rider Gerry Cooney and trainer H.M. Hartigan.

1948 June 30 Large crowds attended both days of the 1948 fixture, where the chief honours went to the Clonsilla jockey, Mickey Gordon, who rode four winners from five mounts. Two of his winners were for Maxie Arnott, who was the only trainer to have more than one winner. Mickey Gordon was a very versatile jockey, being able to do near eight stone on the flat. To illustrate his versatility, two of his four wins were over fences, one over hurdles and the other one on the flat. Gordon opened proceedings on the first day when he rode *Dab* to win the Meath Hurdle for owner/trainer Mr H.B.Surman. For good measure he rode the winner of the last race, when *Smiling Marcus* supplemented his course win of the previous year, in the Duleek Chase for trainer Maxie Arnott. Another horse repeating his course win of the previous year was *Sir Gabriel*, for owner/trainer Patrick J.Ryan, this time ridden by his son, Mr J.Ryan, in the Amateur Hurdle. The featured Drogheda Tradesmen's Chase went to the John Kirwan-trained *Astra*, under Thomas Foran, with the luckless *Athlone Calling* second again, beaten by a short head. *Moss Trooper* sprang a 20/1 shock when beating twenty-one others to win the Bumper for trainer J.J.Long and jockey Mr T. O'Connell. The other race of the day, the one-mile flat handicap was won by the George Robinson-trained *Dawros*, under Jimmy Eddery.

July 1 The second day opened as usual with the Crockafotha Handicap Hurdle and here Paddy Sleator had the first two placings, with *Gay Rosalinda* landing a nice touch to win under Chris Sleator, the trainer's brother. *Fanny's Way* proved best in His Majesty's Plate for C. Brabazon and T.P. Burns. The three-mile chase provided another win for jockey Mickey Gordon, when *West Wind*, trained by Peter Connolly proved successful. *Murrisk*, for the Coonan family, won the Shallon flat race for rider Mr J.A. Osborne. In the Legganhall Chase, *Lonely Boy*, for enthusiastic North Dublin owner/trainer Charlie Lawless was the winner for jockey Brendan O'Neill. Maxie Arnott and Mickey Gordon closed out the meeting when *Count Gabriel* justified favouritism in the one-mile maiden.

1949 July 6 Ratoath trainer, Charlie Rogers, dominated the opening day of the 1949 Bellewstown meeting with three winning favourites. He won the first two races on the card with horses owned by eccentric owner, Ms Dorothy Paget, *Jack Loo* winning the

Meath Hurdle with T.P. Burns in the saddle, Mr P.P.Hogan steered *Iceflow* to success in the following Amateur Hurdle. Hogan completed his double in the Bumper on Rogers' owned and trained *Prince Resenda*. In the Drogheda Tradesmen's Chase, the P.J. Lenehan-trained *Crafty Prince* got the better of *Bright Cherry* with Martin Molony in the saddle. George Robinson had a good strike rate at the course and he saddled *Solifa,* with Phil Canty in the plate, for another win in the one-mile handicap. Another famous racing family, the Taaffes, won the Novice Chase, with *Wuhu*, and a youthful Pat Taaffe, then an amateur, in the saddle for his father, Tom.

July 7 Yet another iconic racing family, the Cox family, started the second day off well, by winning the handicap hurdle with Mr J.R. Cox steering *Gangster* to win for his father. The following race, His Majesty's Plate, saw the complete outsider of the six runners, *Anthony Wakefield* at 20/1 make all the running to win for Barney Nugent, thus providing his young jockey, Paddy Cowley, with his initial riding success. Martin Molony notched up his second win of the meeting by winning the Wintergrass Handicap Chase on Joe Osborne's mare, *Pastime*. *Statistic* won the first of his three consecutive wins in the Shallon Handicap for Maxie Arnott and jockey Liam Ward. Mick Browne piloted *Dark Ivy* to win the novice chase for north of Ireland trainer, Major Carson. P.J. Prendergast closed proceedings with a win in the Corporation Maiden with *Hyland Dew*, ridden by Paddy Powell Jnr.

1950 July 5 The 1950 meeting was a very successful affair with fields on both days being of highly satisfactory proportions. The Tote takings on the first day constituted a course record, but that figure was far surpassed on the second day. Most successful jockey at the meeting was Jimmy Eddery, who notched up three winners, while there were doubles for both Pat Taaffe and Martin Molony. Dan Moore was the only trainer to have more than one winner, winning the last two races on the first day.

The main event of the first day, the Drogheda Tradesmen's Chase, was won by *Bright Cherry,* for the Baker family from Malahow, near the Naul, trained by Tom Dreaper and ridden by Pat Taaffe. While Bright Cherry was a great prolific mare, she attained greater fame in racing history as the dam of the great *Arkle*. In an ironic twist of faith, it is interesting to note that Nas na Riogh, dam of *Arkle*'s great rival, *Millhouse*, also won the Drogheda Tradesman's Chase in 1953 for the Lawlor family from Naas. The opening race, the Meath Hurdle saw Mr George Dunwoody return to the saddle after a long absence through injury, winning on his own horse, *Cloncaw*, trained by R.G. Patton. In the next race, *Slippery Hill,* owned by Lieut. Col. E. Shirley, a steward at the meeting, finished first in the Ardcath Maiden, but he was subsequently disqualified in favour of *Golden Strand*, ridden by James Tyrell. *Golden Strand* was trained by Harry Ussher and, as it turned out, it proved to be his last winner at the course, where he had enjoyed unparalleled success as a trainer between the two world wars. Seamus McGrath and Jimmy Eddery won the 1-mile handicap with *Ladastra*. In the last two races, Dan Moore was the successful trainer with *Embarkation* in the Bumper under Mr J.R Cox and with *Buy Me* in the Duleek Chase, ridden by young amateur, Mr R. Knowles.

July 6 The second day opened with the Handicap Hurdle and here *Murrisk* repeated a previous course win for the Coonan family and Pat Taaffe. The King's Plate saw George Robinson provide Jimmy Eddery with the first of his brace with *Radiant Guinea,* which was completed in the last race of the day by the P.J. Higgins-trained *Garryro* in the famous Kerr silks. Martin Molony also completed a double first with the P.J. Lenehan-trained *Lucky Sprig*, in the three-mile chase. He also won with *Scrambler* from the Joe Osborne yard in the other chase on the card, where the second horse, *Red Knight*, was ridden by Martin's brother, Tim. *Statistic* won the Shallon Handicap for the second year in a row for Maxie Arnott, this time ridden by W. Howard.

1951 July 4 This year's annual meeting at Bellewstown was very eventful and while the weather on Wednesday was fine, the second day was marred by continuous rain. The ground became extremely slippery and there were several mishaps in one of the flat races. Charlie Rogers saddled another three winners, while jockeys Eddie Newman and Martin Molony both recorded doubles.

In the opening race of the meeting, Rogers and Molony combined to win the Meath Hurdle with *Mountrath*. Rogers completed his first day double by saddling Ms Dorothy Paget's *Persian Lad* to win the bumper under Mr P.P. Hogan. In the second race, apprentice P.F. Conlon atoned for his disqualification of the previous year, by steering Dick McCormick's *Still Waters* to win the Ardcath Maiden. Eddie Newman rode both chase winners on the opening day, first with *Still Prudent* for trainer Danny Morgan in the featured Drogheda Tradesmen's Chase. He followed up by winning the Duleek Chase on *Noble Scion* for trainer Capt. Denis Baggallay, later to become Secretary of the Turf Club. In the other race on the card, Dan Kirwan made the long trip from Co. Kilkenny worthwhile, when his owner/trainer *Free Entry* obliged for Jimmy Eddery in the Hilltown Handicap.

July 5 Dan Moore could always be relied on for a winner at Crockafotha and in the opening handicap hurdle of that name, *Count Idol* justified strong market support, to win for owner Mrs A.W. Riddle-Martin and rider T.P. Burns. The King's Plate was usually the second race on the second day of the meeting and in the fifties, legendary trainer P.J. Prendergast had a great record in it. This year his *Rose Dentelle* justified short odds to win for jockey Jimmy Mullane. The reputation of the time-honoured Wintergrass Handicap Chase over three miles as a genuine Galway Plate trial, held up when *St. Kathleen II* obliged for trainer Willie O'Grady and jockey Pat Doyle, before going on to win the Ballybrit feature. *Statistic* won his third Shallon Handicap in a row, this time for new trainer Ger Flood and local jockey Andy (Tiny) Duff. In a grief-strewn Corporation Maiden Plate, Mick Hurley's *Fijian*, under Georgie Wells, avoided all the mayhem to oblige for owner Mr Terence J.S. Gray. In the concluding Legganhall Novice Chase, *Knight's Harp* completed doubles for Ms Dorothy Paget and jockey Martin Molony and a treble for trainer Charlie Rogers.

1952 July 2 The annual fixture took place on July 2nd and 3rd this year and proved as enjoyable as ever. Apart from a two-horse contest on the first day, fields were of good strength throughout with only trainer John Cox winning more than one race. However there was an initial success for Toss Taaffe, since joining the professional ranks and a first riding success for 16-year-old apprentice John Flanagan.

Toss Taaffe's success came in the opening Meath Hurdle when he steered *Dovetail* to win for Joe Osborne. In the second race Tony Riddle-Martin trained *Orange Torney* to win the one-mile five-furlong maiden for his mother-in-law, Mrs Lewis, with apprentice Francis McMahon in the saddle. The main event of the day, the Drogheda Tradesmen's Plate, saw the Rathfeigh stable of Jimmy Brogan prove successful when the prolific veteran *Royal Bridge* won under Christy Grassick. *Noble Scion* repeated his course success of the previous year by winning the Duleek Chase for trainer Capt. Baggalay and rider Eddie Newman. The one-mile Hilltown Handicap went the way of *Rathregan* for John Cox and T.P. Burns, while the last race of the day, the Bumper, saw the Patton family's *La Tinta* win for rider Mr S. Patton.

July 3 Trainer John Cox secured his second win of the meeting when his own horse, Little Roger, won the opening Crockafotha Hurdle for rider Pat Doyle. Brud Fetherstonhaugh won the second race of the day, His Majesty's Plate, with *Excelsa* for famous owner Capt. Cecil Boyd-Rochfort, who justified odds-on support for rider *Herbert Holmes*. The Kirwan stable from Gowran, Co Kilkenny invariably had a winner at the meeting and here Dan Kirwan owned and trained *Grange Silvia* to win the 3-mile chase. Another trainer with a good record at the course, George Robinson, supplied the winner of the Shallon Handicap, with *Third Estate* winning for Jimmy Eddery. *Mighty High* atoned for some previous disappointments when leading all the way to win the 1-mile Maiden and thus provided 16-year-old John Flanagan with his initial racecourse success for his boss Mick Hurley. In the concluding Legganhall Novice Chase, *Baby Power* showed no ill-effects from his second placing in the Bumper on the first day and his owner/rider Mr Wilfred McKeever putting up three pounds overweight, by winning easily. Mr McKeever also trained him.

1953 July 1 The meeting in 1953 was held on firm ground, in spite of which the fields held up very well. On the opening day, Pat Taaffe rode the winner of both chases, while on Thursday, Dan Kirwan and jockey Tom O'Brien combined to win both chases.

The most famous horse to win at the meeting was *Nas na Riogh*, later to become dam of the famous *Millhouse*. In winning the featured Drogheda Tradesmen's Chase, she was winning the same race as Arkle's dam *Bright Cherry* who had won three years earlier in 1950. *Nas na Riogh* was owned by the famous Lawlor family from Naas and ridden by Pat Taaffe for his father, Tom. Tom Dreaper supplied Pat Taaffe with his second winner of the meeting when *Nice Work* easily won the Duleek Chase. The meeting had opened as usual with the Meath Hurdle and here 'The Ward' trainer Barney Nugent supplied the winner with *Le Plaisant* under Paddy Cowley. The two flat races on the card went firstly to the Kevin Kerr trained *Sir Norman* who won the Ardcath Maiden for Jimmy Mullane. The Hilltown Handicap was won by *Lady Gracefield* for jockey Paddy Powell Jun. and trainer Willie Byrne. The concluding Bumper, the Bellewstown Plate, provided one of the most popular local successes ever at the course when *Little Horse*, owned and trained by Leslie Ball at Wintergrass, Bellewstown (about a mile from the track), won at the rewarding odds of 20/1. He was ridden by Mr E. J. (Ted) Kelly and was led up by James (Mousey) Black, a very popular local character. Mr Kelly later became a long serving Turf Club official. *Little Horse* was second in the Meath Hurdle here the following year and later was sold on to the Newell family from Drumree for whom he won several races including winning on successive days at the 1962 Punchestown Festival as a 14-year-old, one race being the 4-mile, 2-furlong La Touche Chase over the banks course.

Mousy Black with Little Horse

July 2 The second day, held in ideal weather, saw *Fair Bachelor*, trained by J.T. Doyle, win the opening Crockafotha Hurdle for amateur jockey Mr M.R. Magee. P.J. Prendergast won the King's Plate with *Foxella* under Liam Ward and the McGrath family provided the winner of the Shallon Handicap for apprentice John J. Eddery with *Flandria*. In the 1-mile Maiden, the C. Sheridan-trained *Stalenger* proved successful for owner Mrs E.J. King and jockey Nicky Brennan. The two chases on the card were both won by Dan Kirwan trained and Tom O'Brien ridden horses, with *Rambling Girl* winning the 3-mile chase and *Bell Wave* winning the concluding Legganhall Novice Chase.

1954 July 7 Jockeys T.P. Burns and Mr J. R. (Bunny) Cox were the only ones to score doubles at the 1954 meeting, held in pleasant weather conditions.

The meeting opened with a win for *In View* in the Meath Hurdle for Dan Moore and jockey Pat Doyle. Nesbitt Waddington, who resided at Beaulieu House, Drogheda, and was a steward at the course for a long number of years including serving as chairman of the stewards for a considerable time, had the pleasure of owning the winner of the Ardcath Maiden, when *Pearl Chariot* won for jockey Gerry Cooney and trainer H.M. Hartigan. Capt. E.A. Gargan, who owned *Southerntown*, the 20/1 winner of the Duleek Handicap Chase, had strong family links with the Bellewstown area. In winning, *Southerntown* was providing his trainer, W.J. Magnier, with his first success since taking out a license and he was ridden by E.L. McKenzie. The Michael Dawson-trained *Soir* proved too good for his rivals in the featured Drogheda Tradesmen's Chase, under C.F. McCormick. The Hilltown Handicap provided a thrilling finish when Seamus McGrath's

Keimaneigh dead-heated with *Rathregan*, trained by T. O'Sullivan. The jockeys involved were Jimmy Eddery and T.P. Burns respectively. It was only when he arrived at the course that Pat Rooney decided to run *Arctic Flame* in the Bumper. He had intended keeping him for a chase on the Thursday, but when he found out that Mr J.R. Cox had no mount in that race, he changed his mind and sent home for **Arctic Flame**. Mr Cox took the mount, with happy results for all concerned. *Arctic Flame* also ran in a chase on the next day, but fell.

July 8 Mr J.R. Cox won the last race on Wednesday and started off in style by winning the first race on Thursday, when *Little Roger* won the Crockafotha Handicap Hurdle, thus repeating his win of 1952 in the same race. P.J. Prendergast won another Queen's Plate, this time with *Itaissu*, ridden by T. Wallace. George Robinson had another Bellewstown winner when *Reinstated* won the Shallon Handicap for T.P. Burns. The gallant 15-year-old grey *Game Toi* pulled up in a chase on the previous day, but showing no ill-effects he out-battled *Carey's Cottage* to win the 3-mile Handicap Chase for Johnny Lehane and trainer R.P. O'Connell. Miss Dorothy Paget had another Bellewstown winner when *Scroll* won the 1-mile maiden for Charlie Rogers and Phil Canty, while the concluding Novice Chase was won by *Spicey* for the Taaffe family, this time ridden by Toss.

1955 July 6 One of the most successful fixtures ever took place in glorious weather conditions. With the going riding good, there were plenty of runners, indeed the Bumper on the first day had to be divided. P.J. Prendergast was the only trainer to record more than one winner, with a winner on each day.

The main event of the day, the Drogheda Tradesmen's Chase, resulted in a great local win for local trainer George Barry, who trained at Balgeen about two miles from the track. His horse, *Camofly*, was owned by Pat Purfield and ridden by Micky Regan. Micky, along with his brother, Timmy, were mainstays of the Delany stable, Corbalis, Laytown for a long number of years. The meeting had opened as usual with the Meath Hurdle and here *Kilkilogue*, owned and trained by Bobby Patton, justified favouritism for jockey Paddy Crotty. Chairman of the race committee, Lt. Col. E. Shirley, had a nice win in the Ardcath Maiden when his *Low Cloud* provided P.J. Prendergast with his first win of the week, under rider T. M. Burns. The bookmakers went 6/1 the field in the 19-runner Duleek Chase and one of the co-favourites, *Belrobin*, obliged for Dundalk trainer John Cox and jockey Toss Taaffe. Charlie Weld provided the winner of the one-mile maiden, when *Rocint* scored for T.P. Burns. The Bumper was divided and Dan Moore trained the winner of the first division with *Royal Courier* scoring for Mr Brian Lenehan. Division Two went to the Wilfred McKeever-trained *Irish Tara* for Mr Eddie Harty.

July 7 Racing on Thursday took place in heat-wave conditions and the scene presented more in the nature of a picnic than a race meeting. Tom Dreaper sprang a bit of a surprise in the opening Crockafotha Hurdle when Martin Murray rode Lord Bicester's *Merry Rock* to win at odds of 10/1. *Itaiassu* won the Queen's Plate for the second year in succession for P.J. Prendergast, this time ridden by Liam Ward. The Shallon Handicap, over 1-mile, 5 furlongs, was won by *Master Melody*, trained by Tony Riddle-Martin for his wife, with

Gerry Carroll in the plate. The 3-mile Handicap Chase resulted in a win for the Joe Osborne-trained *Rosegg,* ridden by Michael Magee. J.M. Rogers had a rare Bellewstown winner, when *Dusty Bridge* won the one- mile maiden for apprentice Willie Burke, who later achieved everlasting fame when he steered *Santa Claus* to win the 1964 Irish Sweeps Derby for his boss, Mickey (J.M.) Rogers. The meeting concluded with a big field for the Legganhall Novice Chase and here Michael Dawson's *Waterview* won for C.J. McCormick.

1956 July 4 The Taaffe brothers, Pat and Toss, both rode two winners at this year's meeting at which the opening day was marred by continuous rain, which left the small attendance fully exposed to the elements on the 'Hill'. Tom Dreaper was the only trainer to score more than one winner, recording a double on the opening day.

Dreaper opened proceedings by winning the Meath Hurdle, with *Nicholaus Dream* under Pat Taaffe. Toss took over in the saddle for Dreaper's second winner, when *Caduceus,* owned by his brother, Dick, won the Duleek Chase. Lt. Col. E. Shirley, P.J. Prendergast and jockey T.M. Burns repeated last year's success in the Ardcath Maiden when *Duckling* obliged at short odds. The Drogheda Tradesmen's Chase saw jockey Toss Taaffe complete his double on his father's *Honor's Ray* and Dan Kirwan had another course win with *Eleanor M* winning the Hilltown Handicap under Herbert Holmes. In the concluding Bumper, *No Surprise,* despite whipping around at the start, won easily for Paddy Sleator and jockey, Mr Francis Flood.

July 5 The weather improved for the second day and both *New Hope* and *Soir,* who had failed at the opening day, recouped their losses. *Soir,* who had fallen in a chase on Wednesday, got loose and galloped almost four miles on a nearby road before being caught. None the worse for his exertions, he took the opening Crockafotha Hurdle for the McDowell family, thus completing Pat Taaffe's brace of winners for the meeting. The Queen's Plate provided Michael Dawson with another win with *Infidel,* winning for Liam Ward. Dan Moore's *Tracassin* won the Shallon Handicap for Frank McKenna and owner Mr Brand. *New Hope* made his overnight stay worthwhile when he took the 3-mile Wintergrass Chase for owner/trainer W.L. Cullen and pilot Danny Kinane. Mickey Rogers repeated last year's success in the Corporation Maiden when *Corraith* proved an easy winner for Paddy Powell Snr., and George Wells trained the concluding winner when *French Sky* won the Novice Chase for then amateur Mr G.W. Robinson.

1957 July 3 Trainer George Robinson was the trainer in form at this year's meeting, saddling three winners over the two days. Owner Dick McIlhagga owned two winners while trainer George Wells and jockey Jimmy Magee combined with a winner on each day. Unfortunately, Magee was injured in a later race, receiving serious injuries.

George Robinson recorded a double on the opening day, his first winner coming when Mr Dick McIlhagga's *Lime Cordial* won the Ardcath Maiden with the trainer's son, Willie, in the plate. He rounded off the day by winning the concluding Bumper, when Mr Frank Prendergast steered *Mr Wain* to a narrow success. The meeting opened with a first win for trainer Clem Magnier at the course, when *Regal Token* won the Meath Hurdle for rider Dan O'Donovan. Cecil Ronaldson owned, trained and rode the winner of the Duleek Chase with *Another Jungle*, beating the favourite, *Wild Cherry*, into second place. *French Sky*, repeating his course win of the previous year, won the featured Drogheda Tradesmen's Chase for trainer George Wells and Jimmy Magee. Australian jockey, E.J. Fordyce, paying his first visit to the course, rode a dashing race on Mr Bert Kerr's *Cheer Up*, to win the Hilltown Handicap for trainer P.J. Lenehan.

July 4 Five clear favourites and a well-backed second choice delighted punters on Thursday, where the attendances did not seem to be as large as in recent years. In the opening race, McIlhagga, Wells and Magee combined to win the Crockafotha Hurdle with *Turkish Princess*. In second place here was Ms Maura Callan's gallant mare, *Mona Pearl*, ridden by Timmy Regan. P.J. Prendergast won another Queen's Plate when T.M. Burns steered *Steel Flash* to an easy success. George Robimson had his third winner of the meeting with *By-Passed* winning the 1-mile handicap, again ridden by his son Willie. The 3-mile Wintergrass Chase was marred by the fall of *Cullenroi* at the last fence, first time round, pinning his jockey, Jimmy Magee, to the ground, causing him serious injuries. The race went to the Tom Dreaper-trained *Villain of Lyons* for Pat Taaffe, who fended off the gallant *Tracassin* by a neck. John Oxx had a rare Bellewstown winner when *Scented Slipper* recorded an easy win in the one-mile maiden under John Power. The concluding Legganhall Novice Chase went to the Davy Brennan-trained *Captain Hanley*, who scored under Liam Brennan, who later as a trainer master-minded the famous Yellow Sam coup for Barney Curley in 1975.

1958 July 2 The 1958 meeting at Bellewstown will long be remembered by those who attended the old established venue. On the first afternoon, it was touch and go as to whether racing could take place as a thick fog hung over the course. After a long wait, it was decided to go ahead with the races which began fifteen minutes late. While punters were delighted that racing went ahead, with four favourites winning, from a racing point of view it was pretty farcical as only the last fifty yards or so could be seen. On Thursday, viewing conditions were perfect with another four favourites winning.

Tom Dreaper and Pat Taaffe combined for a double on the Wednesday, winning the opening Meath Hurdle with *Villain of Lyons* and completing it in the featured event, the Drogheda Tradesman Chase, with *The Big Hindu*. Willie Byrne trained the winner of the second race, when *Ancient Silver* obliged for Jimmy Mullane, while in the Duleek Chase Johnny Lehane steered *Cuilapuca* to victory for Rathfeigh trainer Jimmy Brogan. Doug Page landed *Brogeen Oir* in front close to home, to win the Hilltown Handicap for trainer Paddy Kearns and owner/trainer Pat Rooney combined once again with Mr J.R. Cox to win the Bumper. A welcome visitor at the track on this day was Sir Gordon Richards, many times champion jockey in England.

July 3 Thursday's racing featured a double for the Paddy Sleator/Bobby Beasley combination. Mrs Paddy Meehan's *Havasnack* won the opening Crockafotha Hurdle for them and went on to win his next five starts while the double was completed with *Pass*

Friend winning the 3-mile chase. The President of Ireland's colours had a successful outing when *Tula Riona* won Her Majesty's Plate for jockey John Power and John Oxx. The distance of this race was reduced to 2 miles from 2 ¼ miles for the following years. The Dundalk trainer, John Cox, maintained his good strike rate at the track when his own horse *Good Score* won the Shallon Handicap for Liam Browne. Before the start of the Corporation Maiden Plate, a dramatic incident took place. As the horses were being mounted in the parade ring, Mick Hurley's horse, *Bearna na Saileach* bolted and jumping out of the parade ring, he ran straight through the Bookmakers ring, knocking a few bookies off their perches. He then burst through the iron railings into the outside enclosure, scattering people as he went and ran down the Bonfire Bank road. Miraculously, no-one was injured and he was caught a short time later, unscathed. In the race itself, Kevin Bell's *My Prayer* justified odds on in the hands of Liam Ward. The concluding Legganhall Novice Chase was won by the M.J. Fanning owned and trained *Clane Beau* in the capable hands of G.W. (Willie) Robinson. Unplaced in this race was Mr Fred Hoey's *Gay Navaree*, who subsequently ran some fantastic races in the Aintree Grand National, first for Fred Hoey and later for Mr Fred Pontin who renamed him *Pontin Go*.

Bellewstown Races in the 1950s

1959 Bellewstown Race Card

1959 July 1 Kilsallaghan trainer, Tom Dreaper, had a successful time at this year's meeting, saddling a double on both days. Pat Taaffe combined with Dreaper for his opening day double. The only other to record more than one winner was Bobby Beasley, who won the opening race on each day. The quantity of runners was somewhat depleted after a prolonged dry spell and unfortunately some rain fell on both mornings of the races, rendering the ground somewhat slippery.

Dreaper and Taaffe combined to win both chases on the card. Mr George Ansley's *Wild Cherry* won the Duleek Handicap Chase and *The Big Hindu* repeated his win of last year to win the final running of the Drogheda Tradesmen's Chase, which had been a feature of the meeting since chasing was introduced to the course in 1873. In the opening Meath Hurdle, John Cox's *Headwave* overturned the favourite *Mazzibell* to score for Bobby Beasley. The unfortunate *Mazzibell* finished second in his next race, the Galway Plate, but collapsed and died shortly after passing the post. *King's Charter* won the Ardcath Maiden Plate for John Oxx and jockey John Power. The other flat race on the card, the Hilltown Handicap, saw Jimmy Mullane get the Dick McCormick-trained *Good Spelling* up close home to win narrowly. The concluding Bumper went the way of the outsider, *Ill Wind*, who scored for South of Ireland trainer, J.J. Purcell and Mr John Cash.

July 2 Tom Dreaper's double on the second day was initiated by one of his flat summer specialists, *Mesroor*, who justified odds-on for jockey Mick Kennedy. The double was completed by *Digby Diver* who won the Wintergrass Chase for Mr Mark Hely Hutchinson, riding for his father, Lord Donoughmore. Paddy Sleator repeated his success of the previous year in the opening hurdle race, this time with *West Bank*, again ridden by

Bobby Beasley. In second place here was *Polyboea*, owned and trained by Mr Vincent Eivers, near Boardsmill, who despite several attempts never succeeded in winning at the 'Hill'. T.P. Burns and Charlie Weld combined to win the Queen's Plate, with *Maid of Galloway* at prohibitive odds. In the other flat race, Clonsilla trainer, Sir Hugh Nugent, trained his first winner at the course with Mrs King's *Barslipper*, in the Corporation Maiden Plate under Paddy Powell Jun. The final race of the meeting, the Legganhall Novice Chase, saw Mr Willie Rooney train and ride *Hall Star* to victory, beating the Duchess of Westminster's *Suirvale* into second place.

1960 July 6 This year's meeting produced some entertaining racing on both days despite fields being of moderate size due to the firm ground. As is customary, several horses were saddled twice and two of them, *Blueville* and *Little Champ*, won a race apiece on each day for the Hoey and Dunwoody stables respectively.

Jockey Mick Kennedy was the man in form on the first day, scoring a treble in the three flat races, two of them for owner Mr Bert Kerr. His opening winner came in the Ardcath Maiden with *Celtic Park*, trained by the owner's brother, Kevin Kerr, at Clonee. He followed up in the next race, a two-mile flat handicap, when *Snow Trix* made use of the 2½ stone he was receiving from that great horse *Fortria*, to win for owner/trainer John Cox. Kennedy's treble was complete when *Cheer Up* won the 1-mile Hilltown Handicap in the Kerr colours, this time trained by P.J. Lenehan. The meeting had opened, as usual, with the Meath Hurdle, when *Sparkling Flame* warmed up for his Galway Plate triumph later in the month, by winning for the formidable alliance of Paddy Sleator and Bobby Beasley. In the only chase on the card, *Little Champ* proved successful in the famous Catherwood colours for trainer George Dunwoody and rider Christy Kinane, who was making his first visit to the course. In the concluding Bumper, *Blueville*, trained nearby at Julianstown by Dick Hoey, won easily by ten lengths from *Callarin* and was ridden by Mr Kevin Prendergast.

July 7 The Crockafotha Handicap Hurdle opened proceedings on the second day with *Blueville* showing no ill effects of his win on the previous day, winning again this time with Cathal Finnegan in the saddle. Uniquely, *Callarin* was once again second, this time reducing the winning margin to just a neck. *Callarin* gained his just rewards by winning his next race at Baldoyle a week later. The other horse to win on both days was *Little Champ*, who showed his durability by winning the 3-mile Handicap chase, again ridden by Kinane. The Queen's Plate was won by Mrs Nolan's *Deal Sma*, who was pulled up the previous day due to a slipped saddle. She was ridden by Peadar Matthews and trained by Matt Geraghty at Balrath. *Clane Beau*, who had won a chase at the meeting two years earlier, showed his versatility by winning the Shallon Handicap, thus completing a brace of winners for Paddy Sleator and a welcome winner for jockey Bobby Moylan. The other flat race on the card, the Corporation maiden, went the way of *Peter's Town* for Danny Morgan and T.P. Burns. The last 2-mile chase at the course was run this year, as it started along the wall between the Gate Lodge and the Barracks, where at the time there was no road. A roadway was put there the following year. The race was won by

Hyseller, owned by Mr Dicky Murray, from nearby Irishtown, trained by Dan Moore and ridden by Willie Robinson.

1961 July 5 (Firm) Two brilliantly sunny days attracted crowds of record proportions to the course this year. Considering the prevailing firm state of the ground, there was quite a good supply of runners over the two days. Jockey Paddy Powell Snr rode three winners at the meet while Tom Dreaper was the only trainer to score more than once.

A new sponsored race was introduced to the card this year with Joseph Bellew and Co. Ltd., Seed Merchants Drogheda, sponsoring the Joseph Bellew Handicap Hurdle. In a very competitive race, Tom Dreaper supplied the winner in the famous Col. John Thomson silks, *Spanish Hawk* obliging under Pat Taaffe. The opening Meath Hurdle was won by *Copper Cottage* which was ridden by Frankie Carroll for northern trainer E. Ahern. When the Eamonn Delany-trained *Narcotic Nora* won the Collierstown Handicap, she was bridging a twenty-year winnerless gap for the local Corballis, Laytown stable, going back to when Silverfizz won in 1940. Patrick O'Hagan's mare was ridden by Timmy Regan, his first winner at the course. Another North of Ireland trained winner came in the Duleek Chase, with *Hall Star* obliging for Willie Rooney and his son Mr Gerry Rooney. Paddy Powell Snr rode the last two winners of the day, winning the Hilltown Handicap with David Ainsworth's *Last Count* and closing the first day with an easy win for the Sir Hugh Nugent-trained *His Shoes* in the longer-distance Maiden.

July 6 (firm) Paddy Powell resumed where he left off on Wednesday by winning the opening Crockafotha Handicap Hurdle on the John Cullen-trained *Breaker's Hill*, which landed a nice little gamble in the process. John Oxx saddled *Dante's Hope* to an easy win in the following Queen's Plate, with Paddy Sullivan in the Plate. The Shallon Handicap provided a rare flat race winner for Tom Dreaper when Mick Kennedy landed the odds-on *Mesroon*, who beat Mr D.J. McNello's *Inniskeen* into second place. The Wintergrass Chase provided *Lucky Touch* with compensation for his second placing on the opening day, winning under jockey Tony Redmond. Mr Frank Yorke's owned and trained gelding had an eventful trip before securing the prize. His saddle started to slip back after only a mile, being prevented from going right back by the breastplate. Then a bandage on his off-fore became unwound and trailed out behind him while at the last fence, which *Lucky Touch* clouted, jockey Redmond lost his whip. Clem Magnier trained his wife's *Chignon*, which won the mile maiden under Doug Page, while in the concluding Bumper, *Straight Lady* completed a good meeting for North of Ireland trainers, winning for John Woods and well-known owner/rider Mr Archie Watson.

1962 July 4 Owing to the firm ground, fields were smaller than usual, but despite this, racing was excellent, with several close finishes on both afternoons. Local trainer Eamonn Delany and Curragh-based Charlie Weld both had a winner on each day, while in the riding category, Paddy Powell Jun. shared Weld's double. Laytown trainer Eamonn Delany saddled the first winner on both days and in the opening Meath Hurdle, his own horse, *Erindale Boy*, won narrowly, ridden by his son, Mr E. D. Delany. In the best endowed event of the day, the Joseph Bellew Handicap Hurdle, the complete outsider of the field, *Killykeen Star*, under a dashing ride from Frankie Short won for Co Westmeath permit-holder Mrs Rochfort Hyde. Unplaced in this race was the now venerable *Quita Que*, who in 1959 won the first running of the 2-mile Champion Chase at the big Cheltenham festival meeting. In an unusual turn of events, Tom Dreaper and Pat Taaffe's only winner at the meeting this year came in the 2-mile flat Handicap, when course specialist *Duffcarrig* landed the spoils. Tax Law showed his liking for the course by winning the Duleek Chase for trainer Danny Morgan and Timmy Hyde, beating the hot favourite *Castle Falls* into second place. Those with a long memory will remember *Castle Falls* in Michael O'Hehir's famous commentary of the 1967 Grand National, which *Foinavon* won, after the mayhem at fence number 23. Charlie Weld and his jockey Paddy Powell Snr combined for their first win of the meeting, when the gray *Donora* had a thrilling short-head victory over another course specialist *Migoli Slipper* in the one-mile handicap. In the Ardcath Maiden, Brud Fetherstonhaugh saddled *Illustrious* to win for jockey Peter Boothman.

July 5 Trainer Eamonn Delany once again started off the second day's racing with a win, when Timmy Regan steered his wife's *Thorny Path* to victory in the Crockafotha Handicap Hurdle. Chally Chute had his only winner ever at the course when he trained *Medusa III* to win Her Majesty's Plate for his brother-in-law Lord Harrington, ridden by Nicky Brennan. In the Shallon Handicap, Sir Hugh Nugent and Mick Kennedy combined for a win with *Sandshoes*. 'If at first you don't succeed, try, try again' was surely the motto for Oliver Hardy Eustace-Duckett's stalwart chaser, *Yonder-He-Goes*, who finally won the 3-mile Wintergrass Handicap Chase at the fifth attempt, ridden by Willie Robinson. Charlie Weld and Paddy Powell Jun. completed their brace at the meeting when *Elle Meme* won the Corporation Maiden Plate. North Dublin trainer, Pat Rooney, and jockey 'Bunny' Cox combined once more to win the bumper, this time with *Arctic Find*.

1963 July 3 With the ground riding good for a change, runners were more plentiful than of late at this year's annual reunion. Trainer Danny Morgan was the only trainer to have more than one winner, with a mixed double on the opening day and lightweight jockey Nicky Brennan rode a winner on each day.

Charlie Rogers trained many winners at Bellewstown over the course of his career, but now retired from that role, he had the pleasure of seeing his horse *Prairie Wolf* oblige in the opening Meath Hurdle, for Dan Moore, thus providing Tommy Carberry with his first win at the course. In the featured Jos. Bellew Handicap Hurdle, course specialist *Duffcarrig* once again obliged for Tom Dreaper and Pat Taaffe. Danny Morgan's first success of the day came in the 2-mile flat handicap when Paddy Powell Snr. delivered the goods once again on *Kilcrohane* and Morgan followed up in the Duleek Chase with *Tax Law* repeating his success of the previous year, once again ridden by Timmy Hyde. The following Hilltown Handicap was won by the Paddy Norris-trained *Sedandun* for young apprentice Tommy Enright and the concluding one-mile maiden saw Stephen Quirke provide Nicky Brennan with his first winner of this year's meeting in the colours of his famous father, Martin Quirke.

July 4 The McElroy family from the North of Ireland won the opening event of the second day with *Great Time* obliging for his young jockey Richard McElroy. Nicky Brennan completed his brace of winners at the meeting by steering *Baymoon* to win the Queen's Plate for Curragh trainer David Ainsworth. The one-mile Shallon Handicap proved a red-letter day for young English-born jockey Owen Weldon, when *Steel,* the complete outsider of the field, provided him with his initial riding success. *Steel* was trained by Christy Grassick. *Burton Brown II*, trained by Paddy Murphy and ridden by Frankie Shortt, proved too good for his rivals, which included the doughty veterans *Tracassin* and *Yonder-He-Goes*, in the 3-mile chase. Jockey Paddy Sullivan had a welcome change of luck after two months out of action with illness, with *Panama Mail* winning the Corporation Maiden for trainer John Oxx. The concluding bumper saw the Michael Dawson-trained *Tralee Bay* win, in the very capable hands of Mr Kevin Prendergast. In second place here was *Cold Scent*, ridden by Mr Niall Delany, for long a chairman of the race committee at Laytown and also an invaluable member of the Bellewstown Committee.

1964 July 1 An opening day treble for Tom Dreaper, two of which were partnered by Pat Taaffe, and a double for Curragh trainer Kevin Bell in the final two races of day one, were the highlights of this year's festival, held in glorious weather conditions. Fields were reasonably-sized on both days.

In the Meath Hurdle, the favourite *Ronan*, from the Dreaper stable, was clear coming to the last hurdle, but he made a total mess of it and came down, leaving his stable companion, *Celdado*, to go on to win for jockey Paddy Woods. Course specialist, *Duffcarrig*, provided Dreaper with his second win of the day in the featured Joseph Bellew Hurdle, repeating his success of the previous year in the corresponding race, with Pat Taaffe again in the saddle. The promising *Titus* completed a good day for the Dreaper/Taaffe combination, by winning the Duleek Chase. Kevin Bell trained the last two winners of day one, winning the Hilltown Handicap with *Cool Pace*, ridden by apprentice Vivian Kennedy and the Ardcath Maiden with *Royal Graney*, who prevailed by a short head, under T.P. Burns. The other event on the opening day was won by Miss Sheila Dowley's *Kitty Sick*, from Clem Magnier's Rathvale yard, ridden by his promising Drogheda-born apprentice, Joe Larkin.

July 2 The opening race on day two saw Dan Moore have another course success, this time with Mrs T.K. Cooper's *Clancy Junior* ridden by Tommy Carberry. The Queen's Plate was won by *Tarmac* for Seamus McGrath and Johnny Roe. *Talgo Abbess* was Kevin Prendergast's first training success at Bellewstown, winning the Shallon Handicap. In the intervening years, he has become the most successful trainer at Bellewstown with 56 winners. *Talgo Abbess* was ridden by his apprentice Pat Black, from nearby Bettystown. *Proud Glen* won the 3-mile chase for trainer L.J. Mahon and jockey, Liam McLoughlin, benefiting from a dreadful last-fence mistake by the previous year's winner

Burton Brown. The evergreen *Tracassin* had his usual two runs at the meeting this year, having won at the meeting as far back as 1956. Mrs W. McAuley and her trainer Alan Auld had compensation for the defeat of *River Whistle* earlier, when Nick Brennan rode *King's Highway* to a good win in the Corporation Plate. A popular wind-up to the fixture was the success of the favourite *King's Ribbon* in the bumper for the Cox family.

1965 July 7 (going firm) This year's fixture was held in fine weather, where race-goers got their first view of the new 5-furlong track, though to be fair, they would not have been able to see the first two furlongs which are out-of-view. Another welcome innovation was the new sponsorship of two races, by Grant of Ireland Ltd. Tom Dreaper continued his domination of the National Hunt events with three winners, two of them ridden by Pat Taaffe. Others to have doubles were trainer Kevin Prendergast and jockey Ben Hannon, who won the opening race on both days.

While sprint races were new to the modern course here, from as far back as the 1860s, flat races were run at the course over 4 fur., 5 fur., and 6 fur. until they were discontinued in 1905. (For the record, the 1905 winner of the Bellewstown Plate over 6 furlongs was a horse called *Herbert Vincent*, owned by Mr R. (Boss) Croker, and was ridden by the leading flat jockey of the time, John Thompson.) When sprinting resumed at the track this year, the honour of winning the inaugural 5-furlong race went to Mr P.J. Conlon's *Abbey Liffey*, trained by Kevin Prendergast and ridden by Nicky Brennan. *Abbey Liffey* was completing a double for Prendergast, as earlier he had won the sponsored Preston 10 stakes, with *Miss Sherlock*, ridden by apprentice David Dunn. Tom Dreaper's double was initiated by *Ronan* in the Jos. Bellew Handicap Hurdle, under Pat Taaffe, while *Celdado* replicated his course win of the previous year, this time winning the Duleek Chase, again ridden by Paddy Woods. John Cox's *Scoil* won the opening Meath Hurdle, for rider Ben Hannon, while in the concluding Hilltown Handicap, *Migoli Slipper* enhanced his reputation as a course specialist for owner/trainer Sir Hugh Nugent and Mick Kennedy.

July 8 The opening event of the second day began with Barney Nugent, saddling his last ever winner when Mr ffrench-Davis *The Hedger* obliged under Ben Hannon in the Crockafotha Hurdle. Ben Dunne's *Musical Chairs* won the Queen's Plate for Clem Magnier and his apprentice James O'Grady. The second five-furlong sprint of the week, the Regency Sherry Handicap was won by Paddy Norris's *Whistling Lady* under T.P. Burns. The best horse on view at the meeting was *Arkloin,* a dual Cheltenham Festival winner and he defied the steadier of 12 st. 7 lbs to win the Wintergrass Chase over three miles for Tom Dreaper and Pat Taaffe. In the Corporation Maiden Plate, Paddy Prendergast Junior got on the score sheet at the course with *Pinard* scoring for Peadar Matthews. As usual the Bumper concluded affairs and here *East Wind*, who was beaten by a short head on the opening day, displayed all the toughness of the Delany summer performers, to wear down the favourite *Roman Thistle*, to win by a neck under Mr E.D. Delany.

1966 July 20 (firm) The annual reunion this year was moved from its usual slot in the first week of July to the third week and the gloriously sunny weather on both days contributed to a large attendance. Fields were of good strength at the first stage, but with the ground remaining so firm, they cut up somewhat on the Thursday. Mick Connolly was the only trainer or jockey to have more than one winner, with a double on the second day.

There was a minor sensation in the final stages of the Duleek Chase on the opening day. After clearing the final fence, *Hot Contact* looked sure to win, but jockey Mick Ennis, head down and riding hard, continued on the chase course, instead of veering right for the finishing line. By the time he realised his error, it was too late and he had to pull up, leaving the favourite, *Felspar* from Tom Taaffe's yard, to score for Ben Hannon. Dan Moore, who trained *Hot Contact*, had earlier won the opening Meath Hurdle, with *Appollon* ridden by Tom Carberry. With the sponsored Jos Bellew Hurdle running its course, the second race was now an amateur hurdle and here Mrs Catherwood's famous colours had another course success with *Flaxen King* scoring for John Cox and rider Mr Francis Flood. The Preston 10 Flat Maiden over a mile went to the Brian Alexander-trained outsider *Ballysax Kuda* for rider Paddy Sullivan. The final two races of the day saw Sir Hugh Nugent and apprentice Joe Larkin combine to win the sprint, with *Tic Tac*, while Dick McIlhagga silks were back in the winners enclosure here, after a long gap, when *Terossian* obliged for George Wells and T.P. Burns.

July 21 *Arkloin*, from the Dreaper stable, was the star turn again on the second day, when, with another welter-weight of 12 st. 7 lb., he cruised to his second win in a row, in the three-mile chase for Pat Taaffe. Paddy Murphy's gelding *A.S.R.* was a 10/1 winner of the opening Handicap Hurdle for Frankie Shortt, while in the Queen' Plate, Mick Connolly initiated his double with Bert Kerr's *Irish Independent* scoring for George McGrath. Connolly's double was completed by *Star Clipper* in the featured Regency Sherry Handicap over five furlongs for Johnny Roe. Mick Hurley had a habit of winning maiden races here and *Mr World* did just that by landing the Corporation Maiden for rider J.V. Smith. The concluding bumper, the Legganhall Plate, saw Danny Kinane make the long trip from Tipperary worthwhile by saddling *Most Seen* to win for owner/rider Mr Ian Williams.

1967 July 19 (firm) This year's fixture proved a profitable one for bookmakers with only one favourite scoring over the two days. Clem Magnier was the only trainer to have a double, while Johnny Roe rode a winner on each day.

The opening Meath Hurdle was an augury of things to come as far as favourite backers were concerned, with the complete outsider of the field *Around the World* springing a 50/1 shock. The favourite *Nostra* from the Delany stable was badly hampered in the vicinity of the last hurdle, when making her challenge, leaving *Around the World* to score for trainer John Sherwin and owner Harry Boylan. The winner provided a first success for jockey Paddy McDonnell from Clonee and it turned out to be his only winning ride ever. That marvellous horseman from Co Cork, Mr Bill McLernon, made his first visit to the course a winning one, when he won the Amateur Hurdle on *Hydra-Z* for trainer Clem Magnier, who completed his double in the following race with *Telling* winning the Preston 10 stakes, piloted by Johnny Murtagh, who, like Bill McLernon, made his first ride on the course a winning one.

The only chase on the card, the Duleek Steeplechase, was packed with drama. The early leader, *Marvellous Tack*, made a dreadful mistake at the fence in front of the stands, dropping right back to the rear, with the lead constantly interchanging. The odds-on favourite, *Vulnagrena*, eventually got to the front. He was clear at the final fence where he crumpled on landing and being brought to a standstill, jockey Pat Black did wonders to stay aboard. This left *Lough Keel* in front, but he got interfered with, handing the initiative to a resurgent *Marvellous Tack*, who stayed on grimly to take the prize for Clonsilla trainer Jimmy O'Connell and jockey Bobby Coonan. The 5-furlong sprint went the way of the Charlie Weld-trained *Sweet Chupati*, ridden by Australian jockey Laurie Johnson. Two real course specialists fought out the finish of the Hilltown Handicap and at the winning post, *Mignoli Slipper* proved just too good for *Duffcarrig*. Johnny Roe was in the saddle this time on Sir Hugh Nugent's old stalwart.

July 20 (firm) The Tormey family from Bunbrosna, Co Westmeath, had a great win in the opening Crockafotha Hudle with *Peaceful Pat* turning over the favourite *Prince Tino* in the hands of young Mr Tom Tormey. The only favourite to win at the meet was *Pawn Office*, who easily won the Queen's Plate for Kevin Prendergast and Laurie Johnson. For the second successive year, *Star Clipper* won the Regency Sherry Handicap for Mick Connolly and Johnny Roe. The Wintergrass Chase proved a lucky spare ride for Tony Redmond, who had a comfortable win on Peter McCreery's good stayer, *Fairy Pack*. Paddy Prendergast Junior trained *Tangleberry* to win the Corporation Maiden under Peadar Matthews, while in the concluding bumper Mr Cecil Ronaldson scraped home by a short head on *After Eight* for Trim handler Vincent Keane.

Pawn Office ridden by Laurie Johnson winning Her Majesty's Plate 1967

1968 July 3 This year's fixture reverted back to its normal date, the first week of July, after two years relocation to the third week of July. Fields held up reasonably well over the two days and riders Mr Arthur Moore and Lauri Johnson registered doubles, as did trainer Kevin Prendergast.

Paddy Sleator and Bobby Coonan combined to win the opening Meath Hurdle, with odds-on favourite *Treasure Time*, after a good tussle with *Meddling Polly*. The prolific *Kilcoo* brought his tally of successive wins up to five, with an easy win in the amateur hurdle, when Mr Arthur Moore, deputising for his absent owner, Tony Robinson, had the mount which was trained by his father Dan. Mick Hurley's propensity for training maiden winners at the course continued with *Persian Tiger*, scorching clear in the hands of Gail McMahon to win by ten lengths in the Ardcath Maiden. *Home Alone II*, who had fallen last time out, made amends when taking the Duleek Chase in a good finish with *Bar Lough*, for Moynalty trainer Charlie McCartan and jockey Cathal Finnegan. The best finish of the day came in the five furlong sprint with the John Murphy-trained *Lucky Plum* holding off *Tu-Va* and *Lenin* to score narrowly for Johnny Roe. In the final race of the day, Christy Roche had an easy task on the favourite *Gay Bruce*, which won the Hilltown Handicap for trainer Michael Connolly.

July 4 Arthur Moore completed his double at the meeting in the second day's opening Crockafotha Hurdle on *Night Assault* for the Brian Alexander stable. Kevin Prendergast and his Australian jockey Lauri Johnson combined for a double with *Copper Gamble* in the Queen's Plate and *Fantastic Lady* in the longer distance maiden. Seamus McGrath's filly *Wild Bee* came back to form to win the second day's sprint for his namesake George McGrath. Mrs K Harper's *Fairy Pack*, trained by Peter MvCreery, gave an encore of her win the previous year in the Wintergrass Chase, this time with Frankie Shortt in the saddle. In second place was the good stayer *Rosinver Bay*, while Mr Richard Filgate rode the family's *Horse Radish* into third place. The most popular win of the day came in the concluding Legganhall Plate, when Mr N.D. (Declan) Winters from Drogheda, on his father's filly *Eau de Vie,* scored an impressive win for trainer Mrs Nolan.

1969 July 2 Trainer Kevin Prendergast took the main honours at this year's fixture, saddling three winners on the second day, two of which were ridden by Gabriel Curran, scoring his first ever double. Owner/trainer Mick O'Toole also had two winners at the meeting, which was held in ideal conditions.

On the first afternoon, only one favourite obliged, *Struell Park* and he had to survive an objection, before claiming the prize for North of Ireland trainer, Leslie Crawford and jockey Tommy Kinane. The meeting had opened as usual with the Meath Hurdle and here brothers John and 'Buster' Harty combined for a good win with *Cincinnati*. The Mount Hanover Amateur Hurdle produced a good finish between two Drogheda-born jockeys with Mr Edmund Collins on *Autumn Girl* getting the better of Mr Declan Winters on *Eau de Vie*. Mr Collins is the brother of Joe Collins, long-time Turf Club official and secretary/manager of Bellewstown from 1974 to 1992. Vincent Keane was the successful trainer. Curragh trainer, Mick Hurley, had another win in the one-mile maiden with *Lodola* getting up late to win for Gail McMahon. Although a sprint, the Collierstown Handicap produced the easiest winners of the day, with Mick O'Toole saddling the 20/1 shot *Gold Spot*, to score for young Martin Nolan. In the concluding Hilltown Handicap, trainer George Dunwoody enhanced his good strike rate at the track, with Peter Boothman pushing *Aldave* clear, close to home.

July 3 Kevin Prendergast dominated day two of the fixture, winning all three flat races on the card. Mick O'Shaughnessy had an easy task on *Eternal Hope* in the Queen's Plate and Gabriel 'Squibs' Curran likewise had no problems, winning with *Arctic Talisman* in the sprint and *Khailas* in the longer distance maiden. Mr Raymond Guest's famous silks had a successful airing in the opening Crockafotha Hurdle, when Tommy Carberry got *Trentina* home in front for Dan Moore. *Indian War* proved an easy winner of the Wintergrass Chase for owner/trainer Desmond Ryan and gave Ben Hannon a welcome change of luck. Leading amateur, John Fowler, combined with Mick O'Toole to win the concluding bumper on *Red How*.

1970 July 1 Three winners for veteran trainer Tom Dreaper and a second day treble for apprentice Gabriel Curran were the highlights of this year's reunion. There were also doubles for trainer Kevin Prendergast, while Pat Taaffe and Tommy Carberry had riding doubles. Showers on the opening day left the track slippery on the bends and there were a number of fallers as a consequence.

Tom Dreaper opened the day, by winning the Meath Hurdle with *Fortina's Dream*, ridden by Pat Taaffe and he completed his double on the opening day with *Black Secret* winning the Duleek Chase, ridden by his son, Mr Jim Dreaper. (The renowned trainer never won the Aintree Grand National but in 1971 *Black Secret* came within a hair's breath of the great prize, being just touched off by *Specify*.) There was mayhem in the amateur hurdle with four of the nine runners slipping up on the far bend, leaving Ballydesmond to win for northern trainer John Woods and jockey Mr E. Rice. The Ardcath Maiden over a mile was won by the favourite *Welcome Home*, trained by Seamus McGrath and ridden by his namesake George McGrath. The sprint over five furlongs saw *Black Gnat* in front from flag-fall, to score handily for Clem Magnier and his promising young apprentice Michael Teelin. In the concluding Hilltown Handicap, trainer George Wells and jockey Tommy Carberry combined for a win with the well-backed *Vector*.

July 2 The highlight of the second day was a treble for Gabriel Curran in the three flat races. Squibs, as he was better known, had a fantastic record on the course, particularly for his boss, Kevin Prendergast. However, his first winner this day was on the Christy Grassick-trained *Galesian*, who defied the steadier of 10st. 9 lb. in the sprint. Curran's other two winners were for his boss, with *Copper Gamble* having a bloodless victory in the Queen's Plate and *Credulous* scoring in the Corporation Maiden Plate. In fourth place here was *Allangrange*, who after this won five successive races, the last of which was in the Irish St Leger at the Curragh. Tom Dreaper had opened the second day by winning the Crockafotha Hurdle with *Nobska*, which made all the running for Pat Taaffe. Mrs Stewart Catherwood owned the other two winners on Thursday, firstly with *Carriglea Lady* in the Wintergrass Chase for Dan Moore and Tommy Carberry, while in the concluding bumper, her *Partian Ranger* justified favouritism for Mick O'Toole with Mr Dermot Weld in the saddle. As a result of the falls on the flat that year, work was undertaken to try to remedy this problem. After the 1970 meeting, a new cambered bend was put in on the west side, and after the 1971 meeting, a similar exercise was carried out on the bend in front of the stands.

1971 June 30 Some wretched weather on the opening afternoon of the annual two-day fixture was somewhat balanced by a fine second day. The new bend, at the top of the course, was particularly favourably commented upon by the jockeys. Trainers Mick O'Toole and Al O'Connell had two winners each, while the only rider to achieve the same distinction was apprentice Paddy Mooney.

The opening Meath Hurdle had often provided trainer Paddy Sleator with a winner and this year *Dicasee* confounded his weakness in the market, to score for Liam O'Donnell. The following Amateur Hurdle saw the Williams family from Co Limerick score, with the favourite *Credulous*. In second place here was Noel Meade, riding his own horse *Tu Va*, while steward at the course, Mr Thomas Matthews from Dunleer, rode his own mare *Beatrix* into third place. The Fitzsimons brothers, Frank and Brian, who often act as stewards at the meeting, also rode in this race. Mick O'Toole had the first of his two winners at this year's meet, when apprentice A.C. Brennan steered *Bert Satin* to an easy success. The Duleek Chase saw Tommy Carberry avail of a last fence mistake by *Razor's Edge*, to land Willie Rooney's Little Tom the prize, for his daughter Ann Ferris. *Black Gnat* repeated her success of the the previous year in the Collierstown Handicap over five furlongs, for Clem Magnier and Michael Teelin. To illustrate the toughness of the Magnier horses, Black Gnat won a hurdle race at Thurles two days later. Al O'Connell and Paddy Mooney had their first success of the meet, when *Big Jack* had a comfortable win in the concluding Hilltown Handicap.

July 1 The second day opened with the O'Connell/Mooney combination, winning the Crockafotha Hurdle with *Sapphire Star*, which carried the well-known brown and white colours of Barney Lawless. Kevin Prendergast won Her Majesty's Plate for the fifth year in a row, with *Le Levanhot* scoring for Gabriel Curran. Last year's winner of the Shallon Handicap, *Galesian*, found the weight concession of 27 lbs. to *Mezlam Prince* just too much, thus providing Mick O'Toole with his second win of the meeting, *Mezlam Prince* being ridden by Paddy Sullivan. Old stager *Rosinver Bay*, owned and trained by Tony Riddle-Martin, belied his years to win the Wintergrass Chase, beating local horse, *Blue Blazes*, into second place. Conditional jockey, Mervyn McNeill, was seen to good advantage on the winner. Mrs J.R. Mullion's *Paul Revere* at last had his turn, winning the longer distance maiden. Christy Roche took up the running after a couple of furlongs and made a long run for home, outstaying the opposition, for flat training legend P. J. Prendergast. Trainer Tom Dreaper, now in the twilight of his great career, saddled his last winner at the course, when *Veni Vici* stayed on doggedly to win for owner Omer Van Landeghem. Appropriately his final winner at the course was ridden by his son, Mr Jim Dreaper. During his long career, Tom Dreaper trained 32 winners at Bellewstown. For Bellewstown races, he always stabled his horses at Mick and Mag Arnold's stables, which were located just below where the old one-mile start was situated.

1972 June 28 The meeting in 1972 was held in contrasting weather conditions and a week earlier than usual. On the first day heavy showers, mixed at times with hailstones, made things testing for man and beast, but on the Thursday brilliant sunshine favoured the punters. With the going riding good for a change, runners were plentiful over the two days. It was a memorable meeting for three jockeys, amateur riders John Nicholson and Homer Scott and apprentice Martin Kinane, all of whom rode their first ever winner.

The meeting opened with Paddy Mullins recording the first leg of a training double, when *Shevatroon*, partnered by Michael Brennan, won the Meath Hurdle. He completed the double in the last race of the day, with *Saucy Society* and 'Buster' Parnell in the saddle. *Saucy Society* showed no ill-effects from finishing second at Mallow the previous evening. Trainer Liam Brennan saddled the top weight *Journalist* to win the Mount Hanover Amateur Hurdle, with Mr Timmy Jones in the saddle. The third race of the day, the Ardcath Maiden, was run in a shower of hailstones, which surely made things very difficult for the jockeys. The race was won by the newcomer *Fledgeling*, starting at 20/1, for the formidable alliance of jockey Tommy Murphy and Clem Magnier, who combined for a win on both days. The only chase on the card, the Duleek Chase, saw *Truly Merry*, benefiting from the early fall of the favourite *Escari,* win for the father/son combination of Tom Nicholson and John Nicholson, riding his first winner. Another first time winning jockey, Martin Kinane, rode the winner of the sprint, with *Snow Moss* obliging at 33/1 for trainer Daniel O'Donnell.

June 29 The second day opened with another first-time winning jockey, when Mr Homer Scott grimly held on, to win the handicap hurdle on his mother's horse, *Lisheen,* who was trained by Paddy Norris. The Queen's Plate was won very snugly by the odds-on favourite *Census* for John Bryce Smith and Christy Roche, while Australian jockey Bruce Marsh had only a short head to spare on *Paul's Pet*, who won the sprint for Paddy Prendergast Jnr. An unusually big field of thirteen went to the post for the Wintergrass Chase over three miles and Tom Costello made the long trip from Co. Clare worthwhile, winning on *Westland Boy* for Jackie Cullen. Clem Magnier and Tommy Murphy had their second winner of the meeting with *High Beech* winning the Corporation Maiden. The concluding Legganhall Plate produced the easiest winner of the day, with the well-backed *Conninbeg* scoring easily for Wexford handler Padge Berry and top amateur Mr Bill McLernon.

1973 June 27 (Going firm) In contrast to the previous year, a prolonged dry spell resulted in rock-hard ground at this year's reunion, which meant there was only an average of six runners per race.
Punters got a shock in the opening Meath Hurdle, when one of the outsiders, *Wadi Halfa,* owned by Ms Anna Buggle and trained by Seamus Buggle, proved too good for his rivals, in the hands of Ben Hannon. Jim Dreaper, now training at the famed Greenogue stables, saddled his first Bellewstown winner, when Mr James Duffy's *Brissago* won the amateur handicap hurdle, ridden by Mr Martin Murray, son of the stable's long-serving headman Paddy Murray. The only trainer to have more than one winner at this year's meeting was Dermot Weld, who won both maiden races. On the first day, *Boquet* justified odds-on to score for Buster Parnell. In the Duleek Chase, Dreaper's near-neighbour, Al O'Connell, produced *Native Clover* in fine fettle, to score for his apprentice Paddy Mooney. The five-furlong Collierstown Handicap went to another apprentice, Eddie Downey, on Liam Browne's *Spruce Street*, while the Kevin Prendergast/Squibs Curran alliance finished off the day well for backers, winning the Hilltown Handicap, with *Bilbo Baggins*.

June 28 Hard ground or no, it didn't prevent *Lady Alymer* from winning the second day's opener, the Crocafotha Hurdle, after running fourth in the previous day's finale. She was trained by Andy Geraghty and ridden most capably by John O'Gorman. Only two horses went to the post for the Queen's Plate, which resulted in an easy win for P.J. Prendergast's *Meadow Manor* in the hands of Christy Roche. Another Prendergast, this time Paddy Junior, trained the winner of the Shallon Handicap with *Supercoe* scoring for Noel O'Toole, his second winner. Although only three went to the post for the three-mile Wintergrass Chase, it developed into an enthralling battle between the top-weight *Rough Silk* and the local horse *Top Up*, which was trained about 100 yards from the track by enthusiastic steward, Christopher Morshead and ridden by his son, Sam. At the winning post, *Rough Silk* was a neck to the good, for trainer Edward O'Grady and his young amateur, Mr Michael Morris. Dermot Weld and his jockey, Buster Parnell, had their second winner of the meeting with *Caralgo* in the Corporation Maiden. Owner, breeder and trainer James J. Reilly had the pleasure of winning the last event of the meeting, the Bumper, with *Rosaveal*, and for good measure, he rode the horse as well.

Bellewstown Racing in the 1970s

1974 June 29 (firm) Bellewstown broke new ground this year, by holding an additional fixture towards the end of August. The annual two-day meet was held on the last week in June, with fine weather resulting in the ground riding firm as usual. Seamus McGrath had a training double on the second day, both of which were ridden by George McGrath.

Jim Dreaper's *Coniff* didn't look to have much to beat in the opening Meath Hurdle and he accomplished his task with as little fuss as possible, making all the running for Tommy Carberry. The father and son team of Ruby and Ted Walsh combined to win the amateur hurdle, in a close finish with the favourite *Rough Silk*. *Nakilts* sprang a 20/1 shock in the one-mile maiden for trainer Christy Grassick and jockey Mick Kennedy, for whom, surprisingly, this was a first winner of the year. The following Duleek Chase proved an eventful affair. With the favourite *Brigand Prince* falling when clear at the last regulation and Larry King's *Fairy Dreams* falling two out, when looking sure to score, it left Peter McCreery's *Glittering Gold* to come home, clear of the only other finisher, *Punch Bar*, for Joe Bracken. Young Robert Connolly, riding for his father, Mick, scorched out of the gate in the five-furlong sprint, to win comfortably, while in the concluding Hilltown Handicap, trainer Al O'Connell had another Bellewstown success, with *La Grisette* scoring by a head from *Mooneen*, under Christy Roche.

June 30 *Coniff*'s rider, Tommy Carberry, rode the first winner again on the second day, when *Colonial Prince* made all the running in the Crockafotha Hurdle for Dan Moore, to defeat the favourite, *The Disturber*, from the Delany stable. The unrelated McGraths had their first success of the day with *Baltic Star* having a bloodless win in the Queen's Plate and they completed their double with the outsider *Surcingle* in the Corporation Maiden. There was an audible groan from punters who had supported the Dreaper horse *National Lion*, at odds-on, when he fell at the regulation fence and this left Leslie Crawford's *Casquette* to score for his long-time stable jockey Sammy Shields. There was a popular conclusion to the meeting when Paddy Woods's sixteen-year-old son Edward rode his first-ever winner, *Kilmore Boy*, in the Leggan Hall Bumper Race for owner Mr P. R. Lyons.

August 28 1974 saw the introduction of a one-day meeting in August and this continued for four years (1974-1977 incl.). From 1978, this extra day's racing was joined to the July festival, making it a three-day festival for the first time in the modern era.
This meeting saw the running of a two-year-old race, for the first time here since 1905. Here the colourful Australian, R.F. (Buster) Parnell, guided the Sir Hugh Nugent-owned and trained *Spare Slipper* to a comfortable win. Dan Moore and Tommy Carberry combined to win both jumping races on the card with locally owned *Saucy Slave*, a first winner for Timmy Murray and course specialist *Colonial Prince* won the Bolies Chase. *Kitty O'Shea* won the maiden race for the McGraths and John Murphy and apprentice Tommy Carmody won the one-mile handicap with *Carol Barnett*. Peter McCreery and Ted Walsh had a profitable alliance over the years and they won the concluding bumper with *Gay Boris*, justifying strong market support.

1975 June 25 (Going firm) Tropical heat on the first afternoon and eight winning favourites made this year's meeting a pleasant one for racegoers. Trainer Padge Berry had a double on the first day, while course specialist Kevin Prendergast did likewise on the Thursday. 1975 will always be remembered for the *Yellow Sam* gamble, which Barney Curley planned so meticulously. Dave Barker, the Irish Field's representative at the meeting, reported on the *Yellow Sam* race as follows:
'Rank outsider in a field of nine for the Mount Hanover Amateur Handicap Hurdle, *Yellow Sam* confounded the vast majority, but not all, in beating *Glenallen* and *Silver Road* by two and a half lengths and the same.'
As the size of the massive gamble only became evident much later, the under-stated tone of the report is understandable. *Yellow Sam* was trained by Liam Brennan and ridden by Mr Michael Furlong. See Barney Curley's account of the betting coup later in the book.

The meeting had opened in a more mundane manner, with the long-odds-on favourite *Auburn* initiating Padge Berry's double in very easy fashion for jockey Christy Seward. The double was completed in the only chase on the card, when Drop Even survived a late rally from course specialist *Colonial Prince*, to score for Frank Berry. Liam Browne and his apprentice Tommy Carmody joined forces to win the one-mile maiden race, while in the sprint, top-weight *National Note* gained a narrow success for Paddy Prendergast Junior and Christy Roche. The concluding Hilltown Handicap produced as gripping a finish as had been seen for some time, with jockeys Wally Swinburn and Gabriel Curran battling it out, neck and neck, with the photo-finish camera revealing that the former had prevailed by a short head, on the Richard Annesley-owned and trained *Le Gaulois*.

June 26 (Firm) Course specialist *Colonial Prince*, none the worse for his second-placing in the chase on the previous day, made all the running to win the Crockafotha Handicap Hurdle for the second year in a row for Dan Moore and Tommy Carberry. Kevin Prendergast won another Queen's Plate, this time with *Safari* ridden by Jimmy McCutcheon. He completed his double by saddling *Wee Robin*, to win the Corporation Maiden for jockey Gabriel Curran. Clem Magnier enhanced his good strike rate at the track with *Nuaguese* winning the Shallon Handicap over the sharp five-furlong track. Mr J.J. McDowell, owner of *Caughoo*, the winner of the 1947 Aintree Grand National saw his colours carried to success by topweight *Escari*, from the Cox stable in the Wintergrass Chase. He was ridden by Pat Black, who was renewing, on a winning note, his partnership with trainer 'Bunny' Cox. The meeting closed with John Fowler owning, training and riding *Mersheen*, to win the Legganhall N.H. flat race.

August 27 (firm) Small fields attracted a smallish attendance to the August meeting, which was held in ideal weather conditions. Peter McCreery and his jockey, Joe Bracken, opened the day by winning the maiden hurdle with *Mariner's Barge*, while in the following Bolies Chase, trainer Frank Prendergast had an overdue win with *Own's Mill*, partnered by Frank Berry. This low-key day's race was significant for the fact that it turned out to be the last time that T.P. Burns rode a winner in his long and successful career. The horse in question was *Festive Diplomat*, running in Division 1 of the Dardistown Handicap and trained by Burns's great friend G.W. (Willie) Robinson. The second division of this race went to *Thornproof*, ridden by Pat Clarke and trained by Frank Ennis, his first training success on the track. Trainer Richard Annesley and Wally Swinburn supplemented their win at the course in June, with *Duetto* winning the Lisdornan Maiden, while the concluding bumper went the way of *Wurrabi*, owned by Mr Rex Beaumont, trained by J. F. Tormey and ridden by his brother, Tom.

1976 June 23 Since the previous year's racing a new stand, with a bar underneath, had been built, and was much appreciated by race-goers in the sweltering heat on both days. Despite the firm ground, there were plenty of runners, with Paddy Mullins having a mixed training double on the first day. Trainer Dermot Weld and jockey Wally Swinburn also had a winner on both days.

The meeting kicked off with the Meath Hurdle and here Danny Kinane landed a tidy gamble with *Three Million*, ridden by Bobby Coonan. In the following amateur hurdle, the Macauley family from the North of Ireland had a welcome win with *Perfect Blue* benefiting from the last hurdle fall of favourite *Artistic Prince*. The one-mile maiden was divided, with the first division going to Kevin Prendergast's *Irish Advocate,* ridden by Gabriel Curran and the second division saw Wally Swinburn force Pat Lally's *Ballyglass* home in a finish of short heads. The versatile Paddy Mullins won the two-and-a-half mile Duleek Chase with *Kiltotan,* ridden by Ferdie Murphy and followed up in the next race, the five-furlong handicap with *Pierre the True,* with 'Buster' Parnell in the saddle. The concluding Hilltown Handicap saw a rare 20/1 winner for Dermot Weld, with the lightly-weighted *Serissa* scoring for Ken Coogan.

June 24 The opening event on the second day saw the shrewd northern handler, Brian Lusk, who owned and trained *Bamber's Security,* winning the Crockafotha Hurdle, under Michael Morris. Dermot Weld and Wally Swinburn combined to win the two-year old maiden with *Borsalino,* and in the three-mile chase, *Gone Out* prevailed for the long-standing alliance of Francis Flood and Frank Berry, beating the gallant *Hope's Choice,* from the Fitzsimons family of Co. Down, into second place. Young apprentice Norman Cassidy rode his first ever winner for his boss, Seamus McGrath, on 10/1 shot *Moctezuma*, while Raymond Caroll had an easy task landing John Oxx's *Whistle for Gold*, to win the Queen's Plate. The only local trained winner at the two-day meeting came in the concluding bumper, when the Tony Cameron-owned *King or Country* obliged for Julianstown trainer Dick Hoey and top amateur Mr John Fowler.

August 25 The scorching hot weather again prevailed for the August meeting, with runners thin on the ground. While only three horses went to the start of the opening Bolies Chase, there was no shortage of incident, with the favourite, *Scar Bridge*, falling six fences out and his market rival, *Flipper*, tipping up at the next, leaving the 10/1 outsider, *Collins*, ridden by Ferdie Murphy for Ger Hogan, to score unchallenged. The other two re-mounted to finish in their own time. The following maiden hurdle provided the biggest field of the day and here Peter Russell landed the even-money favourite *Intervention*, an easy winner for trainer Tony Redmond. Seamus McGrath trained the winners of the next two races, with *Jean Fabre* winning the two-year old maiden for rider George McGrath, while Mick Kennedy got *Fickle City* home in front in the one-mile handicap. Mick Kennedy completed a double in the Lisdornan Maiden for trainer John Power. In a repeat of the first race, only three went to the post in the Bumper and once again, the odds-on favourite was well and truly beaten. The winner, *Bar You Forget,* was owned by Mr Paddy Griffin from Rolestown and was ridden by Mr Edward Woods for his father, Paddy.

1977 June 22 (firm) Bellewstown took the plunge into evening racing for the first time on the second day of this year's fixture. With the weather beautifully sunny on both days, the venue was crowded, although many of the attendance preferred to stay on the outside. Jockey Bob Townend took the honours of the meeting by riding a double on the first day and trainer Christy Grassick had a winner on each day.

The Meath Hurdle was divided for the first time in its history and in the first division Bob Townend had the first leg of his double when *Coco Boy* completed his hat-trick for Curragh trainer, John Murphy. The second division went the way of another Curragh based trainer, when market drifter *Knocknarea* scored for Tony Redmond and Frank Berry. The following amateur hurdle resulted in another success for local trainer Dick Hoey and Mr John Fowler, with the veteran *Autumn Wonder*, which he trained for his sister, Mrs J.P. McGuinness. The formidable alliance of Dermot Weld and Wally Swinburn won the one-mile maiden with *Gigitpoke* and in the last year of steeple-chasing at the course, Frank Ennis produced the enigmatic *Mayfield Grove* in fine fettle to win the Duleek Chase and complete Bob Townend's double. Colourful Co. Clare owner Noel Glynn and his more reserved trainer Peter Russell both had their first ever racecourse win, when *Strip Light* landed a nice little gamble to win the 5-furlong sprint, under excellent lightweight jockey Ken Coogan. Apprentice Robert Eddery was seen to good effect on the outsider *Melody Music*, who narrowly won the concluding Hilltown Handicap, for trainer Christy Grassick.

June 23 (firm) Christy Grassick resumed where he left off the previous day, by winning the opening Crockafotha Handicap Hurdle with *Gallop'n Inflation* in the hands of Bobby Coonan. The final running of the Wintergrass Handicap Chase over three miles went to the Bert Poot's owned and trained *Little Bug* for Michael Cummins, thus relegating the old favourite *Hope's Choice* to second place once again. Declan Gillespie and trainer Liam Browne combined to win the two-year old sprint with *Always Late* and in the Corporation Maiden, the John Oxx-trained favourite *Surely A Boyo* had an easy win for Raymond Carroll. The Co. Wexford trainer Padge Berry had a rare-enough flat winner with *Borallez*, which won the Queen's Plate under a confident Tommy Murphy. The concluding Leggan Hall Plate was divided, with Bunny Cox's *Readypenny* winning the first division for Crickstown amateur Mr Richard King and the Paddy Norris-owned and trained *Arctic Sunset* took the second division for Mr Andrew Tyrell.

August 24 (Good to Firm) This was the last of the one-day meetings held in August and it was held in miserable weather conditions. Heavy rain during the late morning combined with a dense mist, which came in after the first race and lasted for four races, after which it cleared into a lovely sunny evening. There was some compensation for punters with six of the seven favourites obliging, two of which were supplied by Kevin Prendergast and Gabriel Curran.
The day opened with the Bolies Chase, which turned out to be the last Steeplechase to be run at the course, the chase course being first used in 1873. The honour of winning the final chase went to *Mill Grange*, owned and trained near Dundalk by Philip Smyth. She was ridden by Joe Byrne. The other jockeys to ride in the last chase were Frank Berry, Paddy Kiely and Bellewstown lad David Whearty, who parted company with *Mullaharry* six fences out. Mr Peter McCarthy rode his own *Gougan Barra* to win the maiden hurdle for his father-in-law Paddy Mullins and in the following Carnes two-year old maiden, P.J. Prendergast notched his first juvenile success of the season with the Christy Roche-ridden *Real Character*, surely an interesting and unique fact in the long career of the Rossmore

Lodge maestro. The one-mile handicap was divided, with *Love Child* winning the first part for Richard Annesley and George McGrath and the Kevin Prendergast/Curran combination won the second division with Engage. Stephen Quirke and his jockey, Dermot Hogan, won the maiden race with *Lady Lantern*, while the final race completed the Prendergast/Curran double with *Sneem* in the five-furlong Kilsharvan Maiden.

1978 June 20 Bellewstown's first ever three-day meeting, in modern times, was not a great success. Attendances were down on previous years, with a number of factors contributing to this. There was bad weather on the Wednesday and Thursday, while both Tuesday's and Thursday's meetings clashed with other Irish meetings as well as Royal Ascot. There were no steeplechases and also the World Cup Finals were being broadcast on T.V., all of these things combined to make it the drabbest meeting for some years.

Racing got under way on Tuesday evening, the highlight of which was a double for Clem Magnier. He won the opening Meath Hurdle with *Red Due*, partnered by Tommy Carberry and also won the maiden sprint with *Mariko*, under stable apprentice Benjy Coogan. John M. Kennedy, from Co. Kilkenny, had a welcome winner in the Bolies Flat Handicap when *Lady Annie* obliged under Philip Lowry, while *Buck Royale* landed a nice touch for Limavady permit holder, John McNicholl, in the Bumper, under Mr John Queally.

June 21 The middle day's racing will long be remembered by Newcastle, Co. Dublin trainer, Frank Oakes, who had his first ever double. The first leg of the double came in the Amateur Hurdle, with *King Herbert* winning at 10/1, in the hands of Mr Frank Codd, and the double was completed by *Wallis* scoring in the mare's maiden hurdle for claiming jockey Peadar McCormick. Kevin Prendergast and Gabriel Curran also recorded doubles, with *Water Witch* in the Ardcath Maiden and followed up in the last race with *Pollardstown*, which went on to be a top hurdler, when sold on to race in the U.K.

June 22 The final day of the meeting opened with *Kingstown Pride* winning for Francis Flood and Frank Berry, owned by Warrenpoint sportsman, Patrick McAteer. Tommy Carberry had a double on the day and his third win of the week, by riding two flat race winners, firstly for Stuart Murless on *Tudor Earl* and then for Clem Magnier, on *Lovely Bio* in the Queen's Plate. Mr Ted Walsh and his father, Ruby, won the concluding Leggan Hall INH Flat race, when *What a Pleasure* overturned some better-fancied rivals.

1979 June 19 This year's three-day meeting proved satisfactory for the organisers with attendances up on the previous year. The first two days were run off in glorious weather, but the final evening was held in miserable conditions. Two apprentices, Joe Deegan and Pat Gilson recorded doubles, while of the trainers, only Dermot Weld managed to win more than one of the twenty races decided.

There were two hurdle races on the opening card and in the Beaumond Maiden Hurdle, John Harty produced *Joann's First*, after the last flight, for a cosy win for Grangecon trainer, Willy Bourke, while in the three-mile Handicap Hurdle, *Delightful Buck* rolled back the years for the Patton family from the North of Ireland, with a thrilling short head win over the game mare *Pigeon's Nest*, who won nine races later on in the year.

Dermot Weld had his first winner of the meeting in the opening two-year old maiden, with *Sunderland* winning for Joe Deegan. Jockey Pat Gilson had his double on the opening day, for two trainers with small strings. He rode *Hutnage* to victory in the Dardistown Handicap for Co. Tyrone trainer Ronnie Walls and Larry Greene supplied him with his other winner. The bumper was divided with Jim Dreaper and his neighbour Mr Edward Woods combining to win division one and veteran jockey, Mr Cecil Ronaldson, won the second division with *Three Clouds*, which he also owned and trained.

There was a dramatic incident after the final race. As the field approached the final elbow, Mr John Sleator's mount, *Beau Cheval*, had his head cocked ominously and in spite of his rider's best endeavours, charged into the horse-box parking area, where young Christy Cole was holding *Cradle Days*, a runner earlier in the day. Having deposited Mr Sleator on the bonnet of a car, *Beau Cheval* knocked down Cole, resulting in *Cradle Days* running off in a frightened state, after the tail-end of the field. He jumped into the infield in front of the stands, scattering spectators, jumping parked cars and generally causing mayhem, until eventually he became exhausted and was caught.

June 20 The second day featured a new race, the Sean P. Graham Amateur Handicap Hurdle, and here Clem Magnier's *Accipiter* won for his son Colin, then emerging as one of the best amateur riders ever. *Tishoo* finished third here, with a young Mr Peter Scudamore in the saddle. The other hurdle race on the card, the Meath Hurdle, was won by *Greenane Prince*, which Tommy Kinane trained and rode himself. Of the four flat races on the card, three of them were won by top trainers, Seamus McGrath, Kevin Prendergast and Mick Connolly, while the Hilltown Handicap was won by John Bryce Smith with *Hodelsing*.

June 21 The final evening's racing opened with Dermot Weld and Joe Deegan completing their brace of winners at the meeting, with *Sound Reality* in the two-year-old maiden. The following Corporation Maiden, for 'conditional' jockeys, saw Raymond Keogh's *An Tig Gaelige* land some some tidy wagers in the hands of Paddy Parnell. Mr Keogh was a long-time Master of the Ward Union Hunt, with a 'stag's head' featuring on his colours. The Crockafotha Handicap Hurdle was fought out by two horses from the neighbouring village of Curragha, with *Valace*, trained by Charlie Smith and ridden by his son-in-law Paddy Mooney, winning over Larry King's *Dryrot,* ridden by his son Richard. Trainer Richard McCormick and apprentice Michael Murphy combined to win the one-mile handicap with Up Front. The mare's maiden hurdle was divided and division one went the way of the outsider *Zarina Lady*, owned, trained and bred by Paddy Beggan, near Drumree, Co. Meath. Beggan was father-in-law of popular race-course committee member, Tom Jenkinson. The second division was another bookies' benefit, with another 12/1 shot, *Hazelwell*, winning for trainer John Fowler and his young amateur rider, Mr Martin Lynch. The Leggan Hall flat race concluded the meeting, with a very popular success. Owner/trainer Basil Brindley celebrated his fifty-second birthday by partnering his horse, *French Trail*, to a memorable victory. This must have been a very sweet victory for the colourful racing enthusiast, as the jockeys filling the next four placings were Ted Walsh, John Queally, Colin Magnier and Willie Mullins, who were among the most competitive amateur riders to grace the Irish racing scene.

1980 July 1 With the annual meeting now back in its rightful slot on the first week in July, attendances were satisfactory and plenty of runners ensured interesting racing. Since the previous year, most of the course now had a permanent fence on both sides of the track, with the flat track now moving to the inside and the hurdles course on the stands side. In addition to the safety factor, the changes permitted the Committee to mix flat and hurdle races throughout the programme, without the cost or worry of moving hurdles.

Jockey Mick Kinane was the man in form with a winner on each day, with course specialist Gabriel Curran, amateur Colin Magnier and apprentice Jimmy Corrigan all recording two winners each. On the training front, Michael Kauntze, Clem Magnier, Kevin Prenderdast and Seamus McGrath saddled a brace each over the three days.

The weather was chilly but dry for the opening day, which saw both Michael Kauntze and Noel Meade record their first winners at the track. The former combined with Mick Kinane to land the first division of the Fillies Handicap over a mile, with *Collector's Item*, owned by Mr Christopher Gaisford St Lawrence. Noel Meade saddled the winner of the second division with *Palmalina,* in the hands of Stephen Craine. Trainer Dick Nevin made his long trip to the meeting worthwhile when *Laurentino* ground out a hard-earned win in the three-mile hurdle for John Maher, gaining his second win. Frank Berry came from last to first, to win the other hurdle race on the card, on the 10/1 *Chance The Downs*, trained by Andy Geraghty.

The Sean Graham Hurdle was again the feature on the second day, with the father and son team of Clem and Colin Magnier repeating the previous year's success, this time with *Welsh Thorn*. Michael Kinane will always have fond memories of *Muscari*, who gave him his first racecourse success at Leopardstown in 1973 and the veteran, now ten years old, proved too sprightly for his younger rivals in the Collierstown Handicap, over the sharp five here. Likewise Martin Kinane, who had ridden his first-ever winner here in Bellewstown back in 1972, rode the winner of the Meath Hurdle on Bobby Coonan's *Old Matt*. Curragh permit-holder Paul Kelly saddled his first-ever winner, when *Balmy Grove* won the Ardcath Maiden under Joe Deegan. This day's racing marked the end of an era, with the final running of Her Majesty's Plate, which had been run continuously since 1800. Although be-devilled sometimes with very small fields down through the years, seven went to the post in this final running and, with a hint of irony, the prize went to the Seamus McGrath-owned and trained *Weaver's Pin*, ridden by apprentice Jimmy Corrigan.

After a chilly opening on the Tuesday, followed by glorious weather on the middle day, the final session on Thursday evening was strictly for the ducks. Continuous rain made it thoroughly unpleasant for the race-goers, although the pain was lessened somewhat by the success of four favourites. Seamus McGrath and his apprentice Jimmy Corrigan, Kevin Prendergast and Gabriel Curran all completed their doubles in the opening two races. *Yellow Sam*'s trainer, Liam Brennan, again showed his skill for having one ready for a handicap hurdle, when *Ailwee Caves* justified some nice support to win for young English-born conditional, Melville Drake. Mick Kinane completed his treble and Michael Kauntze his double, with *Public Opinion*, in the Hilltown Handicap. Padge Gill ended an eight-month spell without a win by winning on Pat Brennan's *Marand* in the first division of the Mares Maiden Hurdle and *Moss Fairy* made the long journey from Co. Donegal worthwhile for Michael Lafferty and jockey Gerry McGlinchey in Division II. The meeting closed when the Brian Malone-trained newcomer, *Miss Jordan*, sprang a 25/1 shock in the hands of Mr Martin Lynch, in the bumper.

1981 June 30 The main feature of the meeting this year was the number of doubles recorded, nine in all. Seven trainers, Ted Curtin, Jim Dreaper, Francis Flood, Andy Geraghty, Arthur Moore, Kevin Prendergast and Dermot Weld and two riders, Dermot Hogan and Mr Tony Powell, achieved this feat. Attendances were good throughout, with the middle evening providing a record Tote aggregate for the track.

The main interest in the opening day's proceedings came with local winners in the two jumping races. *Charfran* which was trained at Curragha by Charlie Smith for his wife, won the Beamond Maiden Hurdle in the hands of their son-in-law, Paddy Mooney, and in the 3-mile Bolies Handicap Hurdle, the Ken Morgan-ridden *Belassie* made all the running to score for Jim Dreaper and Balbriggan owner Maurice McAuley, who was a member of the committee for a long number of years.

July 1 The middle day of the festival saw some well-known colours carried to success. Ben Dunne owned the winner of Division II of the Ardcath Maiden when *Polish Prince* obliged for Mick Connolly and Christy Roche, while in the 5-furlong sprint, one of Nelson Bunker Hunt's lesser lights, the course specialist, *Waiting Night,* won for trainer Ted Curtin and Dermot Hogan. When Wally Swinburn and Dermot Weld teamed up at this track, they had a good strike rate and *Triumphal March* enhanced their record by scoring in Bert Firestone's famous colours in the Hilltown Handicap. The concluding Bradain Maiden went to Jim Dreaper's *Persian Wanderer*, which Ted Walsh had to keep at full stretch to win for local owner and steward at the meeting, Brigadier Tony Wingfield.

July 2 Several heavy and prolonged showers during the course of the final afternoon made matters very unpleasant for race-goers and underlined the absence of covered accommodation for race-goers. On the track Tom Morgan emulated his brother Ken, who had a winner earlier, by riding the winner of the Crockafotha Hurdle for owner John Harte and trainer Andy Geraghty. Dermot Weld and Michael Kinane combined to win the Corporation Maiden on Walter Haefner's *Airbus*, while the father-and-son team of Paddy and Edward Woods won Division 2 of the Mares Maiden Hurdle on *Highway's Last*. There was a dramatic conclusion to the meeting in the Leggan Hall INH flat race. *Sicilian Answer*, whose name did not appear on the race-card, sprang a 25/1 shock in a race where a number of horses slipped up at the stand bend. He was trained by Francis Shortt and ridden by Mr Patrick Gallagher.

1982 July 6 Champion jumps jockey, Frank Berry, could not have had a better Bellewstown this year. He rode in one race on each day and won in all three, and after scoring on *Tamer's Belle* in the opener on the final day, he dashed off to Thurles and rode another winner there. Declan Gillespie also rode three winners at the meeting, including a double on the middle day.

The opening day saw Berry win the Beamond Maiden Hurdle for Tony Redmond on *Sinead's Princess* and Edward O'Grady and jockey Pat Gilson combined for a good win with *Truculent Scholar* in the Dardistown Handicap. Ivan Keeling partnered his own mare, *Rugged Maid*, to win the Bumper and she turned out the following day, finishing second in the Mares Maiden Hurdle.

July 7 The second day included doubles for Kevin Prendergast and Squibs Curran, who won both divisions on the one-mile maiden. Declan Gillespie rode *Senta's Girl* to win the sprint for Harry de Bromhead and then *Sanmara* to win the Hilltown Handicap for his boss, Jim Bolger. The most popular win of the middle day came in the featured Sean Graham Amateur Hurdle when Half Shot won for veteran trainer Pat Rooney. He was owned by Jimmy Curran, for long one of the main driving forces at the track and ridden by young amateur Mr Tom McCourt, thus providing him with his first Bellewstown win. Mouse Morris had a rare enough winner at the course when *Hi Harry* won the amateur rider's race with the excellent Mr John Queally in the saddle.

July 8 The ground had firmed up by the start of racing on the third day. Tamer's Belle kept Frank Berry's 100% record at this meeting intact, foiling *Half Shot's* attempt at the double. Dermot Weld and Wally Swinburn joined forces to win the Shallon Two-Year-Old Maiden and in the one-mile handicap *Loose Goose* was an emphatic winner for Michael Cunningham and Declan Gillespie. Amateur rider Mr John Fowler rode his own horse, *Ballymacarrett* to win the mare's maiden hurdle. There was a popular local win in the concluding bumper, when Paddy Griffin, from Rolestown in North Dublin, owned and trained *Wingate* to land a nice little touch with Mr Ronnie Beggan in the saddle.

1983 July 5 The weather was ideal on all three evenings at this year's festival, which saw Noel Meade have a mixed double on the opening day and trainer Bunny Cox and leading amateur Mr John Queally combined for a double on the middle day, a feat trainer Ted Curtin and his Australian jockey Kevin Moses also achieved.

Noel Meade's double on the opening day was initiated by Mr Noel Coburn's *Daltmore* ridden by the excellent Tommy Carmody and in the following 5-furlong Kilsharvan Maiden, he landed some nice bets with *Two Touches*, ridden by Stephen Craine. The bumper on the opening day went the way of the Bobby Coonan-trained *Ballycahan Boy*, ridden by Mr John Shortt.

July 6 Seamus McGrath had a rare jumps win in the middle day's opener, when Joe Byrne steered *Pasquinal* to an easy win in the Meath Hurdle. Ted Curtin and Kevin Moses's double both were in the Nelson Bunker Hunt silks, with *Tetradracham* winning the Ardcath Maiden and *Waiting Knight* again showing his liking to Bellewstown's unique five furlong track. Desmond O'Hagan, another long-standing steward at the meeting, got Bunny Cox's double started when *Wren's Lass* won the Amateur Hurdle and *Little Mills* finished off the day well for both Cox and his jockey, John Queally in the concluding Bradain Maiden. *Wingate*, successful in a bumper here the previous year, was on the mark again, this time winning the Hilltown Flat Handicap for rider Joe Deegan.

July 7 Racing on the concluding day opened with the Mares Maiden Hurdle and here Victor Bowens sent out *Dual Express* to win, with Martin Lynch in the plate. Mick Connolly and Christy Roche combined to win the Shallon Two-Year-Old Maiden over the sharp five, with Frank Glennon's *Whistling Deer*. Kilbride, Co Meath, publican, John Sweeney was in good fettle after his old favourite *The Chancey Man* won the Drogheda Handicap for Jim Bolger and Declan Gillespie. *Roaminoer* appreciated the firm ground, to win the Crockafotha Handicap Hurdle for North Meath handler, Paddy Farrell and young jockey J.N. Brady. Michael Kauntze had his second winner of the meeting, when *Private Opinion* was a shock winner of the Corporation Maiden and so provided Christy Barker with his second winner. The Goold family from Co. Cork sent out *Zaratino* to justify favouritism in the concluding bumper, with Mr Ted Walsh doing the steering.

1984 July 3rd, 4th, 5th The layers had a cantering win on the opening evening of this year's festival as the first five favourites were beaten and the only relief for punters came in the concluding bumper, with one of the joint favourites obliging. The weather was favourable on all three evenings.

Trainer Kevin Prendergast and jockey Gabriel Curran both had doubles on the opening evening, and also shared a winner on the other two days. Curran's opening winner came in the Kilsharvan Maiden over 5 furlongs with *Recent Events*, scoring for Paddy Norris and owner Mr. Davy Brennan. Trainer John Bryce-Smyth and Michael Cummins combined to win the maiden handle with *Ballyglunin*, and in the other hurdle race on the card *Retinue Dual,* for popular handler Christy Kinane, got the better of the favourite *Laurentino,* to win for jockey Michael Byrne. *Pauper's Spring* and *Mullingar Boyo* were inseparable in the market for the bumper, the Lisdornan Flat Race, and in the race itself were equally close, with the former winning by a head after a protracted battle. Mr. Maurice Phelan piloted the winner for Francis Flood and owner Capt. J. P. Roche.

The second day opened with a win for the Magnier family, when *The Centaur* outclassed his field, with Joe Purfield's *Some Choice* staying on into second place. Michael Kauntze provided the winner of the Hilltown Handicap when *Commanding Heights* obliged for David Parnell and owner Mr. Peter McKeever. Kauntze's brother in law Jim Dreaper also got on the score sheet when *Deputy's Pass* owned by George Dobbs justified favouritism in the Amateur Hurdle for Mr. David O'Connor. The final race on the middleday the Bradain Maiden for amateur riders resulted in a popular win for Mrs. Thomas Matthews's *Black Economy*, trained by 'Bunny' Cox and ridden by Mr. John Shortt.

Trainer Michael Connolly and jockey Mick Kinane started off the final day's racing well, by winning the first two races with *Torresol* and *Jaflora*. Yorkshire born jockey Pat Farrell, was in the saddle when *Prince Constance* won the Crockafotha Handicap Hurdle for trainer Frank Ennis. Kevin Prendergast and his jockey Gabriel Curran completed a good meeting (4 winners in total) when *Michaela* won the long distance maiden in the well-known colours of Mr. Charles St. George. The most popular winner of the meeting came when *Call Me Anna* won the Bellewstown Mares Maiden Hurdle ridden by Mr. Michael Halford. *Call Me Anna*, who had finished second the previous evening, was trained by Philip McEntee, who was born at nearby Lisdornan, where his father, Paddy, supervised the kennels for the Little Grange Harriers. Philip was champion apprentice in Ireland twice in the early sixties when apprenticed to Seamus McGrath. He later moved to England to train with some success, and his son, also Philip, continues to train in England.

1985 July, 2nd, 3rd, 4th This years' meeting started in a welter of controversy when the photo finish equipment failed to arrive at the course, and in the opening sprint, the tape broke, resulting in that race being started by flag. In this opener *Winds Light*, trained by Paddy Mullins, for his daughter Sandra, obliged in the hands of Stephen Craine who went on to ride a winner on each day. John Bryce-Smith trained the winner of the Beaumond Maiden hurdle for the second year in succession, this time with *Helen's Birthday* ridden by Tom Taaffe. Bunny Cox and his amateur jockey Mr. John Shortt combined for another win at the course when *Fort Invader* won the Potato Growers Hurdle. Donegal man Terry Casey, who later in his career trained *Rough Quest* to win the 1996 Aintree Grand National, saddled *Aqualon* to win the second division of the Drogheda Handicap over one mile. The concluding bumper saw the market rivals *Bonnie Buskins* and *Knight's Maid* slog it out, toe to toe, over the final mile, and, after a battle royal, the near venerable *Bonnie Buskins* just prevailed. He was trained at Castleknock by John Daly for his wife and was ridden by Mr. Paul Larkin.

Apprentice Donal Manning who had ridden *Silver Lark* to win on the opening day was the jockey in form on the middle day, riding a double. His first winner came aboard *Joe Denby,* in the Hilltown Handicap, for Ian Duggan who trained a small string at Kentstown, and he completed his double on Mick O'Toole's *Formalist* in Div. II of the sprint handicap. The conditions of the Meath Hurdle, allowed Galway Hurdle Winner *Pinch Hitter* to meet his rivals at level weights, but in the event, his jockey Pat 'Shorty' Leech had to keep him at full stretch to justify his odds-on status for Noel Meade. The former great rivals on the track, Tommy Carberry and Frank Berry, combined to win the Jack Penny Memorial Handicap Hurdle with *Hasty Prince*, and another great 'jumps' rider of the past, Tony Redmond, sprang a 20/1 shock when he trained *Another Deb* to win a division of the sprint handicap. Clem and Colin Magnier had another winner at the track when the joint favourite *Polar Bee* won the Bradain Maiden for owner George Mayers.

There was another big turnout on the final evening, resulting in record attendances and betting turnover at the historic track. Controversy reigned after the opening race when Kevin Prendergast's *Song an' Dance Man* was promoted to first place on the disqualification of Oliver Finegan's *Auction Girl* in Div. I of the Shallon Two-Year-Old

Maiden. Owner/trainer Brian Malone combined with Jimmy Coogan to win Div. II of the same race with *Caroline Anne*. Paddy Molloy who trained briefly at the Cloghran Stud, near Dublin Airport, won the Mares Hurdle with *Call Me Kiri*, under a strong drive from Mr. Martin McNulty. The other hurdle race on the card was won by Mick Manning's *Cuban Crisis*. None the worse for finishing second to *Pinch Hitter* on the previous day, *Cuban Crisis* was a first winner for Dunboyne permit holder Mick Manning and was ridden by Peter McCormick. The featured Dardistown E.B.F. Handicap was won by *Irish Folly* for John Oxx and Dermot Hogan, while, in the longer distance flat maiden, Edward O'Grady's *Rage In The Cage* provided Stephen Craine with his third winner of the meeting. The best horse to win at this year's festival was probably *Four Trix* who proved a decisive winner of the concluding bumper. Owned and trained by Bunny Cox he was ridden by Mr. John Shortt. *Four Trix* was sent over to race in Britain and among his numerous wins was the 1990 Scottish Grand National.

1986 July 1st, 2nd, 3rd The opening race of this year's festival, the Kilsharvan Maiden over 5 furlongs went to the Denis Brosnan owned *Island Dandy*, trained by Tom Lacy and ridden by Declan Gillespie. Mick Halford who had a good record at this course, recorded his first training success here when Tommy Carmody steered *McKillop* to win the Beaumond Maiden Hurdle. Apprentice Charlie Swan got the Paddy Mullins trained *African Cousin* home by a short lead in the 2 year old maiden, while in the three mile Potato Growers Handicap Hurdle, *Bavamour*, owned by Mr. Eugene McKeever, was successful for trainer Pat Martin and amateur Mr. John Queally. Local owner Tom Moore from North Dublin was on hand to welcome in *Turf Side VI,* winner of the bumper for Dundalk trainer Bunny Cox, and was ridden by Mr. Colin Magnier.

Day two of this years's meeting proved a disastrous one for punters with only one favourite obliging, and the average price of the other 6 winners worked out in excess of 11/1. The winning favourite to oblige was *Winning Nora* in the Seamus Mulvaney Hurdle from the Michael Hourigan stable and was ridden by Kevin O'Brien. *Winning Nora* was owned by Bettystown native Denis Reddan, who always liked to have a winner at 'The Hill' and capped a memorable meeting by also winning the final race on Day 3, when *Harrington* won the Vincent Keating INH flat race in the hands of Mr. Enda Bolger, making a rare visit to the course. *Four Trix* who had won the concluding bumper at the previous year's meet, won the other hurdle on the day. Now in the colours of Mrs Stewart Catherwood, he was providing J.R. Cox with his second winner of the week, and was stylishly ridden by Mickey Flynn. Permit holder John Costelloe saw his 20/1 shot *Zinzi*, ridden by David Parnell, win Div. I of the sprint handicap. Apprentice Ron Hillis, who had ridden *Dancer's Shoe* to win on the opening day for Robbie Connolly was in sparkling form on day two, riding a double. His first winner came courtesy of *Magic Deer* trained by Mick Connolly and followed up by winning Div. II of the sprint on *Miami High,* for trainer Thady Regan.

The day three opener was won by *Ewood Park*, ridden by Drogheda native Pat Leech. He was trained in Co. Kilkenny by John M. Kennedy, who liked to have a winner here. The second Div. of the Mares Maiden hurdle proved to be a red letter day for David Geraghty, who is a native of Fennor, Ardcath (a few miles from the track). He rode *Ella Rosa* for his boss Tommy Carberry, for his first ever winner. Hindered by rising weight it proved to be his only winner, and following a spell training privately in England for some years, he now has a restricted licence, and has a nice measure of success in that role.

Tipperary trainer Edmund Hayden made his long journey worthwhile when Paudge Gill rode *Crohane Chieftain* to win the Crockafotha Handicap Hurdle. Moynalty owner Pat Cussen, was delighted to win the featured Dardistown E.B.F. Handicap with *Majestic Wolf,* trained by his neighbour Dessie McDonagh, and ridden by John Egan. Dermot Weld and Mick Kinane, who combined for a win on the opening day with *Classic Times*, won the Shallon 2-year-old maiden with *Leszko Le Noir*.

1987 June 30th July 1st, 2nd Good weather brought big crowds to the old venue this year, where the ground was good on the opening two days – it firmed up a bit for the third day. Mick Kinane was the jockey in form riding three winners. Pat Leech was the only other jockey to ride more than one winner, while on the training front, Noel Meade, Michael Cunningham and Paddy Mullins saddled two winners each.

The star of the show on the opening evening was *Pargan* who blitzed his rivals in the Seamus Mulvaney Hurdle. After establishing a long lead, he was never seriously troubled and came home eased down in the hands of Tony Mullins, for his father Paddy. Earlier Mick Kinane had got backers off to a good start when Mr. J.D. Clague's filly *Pas Du Tout* won the two year old maiden for Michael Kauntze. Castletown trainer Noel Meade and his jockey Pat Leech, combined to win the Potato Growers Hurdle with *New Sister* in good style, from his stable companion *Whiteriver Grove. Power and Red* sprang a 20/1 shock for Co. Limerick trainer Gus Leahy and apprentice J.M. Hunter in the Kilsharvan Maiden. Mr. A.J. Martin got on the Bellewstown scoresheet when he piloted *Atlantic Angel* to win the bumper for Michael Cunningham.

The combination of a bumper attendance and a jackpot carry-over, enabled a record Tote aggregate of over £77,000 to be established on the Wednesday evening this year. Michael Kinane recorded a double, winning the opening Five Roads Maiden on *Absence* for his boss Dermot Weld, and then guiding *Flower from Heaven* to win Div II of the 5-furlong sprint for his uncle Christy Kinane. Tom McCourt rode his second Bellewstown winner when the John Harty trained *Saintfield* won the 4 year old maiden hurdle. The other hurdle race on the card went to *Timber Creek*, owned by Mrs. Jean Wade. *Timber Creek* was ridden by Joe Byrne and also trained by him. Michael Cunningham had his second winner of the meet when *Cooliney Chimes*, belying an absence of over two years from the track, took the Hilltown Handicap in the hands of Declan Gillespie. David Parnell piloted *Haulboulder* to win Div I of the 5-furlong sprint for Peter Russell, while in the featured Sean P. Graham Flat Race, Mr. John Berry got *Never Be Great* home in front for Grangecon trainer Francis Flood.

Bunny Cox enhanced his strike rate at the track by winning Thursday's opener, The Bellewstown Maiden Hurdle, with *Black Trix,* under John Shortt. *Montagnard,* in Lord

Iveagh's silks won the Corporation Maiden for Kevin Prendergast and "Squibs" Curran. Co. Louth owner Niall Coburn always liked to have a winner at the course and his *Fane Prince* obliged in the Crockafotha Hurdle, thus providing Noel Meade and "Shorty" Leech with their second winner of the week. The Bowens family's *Top Cut* won the Shallon 2-year old maiden, while Paddy Mullins had his second winner of the week when *Hazy Bird* won the featured Dardistown EBF Handicap, for effervescent rider Stephen Craine. The concluding bumper was a very slowly run affair with Mr. J.P. O'Brien riding for his father Frank, getting the favourite *Mid-Day Run VI* home in front.

1988 July 5th, 6th, 7th Honours were spread very evenly over three days, with trainers John Harty and Pat Martin saddling two winners each, and only Declan Gillespie doing likewise on the jockey front. Pat Hughes saddled a rare 2 year old winner in the opening maiden, when the newcomer *Country Clover* scored for owner Mr. M.J. Clancy and jockey Stephen Craine. In the following Potato Growers Hurdle over 3 miles, the tough as teak *Sandymount* outstayed his rivals for the father and son combination of Frank and Kevin O'Brien. Trainer Ted Curtin and John Egan combined to win the older-aged sprint maiden with *Sweet Hollow* in the colours of Franklin N. Groves. Jessica Harrington owned and trained *Gallant Boy* to win the featured Seamus Mulvaney Hurdle for Anthony Powell. The Murphy Sand and Gravel Handicap was divided. Division I was won by *Persian Valley* for trainer Michael Grassick and jockey Niall McCullagh, while appropriately Div. II was won by the Pat Martin trained *Mr. Mystery* in the colours of the sponsor, Seamus Murphy, for long one of the best supporters of the meeting, both as steward and sponsor. *Mr. Mystery* was ridden by Pat Gilson. The final race of the first day was won by *Dalus Dawn*, trained by Willie Tracey and ridden by his grandson, Mr. Niall Kennedy.

The opening race on the middle day provided a first winner at the track for Brendan Sheridan, who officiated at the track in different positions, including Clerk of the Course. He rode *Gemini Way* to win the 4 year old hurdle for Paddy Norris. Trainer John Harty saddled the first of his brace, when *Nec Precario* won the 1 mile maiden, ridden by apprentice Eddie Leonard. *Valtron Lad* proved a welcome winner for trainer Alfie Evans and his son David, when he won the Ladies Day Handicap Hurdle. Now trained by Robbie Connolly, *Profligate* won the 1¾ mile flat Handicap, in the capable hands of Christy Roche. M.J. Kinane produced an inspired ride on *Flower From Heaven* to repeat her previous year's success in the same race (5 furlong handicap) for owner Mr. W. Granville and trainer Christy Kinane. In the final race of the day Mr. Willie Mullins had an easy task steering his father's *Innocent Choice*, to win the featured Sean P. Graham flat race.

The Heineken E.B.F. Handicap over 1 mile was the featured event on the final day of this years proceedings. Many regulars at the course were delighted to see *Ballatico* score for Dean Hill trainer Oliver Finegan, and in some way making up for the harsh disqualification of his *Auction Girl* at the course in 1985. *Ballatico* was owned by Mr. Frank Cullen and ridden by David Smith. In the opening maiden hurdle Mick Halford and Tommy Carmody teamed up for another win with *Golden Wood*, while in the next race John Harty had his second winner of the meet, with *Mizuna* scoring for Declan Gillespie in the longer distance flat maiden. Pat O'Leary owned and trained *Troville Lady,* the winner of the Crockafotha Handicap Hurdle, and he was well ridden by Noel O'Toole. Declan Gillespie's second winner of the day came when *Evanna's Pride* pounced late to win the 1 mile, 2 year old maiden for trainer John Hayden. The concluding bumper was won by the favourite *Slaney Queen*, trained by Pat Martin and ridden by Mr. John Queally.

1989 July 4th, 5th, 6th The prolonged dry spell during June and early July prompted the executive to water the course for the first time in the course's history. This meant filling slurry tankers with water from the River Nanny at Beamond Bridge, and travelling 1 ½ miles up the hill, and then spraying it on the course with a boom. The herculean effort kept the going good for the three days and trainers in general were loud in their praise for the committee's efforts. Dermot Weld and Mick Kinane were the men in form with 4 winners apiece, while Kinane also rode another winner for his old ally, Michael Kauntze.

Pargan rolled back the years by repeating his win of 1987 in the Seamus Mulvaney Hurdle for the Mullins family, and in the other hurdle race on the card Bunny Cox owned and trained *Black Trix,* who had also won at the course in 1987, to win the 3 mile handicap hurdle under Conor O'Dwyer. Earlier Mick O'Toole had started off the meeting well by winning the 2 year old Fillies Maiden with *Bold Starlet*, ridden by Johnnie Murtagh. Michael Kauntze had a winner on both Tuesday and Wednesday with *St. Joachim* winning the older maiden sprint for Pat Shanahan. Dermot Weld and M. J. Kinane won both divisions of the one mile flat handicap and in the bumper Jim Dreaper produced *Bee Friend* to win for Galway owner Mrs. Annette Mee, and his stable amateur Mr. Martin McNulty.

Mick Kinane rode another two winners on the second day. He displayed all his artistry to get the one eyed *Orembo* home in the Ladies Day Handicap, for Michael Kauntze, and in the Bellewstown Race he had *Picture Perfect* in front where it mattered, for his boss Dermot Weld. *Flower from Heaven*'s bid to win the 5 furlong sprint for the third year in a row, came unstuck when Johnnie Murtagh forced *Littlepace* up close home to win for the Keaney family from Clonee. There were two hurdles races on the card. Willie Mullins trained *Toohami,* who won the 4 year old Novice hurdle while Dick Donoghue's *Derrynap* defied top weight to win the Potato Growers Handicap Hurdle for Robbie Byrne.

On the final day the East Meath Racing Club had a great win in the Bernard Barry Crockafotha Hurdle when *Corporate Raider* ran out an easy winner in the hands of Niall Byrne for Stamullen trainer Tom McCourt. Kevin Prendergast's only winner at this year's meeting came in a hurdle race, when Charlie Swan steered his wife's charge *Dance on Lady* to win the maiden hurdle. Dermot Weld and Mick Kinane completed their good week's work when *Albakht* won the Hilltown 2 year old Maiden for absent owner Hamdan-Al-Maktoum, for the second year in a row. Pat Martin trained the winner of the concluding bumper when *Sunset Travel* obliged for owner Mrs. Audrey Healy.

The winner was a spare for Mr. Francis Flood as the intended jockey had forgotten to renew his licence.

1990 July 3rd, 4th. 5th Tuesday, the opening day of this year's festival, was not remembered fondly by punters as a sequence of shock results left them badly out of pocket. Philip McCartan completed a long-priced double, and added a third winner on the second day.

Philip McCartan's training double was initiated when *Sam Weller* won the 3 mile handicap hurdle in the hands of Pat Clarke, and completed it in Div. I of the one mile handicap, when Johnnie Murtagh got a dream run up the rails on *Nukonnen* to win, after being last for most of the way. Earlier, the Sue Doyle-owned and trained *Hitchin-A-Ride* had sprung a 20/1 shock, in winning the 5-furlong maiden, with Mickey Fenton in the saddle. In the other 5-furlong sprint for 2year olds, Kevin Prendergast had the first of his two winners at the meeting when his Australian born jockey Wayne Harris eased *Downeaster Alexa* to a comfortable success. Course specialist Never Be Great, now owned by Mr. Patrick McAteer, strolled to victory for Conor O'Dwyer and Francis Flood in the featured Seamus Mulvaney Hurdle. In Div. II of the 1-mile handicap Jim Gorman and lightweight jockey Andy Nolan combined for an easy win with *Slightly Shy*. The concluding bumper resulted in a popular local win with *Bel Slipper* owned by Ashbourne auctioneer Paul Grimes. He was trained by Martin Murray at Kilsallaghan and was ridden by Mr. Charlie McCann, Jnr., son of the long serving Ward Union Huntsman of the same name.

Wednesday turned out very wet, windy and dismal for patrons. Fortunately, both the stands had been roofed since the previous year to allay some of the adverse climatic conditions. Unusually, trainer Jim Bolger recorded a National Hunt double, firstly when Liam Cusack piloted *Orbis* to win the Potato Growers Handicap Hurdle, and in the last race of the day Mrs. Margaret Heffernans's *Latin Quarter* ran away from his rivals to win the Duleek Q.R. Race for Mr. Aidan O'Brien. The opening maiden hurdle resulted in a win for *Say Goodbye* for Curragh trainer John Murphy and was ridden by Mickey Flynn. *Say Goodbye* was bred locally at Clinstown by Jarlath Folan. Another locally-based owner, Mrs. Desmond Grant, won the 1 mile maiden with *Burella*, which was trained by P.J. Finn and ridden by Gabriel Curran. This was the last winner 'Squibs' rode at the 'Hill' where he enjoyed so much success, particularly for his boss Kevin Prendergast. The latter won the Ladies Day Handicap with *Montezuma,* ridden by apprentice Robbie Burke. Philip McCartan's third winner of the meeting came in the sprint handicap with *Majesty Nurse* winning for a young Richard Hughes. In the other race of the day, Dermot Weld and M.J. Kinane combined to win the Bellewstown Inn Race with *Gaze Upon*.

The final evening took place in much better weather conditions, although the ground was soft after all the rain. The featured Heineken Handicap was won by *Blue Sceptre*, who was following up on her Curragh win at the week-end for Michael Kauntze and his jockey Warren O'Connor. In the opening Novice Hurdle the Kinane family had a nice win, with *Gentle Lad* winning for trainer Christy and his son of the same name. Dermot

Weld and Mick Kinane had their second win of the meet with Arabian Nights, winning the Garristown Race. The Crockafotha Handicap Hurdle went to *Hero to Zero* who was trained by Ms. Sandra Duffy, and was ridden by Kentstown jockey Philip Carey. *Hero to Zero* was owned by Mr. Philip Smyth, who trained *Mill Grange* to win the last steeplechase to be run at Bellewstown in 1977. Jim Bolger's third winner of the festival came with *Nordic Sun* winning the one mile, two year old maiden for Christy Roche. There was a popular win in the maiden hurdle, when the Farrell family, who own the Brock Inn, saw their good horse *The Ridge Boreen* win under Tommy Carmody. The concluding bumper resulted in another family success, this time for the Mullins family with *Pit Runner* obliging for their daughter, Mrs. Sandra McCarthy.

1991 July 2, 3rd, 4th   Blazing sunshine greeted patrons, at the opening of this year's session at Bellewstown. The ground rode good on all three days with jockey Johnnie Murtagh the only one to win more than two races.

Trainer Edward O'Grady trained a double on the first evening, including winning the opening 2-year old maiden with *Lute and Lyre*, the complete outsider of the field at 25/1, for rider Timmy O'Sullivan. O'Grady completed his double in Div. I of the one-mile handicap, with *Morris Dancer*, ridden by Niall McCullagh. Div II of this race, went to the Barry Kelly trained *Mejeve*, ridden by Sephen Craine. There were two hurdle races on the card, and in the Collierstown Hurdle, *Viola Quay* from the Jimmy Coogan stable had a comfortable win for Pat Davey. The other hurdle race in the card, the 3 mile handicap hurdle resulted in a thrilling finish between *Twilight Gale* and *Muzahim*, with the former prevailing by a head. *Twilight Gale* was owned by a consortium which included local Ardcath men Johnny Corry and Malachy Tuite, and was trained in Co. Cork by Kenty Riordan and ridden by Denis Leahy. The Aga Khan, John Oxx and Johnnie Murtagh had the first of two winners at the meeting when *Siwana* won the 5-furlong maiden, while in the concluding bumper the Finn family from Co. Limerick had a nice win, with Mr. David Finn steering *Heloonium* home for his mother, Mrs. Edwina Finn.

Owner Aidan Comerford and trainer Tony Redmond were the men in form on the middle evening with a mixed double. Firstly, *Harristown Lady* obliged in the 2 mile handicap hurdle for Pat McWilliams, and in the Anglo Print Handicap Mick Kinane got *Prince Yaza* home in front. In the opening novice hurdle Joe Byrne trained and rode the winner *Cellatica* for Mr. A.J. Gleeson, while in the following one mile maiden, Kevin Predergast had his only win of this year's meet with *Mutarjam*, ridden by his new Australian jockey Rod Griffiths. Paddy Prendergast also got on the scoresheet, courtesy of *Simply Amber* in the sprint handicap, for rider David Smith. Vincent O'Brien broke new ground at the track this year by training his first and only winner at Bellewstown, with *News Headlines*, winning the Bellewstown Inn Race with Pat Gilson in the saddle. The concluding qualified riders race went the way of the Michael Grassick trained *Judicial*, ridden by Mr. Ross Neylon.

There were doubles on the closing day for jockey Johnnie Murtagh and trainer Ted Curtin. They combined to win the featured Heineken Handicap with *Radley*, who was second in this race last year. Johnnie Murtagh's double was completed when *Banour* won the long distance maiden for John Oxx and H.H. Aga Khan. Ted Curtin completed his double in the concluding bumper, when *Moresque* won for Mr. Ted Walsh. Earlier Declan Gillespie had saddled *Pennine Pass* to win the 1-mile two year old maiden, ridden by Stephen Craine. There were 3 hurdle races on the card and in the opener Barry Kelly saddled *Katesville* to win with Mr. A.J. Martin in the saddle, while in the following Stamullen Maiden Hurdle, Mickey Flynn rode *Pylon Sparks* to victory for Eddie Harty. In the other hurdle race, the Crockafotha Handicap Hurdle, there was a bit of controversy when Philip Carey on the previous year's winner *Hero to Zero*, rode a finish a circuit too soon, thus forfeiting any chance he may have had. When they did finish at the correct time Donal Bromley had *Kayrawan* in front to score for owner/trainer Dessie McDonagh.

1992 June 30th, July 1st, 2nd Mick Kinane was the man in form at this year's reunion riding five winners, three of which were for his boss Dermot Weld. Mick O'Toole also saddled three winners at the meeting.

Mick O'Toole and Mick Kinane shared a winner on the opening evening with *Imprimatur* winning the 5-furlong Maiden. Earlier O'Toole had won the Novice Hurdle with *Head of Chambers* ridden by John Banahan. Mick Kinane had opened the meeting by winning the 2 year old maiden on *Gate Lodge* for his old boss Michael Kauntze. *Maridya* won the Bambury Bookmakers Handicap for HH Aga Khan, John Oxx and apprentice Declan O'Shea, and in the 3 mile handicap hurdle *Harristown Lady* replicated his course win of the previous year for trainer Tony Redmond and jockey Anthony Powell. Trainer Frank Dunne had the top weight *Happy Rover* in fine fettle for his seasonal debut, and he made light of top weight in the 1-mile handicap for apprentice Robbie Burke. Michael Halford turned out the winner of the bumper, with *Turning's Lass* justifying favouritism in the hands of Mr. Charlie Farrell, who had spent the previous two seasons in Britain with Charlie Brooks.

In the first race on Wednesday, *Earl of Barking* spread-eagled his field in the 1 mile, 2 year old maiden, winning by 10 lengths. Trained by Kevin Prendergast and ridden by Rod Griffiths, *Earl of Barking* improved to become a stakes winner in the U.S. and returned to stand as a stallion in Ireland. There was a locally owned winner of the 4 year old Novice hurdle with *Tymoole* winning for Noel Meade and jockey Harry Rogers. *Tymoole* was owned by Mr. Robert Gogan from Ardcath, and he nowadays lives near the course at Hilltown House. Dermot Weld and Mick Kinane combined for their first win of the week, with *Damister's Pet* winning the one mile maiden. There was a divide in the 1-mile handicap, with *Drumaleer* winning Div. I for Eddie Lynam and Mickey Fenton, while Div. II went to the Coogan brothers, Jimmy and Benjy, with *Tombara*. Noel Meade had his second winner of the day in the featured Tayto Growers Handicap Hurdle, with *Beau Beauchamp* in the colours of Dunleer businessman Donal Kinsella, scoring in the hands of Charlie Swan. Jim Bolger and Christy Roche followed upon their Irish Derby win with *St. Jovite* at the weekend, by winning the sprint handicap with *Osvaldo*, and in the concluding amateur riders race Mr. David Marnane got *Enqelaab* home in front, for Mick O'Toole's third winner of the week.

The weather of the closing day took a turn for the worse, with intermittent rain and a cold breeze, spoiling the holiday atmosphere somewhat. Mick Kinane had another double, combining with Dermot Weld to win both the opening 2-year old, one mile maiden with *Lantansa*, and the Derek Plant Maiden Race on *Cliveden Gail*. Trainer Declan Gillespie and Mickey Flynn combined to win the maiden hurdle with *Oatfield Lad*, and in the Novice Hurdle Mr. B.H. Leneghan owned *El Bae* won for Arthur Moore and his stable jockey Tom Taaffe. The Featured Heineken Handicap was won by *Classic Match*, trained by Danny Murphy and ridden by Pat Gilson. Pat Malone, now a Turf Club official, rode the Jeremiah O'Neill owned and trained *Pearltwist* to win the Crockafotha Handicap Hurdle. The concluding bumper saw the colourful Stamullen trainer Peter Casey train his first winner at the course with *Bellecarra* scoring in the hands of Mr. Peter Casey Jnr.

1993 July 6th, 7th, 8th The opening day of this year's fixture was marred by a bad accident to jockey Warren O'Connor in the Murphy's Sand and Gravel Handicap. Just after the road crossing in this one mile race, a general tightening of the field resulted in O'Connor's mount *Sans Ceriph* falling, and bringing down *Rafferty's Inner*, the mount of Robbie Fitzpatrick. The latter received bruising to a leg, but the unfortunate Warren O'Connor fractured an ankle, ruling him out of action for some time. In the race itself, *Happy Rover* repeated his success of the previous year, for trainer Frank Dunne and this time he was ridden by Johnnie Murtagh.

The meeting had started with the Kilsharvan 2-year old maiden over 5 furlongs, and here John Egan swooped late on *Nurmi,* trained by Pat Flynn to claim the prize. In the next race, the Hilltown Hurdle, *Cabra Towers* belied his odds of 33/1 to win for Banbridge trainer Jerry Cosgrave and provided jockey Michael Mackin with a rare winner. Richard Hughes and Michael Grassick combined to win the 5-furlong maiden with *Kileen Star*, while in the Oldbridge Concrete Handicap, *Angareb* obliged for Mick Halford and Pat Gilson. *Pearl Twist* won a race over 2 ½ miles at the meeting the previous year, and now stepped up to 3 miles, he won the Bolies Handicap Hurdle for Jerry O'Neill and Pat Malone. The concluding bumper was won by Mrs. Jacqui Mullins on *First Session*, trained by her husband Willie.

Kevin Prendergast had a double on the middle day, winning the 4 year old Novice Hurdle with *His Way* ridden by Mickey Flynn, and winning the 1 mile maiden with *What a Pleasure*, and apprentice Barry Walsh in the saddle. Pat Beirne, a permit holder from Summerhill, Co. Meath, saw his appropriately named *Summerhill Special* justify favouritism in the 2 year old Auction Race for rider Johanna Morgan. The 1 mile handicap was divided, with *Mejeve,* a course winner in 1991 winning Div. I for Barry Kelly and Stephen Craine, and in Div. II, The Bower, trained by Con Collins for his wife scored under Robbie Burke. Tony Mullins trained *Aquinas* to win the Tayto Growers Handicap Hurdle for owner Bill Hennessy and his jockey son, Robbie Hennessy.

The Anglo Printers Handicap over the sharp 5 furlongs, produced a tremendous finish with the outsider *Afterglow*, trained by Colin Magnier and ridden by Liam O'Shea getting up on the line to deny the favourite *Lady President*. The judges' verdict did not meet with unanimous approval and a large group of punters gathered at the weigh-room door demanding to see the photo finish prints. When the prints became available, it showed that *Afterglow* had won clearly, if very narrowly. While most punters accepted the verdict, there were still some who continued to haggle. The concluding qualified riders' race was won by the Noel Chance trained *Hackett's Cross* with Mr. James Nash in the saddle.

Kevin Prendergast had another double on the final day to bring his tally at the meeting to four. Both of his winners were owned by Mrs. Catherine McNulty with *Oliver Messel* winning the 2 year old maiden for Willie Supple, and apprentice Barry Walsh having his second winner of the week on *Desert Calm* in the featured Heineken Handicap. Dermot Weld had just the one winner at this year's meet and, unusually, this came in a hurdle race with *Open Market* winning the 2-mile maiden under Brendan Sheridan. When Donie Hassett makes the long trip from his Co. Clare base, it pays to take heed, especially when the money is down. His *Morning Dream* was backed down to second favourite in the Novice Hurdle, but at the fourth last he was all of 25 lengths behind the leaders. However, rider Gerry O'Neill kept rowing away and he gradually picked up the leaders, and swept by the Tony Martin-ridden favourite, *Ifallelsefails*, in the last 100 yards. Dessie Hughes and Charlie Swan combined to win the Crockafotha Hurdle with *Song of Cademon* and in the Derek Plant Race, Frank Dunne and Johnnie Murtagh had their second win of the meet with *Safe Conduct*. The concluding bumper was won by the Paddy Prendergast trained *Cloghan's Bay*, ridden by Mr. James Nash.

1994 July 5th, 6th, 7th Aidan O'Brien was the trainer to follow at this years meeting saddling 4 winners, including winning the three races open to amateur riders. The Coogan Brothers Jimmy and Benji started off the meeting well by winning the opening Kilsharvan 2-year old maiden with *Double Risk*, and in the following Novice Hurdle, Kevin Prendergast's *Lake Of Loughrea* just lasted home in the hands of John Shortt. The other five races went to horses trained in the south of the country. Tommy Stack trained *Tourandot* to win the 5-furlong maiden under Stephen Craine, and in the Oldbridge Concrete Handicap, Michael McCullagh's genuine horse *Wesbest* came home in front for his son Derek McCullagh. John Queally made the long trip from Waterford worthwhile, when Mr. Karl Casey's old favourite *Merry People* kept punters happy winning the Long Distance Hurdle under Trevor Horgan. Jim Bolger had another winner at the course, when *Nordic Colours* won the one-mile Handicap for apprentice Seamie Heffernan. In the concluding bumper Aidan O'Brien's *Lancastrian Dream* came home unchallenged in the hands of Mr. Ger Ryan.

On the middle day Noel Meade and his jockey Paul Carberry won both hurdle races on the card. They won the 4 year old Novice Hurdle with *La Cenerentola*, and in the featured Tayto Growers Hurdle Mr. F. Towey's *Dashing Rose* came home in front. Following a downpour after the second race the ground was changed to soft, and in the third race Jimmy Coogan trained his second winner of the week with *Nun's Island* winning the one-mile maiden. Both divisions of the one-mile handicap were won by out-of-form stables. Mick O'Toole and John Egan combined to win Div. I with Blakes Hotel, while in the second division, John McLoughlin trained his first winner for nineteen months with *Noble Choice*, given a good ride by up and coming apprentice, Pat Smullen. The five furlong handicap had to be started by flag, but *Matchless Prince*, the favourite, got away well and made all the running to win for Michael Duffy. Aidan O'Brien trained the other two winners on the card. His newcomer *Hero's Honour* won the one-mile auction maiden for Seamie Heffernan, and in the concluding amateur riders race *Rockfield Native* stayed on well with the trainer in the saddle.

Kevin Prendergast had his second winner of the week, when *Blue Kestrel* won the opening Shallon 2-year-old maiden for Willie Supple. Michael Hourigan made the long journey from his Co. Limerick base worthwhile as *Stevie B* justified favouritism to win the Bookmakers Hurdle for Kevin O'Brien. The featured Heineken Handicap went to *General Chaos*, trained by Con Collins with Stephen Craine in the plate. The 19-year old Naas born conditional David Finegan had an evening to remember when he rode his first ever winner on *Push the Button*, trained by Michael O'Brien in the Tipperary Water Novice Hurdle. Pat Hughes owned and trained *Coin Machine,* winner of the Crockafotha Handicap Hurdle giving Paul Carberry his third winner of the week. When *Huncheon Chance* won the Derek Plant Flat Handicap for Co. Antrim trainer Ian Ferguson, he was providing Tony McCoy with his last flat winner prior to embarking on his career in Britain. Aidan O'Brien and his jockey Mr. Ger Ryan closed out the meeting with *Waterloo Ball* winning the Vincent Keating INH Flat Race.

1995 July 4th, 5th, 6th Just two days after *Celtic Swing*'s demise in the Budweiser Irish Derby, owner Peter Savill (Chairman of the British Horse Racing Board) paid his first visit to Bellewstown to see his speedy colt *Almaty* initiate a double for trainer Con Collins and rider Pat Gilson, in the opening Kilsharvan E.F.F. 2-year-old Maiden. *Almaty* was bred by Turf Club's senior judge Percy Banahan, and was one of the leading two year olds of the year, his wins included the Molecombe Stakes at the Goodwood festival. Collins and Gilson's double was completed, after *Violet's Wild*, owned by Mrs. Avia Riddle Martin won the Maurice McAuley Memorial Maiden. The other two flat races on the card were trained by course specialists Kevin Prendergast and Michael Kauntze with *Multy* and *Dance Academy* respectively. There were three N.H. races on the card, and in the 3 mile handicap hurdle, Cecil Ross saddled Liam Gilsenan's mare *Derravragh Gale* to win for Franny Woods, who rode a winner on all three days. Pat Hughes owned and trained *Cullenstown Lady* to win the Conditions Hurdle for Charlie Swan, while in the bumper Pat Martin enhanced his record at the course with *Harry Heaney*, obliging for owner Kevin Heaney.

The second day opened with a shock 20/1 win for *Better Style* in the 4-year-old Novice Hurdle. She carried the colours of the Beck's Syndicate, based in the well known hostelry, of the same name, at Cushenstown, about 6 miles from the course and provided Garristown trainer Tommy O'Neill with a welcome winner, and a second winner of the week for Charlie Swan. The other hurdle race on the card, the Tayto Growers Handicap Hurdle, was won by *Turning Point* trained by Arthur Moore and was Franny Woods's second winner of the week. There were four flat races on the card, with Kevin Prendergast, Eddie Lynam and Mick O'Toole among the winners. The other flat race on the card, the Anglo Printers Handicap over the sharp 5 furlongs, saw John Joe Walsh make the long trek from his Co. Cork base worthwhile with *Coolowen Flash* winning for apprentice Robbie Burke. The concluding Mullagh Quarries (QR) Race went the way of *Brave Fountain*, who won for Aidan O'Brien, and was ridden by his sister-in-law, Ms. Frances Crowley.

After two glorious days, rain arrived to dampen the spirits of punters on Thursday. Michael Kauntze and his jockey Warren O'Connor recorded their second success at the meeting, when *Sholam* won the 1 mile, 2-year-old maiden in Sheikh Mohammed's famous colours. In the following 2-mile maiden hurdle, Mickey Flynn saddled *Welcome Express* to win for rider David Evans. In the featured Heineken Handicap, Dermot Weld and Mick Kinane had their only winner of the fixture when *Kilconnell*, obliged for American owner Mrs. J. Maxwell-Moran. *No Dunce* from the Paddy Mullins stable won the Novice Hurdle for David Casey while in the Crockafotha Handicap Hurdle, Co. Down trainer, Jeremy Maxwell, saddled *Maid of Glenduragh* to win for Brendan Sheridan. Frannie Woods had his third winner of the meet, when he arrived late on *Touching Moment* to win the Derek Plant Flat Handicap for his boss Arthur Moore. Aidan O'Brien and Ms. Frances Crowley had their second winner of the week in the concluding bumper, when *Clahada Rose* won for Mrs. P. Ryan.

1996 July, 2nd, 3rd, 4th Aidan O'Brien and his jockey Seamie Heffernan were the men in form at this year's festival with a winner on each day. Their winner on the opening day came courtesy of *Cuddles*, in the colours of the Garda Siochana Racing Club in the 5-furlong sprint. The opening 2 year old maiden had gone the way of *Onbendedknee* for the Jim Bolger, Kevin Manning combination. In the 3-mile handicap Hurdle *Arctic Kate* from the James O'Haire stable, won for Gold Cup winning jockey Conor O'Dwyer. *Magic Combination*, who won a 2-year old race at the previous year's meeting, was on the mark again, this time in the Oldbridge Concrete Handicap for Kevin Prengergast and Willie Supple. Pat Shanahan, fresh from his Irish Derby success at the week-end on *Zagreb*, got on the score sheet here, when *Forsake Me Not*, in the well known Norton colours, won the one-mile maiden for his boss Con Collins. The bumper was won by *Moonlight Escapade* for trainer Tony Mullins and leading amateur Mr. Philip Fenton. Because of the small field, the Conditions Hurdle was moved to the last race on the card. It turned out to be a good race for the Casey family from nearby Stamullen with *Siberian Tale* winning, and landing some nice bets in the process (5/1 to 3/1).

Noel Meade started off the second day well, winning the 4-year old Novice Hurdle with *Wesperada*, ridden by Paul Carberry. The one-mile, 2 year old maiden provided Kevin Prendergast and Willie Supple with their second success of the meeting when *Burtown* won. Jim Kavanagh had his first Bellewstown win when *Gerry Dardis* stormed to success in the lower grade one-mile handicap for apprentice Pat Smullen. Pat Martin supplied the winner of the other one-mile handicap, with *Bajan Queen* winning for Jason Behan. *Near Gale* provided the Paddy Mullins / Tommy Treacy combination with the first of their brace for the week, winning the featured Tayto Growers Handicap Hurdle. Aidan O'Brien and Seamie Heffernan won the sprint handicap with *Best before Dawn*, while in the concluding Amateur Riders Race, Mr. David Marnane got the favourite *Celtic Lore* home in front for Dermot Weld and owner Michael Smurfit.

The weather turned a bit unseasonal for the concluding day's racing, nevertheless the biggest crowd of the week turned up. In the opening one-mile maiden for 2 year olds Con Collins, trained his second winner of the week with *Mystic Magic* successful for Pat Gilson. The following Sam Dennigan Hurdle proved to be a red letter day for Ballymoney Co. Antrim trainers John Quinn, who saddled his first winner with *Red Glitter* in the hands of Charlie Swan. The featured Heineken Handicap provided Aidan O'Brien and Seamie Heffernan with their third winner of the week with *Bold and Gorgeous* for owner Finbarr Sheedy. Owner/trained/rider Pat Healy brought *Kilcaramore* on the long haul from his Midleton stables in Co. Cork and he made the journey worthwhile, by justifying favouritism in the 3-mile maiden hurdle. In the third hurdle race on the card, Eddie O'Grady saddled *Shorewood* to win the Crockafotha Handicap hurdle, with Frannie Woods in the saddle. The talented but quirky, *Notcomplaininabut* was Paddy Mullins and Tommy Treacy's second winner of the week, when she won the 1 ¾ mile handicap and in the concluding winners bumper *Supreme Charm* made it two from two for trainer Michael O'Meara and Mr. Philip Fenton.

1997 July 1, 2nd, 3rd   It may have been July 1st, but the opening day of this year's festival seemed more like New Year's Day. Despite the wet and wintry conditions the meeting was well supported. John Muldoon saddled the winner of the opener, the 2 year-old sprint with *Dress Design* winning for Willie Supple. There were a few locally trained winners on the opening day and in the Agrifert Handicap Hurdle over three miles, the father and son duo of Tommy and Paul Carberry combined for a win with *Kilcar*. Tommy Stack saddled *Burnt Toast* to win the 5-furlong maiden, ridden by Johnnie Murtagh, while in the Oldbridge Concrete Handicap, *Jawah* sprang a 10/1 shock for Dermot Weld and apprentice Declan McDonagh. *Jawah* was led up by local lad Gary Reilly, who worked for Dermot Weld at the time. Tom Taaffe saddled two winners at the meeting, and the first of these came when *Welcome Parade* won the Conditions Hurdle, for Conor O'Dwyer. The final two winners of the day both had local interest. Firstly, in the one-mile maiden, Peter Cluskey who trains near Balbriggan, saw his *I Have To Go* spread-eagle his field to win at 20/1 for Wayne Smith. In the concluding bumper local owner Mrs. Denise Reddan had the pleasure of leading in *Hi Jamie*, with trainer Tony Martin in the saddle.

Torrential showers, before the first race, turned the ground conditions to soft on the middle-day. In the opening 4 year old Novice Hurdle, *Snow Falcon* was an easy winner for Tom Taaffe and Norman Williamson. Aidan O'Brien and Seamie Heffernan continued their good run at the track in recent years, winning the one-mile maiden for 2-year olds with *Precise Direction*. The lower grade one-mile handicap was divided, and resulted in wins for *Shahnad*, trained by Don Kelly and ridden by Wayne Smith and *Aurliano* trained by Jim Gorman and ridden by Pat Shanahan. Laytown specialist *Bolero Dancer* won the other one-mile handicap for Tommy O'Neill and Pat Smullen. Michael O'Brien and Tom Rudd combined to win the featured Tayto Growers Handicap Hurdle with *Born to Win*, and in the 5-furlong sprint handicap Gerry Moylan had *Tinker Amelia* in front where it mattered for owner-trainer Jimmy McDonald. *Mudlark Valley Lane*, revelling in the conditions, landed some nice bets to win the amateur rider race for Michael Cunningham and Mr. Philip Fenton.

Trainer Michael O'Brien had his second winner of the meeting, when *Hammelis* won the 1 ½ mile maiden under Eddie Ahern. Noel Meade and his jockey Paul Carberry combined to win the maiden hurdle with *Alambar*. Aidan O'Brien and Seamie Heffernan had their second win of the week with *Eternal Joy* winning the featured Heineken Handicap for Michael Tabor. Owner/trainer Lee Bowles saddled *Kinnegad Girl* to win the 3-mile maiden hurdle, for conditional jockey Jason Maguire, while in the other hurdle race Michael Donoghue owned and trained *Roseaustin* was a long-priced winner for jockey Derek McCullagh. *Sambara* was a short-priced favourite in the 1m.6f. handicap, and he duly obliged for Willie Mullins and Johnnie Murtagh. There was a very popular win in the concluding race when *Jackpot Jimmy* made all the running to win for owner Thomas Farrell, host of the Brock Inn. *Jackpot Jimmy* was ridden by his son Mr. Gerry Farrell who was riding his first winner since *The Ridge Boreen* at Dundalk in 1989.

Tony Collier leading Eloquent Way, winner at Bellewstown 1998

1998 July 1st, 2nd, 3rd The decision to change from the traditional Tuesday, Wednesday, Thursday format to this year's Friday finish certainly seemed to work pretty well. The bookmakers' area was tarmacked since last year, which was well received by punters.

The Prendergast brothers dominated the finish of the opening Kilsharvan 2-year-old maiden, but in a close finish it was Paddy who was in the winners' enclosure with *The Flying Pig* justifying favouritism under Stephen Craine. In the next race Mr. Philip Carberry had a day to remember, when he recorded his first racecourse success on his father's good old stalwart *Native Status*. The John Oxx/Johnnie Murtagh alliance won the 5-furlong maiden with *Sarigon,* for his HH, the Aga Khan, and in the Oldbridge Concrete Handicap, Gerard Cusack saddled the in-foal mare *Generous Lady* to win in the capable hands of Fran Berry. The Bowe family from Gathabawn made a rare excursion to the course, but with the usual front running tactics employed, *Daisy A Day*, with Derek McCullagh in the saddle ran her rivals into the ground. Stephen Craine secured a double on the day, when he steered *Night Scout* to win the one-mile maiden for his boss Kevin Prendergast. There was a local flavour to the winner of the concluding bumper when *Townley Hall* owned by popular Drogheda publican George Kingston obliged. He was trained by Francis Flood and ridden by Mr. Josh Byrne.

Adrian Maguire, suspended in Britain at the time, but able to ride in Ireland on days when there was no N.H. racing in Britain, took advantage of this loophole to steer the Pat Hughes-trained *Mumaris* to success in the 4-year-old Novice Hurdle. Stephen Craine had his third winner of the week, winning the one-mile maiden for 2 year olds with *Alabama Jacks* for his boss Kevin Prendergast. The 0-70, one-mile handicap was divided, with Mick Halford and Johnnie Murtagh combining to win the first division with *New Legislation*. The second division was won by the Peter Cluskey owned and trained *Eloquent Way,* in the hands of apprentice Steven Crawford. The other one-mile handicap on the card was won by *Luminoso*, who was hard driven by David McCabe to land the spoils for Curragha trainer Paddy Mooney. The second hurdle race on the card, the 2-mile handicap hurdle resulted in an easy win for *Southern Man*, trained by Frances Crowley and ridden by Charlie Swan. *Burnt Toast* won the 5-furlong maiden at the previous year's meet, and returned to win the sprint handicap for Tommy Stack and Jamie Spencer. David Hanley produced *Galletina* to win the amateur riders race for Mr. Andrew Coonan.

J.P. McManus's *Fawn Prince* provided Charlie Swan with the first success in his new training career, when he won Div.I of the Sam Dennigan Maiden Hurdle. Johnnie Murtagh had a winner on each day of the meeting, and in the opener he steered *Chaina* to win for his boss John Oxx. The second division of the maiden hurdle fell to Mrs. Rita Polly's *Treasure Dome* for Noel Meade and Barry Geraghty. Sligo trainer Michael McElhone won the featured Heineken Handicap with *Golden Fact*, for rider Pat Shanahan. *Mulligan's Boy* from Stephen Cox's Co. Offaly stable benefitted from a pile up at the 5th last hurdle to win the 3-mile maiden hurdle for rider Garrett Cotter. Kilmoon owner Tony Battersby and trainer Oliver Finegan combined to win the Crockafotha Handicap Hurdle with *Rice's Hill*, for the excellent Pat Malone. Paddy Mullins won the

(1m. 6 fur.) handicap with *No Avail,* for his wife, with apprentice Shane Kelly in the saddle. The concluding bumper was won by *Colin's Double* for Garlow Cross owner / trainer Cathal McCarthy and Mr. Robbie McNally.

1999 June 30, July 1st, 2nd Bookmakers had by far the worst of this year's renewal on the opening day, with all seven winners well backed. New trainer Kevin O'Brien started off the meeting well, winning the Kilsharvan 2-year-old maiden with Johnnie Murtagh in the saddle. *Rice's Hill,* a winner at the meeting the previous year, supplemented that win by coming from the back of the field in the 3-mile Handicap Hurdle for Tony Battersby, Oliver Finegan and Pat Malone. David Hanley sent out *Black Paddy* to win the 5-furlong maiden, with Eddie Ahern in the plate. The flamboyant Stephen Mahon had his first Bellewstown success, when Kevin Manning steered *Undaunted* to success in the Oldridge Concrete Handicap. The second hurdle race on the card, a 2 ½ mile conditions race, went to the Sean Treacy trained *Twin Gale* for 7lb.claimer, Shane McCann. Kevin Prendergast has often won the one-mile maiden here, and another win came about with Stephen Craine was a narrow winner on *Saraaf.* The concluding bumper was won by the Dessie Hughes trained *Miss Dale* with Mr. Robbie Walsh riding.

The local trainer Peter Casey landed a nice touch in the Bambury Bookmakers Handicap. Owned by his wife Junie, *Society Queen* just got up in the last couple of strides in the hands of the trainer's son Oliver. Grangecon trainer Willie Bourke had a meeting to remember, saddling three winners, including a double on the middle day. He initiated the double on Mrs. L. Carberry's game old mare *Treora* in Div I of the Old Mill Handicap for apprentice Darren Stamp, and the double was completed when Mr. Colm Cronin got *Monty's Fancy* home in front in the amateur riders race. The meeting had opened with Gerry McArdle's *Abuhail* winning the Novice hurdle for Charlie Swan, and in the following one-mile maiden, Pat Shanahan steered *Neutron* to success for Ms. Frances Crowley. 19-year old apprentice Alan Fagan rode his first ever winner when he rode *Ger's Gold* to win Div. I of the Old Mill Handicap for Curragh trainer Jeremy Harley. The rider's father Dermot Fagan is an integral part of John Fowler's stable, and has ridden a good number of winners for him. Shane McCamn had his second winner of the meet, when he forced Gerry Keane's *Cheeky Harry* home by the narrowest of margins, with the locally owned *Magua* in second place in the 2-mile handicap hurdle. Pat Martin kept his strike rate at the course ticking over when *Magic Annemarie*, with Eddie Ahern in the saddle won the 5-fur. sprint handicap.

Dermot Weld, without a winner on the opening two days, redressed the balance by saddling a double on the closing day. Both winners were partnered by Pat Smullen. The other flat race on the card went to *Snow Falcon*, a hurdle winner at the course previously, who won the Derek Plant Handicap, for Noel Meade and Fran Berry. There were two maiden hurdles on the card with Eddie O'Grady's *Okay Ocee* winning the shorter maiden for Jason Titley, and Barry Geraghty rode *Outrigger* to win the 3-mile maiden for Ms. Frances Crowley. The Crockafotha Handicap Hurdle, sponsored by Seamus Mulvaney was divided. In the 1st Div., after a stewards' enquiry, *Duinin* from the Pat Hughes stable, was promoted to first place. The second division was won by Charlie Swan on

Savo Sea, trained in Co. Wexford by Michael Doran. Trainer Willie Bourke capped a memorable week by winning his third race of the meeting when *Scary Spice* won the bumper with Mr. Josh Byrne in the saddle.

BELLEWSTOWN'S BIG RACING COUP

BARNEY CURLEY: I'M PULLING OFF A BIG COUP TODAY
(From *GIVING A LITLE BACK* (1999) CollinsWillow) p. 152-172)

You'd visit the country track of Bellewstown in County Meath for the wonderful scenery alone. In the midst of golfing country, the views are spectacular. It's about twenty-three miles north of Dublin as you head towards Belfast, then turn off towards the coast down winding lanes. Perched high up on the Hill of Crockafotha beside the village, with the Mountains of Mourne in the distance, its more romantic visitors associate it with the smell of strawberries and cream and freshly mown hay. Its sharp, left-handed, nine-furlong track only had an outside running rail added in relatively recent times. For many years a makeshift barrier was provided by horse boxes and trailers and that was to stop the horses colliding with picnic parties just out to enjoy a day's racing and taking the bracing air.

But on Wednesday 25 June 1975 I wasn't there for the benefit of my health, only the health of my rocky finances. In those early years, after Lester and Roberto had been my saviours three years before, there were a couple of tricky moments but then I 'hit the wall' again in a serious way. I'd had a very bad run and had already sold the show-jumpers to try and make ends meet.

I had a chat with Liam Brennan and told him, 'I badly need to pull off a "touch". Let's go through these horses and see what horse is capable of doing it.' We didn't have much of a choice really because, being summer, we needed a horse that would go on firm or good ground. Most of our better horses were resting, awaiting softer going in the autumn, or were away on their holidays at grass. After a couple of days, he came back to me and said, 'You know, Barney, this horse *Yellow Sam*, I think he's improved a bit.' I said, 'Give him a bit of work over the next couple of days and we'll see how he goes.' Well, predictably enough, he didn't work like *Arkle* but he did produce enough to show us that he was capable of winning a bad race, with everything going in his favour. Liam wasn't a trainer who'd ever make the big time, but I had total faith in him. He was a good judge. As we say in Ireland, 'he wouldn't count his sheep as lambs.' *Yellow Sam* was really the only possibility anyway, so we decided we'd have a go and we lined him up for Bellewstown in three weeks' time.

Bellewstown is one of Ireland's oldest racecourses, with records of its races going back to 1726. At one time it had a royal connection: King George the Third was persuaded by George Tandy, former mayor of Drogheda and brother of Napper Tandy, arch-rival of Wolfe Tone, to sponsor a prestigious race there in 1780; it was named His Majesty's Plate and was worth £100 to the winner. Every English monarch continued to support the race until 1980, when the present queen discontinued the practice. The course stages only one three-day summer meeting, when the attendance is swelled by holiday-makers and is the Irish equivalent of, say, the Cumbrian track of Cartmel. Just along the coastline to the east is Laytown, which boasts a stretch of golden sand where, on one day a year only, horseracing takes place on the beach. Informality is the key word. There are no reserved enclosures and holiday-makers mix with the professionals of both sides of the betting ring. But for all its charm, Bellewstown was, and is, very much a third division track. One thing we could be assured of, that admirably suited our purpose, the poor quality of the racing. As races go, the Mount Hanover Handicap Hurdle for amateur riders, over two and a half miles, in which Liam had entered our horse, was probably worse than most races staged there.

I had bought *Yellow Sam* as a yearling and named him after my father's nickname. They used to call the old fellow 'Yellow Sam' because he had a sallow, almost a jaundiced complexion. I have no idea where 'Sam' originated from. The horse was a brown gelding, sired by *Wreckin Rambler* out of a mare called *Tudor Jest*. He was unexceptional-looking and never very good. In all honesty, he was one of the worst horses I've ever owned. He had been unplaced and had shown very little in eight runs over two seasons, although, admittedly, some had been at decent tracks where competition would have been stiff. Wherever Liam ran him, he always seemed to finish in the middle somewhere. His best placing was eighth. (Coincidentally, in one of his races he had been partnered by the top amateur Tim Jones who had ridden *Gay Future* to victory at Cartmel in the notorious coup there on August Bank Holiday.) No way, until this moment, could you have looked at this fellow, glanced at his form and imagine he would ever pull off a 'job'. His only redeeming quality was that he was an excellent jumper. He hadn't much pace; in fact he was a slow horse, but he could make two or three lengths at every hurdle. He was as good a jumper as *Persian War*. An indication of how bad he was can be gleaned by studying his record before Bellewstown.

Season 1973-74
8 December 1973, Fairyhouse (soft), 1m 6f 3-y-o hurdle, unplaced, not in the first nine of twenty.
26 December 1973, Leopardstown (soft), 1m 5f 3-y-o hurdle, ninth of fifteen.
26 January 1974, Naas (heavy), 2m 1f maiden hurdle, eighth of seventeen.
17 April 1974, Fairyhouse (firm), 1m 6f maiden hurdle, ninth of seventeen.

Season 1974-75
28 December 1974, Punchestown (heavy), 2m handicap hurdle, not in the first nine of fourteen.
17 March 1975, Limerick (heavy), 2m 5f handicap hurdle, ninth of sixteen.
29 March 1975, Mallow (good), 2m 5f handicap hurdle, not in the first nine of twenty.
14 May 1975, Navan (soft), 2m 5f handicap hurdle, not in the first nine of twenty-nine.
His modest performances meant that at least he was very well handicapped. He did have a semblance of ability, if not a lot, and these events at country tracks in Ireland on firm ground in the summer can be extraordinarily bad races. Understandably, some cynics might suggest that he hadn't been trying before, that he had been set up specifically for this race for a long time. Well, it was true to say that I had set up horses with Liam in the past. But there was no truth in it this time. We just needed a horse to do a job and he was the only conceivable possibility. He was a big horse who would always be likely to

require time to develop and come to his best and he just suddenly began to show that he was sparkling. We knew that he'd go on the ground. All but two of his previous races had been on soft or heavy going. On the one occasion he had encountered firm ground, at Fairyhouse, he had finished ninth out of seventeen in a maiden hurdle. Although that might not seem encouraging, it must be born in mind that Fairyhouse is a metropolitan track where the racing is invariably of good quality. To now bring him to Bellewstown would be like a horse running at Sandown, then being sent to Fakenham. It was a different class altogether, a significant step down. If some of the firm ground winners at courses like Bellewstown were sent over to England to race they'd still be at the second-last hurdle when the victor was passing the post.

We had the horse. We had the race. Now the crucial, but most difficult, part was getting the money on in sufficient quantities and at suitably rewarding odds. For weeks, I didn't leave my home at Wicklow. I sat in my office and prepared everything down to the last detail, like a general massing his troops before going into battle. Only the enemy, on this occasion, were the bookmakers. Maybe a better analogy was a bank robbery. The timing had to be right and I had to trust my collaborators implicitly. Apart from the paucity of its racing, I chose Bellewstown because I knew that the rarely used, remote course only had one public telephone which was the only means the on-course bookmakers had of receiving intelligence of market moves. And it was their pricing of the horse which would decide its all-important starting-price (SP). Not that I would be betting with them. They probably would have hardly taken a pound on *Yellow Sam* all afternoon. The betting shops were my targets and I intended to have my men put the money down in offices in every large town in Ireland. I aimed to cover about 150 shops in total, from Bantry and Skibbereen in the far southwest of Ireland to Coleraine and Ballymena in the northeast, with the bets going down roughly at the same time, just before the race and all in such small quantities that nobody would pick up on what was going on.
That was the theory, anyway. In practice, this was a far from simple task. It was not a question of quietly going round at eleven o'clock or twelve noon and placing tens or twenties without question. The bookmakers were beginning to smell my horses from afar. Looking back, I had been seriously optimistic to assume that we could get the bets on without causing the slightest ripple of interest in those offices. There's an old adage – 'Loose lips can sink ships' – and that was in my mind constantly as I sat and schemed. One word out of place could scupper the operation, or at the very least drastically reduce its effectiveness. I like to think I am a good judge of people and I chose people I believed I could trust. Eventually I had compiled a list of 25 men and as the days passed I'd strike names out and replace them with others if any doubts about individuals crept into my head. It was vital that no one broke the line. Eventually I ended up with 12 generals and instructed them to recruit soldiers they could trust to put money on. Eamon and Bernard Bradley, who had run one of my first betting shops in Enniskillen, were involved and another key figure was a chap named Brian Donovan, one of our nearest neighbours in Wicklow, who owned a meat business in Dublin. He had on a substantial amount of money for me. All my men got around £1,200 each, but a lot of them just got involved for the sheer thrill of it.

I was like a recluse as I sat in my little room at the Boswell Stud with my maps and my lists. Maureen had a fair idea about what was going on, but this was something I had to plan alone. I spent hour upon hour, over many weeks, poring over my lists and maps, striking names out if I wasn't sure about them, to make sure I had the best possible team and ones that were completely trustworthy. It was not that I feared they would be traitors, just, that too many men cannot be charged with keeping a secret. They would obviously have to contract out and a lot of men I finished up with would have been punters in the betting shops all over the country, whom I'd known down the years from my days with the show-bands. They backed horses all the time and would not provoke any undue suspicion. I never told anyone directly of my plans; not Maureen, not my parents. Even Liam didn't know precisely what I was going to do, or the extent of it. Everything was kept as low key as possible. Just one whisper could have jeopardised the whole operation. That strategy worked because not a whisper got back to the track until it was too late. It was a massive operation and I put a lot of thought into it.

The most vital link in my chain of command was my man who would effectively block the one racecourse telephone, but without drawing attention to the fact. If he didn't do his job properly the whole thing would be blown wide open. I chose a fellow named Benny O'Hanlon, who had worked for me in my betting shops and was then manager at Lisnaskea in Fermanagh. No man could have possessed more integrity than Benny. If you told him to do something, then that was it; he'd obey you implicitly. As for his honesty, he wouldn't steal a pound if you left it in front of him for a year. Benny was a balding, heavily-built kind of fellow, a tough sort that you wouldn't want to get into an argument with. He was a man I could trust with my life. He would let no one pass. To get him off the phone it would need a man to get out a gun and shoot him. And the important thing was he was a great talker.

Benny was a little older than me, and from a very well thought-of family who ran a shop in Irvinestown, selling clothes. He was a real character who had held down every sort of job in his time, from buying and selling jute bags to working for a time as a barman in London. He was once so short of cash, the story goes, that he confessed to being the serial killer John Christie in order to get a police cell for the night. I went 'nap' on him as my 'phone man' without any reservations. He was more than just an employee. Maureen and I were great friends with him. He wouldn't have dreamed of stealing £20 from my shop, but he didn't think twice of blocking that phone box because he trusted and believed in me implicitly. He was a worrier too. He was always going on about how the day had gone against him, how so-and-so had taken a lot of money off us. To listen to him, you'd think we'd never come out on top. He forgot all the times when the punters went down. For that reason I never explained how big this operation was, and how major his part. He would have been quaking in his boots.

Normally one of Sean Graham's men would be on the phone in question to make sure that money came back to the course. Sean, who died a few years ago, was one of Ireland's biggest and best-known bookmakers and the family bookmaking business in his name still flourishes today. We were both from Northern Ireland and I'd known him as a friend for fifteen years, ever since those nights at Celtic Park when we both made books. We were both operating on the Southern circuit and it was inevitable that we should lock horse and there was always a bit of needle between us. Back in the summer of 1975, the stark fact was that I owed around £30,000, and I couldn't pay. 'I've hit a brick wall, Sean,' I told him about a week before the big day. 'I need your help. I could do this without you, but I'd rather I had your help. You'll have to give me your word you'll not tell a soul.' He agreed, as long as I didn't go anywhere near his betting shops. I didn't go into details straight away, just, that I was going to back a horse. I could have blocked the phone without telling him, but it would have aroused his suspicions anyway, so I thought it best to put him in the picture. I knew I could trust him to keep quiet and he told no-one. The knowledge that my horse was fancied and was a 20-1 chance was very useful to him.

Normally, off-course bookmakers, whether it's Ladbrokes today or small Irish chains of shops then, transfer their liabilities to the on-course market – some of us would say manipulate the market – which brings down a particular horse's odds. With today's communications technology it's a simple matter. Even then all it should have taken was a phone call. But my plan was that the calls would never get through – until it was too late. It might be asked, why didn't my men take a price and avoid all the subterfuge? Well, the simple answer is that the shops would not give a price – especially on one of mine. It was safety first. They'd only offer an SP on bets, and if liabilities started mounting up would send the money back to the track so that, in theory anyway, there would be a balanced market. By now, I'd begun to instil fear into the Irish bookmakers. When the money was down they'd fear my horses. Over three years I'd built up a bit of a reputation.

When the declarations were made, we could not have hoped for a better race, or to be strictly accurate, a worse race, in which to pull off our scheme. This event, whichever way you looked at it, was a dreadful race. One of our rivals had won a maiden hurdle, and another had been placed, but they were just in equally poor summer maiden hurdles. They wouldn't have been worth a dollar, those horses. And the ground was just as we wanted it – firm.

Because of his previous moderate displays Yellow Sam was allotted a weight of 10st 6lb in the field of nine runners, of whom the top weight carried 12st. He was third lowest in the weights. It was hardly a great burden given the mediocre standard of his opponents. But his likely starting price of 20-1 was not over-generous, it was the price represented on all known form. As for the riders, there were some decent names taking part. They included Sam Morshead, Willie Mullins, Ted Walsh, John Fowler and Mrs Ann Ferris, who in 1984 would become the first lady jockey to win the Irish Grand National. But our jockey Michael Furlong – later associated with that fine chaser Bannow Rambler, brought down by the fatal fall of Lanzarote when heavily backed in the 1977 Cheltenham Gold Cup – was no mug either. That year, he was runner-up in the amateur jockey's championship, beaten to the title by Ted Walsh by only one race.

The morning of the race I set out to drive the fifty-mile journey from Wicklow in great spirits, but strangely felt the urge to talk to someone whom I knew I could trust and respect. Back at Mungret I had become quite friendly with Barry Brogan, who, like Tommy Stack and Bobby Barry, had been lay pupils at the college. Barry developed into a successful jump jockey on both sides of the Irish Sea, and rode for me on several occasions, although he also became a heavy gambler and an alcoholic and, by his own admission, fixed races to pay his betting debts. Barry was exceptionally talented, possibly as gifted a rider as Richard Dunwoody or Graham Bradley, but he went off the rails in a major way. Initially, I tried to make excuses for him and tried to sympathise with him. Being charitable, I can only put it down to witnessing the death of his trainer father, Jimmy, who suffered a heart attack on the gallops. It was a terrible thing for a young man to experience. Both Liam, for whom he rode out, and I tried to help him by giving him rides when others were spurning his approaches.

Barry had been riding *Yellow Sam* in his work, and he quickly realised the horse had a race in him. 'He was moving exceptionally well,' Barry was to comment later. Yet, I was determined that Barry Brogan would be the last to know about what was afoot. He was a liability. You simply could not trust him. He was too close to several other professional gamblers and bookmakers and he had loose lips, even more so when the drink was flowing. Barry was the eldest of four children and had been followed by Ann, and twins Peter and Pamela. The whole family was involved in some way with horses, and Ann, who was a lovely girl and a joy to talk to, though she was a lot younger than me, became a particular friend. We had a lot in common, sharing a religious faith and a love of horses. She was a very good point-to-point rider and, later, also had several winners as an amateur under rules. Ann was never a very worldly sort of girl and always thought she was destined to be a nun.

The Brogans lived at Rathfeigh, about four miles from the course at Bellewstown, a bleak outpost of a place on top of a hill, and on the way I decided to call in. It was always a nice welcoming house, and they'd sit you down with tea and cake. I suppose I felt a tinge of excitement and just needed someone to talk to. Ann was a great listener. I could barely contain myself about what was planned, and couldn't help just throwing into the conversation casually, 'I'm pulling off a big coup today, and if it comes off I might end up in the *Guinness Book of Records*.' I didn't add that if it didn't, I might end up in an alms-house.

At that stage I still didn't really know what it could mean financially. For all my planning, there were so many unpredictables. Calling in one or two debts of my own, I had around £15,000 to play with. Even when I have been in really dire straits, I've always kept spare cash for such purposes. I didn't really know how much money would get on, or whether the price would stay at 20-1. All I knew was that if all went to plan and my men did their job, it would be the equivalent of my six numbers up - and the bonus ball.

I don't think Ann really took it all in and she probably thought I was talking about a few thousand. She asked me where it was taking place. 'Over at Bellewstown,' I told her, and added as an afterthought, 'Would you come up with me?' It was unusual for me. I usually prowled the racecourse like a lone wolf stalking his prey, but that day the build-up was such that I needed a confidante while I waited for the race to start. I felt like a boxer, prepared for months with road work and gym, and itching to land the knockout blow.

I said to her, 'Now listen, Ann, I can't afford to be seen.' So she agreed to drive me up to the racecourse, but, under my instructions, kept well away from the hurly-burly of the public enclosure. I knew it would be well attended, with maybe a couple of thousand packing the place. I never went near the entrance until afterwards. I knew people would have been looking out for me because my horse was running. And that would have been a sign that it was fancied. The back-straight of the track is along the side of the road, so she stopped half-way along and we crossed over the course itself, without anyone seeing us, and me with my hat pushed down as far as it would go. I probably resembled George Cole playing the gambling spiv in the St. Trinian's films, as we positioned ourselves out of sight in the centre of the racetrack. That was how, on this fine, sunny day, as the minutes ticked slowly by to the 'off', I came to be hiding in some gorse bushes with Ann Brogan, somewhere in the middle of Bellewstown racecourse.

Meanwhile, all over Ireland, my troops were moving into action. I told my generals at a quarter to two. But it wasn't until fifteen minutes before the race, due off at three o'clock, that they told their own men. Each man put on anything from £50 to £300, depending on the size of the shop, and all totalling £15,300. Deliberately, I selected mostly independent bookies so that there would be less of an intelligence network. The offices were happy to accept the bets fifteen minutes before the race, thinking they'd have no trouble in laying it off. All they would have to do was pick up the phone and have it backed on the race-track. Of course they would be pickled come five to three when they couldn't get through and no other off-course bookmakers wanted any money for the horse. They would have to sweat it out and see if *Yellow Sam* got beaten.

But all that presumed a lot on my part and specifically that Benny carried out my instructions to the letter. Benny was told to go into that phone box twenty-five minutes before the race start with strict orders: 'No matter who comes to the phone, do not leave it under any circumstances until the commentator announces "They're off".' It was a huge responsibility. Such was the crowd that day that to keep the phone occupied for half an hour required a stroke of genius. But as I have already said, he was as garrulous as they come. He got talking to some non-existent hospital in nearby Drogheda, where he had an aunt who was dying. Every few minutes Benny would announce his relative's state of health, 'Oh, alright then, that's not so bad… oh dear, she's taken a turn for the worse again.' It was the mundane kind of thing people say when they're inquiring about someone in hospital, but it did the trick. Never has a patient gone through so much recovery and relapse in half an hour. She was about to die and then she got better; she was about to die again and then she rallied. It was all total nonsense, but he carried it off brilliantly. Just as insurance, I placed another chap nearby, just in case it turned nasty and there were fisticuffs. Benny just picked him up on the way and told him to be first in the queue and not budge for anyone. He was there as a kind of minder, to keep a bit of control outside the phone box.

The result was that, with no money to speak of on-course and no word from the 'layers' off-course, the price of *Yellow Sam*, the outsider, remained static on the bookmakers' boards as the field set off on their eighteen-furlong journey, with 20-1 the officially returned SP. That phone would have been hot with people trying to get through as the money went on in the shops, and once Benny relinquished his position, it had the same effect as a dam bursting.

Meanwhile, out in the parade ring, Michael Furlong, who probably thought he was on a no-hoper, got his first hint of what was really expected of the horse. He had absolutely no idea at all of what he was involved in. He was given simple instructions by Liam, basically told to bide his time and hit the front when he thought it was the right moment. As he was legged up into the saddle, he heard just two words, 'You'll win.' Knowing my reputation, and Liam's, he would have understood the message without need of repetition.

Behind that gorse bush in the middle of the track, watching the race through my binoculars, I could see precious little of the finish. And frustrating it was, too. It sounds ridiculously surreptitious on my part, but those bookies were no mugs, and a whiff of my presence would have them scenting a scam. Ann's mother, Betty, was at the races and, apparently, there was a real buzz about the place, as it became apparent that a 'job' had been done. If you imagined I'd be nervous during the four minutes and fifty-one seconds duration of that race, you'd be quite wrong. Once I got to the course, I was ice-cold, even though defeat would have wiped me out. That has always been my way. You couldn't read me at the races and the day that doubt and anxiety enter my thoughts as I walk in through the gates is the day that I'll retire from the game. Yet, I knew that all it would take would be a fall or blunder at any one of the thirteen flights of hurdles and I'd kiss the money, all £15,300 of it, goodbye. But I had faith in my horse's jumping ability and the expertise of his partner. And neither let me down. Ann and I were a couple of hurdles up from the finish post, so we were well placed to watch the majority of the race. We witnessed Yellow Sam progress from midfield to assert his authority after four flights, then take up the early lead on the inside from *Satlan* and *Philipine Hill*. Michael gave him an excellent confident ride; he was always a great jockey at getting horses to jump and he always looked to be going better than anything else. He held on with something in hand, officially two and a half lengths, by the line.

Or so I found out later. From our vantage point, we only got a rapidly disappearing view of horse hindquarters, the back of jockeys and whips waved like conductors' batons - I couldn't actually see who had won. I thought we had done it, but, in the circumstances, it was too close for comfort. Only getting a rear view, you can never be certain what has won and we couldn't hear the commentary... I wasn't absolutely sure, so we dashed across the racetrack, back into the car and drove round to the entrance. I did not know quite what to say. I didn't want it to appear as though there was anything wrong. I just stood there, lost for words, then somebody said 'Well-done, Barney' to me, and then I knew I could relax. As you can imagine, at that price and with his form, the majority of the crowd, who would have been ignorant of what had been going on, weren't exactly ecstatic.

For the record, this was how they finished:

Mount Hanover Amateur Riders' Handicap Hurdle, 2m 4f:
1st *Yellow Sam* 5-10-6, M.J. Furlong, 20-1
2nd *Glenallen* 7-9-11, H.C. Morshead, 12-1
3rd *Silver Road* 7-10-11, W. Mullins, 4-1
4th *Satlan*, 7-10-8, A. Tyrell, 9-2

Portballintrae, 6-11-2, Mrs H. Ferris
High and Mighty, 6-10-9, T.M. Walsh
Philipine Hill 7-10-13, E. Woods
Gerties Beauty 8-10-3, T. McCartan
Deadlock 4-10-9, J.R.Fowler
Distances: Two and a half lengths, two and a half lengths, two and a half lengths.
Time: 4 min 51.20 sec. Tote: win paid £31.54.

I hung around for about ten minutes to watch the effect of his win and I saw at least one bookmaker, with off-course liabilities, kicking up a right fuss. All hell broke loose. All the shops were at last getting through on the phone in the box which Benny had now long vacated, and the men at the course were realising that the off-course offices had been caught, although even then, I don't think at that moment, they realised the gravity of the situation. I thought it was an appropriate moment to make a diplomatic departure, and Ann drove me home for a cup of tea. Her mother and Jim Dreaper, who has trained Betty's horses for her for many years, and is one of Ireland's great gentlemen, and Liam were also there, and into the middle of this intimate gathering entered Barry Brogan still oblivious to what had gone on.

Apparently, he had sauntered into the racecourse after the race and been told by the gateman that Brennan had a big winner. Liam perpetuated the deception by declaring, when Barry congratulated him, 'Oh, don't talk to me, I'm sick. Michael came through on him and we didn't expect him to win. Barney is furious.' Al total nonsense, of course, but even afterwards it would not have been prudent to reveal the truth to Barry immediately. Not a word was said at our post-race tea party either. Indeed, I had to borrow a fiver from Mrs B. to buy some petrol to drive home, not being a great one for carrying cash. Nor was anything said next morning at the stables after Barry had ridden out, and it was not until the following evening that he finally bought an evening paper and saw the headline emblazoned, 'Biggest SP job ever landed in Ireland – *Yellow Sam* at 20-1!' He nearly collapsed with the shock of it all.

Most people would expect that an Irishman having a successful major punt should be out revelling to the early hours, keeping the whole village or town in drink. I'm probably a major let-down to the image of Irish tradition and culture, but there were no celebrations. I simply drove home and went to bed, feeling quietly satisfied at a job well done. It was still on my mind that if the bet had gone down I'd have been in serious trouble. The tank would then really have been empty. My sense of exhilaration was tinged with more than a hint of relief. Before I fell asleep, I just mentioned to Maureen, 'We've had a "touch".' I still had no idea how much I'd won. It took a few days to collect it all at our base, a hotel near home, back in Wicklow. I didn't dare get my men to bring it to the stud, because I feared that the boys with shooters might turn up. Whatever the total, in one pound and one punt notes, it took a lot of space, and we had to put it in one hundredweight bags before we moved it to the bank.

By next day, the whole world knew about it. According to the newspapers some bookmakers were refusing to pay. There was a desperate hullabaloo, but my initial fears proved unwarranted. My men had gone round to collect and most had paid out. Just a few prevaricated. You have to bear in mind that although the pay-out was massive for the time, about £300,000 – equivalent to around £1.4 million nowadays – it was spread relatively thinly. No individual shop had to pay out more than £6,000. It wouldn't have put any out of business, but a sizeable pay-out like that might have damaged their profits for the next couple of months. There wouldn't have been much other betting on that race, not on an amateur riders' handicap hurdle on a Wednesday afternoon.

As I've already explained, gambling debts are not recoverable by law, but the 'layers' probably realised that if they hadn't paid I'd have kicked up a real commotion. Had they continued to withhold payment my recourse would have been to object to their licence next time they tried to renew it. But I must say that, ultimately, there was not a space in my betting book where people owed me money. Bookmakers as a breed are a lot more honourable than people imagine. At least, they were then. If I pulled the same stroke nowadays in Britain, I could envisage that big multiples like Ladbrokes and William Hill would refuse to pay out. I don't remember anyone that didn't pay eventually. There were a lot of cracks about me afterwards from the bookies, but it was mostly in good humour. I recall one fellow, Harry Barry, being particularly slow, but the guy who had the bet with him got the money out of him somehow. I think it was their pride, which had been dreadfully wounded, which got to them, more than any financial loss. One of those hit was Terry Rogers, who for three decades was an institution at Irish racecourses until he hung up his satchel in 1988. He would make a book on anything within reason and normally paid out with remarkable stoicism. Yet Terry was most grieved by Yellow Sam's success. I can't say I really blame him. Having said that, his was the first cheque in the post. He's always respected me for paying my debts on time and never 'welching'. My own mother and father had only discovered what had been going on by reading about it in the papers. I remember my father calling me up a few days later and saying, 'I see you had a "touch".'

I replied, 'I did.'

He said, 'Did you get paid?'

I said, 'I did.' And all he said was, 'That's what matters.'

Those were the only words we ever exchanged on the subject, although a small part of me regarded the success of the scheme as some kind of retribution for what happened to my father nearly twenty years before.

I'd set out with Yellow Sam merely to recoup some serious losses. As I began to liaise with my men it soon became obvious that there was to be a significant windfall. Even more than what a chairman of a private utility might expect today. The notes just kept swirling from the skies. I had always worked on the basis that Yellow Sam's price would be around 20-1, but I never imagined we'd be successful in piling on so much money at the 150 betting shops I'd originally targeted. It's always been estimated that the bookies paid out around £300,000, but I must confess I have no real idea. I gave up counting. It was a lot more than I had originally bargained for. Terry Rogers calculated it was more than that, and he was to comment later, 'What annoyed me is the revelation that Curley and Graham were in cahoots, which is a bit rich for a guy who is always going on about bookies rigging the market.' I could understand his frustration, although I could never see the rationale of his argument; the simple fact was that the scheme would have worked without Sean's cooperation anyway as the horse's form represented a 20 – 1 chance. The bookmakers continued to make all manner of threatening noises, but they had to accept that there was nothing illegal in what had gone on. Unlike some attempted coups, I didn't hide anything about what had happened. There were no 'ringers' involved. It was quite simply one man's brains against the bookmakers. I'd outwitted the system and taken advantage of unique circumstances. You couldn't do it today. If they had been able to, the bookies would have driven that horse into the ground. If those calls had got through and they'd got the money back to the track, they would have made that horse 6-4 favourite, but that was not their divine right. To do something like that, to kid everybody, and for it all to go so smoothly, gives you a great sense of achievement. There was not a hitch. I had no qualms whatsoever about it. I wish I could do it again. It was there to be done – and it worked. There was nothing illegal about it, and I never considered there was anything immoral about it.

Postscript by John Kirwan
Seamus Mulvaney reckons that he is the only bookie that's now 'standing on the rails', who was present in Bellewstown on the day of the 1975 *Yellow Sam* coup. At that time he had a bookie's shop in Parnell Street, Dublin. He recalls that it was only when he returned to his betting shop later that evening that he became aware of the size of Barney Curley's coup. Partly due to the large sums he had to pay out in the aftermath of the coup, this shop had to be closed down. Notwithstanding these losses, Seamus Mulvaney has sponsored a race at Bellewstown since 1986 and has always enjoyed coming to Bellewstown.

BELLEWSTOWN MISCELLANY

Little Grange Harriers Point to Point at Beamore, near Bellewstown

The Littlegrange Harriers held their Point to Point on the Hoey family lands at Beamore from 1945 to 1959. The venue provided a natural amphitheatre for spectators on Crufty Hill, and was very popular with racegoers in the area.

The first meeting took place on Monday April 17th 1945 and the honour of winning the first race went to the Miss Edna Ross-owned *Willpower,* who was ridden by Mr. V. McKeever. Mr. R.A. Hoey rode two winners on the day, beginning with Mr. W. Hilliard's *Ridge Of Windsor* in the Maiden Race, and in the concluding Farmer's Race he scored on *London Way* for Mr. M. O'Sullivan. The other winners at the initial meeting were *Will March* for owner/rider Mr. F.J. Healy in the Heavyweight Open Race, and Mr. J.A. Farrell's *Cullmullen* in the Open Lightweight Race, ridden by Mr. P.P. Hogan.

Field at the 1946 meeting was very healthy, and featured doubles for the outstanding horsewoman Mrs. G. St. John Nolan and Mr. J.R. Cox. Mrs. Nolan rode the winner of the opening Hunt Cup on *Red Quill*, and also rode the winner of the initial running of the Ladies Race on her own horse *Wetau*. Mr. J.R. (Bunny) Cox, then in the early stages of his outstanding career, rode the winner of the Open Heavyweight Race on *Ballyfeighan* for Mr. J. Coleman. The Hoey family could usually be relied on for a winner at their local track and in the Maiden Race Mr. J.J. Hoey piloted *Roman Days* to success for Mr. J.S. Davison. Bunny Cox completed his double in the Lightweight Race on *Weevil* for Mr. George Malcolmson.

The 1947 meeeting was held on Monday March 31st and the opening Hunt Cup was very much a family affair. The winner was *Gormanstown Lad*, owned by Mr. P. Purfield. He was ridden by Mr. Dick Hoey, and the placed horses were ridden by his brother Jim, and his future brother in law Mr. Leslie Ball. The Open Heavy Weight race was won by Mr. Standish Collon on his father's horse *Land's End,* and in the Open Maiden, Mr. Pat Taaffe, just starting out on his outstanding career, piloted his father's charge *Autumn* to success. The Ladies Race was a very popular feature at the meeting, and the year's honours went to the Miss B Kearns ridden *Fair Bay* in the famous brown and white colours of Mr. Barney Lawless. The concluding Open Lightweight was won by *Grand Jury,* ridden by Mr. P. Connolly.

No details available on the 1948 meeting.

There was a large crowd at the 1949 renewal, and local owner Mr F. Gradwell had the privilege of owning *Bright Night II*, winner of the opening Hunt Cup Race with Mr. T. Stone in the saddle. Capt. Denis Baggally rode *Kylescarlet* to win the Open H'Weight race, and in the Open Maiden Race, young Mr J.F. Moorehead had his first ever winner on *Crested Muse* for his uncle Mr Frank Rogers. There was a very popular winner of the Ladies Open Race with Mrs. Wilfred McKeever successful on her own horse *Scarva Corner*, with local lady Ms. Marie Malone in second place on *Kill Beauty*. The final two races were won by Mr. J.R. Cox and Mr. J.J. Hoey.

Meet of the Little Grange Harriers in the 1960s led off by Barbara Jennings

The 1950 meeting opened as usual with the Hunt Cup race, and Mr. J.J. Hoey had another course win on his father's charge *Mr. Bonfire*. The Ladies Open Race provided Mrs. G. St. John Nolan with her second win in the race, this time on *Rubina II* for Lord Farnham. The Open Lightweight Race was won by Mr. Desmond O'Hagan's grey mare *Little Trix*, ridden by Mr. J.R. Cox. The other three races were won by Mr. J.J. Ryan, Jnr, Mr. A O'Scannell and Mr. J. Aherne.

Some excellent racing was witnessed by the crowd at the 1951 meeting, and the main honours went to Mr. J.J. Hoey who rode two winners (*Uncle Tim V* and *Reynoldstown's Niece*) for his father Mr. J.F. Hoey. The opening Adjacent Hunt's Race went to Mr. R.W. McKeever on his own horse *Royal Cora*. Mr. J.R. Cox had another course win, this time on *Ednagrena* in the Schwer Cup. The Ladies Open Race was won by Miss Marshall Barnes on *Bright Night II* for J.A. Farrell, who also owned the winner of the Galbraith Cup with *Night of England* with Mr. J. Ahearne in the saddle.

Fields were on the small side at the 1952 meeting where the highlight was a riding treble for Mr. J.J. Hoey, two of which, *Uncle Tim II* and *Morpheus,* were owned by family members. The meeting opened with another local win in the Confined Hunts Cup, when Mr. T.A. Filgate steered *Shannon Breeze III* to success for Mrs. Eileen Boylan of Hilltown House. Owner Mr. Desmond O'Hagan and Mr. J.R. Cox combined for a win with *Scottish Ivy* in the Open Maiden Race, and Mrs. G St. John Nolan once again won the Ladies Open Race, this time on *Hilarious May II* for Mr. G. Donnelly.

The firm ground depleted the fields somewhat in 1953 and saw Mr. J.J. Hoey replicate his feat of the previous year by riding another treble. Once again, two of his winners *Uncle*

Tim II and *Vintage Wine* were for his father Mr. J.F. Hoey. Mr. J.R. Cox also had another winner at the venue his year on *Little Dell* in the Open Maiden Race. The Open Ladies Race was won by Mrs. Gordon Craigie on her husbands's *Pearl's Peach*, in which Miss Vera Hoey was placed third on *Geraldine's Fancy*. The other race on the card, the Open Light Weight Race, was won by *Flaming Boy*, ridden by Mr. Standish Collen for Mr. Barney Lawless.

The 1954 meeting was marred by terrible weather conditions with heavy rain and strong winds buffetting patrons on the windswept hill. Conditions mattered little to *Uncle Tim II* who won the Heavyweight Race for the third year running, with Mr. J.J. Hoey once again in the saddle. The meeting opened as usual with the Confined Hunts Race, and here Mr. Charlie Crinion's *Pig Hill* obliged in the hands of Mr. J.A. O'Connell. Yet again Mr. J.R. Cox was in the winner's enclosure, this time on *Rub Lightly* for Dan Moore in the Maiden Race. Mrs. Gordon Craigie repeated her success of last year in the Ladies Cup, again on *Pearl's Peach*. In the Open Light Weight Race Mr. E.J. Kelly got *Palo Duro* home in front for his father Mr. R. Kelly.

In contrast to the previous year, the 1955 meeting was favoured by a very fine afternoon, when Mr.J.R. Cox recorded a double on *Fabiola* and *Prospect*. The previous year's winning combination in the Confined Hunt's Race, *Pig Hill* and Mr. J.A. O'Connell, were back in the winners enclosure for Charlie Crinion. Mr. C.A. Schorman rode *Exhort* to victory in the Schwer Cup for Mr. J.C. Brady. In the Ladies Open Race Miss A Horsburgh on her own horse *Skaty Kate II* foiled Mrs G. Craigies's attempt at three in a row, and in the concluding Farmer's Open Race *Mr. Ichabod* who had finished second earlier in the afternoon, showed no ill effects to give Mr. J.J. Hoey his only win of the day. He was owned by Mrs. J. Ball.

No details available on 1956 meeting.

Fields cut up somewhat at the 1957 meeting, and in the opening Confined Hunter's Race Mr. J.R. Craigie steered *Rare Sort* to success for Mr. Barney Lawless. Miss A. Horsburgh rode another winner of the Ladies Open Race, this time on *Wandering Winnie*. The Open Maiden Race was won by Mr. C. McCartan Jnr. on *King Borris* for Miss G.R. Marshall Barnes. The other three races were won by Mr. J. Nugent, Mr. E.H. Leonard and Mr. J.D McEnry.

No details on 1958 meeting.

The last meeting of the Little Grange Harriers Point to Point was held on Monday, April 13th 1959. Racing as usual started off with the Confined Hunt Race, which saw Miss Gabriel Waddington have a great win on *Green Record* for her father Mr. Nesbitt Waddington. The Open Heavyweight Race saw Mr. J.A. Wilson's charge *Kilskyre* successful in the hands of a youthful Mr. Eddie Harty. He later won the English National in 1969 on *Highland Wedding* and represented Ireland at the 1960 Olympics in Rome. The Open Maiden Race was won by Mr. Cecil Ronaldson on *Eustace* for Mrs. W. Willis. The final running of the Ladies Open Race saw Ms. M.R. Robinson successful on

Greatchap for Mrs. R. Ross. The other riders who took part in the final Ladies Race were Mrs. C.S. Bird, Miss G. Waddington, Miss Vera Hoey and Miss Helen Bryce Smith. The Open Light Weight Race went to *Glen Weather* for Mr. G. Chesney. Unplaced in this race was *Sam Weller* ridden by Mr. Tony Cameron, but this combination went on to represent Ireland internationally at 3-Day Eventing. The final race at this very popular Point to Point at Beamore was won by *Rosemary's Princess* owned by Mr. T. Duff, and ridden by Mr. J.A. (Al) O'Connell. For the record, the other riders to take part in this race were Mr. J. Nugent, Mr. Frank Prendergast, Mr. Larry McGuinness and Mr. Cecil Ronaldson.

Dick Hoey and Iris Kellett jumping a fence in Beamore at a Meet of the Little Grange Harriers point-to-point 1940s

Little Hack II, dual Irish Grand National Winner

Little Hack II made his debut as a 5-year old in the Farmer's Plate at Fairyhouse on Easter Monday 1904 and finished second, ridden by P. Bannon. She made two other appearances that year, running unplaced at the Meath Hunt Steeplechases at Boyerstown, and finishing third in the Downshire Plate at Punchestown. The Racing Calendar noted 'the first and third horses being the property of tenant farmers received a bonus of 30 sovs. each'. She didn't appear on the racecourse in 1905, 1906 or 1907 (no record of point to points at that time). When she next appeared on the racecourse in 1908 she won the King's Cup (a 3-mile chase for Hunters) at Fairyhouse on Easter Monday with Mr. AB Lawson in the saddle. After finishing out of the money at Punchestown, she won a 'match race' at Dundalk, ridden by Mr. R.H. Walker, which finished her for that year. Her next appearance came in the Irish Grand National in 1909, where once again ridden by Mr. R.H. Walker she won in a canter by 30 lengths at odds of 100/14. Her only other outing that year came in the prestigious Prince of Wales Plate (then worth twice as much as the Irish National) and she finished second to a good horse called *Paddy Maher*. The following year, 1910, she re-appeared in the Irish National but with the distance reduced to 2 ¼ miles which didn't suit her, she finished unplaced. Back to 3 miles next time out, she won the Prince of Wales Plate at Punchestown, this time with Stephen Matthews in the saddle. Following an unplaced effort in a 2-mile chase at Dundalk, she made her only appearance at her local track (Bellewstown) but unsuited to the fast ground and tighter track, she finished last of four, to subsequent Irish National winner *Small Polly*. She made only one appearance in 1911, in the Irish National and finished third. In 1912 she ran again in the National but fell, and her only other race that year saw her winning the Mullacurry Plate at the Louth Hunt and Ardee Steeplechases at Mullacurry, again with Stephen Matthews riding. Now 14 years of age, and on her only race in 1913, she won her second Irish Grand National, to become at the time, the oldest winner of the Fairyhouse feature, for Stephen Matthews. *Little Hack II* took things easy in 1914, not having a race, but the following year, 1915 and now a venerable 16 years of age she arrived at Fairyhouse for another tilt at the National. Setting off in front as usual, she put in her usual bold showing, but she couldn't sustain her effort and was pulled by her faithful partner Stephen. *Little Hack II* was owned and trained for her entire career by Nicholas Markey at Naul Park, Co Dublin.

Anatis

In 1860 the Aintree Grand National was won by Mr. C. Capel's mare *Anatis* which as a 3 year-old had started her racing career in Ireland, then called *Bellewstown Lass* (by *King Dan*), when owned by a Mr. Langan. On 30th September 1854, running in the name of Mr. Keating she won the maiden plate at Jenkinstown, Co. Kilkenny. Later she was owned by Capt. Hutchinson, Sir E. Hutchinson and a Mr. Dunlop for whom she won the Kilrue Cup on 4th May 1855 and a 3-mile race at Skerries 5 days later. In her Grand National *Anatis* was ridden by a young amateur "Mr. Thomas". His real name was Thomas Pickernell.

Ten of The Best Horses to win at Bellewstown

Drogheda

Drogheda who won the 1898 English Grand National at Aintree, as a 6 year old, had a close association with Bellewstown. He was bred by Mr. George Gradwell at nearby Dowth from his 1887 Irish Grand National winning mare *Eglantine*. Forward enough to run as a two year old, *Drogheda*'s first race was in the Hilltown Plate, a five furlong conditions race for two year olds and upwards, at Bellewstown on 11th July 1894. Ridden by William Wynne from Drogheda, and carrying 7st. he was unplaced. He ran in another two races that year at Down Royal and Baldoyle. Unraced as a three year old, he was sent chasing the following year and recorded his initial win in the Dunboyne Maiden Chase at the Fairyhouse Easter meeting. The following year (1897), after winning a chase at Baldoyle he won the Grandstand H'Cap Chase at Bellewstown, and followed up by winning the Galway Plate on his next outing. He was ridden on all three occasions by Thomas Dowdall.

So impressed was R.C. (Dick) Dawson by his win in the Galway Plate that he bought *Drogheda* for £1,500 with a contingency of £300 should he win the English National. This he duly collected the following year when he defied some of the worst conditions the great race was ever run in. The race was run in a snowstorm and when *Drogheda*'s winning jockey Johnny Gourley made his way to the winner's enclosure, he looked like a mounted snowman. This was a fantastic effort by a 6-year old horse carrying 10st.12lb., but due to ongoing leg trouble he never again reached the heights he achieved that day at Aintree on 25th March 1898.

Shaun Spadah

When *Shaun Spadah* won the 1921 Aintree Grand National he was the only horse to jump all of the fearsome 30 fences without mishap, the other 35 horses either fell or were pulled up. Then owned by Mr. T McAlpine, he was trained by George Poole and was ridden by Fred Rees. Back in 1916 *Shaun Spadah* had the first of his two wins in the Drogheda Tradesmen's Chase for owner Mr. Frank Barbour, who at the time was the dominant owner in National Hunt Racing. When Barbour moved to the Trimblestown estate near Trim in Co. Meath he installed a private trainer and laid out his own racecourse. On this occasion *Shaun Spadah* was trained by Reggie Walker at Rathvale, Athboy, and was ridden by top amateur Mr. Stanley Harrison. *Shaun Spadah* repeated his success the following year (1917) in the Drogheda Tradesmen's Chase when he was trained by Bob Fetherstowhaugh and ridden by Charles Hawkins.

Thomond II

Won 5 races in 1931, among which was the Duleek Chase at Bellewstown, where he was ridden as usual by Mr. Eric McKeever for owner Duke de Stacpoole and trainer Reggie Walker. Sold at the end of that season to wealthy American Jock Whitney to race in Britain, he developed into a top class chaser. Only the presence of the immortal *Golden Miller* prevented him from achieving more success. He finished second to the "Miller" in the 1933 Cheltenham Gold Cup, and third to him in the 1934 renewal. In the 1935 race for the Gold Cup *Thomond II* had a memorable duel with *Golden Miller* only going down by three parts of a length. Also, in the 1934 Aintree Grand National he was placed third to *Golden Miller*.

Hatton's Grace
The best horse ever to win at Bellewstown was probably *Hatton's Grace*, who went on to win the Champion Hurdle at Cheltenham three times in 1949, 1950 and 1951 for Vincent O'Brien and jockey Tim Molony. He was nine when he won his first Champion Hurdle and less than a month later showed his versatility by winning the Irish Lincoln H'Cap at the Curragh over one mile on the flat. Later on that year (1949) he won the Irish Cesarawitch over 2 miles, also at the Curragh. *Hatton's Grace* won 11 of his 29 hurdle races, but didn't see a race track until he was six because of wartime restrictions. Then owned by Commandant Dan Corry of Irish Showjumping fame, the first race he ever won was the Bellewstown N.H. Flat Race at Bellewstown in July 1946. His owner Commd't Corry rode him to that success, and at the time he was trained by Dick O'Connell. Subsequently he was trained by Barney Nugent, before passing into the hands of Vincent O'Brien and Mrs Keogh.

Freebooter
Hatton's Grace won the bumper on the opening day of the 1946 festival at Bellewstown and the other race for amateur riders (on the second day) the Shallon Plate was won by *Freebooter* who went on to win the 1950 Aintree Grand National for owner Ms. L. Brotherton, trainer Bobby Renton, and jockey Jimmy Power. When *Freebooter* won at Bellewstown, he was owned by Mr. J. Johnson, trained by Dick O'Connell and was ridden by JR (Bunny) Cox.

Arkloin
It is not often that a horse comes to run at Bellewstown a few months after winning at Cheltenham Festival but *Arkloin* did. In fact he did so in two consecutive years 1965 and 1966. In March 1965 he won the Sun Alliance Chase with Liam McLoughlin in the saddle, and in July of that year he defied the steadier of 12st.7lbs. to win 3-mile Wintergrass H'Cap Chase, this time ridden by Pat Taaffe. The following year he won the National Hunt Handicap Chase and repeated his success in the Wintergrass H'Cap Chase, on both occasions ridden by Pat Taaffe. *Arkloin* was owned by Mr. George Ansley and trained by Tom Dreaper, who was always a great supporter of the meeting.

Black Secret
About the only major chase never won by Tom Dreaper was the Aintree Grand National. The closest he came was in 1971, when *Black Secret*, ridden by his son Jim, was just touched off by *Specify* ridden by Johnny Cook in one of the closest finishes ever to the great race. In 1970 *Black Secret*, who was owned by Mrs Jean Watney, won the Duleek Chase at Bellewstown and among other races he won was the Troytown H'Cap Chase at Navan later on that year.

Pollardstown

In 1978 *Pollardstown* won the 1m.6f. Hilltown Handicap at Bellewstown for Kevin Prendergast and Gabriel Curran. Sold to race in Britain as a prospective hurdler, he quickly developed into a very proficient performer in that sphere. Among other races, he won the Triumph Hurdle in 1979, and was placed second in the 1981 Champion Hurdle to *Sea Pigeon*.

Almaty

The opening session of the 1995 Bellewstown festival was blessed with a fabulously sunny evening. In the first race *Almaty* put in a scorching display of speed to win the Kilsharvan E.B.F. 2y/o maiden. Owned by Peter Savill (Chairman of the British Horse Racing Board) he was trained by Con Collins and ridden by Pat Gilson. Unusually for a Bellewstown winner, he turned out to be one of the leading two year olds of the year, and among his successes was the prestigious Molecomb Stakes at the Goodwood August Festival. *Almaty* was bred by Penny Banahan, for a long time Turf Club's senior judge.

Liberman

In 2002 Liberman won the Eddie's Hardware/NH flat race at Bellewstown for owner Mr. P.J. O'Donovan, trainer Paddy Mullins and Jockey Mr. Keith Mercer. At the end of the season he was bought by leading English owner Mr. David Johnson and put into training with Martin Pipe. Keeping to the bumper route, he went on to win the Champion bumper at the 2003 Cheltenham Festival and in doing so provided Tony McCoy with his only success there that year.

Mrs Moore, horse-trainer Jimmy (Midge) Tiernan, Ina Kierans, Brendan Kierans and Peter Moore enjoying a day at the races in Bellewstown.

Brigadier Boylan, Secretary of the Turf Club and Keeper of the Match Book

Edward Thomas (Brigadier) Boylan was born in 1894, in Hilltown House, Bellewstown. Growing up in Hilltown, he was naturally involved with horses, taking part in local hunts and competitions, from a young age. He fought with honour in the First World War. On the death of his father in December 1926, Edward retired from the army and moved back to Hilltown to manage the estate.

Edward followed in his father's footsteps, becoming a member of the RDS in 1928 and being elected to the Agricultural Committee of the RDS in 1938. He was elected to the RDS Council in 1946 and to the Executive Committee of the RDS in 1947, becoming Honorary Secretary in 1956. He represented the Society at meetings of the Federation Equestre Internationale in Paris and his great knowledge of all matters connected with international show-jumping was of inestimable benefit to the Society's Shows.

On the outbreak of the Second World War, he rejoined the British army, again playing an active role at the front and was created Brigadier before the end of the war. He retired from the army, back to Hilltown, when the war was over.

1946 was the year that Harold Clarke, long-serving Keeper of the Match Book, retired from the Turf Club. Brigadier Boylan, just home from the war, was the natural choice as successor to Clarke, having already served alongside him as his assistant in the Registry. Brigadier Boylan, formerly Registrar of the Irish National Hunt Committee, became Keeper of the Match Book and Secretary of the Turf Club, a dual job he retained until his death in 1959. He was ideal for the position. Taking over at a period of great progress, his charming personality, vitality and drive helped him to oversee all the developments that took place in the 1950s, including the modernisation of many racecourses and the introduction of the film patrol at all the principal centres. He was a first-class official and held in the highest respect by all involved with the Turf Club. Brigadier Boylan was also a very keen huntsman and was closely associated with the Louth Hunt all his life. He died in December 1959.

The Delany Family, Laytown

The black and gold colours of the Delany Family from Corbal-Lis, Laytown have been prominent in Irish racing for over 120 years. This dynasty was started by Edward Delany, and the first winner came in 1890 when *Teetotum* won a chase at Downpatrick with Capt. Beevor riding. Winners in this decade were getting more frequent and after *Gobo* had come close in 1895, the stable had a great win in the 1898 Irish Grand National with *Porridge* obliging for Bellewstown native Thomas Collier. Another major success came in 1904 when *St. Corinne* won the valuable Conyngham Cup at the big Punchestown festival. The stable continued to turn out a steady stream of winners in the first half of the 20th century. Probably the best horse of this period was *Serpolette*, who after winning at Bellewstown in 1938, went on to win that year's Galway Hurdle and the Naas November Handicap. Edward Delany, who lived to be over ninety, died in 1948. The training licence was taken by Stephen Regan from 1949 – 1959, until Eamonn Delany (nephew of Edward) acceded to the post in 1960. During the 1950's and 60's the Regan brothers, Mickey and Timmy, and Eamonn's sons, Niall and Eamonn, were to the forefront in a revival of the stables fortunes. The latter (Mr. E.D. Delany) won on his first ride in public on *Corbal-Lis* at Laytown Races in 1953. In this era the stable had a number of versatile and durable performers like *Erindale Boy*, *Oue De Bee*, *Narcotic Nora*, *Inniskeen*, *East Wind*, *Fidelis* and *Nostra*. E.D. Delany took over the training licence in 1980. The last big winner to be trained at Corbal-Lis was *Delmoss* in the 1982 Troytown Chase at Navan.

Eamonn Delany with Stephen Reagan and jockey Timmy Reagan in the Delany colours in the 1950s

Bellewstown People in Racing

Thomas Collier was born at Leggan Hall Road, Bellewstown, and was an accomplished National Hunt jockey, both here and in France, in the decades either side of 1900. He rode his first winner on *Ladybird* at Annagassan Strand Races in July 1899 for Mr. A.E. Warren of Leggan Hall House. His second winner didn't come until the Christmas meeting at Leopardstown in 1894, when he rode *Gobo* to win a chase for Mr E. Delany. Riding almost exclusively for Mr. Delany he notched up another 18 winners over the next 4 years in Ireland, culminating in winning the Irish Grand National at Fairyhouse in April 1898 on *Porridge*. Apart from *Gobo* and *Porridge* his other wins for Mr. Delany came on *Nanette* and *Gipsy*, while he also won a chase at Boyerstown, Navan on a horse called *Julianstown* for Mr. F.C. Osborne. Apart from winning races at Baldoyle and Leopardstown, he notched up victories at such diverse places as Mullacurry, Slane, Kells, Carnew, Tullow and Carrickmacross. During this time he was also riding in France, and was particularly successful at Auteuil – he rode 17 winners there in 1897. From 1898 – 1903 he seems to have been riding in France most of the time and his big wins there included the Grand Course de Haies D'Auteuil in 1901 and 1903. From 1903 in Ireland he rode mostly for local owners and trainers, Mr. Richard Courtney and Mr. J.S. Langan, and he rode *Sweet Zephyr* to win the Lloyd Plate at Kells for Mr. Thomas Boylan, of Hilltown House in 1906. His final winner was on *Imaal* for Mr J.M. Ennis at Mullacurry in May 1909.

Paddy Bellew A native of Co. Louth, he settled in Bellewstown after coming to work in the local stables of Mr. Richard Courtney in 1905. His first two winners came when he recorded a double at the Louth Hunt Steeplechases at Mullacurry in May 1900. He won the Farmer's Plate (Steeplechase) on *Princess* for Mr. Ned Delany, and the Stewards Plate (Steeplechase) on *Juno* for Mr Nicholas Markey. He followed up by winning the Corporation Steeplechase at the Bellewstown Festival on *Juno* later on that year and his final win in 1900 came on *Shallon* for Mr. Delany in the Drogheda Hurdle at Termonfeckin Strand Races in August. He had no winners from 1901 to 1904 and in 1905 (now working for Mr. Richard Courtney) he won two races on the prolific *Most Noble* – at Laytown Strand and Skerries Strand Races. On New Year's Day in 1906 Paddy rode *Enchanted King* to win a Steeplechase at Baldoyle, and his other two wins of that year came when *Most Noble* repeated his successes of the previous year at Laytown and Skerries. He rode one winner in 1907, again on *Most Noble* in a hurdle race at the Kells (Lloyd) Meeting. For the next five years (1908 – 1912 inclusive) he did not have a jockey's licence most of the time and didn't ride any winners. However, in 1913 on Mr. Courtney's stalwart chaser *Fond Lucy* he won the Farmer's Plate at Mullacurry. 1914 proved to be his last year in the saddle and he rode 3 winners. His final win came on *Fond Lucy* on Boxing Day in the St. Stephen's Plate (Chase) at Leopardstown.

Richard Courtney trained a small string of horses on his farm at Carnes West, Bellewstown with a fair degree of success, in the early part of the 20th century. The best horse he trained in the 1900's was *Most Noble*, who won a variety of races both flat and national hunt. On one occasion at Bellewstown in 1907 he won the Hilltown Handicap with Steve Donoghue riding. Other good horses he trained were *Enchanted King*, *Enchanted Duke* and *Fond Lucy*. He died in 1922.

Capt. Thomas (Tossie) Martin, from Bonfire Bank, Bellewstown, had a brief flirtation with training horses in 1927 and 1928. The best horse he had was *Aidan* who won three races in each of those years. In 1927, he won races at Kilbeggan, Rosslare Strand and Laytown and in 1928, he was successful at Limerick, Kilbeggan and Claremorris. *Aidan* was unplaced in the Crockafotha Hurdle at Bellewstown in 1928. The other horse he trained was called *Nineteenth Hole.*

Frank Horris A native of Kennetstown, Bellewstown he spent a lifetime in racing, though not much is known of him. He worked in the private stables of Mr. J.V. Rank at Druid's Lodge on Salisbury Plain, England and for some time in the 1940's he held the licence to train there. During that time he trained that great horse *Prince Regent* who was sent to his owner's stables when retired by Tom Dreaper in 1948. The old horse reacted badly to this scenario, so he was put back into training and won twice more.

Philip McEntee A native of Lisdornan, Bellewstown Philip spent a lifetime in racing. He was apprenticed to Seamus McGrath at Glencairn and was crowned champion apprentice in Ireland in 1966. When he retired from riding in Ireland, he moved to England and worked for Lambourn trainer Reg Akenhurst for ten years, before returning to train at the Curragh for a few years. During that time he trained *Call Me Anna* to win a hurdle race at Bellewstown. He returned to England in the late 1980s and eventually started training as a private trainer for Peter Freeman. He moved to train at Newmarket but died prematurely at the age of 52. His son, Philip, now carries on the training.

Tony Collier A native of Bellewstown, Tony's first experience of racing was working at Major C.W.T. Morshead's stables at Bellewstown House. His first mount was on the Major's horse *Bronte's Cottage* in a chase at Bellewstown in 1970. He then worked at Dick Hoey's stables at Julianstown for 13 years, and then went over to Roddy Armitage's in England for about 2 years. He returned home to Ireland after that and went to work at Bill Harney's Tipperary stables. During his time here, he rode his only winner, on *Devon Lark* in a maiden hurdle in Killarney in 1983. Having returned to this part of the country, Tony went to work at Peter Cluskey's stables at Darcystown, Balbriggan as assistant trainer, and during his time here the stable had two winners at Bellewstown – *I Have To Go* in 1997 and *Eloquent Way* in 1998. Tony's most recent assignment was working at the famous Delany stables at Corbal-lis, Laytown, from which he is now retired.

David Whearty Another prodigy of the Major Morshead stables at Bellewstown House, David rode in a handful of races. However, his main claim to fame is that he rode in the last steeplechase ever to be run at Bellewstown in 1977. In this he rode the Major's horse *Mullaharry* in the Bolies Chase, but unfortunately he fell at the sixth jump from home – the race was won by *Mill Grange*. David was a very capable footballer and won a Meath Junior Championship medal with Bellewstown in 1986 – the club's only championship success.

Sam Morshead The Morshead family came to live at Bellewstown House in the late 1960's where Major Christopher Morshead trained a few horses, mostly for Point to Points. It was in this sphere that Sam Morshead first came to prominence on the family's *Top Up* on whom he won a few 'points'. *Top Up* also had a few runs on the racecourse and was narrowly beaten in the 1973 Wintergrass Chase at Bellewstown, with Sam in the saddle. After spells riding here as an amateur jockey for Jim Dreaper and Edward O'Grady, he went to England in 1976 to ride for the famous Fred Rimmell stable at Kinnersley. Sam turned to the professional ranks shortly after this. Always noted for his bold and fearless riding, in eleven years as a professional jockey, he rode over 400 winners until a very bad fall at Worcester Racecourse in 1987 forced him to retire from the saddle. He remained in racing initially as a clerk of the course at some of the Scottish tracks, and he is now manager of Perth Racecourse.

Watching the road-crossing on Hilltown Road

Workers at the Racecourse

Over the years a number of people, mostly locals, have been involved with the races, in the build-up to the days of the races and more particularly on racedays.

Paddy Larkin of the Cosy Bar looked after the course in the early part of the twentieth century. When he died in 1932, the main work was taken over by **Micky Black** and his family. **James Black** took over from his father and continued working until the early 1990s, assisted by his brothers and Nicholas Townley. After that **Oliver Rickard, Kevin Greene, Tom Collier** with **Paul Cudden** and **Padlum Brannigan** all had short periods in charge until Sean (Shuler) Black took over.

There were seven steeplechases on the course up until 1977 which took a lot of maintenance. The main person who carried out this maintenance, over a long number of years, was **John (Carven) Black,** with the assistance of the 'Black Boys'. The hurdle frames were filled with furze from around the course and lacing the frames with the furze was an intricate task. Back in the day, it was carried out by **Jimmy (Mousy) Black** and **Park Brien,** while later on **Paul Ludlow** and **Bobby Power** did this work. Nowadays the hurdles are supplied and maintained by **Eamonn Creighton** from Co. Kildare. Before the permanent post and rail fence was erected in the late 1970s, there was a single rail timber fence, which had to be whitewashed every year. Over the years this task had been carried out by **Paul Ludlow,** and **Jack** and **Kate Slevin.** The last pair to do this were **Michael Brannigan** and **Martin Flynn,** who would have as much whitewash on themselves as on the railings.

On the days of the races, a lot of people helped out. The road crossings had to be manned from about an hour before the first race, controlling traffic etc. The top road was looked after in the past by **Patsy (Mousy) Black, Seamus Collier, Shuler Black, Bobby Power** and **Tommy Farrell.** Nowadays **Pat Brannigan, Robert Power** and **Declan Brannigan** are the men in control. The bottom road in the past was supervised by **Patsy Black, Jack Reilly, Sonny Reilly** and **Tony Flynn.** At present **Tommy** and **James Russell** and **Pakie Reilly** are at the helm.

During the jumping races, each fence is looked after by two people. Among those who have done this in the past were the **Molloy** family, **Joe, Pat, Paddy jnr., Arthur Forbes, Brendan Molloy, Tomty Black. Patsy Halpin, Dermot Molloy, Tony Flynn, Jim (Soldier) Sherry, Patsy Black, Tom Collier, Jimmy Reilly, Paddy Bellew** and **Tommy Farrell.** The present hurdle crew are **Martin Flynn, Anthony Flynn, Paddy Molloy, Tommy Brannigan, Christopher McHugh, Alan Smith, Jim Brannigan, Terry Kearns, Paul Brannigan, David Power** and **Robert Flynn.**

Another important task to be undertaken on race-days was helping the race-starter. When Major Scott was the official Turf Club starter, for many years **Jack Crinion** ably assisted by his two sons **Noel** and **Nicholas,** would attend to his every need. Jack was succeeded in this role by **Mannix Dowdall** who came from Navan and was helped by local man, **Peter Black.** When the photo-finish camera came into use in the fifties, a space had to be kept clear from people, around the winning post. The man entrusted with this task was **Paddy Brannigan snr.** from the Carnes Road and woe betide anyone who stepped into the line of the same camera. **Mick Whearty** looked after the water pump and ancillary services, in the formative years of water coming to the course. **Tosh Healy** was another who ensured the smooth operation of the water system. It is now being looked after by **Olly** and **Ian Hand** from Ardcath.

Mrs Katie Ludlow supervised the Ladies cloakroom for many years and after her came **Lizzie Mills and Betty Brannigan.** Nowadays **Ann Collins** and **Claire Brannigan** do the job. Attendants at the men's facilities have included **Shuler Lynch, Hughie Courtney, Thomas Mills, Dermot Molloy** and **James Myles. John Black** looked after the saddle cloths and numbers in the weighroom. John's brothers, **Michael** and **Pierce** also did this job in turn and later Paul Black took over for many years. **Hugo O'Reilly** looked after the hospitality tent for owners and trainers when it was in vogue, for a number of years. **David Halpin** performed a myriad of tasks both before and during races, as did **Patsy Clerkin. John Joe Collins** supervised the main entrance gate for many years.

Catering at the course was looked after by various companies over the years. In the twenties, **Dinny Reddan** of Bettystown, followed by **Mrs Tippings** of Dundalk, did the catering. **The Gwent Arms,** with **Denis Larkin** catered in the fifties and sixties. In the seventies **Noel Tallon** took over the bar work and **Biddy Watson** did the catering. **Paddy Dunne** of Bellewstown Inn also did the bar for a few years. Eventually all the catering and bar facilities were taken over by **Peter O'Brien Catering** in the early eighties, followed by a variety of catering contractors since then.

BELLEWSTOWN: THE STATISTICS

Race	Winner	Owner	Trainer	Jockey
1900				
July 4				
Hilltown Flat Race 5 Fur	Friary	Mr H. Walker		F. Mason
Stewards H'Cap Chase 3 m	Moondyne II	Mr D. O'Donnell		M. O'Neill
Crockafotha Flat H'Cap 1m	Benoni	Mr. H. Tunstall-Moore		Peter Hughes
Drogheda Tradesmen's Chase 2m	Rose O'Neill	Mr. J.D. Wallis		P. Cowley
Tally Ho Hunters Flat H'Cap 2m	Holy Heroine	Mr P. J. Brophy		J.J.Parkinson
July 5				
Hill Flat H'Cap 6 Fur 80 yds	Achray	Capt. Scott		T. Maguire
Corporation Chase 3m	Juno	Mr N Markey		P. Bellew
Bellewstown Plate Flat 6 fur 80 yds	Mount Dalton	Mr B. W. Parr		Mr H. Nuttal
Grand Stand Plate Chase 2m	Thraneen	Mr J. J. Maher		J. Walsh
Her Majesty's Plate 2 ¼ m	Glenart	Mrs Mc Auliffe		H. Buxton
Meath N.H. Flat Race 2m	Armine	Count Stolberg		Count Stolberg
1901				
July 3				
Hilltown Flat Race 5 Fur	Legganhall	Mr J.S. Langan		John Doyle
Stewards H'Cap Chase 3 m	Juno	Mr N. Markey		Mr. G. J. Ball
Crockafotha Flat Handicap 1m	Esmelee	Mr F. Christie		J Clayton
Drogheda Tradesmen's Chase 2m	Rose O'Neill	Mr. J. D. Wallis		P. Cowley
TallyHo Hunters Flat H'Cap 2m	Night Time	Mr W.H. West		Mr W.P. Cullen
July 4				
Hill Flat H'Cap 6 Fur 80 yd	Roman Child	Mr T. Vincent		D. Condon
Corporation Chase 3m	Kilgreany	Mr R. Thorpe		J. Ward
Bellewstown Plate Flat 6 Fur 80 yd	Leggan Hall	Mr. J. S. Langan		John Doyle
Grandstand Chase Plate 2m	Night Time	Mr. W. H. West		P. Cowley
Her Majesty's Plate 2 ¼ m	Yellow Vixen	Mr W. Jackson		T. Harris
Meath N.H. Flat Race 2m	Armine	Count Stolberg		Count Stolberg
1902				
July 2				
Hilltown Flat Race 5 Fur	Ferriera	Mrs Sadleir-Jackson		J. Thompson
Stewards H'Cap Chase 3 m	Ledessan	Mr H. M. Wilson		P. Cowley
Crockafotha Flat Handicap 1m	Bayleaf	Ms Mansergh		D. Condon
Drogheda Tradesmen's Chase 2m	Duckey	Mr. J. H. Peard		P. Cowley
TallyHo Hunters Flat H'Cap 2m	Aesculapius	Mr E. Delany		Mr H. Nuttall
July 3				
Hilltown Flat H'Cap 6 Fur 80 yd	Zinga	Mr. F. J. Montgomery		J. Clayton
July H'Cap Chase 2m	Cohiltown	Mr A. Lowry		T. Dent
Bellewstown Plate 6 fur 80 yds	Ferriera	Mrs Sadleir-Jackson		J. Thompson
Grand Stand Chase 2m	Minstrel Girl II	Mr E. Rooney		P. Glynn
His Majesty's Plate 2 ¼ m	Balausta	Mr C. Hill		J. Thompson
Corporation Chase	Moondyne II	Mr D. O'Donnell		Mr M. Hayes
1903				
June 30				
Hilltown Flat Race 5 Fur	Alfar	Mr J. Doyle		H. Buxton
Stewards H'Cap Chase 3 m	Duckey	Mr M. Arnott		P. Cowley
Corporation Flat Handicap 1m	Bayleaf	Ms Mansergh		T. Sadgrove
Drogheda Tradesmen's Chase 2m	Mysterious Lady	Mr O.J. Williams		P. Cowley
TallyHo Hunters Flat H'Cap 2m	The Harlequin	Mr G. L. Walker		Mr R. H. Walker

	Race	Winner	Owner	Trainer	Jockey
July 1	Hill Flat H'Cap 6 Fur 80 yd	Elfeet	Mr J. Doyle		H. Buxton
	Annagor Hunters Flat H'Cap 2 ½ m	St Corinne	Mr E. Delany		Mr M. Hayes
	Bellewstown Plate 6 Fur 80 yds	New Antigone	Mr M. Smith		J. McQuillan
	Grand Stand Chase 2m	Glenmore	Mr P. Fox		P. Cowley
	His Majetsy's Plate 2 ¼ m	Piano	Capt. Ashmore		H. Buxton
	Corporation Chase 3m	Band of Hope	Capt. M. Hughes		P. Cowley
1904					
July 6	Hilltown Flat Race 5 Fur	American Boy	Mr R. Croker		J. Thompson
	Stewards H'Cap Chase 3 m	Musicwood	Lord Rossmore		W. Morgan
	Crockafotha Flat Handicap 1m	Most Noble	Mr. R. Courtney		N. Walsh
	Drogheda Tradesmen Chase 2m	Girton M.A.	Major Sellars		E. Sullivan
	TallyHo Hunters Flat H'Cap 2m	Samari	Lord Durham		Mr M. Arnott
July 7	Hill Flat H'Cap 6 Fur 80 yd	Wild Vixen	Mr W. Jackson		F. Morgan
	Annagor Hunters Flat H'Cap 2 ½ m	North Tyne	Mr M. Arnott		Mr M. Arnott
	Bellewstown Plate 6 Fur 80 yds	American Boy	Mr R. Croker		J. Thompson
	Grand Stand Chase 2m	Mida	Lord Dudley		P. Cowley
	His Majetsy's Plate 2 ¼ m	Lord Victor	Mr J. W. Sullivan		W. Higgs
	Corporation Chase 3m	Duckey	Mr M. Arnott		P. Cowley
1905					
July 5	Hill H'Cap Hurdle 1 ½ m	Golden Jubilee	Mr J. Westlake		A.Anthony
	Hilltown Flat H'Cap 6 Fur 80 yds	Signora	Mr JR Markey		H. Buxton
	Drogheda Tradesmen's Chase 2m	Conari	Mr M. Dawson		Mr T. Price
	Tally Ho Welter Flat H'Cap 2m	Grouse	Capt. R.B. Johnson		Mr J. Langan
	Bellewstown Flat Race 6 Fur 80 yds	Herbert Vincent	Mr R. Croker		J. Thompson
	Corporation Chase 3m	Nenemoo'sha	Mr E. Delany		Capt. Stacpoole
July 6	Legganhall Hurdle 2m	Roseland	Mr S. Aries		R. Morgan
	Grand Stand Chase 2m	Rose Graft	Mr R. H. Walker		Mr R.H. Walker
	His Majesty's Plate 2 ¼ m	Rappel	Mr J. Grew		H. Buxton
	Crockafotha Flat H'Cap 1m	Master Mick	Mr E. Mullally		J. Feghan
	Meath Hunters Flat Race 2m	Armine	Count Stolberg		Count Stolberg
	Stewards H'Cap Chase 3m	Shallon	Mr E. Delany		Mr. R.H. Walker
1906					
July 4	Hill H'Cap Hurdle 1 ½ m	Ardee	Mr E. Mooney		J. Lynn
	Hilltown Flat H'Cap 6 Fur 80 yds	Signora	Mr J.R. Markey		A Anthony
	Drogheda Tradesmen's Chase 2m	Bitter Still	Mr B.W. Parr		J. Lynn
	Tally Ho Welter Flat H'Cap 2m	Delphic	Mr M. Arnott		Mr J. Manley
	Corporation Chase 3m	Peter the Great	R. Hamilton Stubber Jun		Maurice Harty
July 5	Legganhall Hurdle 2m	Mt ProspectFortune	Mr T. Vincent		Mr T. Price
	Crockafotha Flat H'Cap 1m	Indiana	Mr R. Croker		J. Thompson
	His Majesty's Plate 2 ¼ m	Gay Man	Mr J. Dowling		P. Hughes
	Grand Stand Chase 2m	Genuine	Mr H. Whitworth		P. Cowley
	Meath Hunters Flat Race 2m	Wheel-Lock	Mr J.P. Maher		Mr JP Maher

Race	Winner	Owner	Trainer	Jockey
Stewards H'Cap Chase 3m	Flight	Mr J. W. Gregg		Mr R.H. Walker

1907
July 3
Race	Winner	Owner	Trainer	Jockey
Hill H'Cap Hurdle 1 ½ m	Too Clever	Mr J. V. Gilligan	T. Bell	Mr JV Gilligan
Hilltown Flat H'Cap 1m	Bahn	Mr W. Rankin	J. Manley	W. Bullock
Drogheda Tradesmen's Chase 2m	Apollo Belvedere	Col. Kirkwood	J. Currid	Mr R. H Walker
Meath Selling Flat Race 2m	Rustic Queen	Mr Silver	M. Arnott	Mr R. H. Walker
Corporation Chase 3m	Red Orchid	Hon. A.H. Ruthven	M. Arnott	P. Cowley

July 4
Race	Winner	Owner	Trainer	Jockey
Tally Ho Welter H'Cap Flat 2m	Rustic Queen	Mr Silver	M. Arnott	Mr R H. Walker
Grand Stand Chase 2 ¼ m	Clear Case	Mr Tim	M. Arnott	G. Brown
His Majesty's Plate 2 ¼ m	Mrs Lyons	Mr J.O'Neill	M. Dawson	S Donoghue
Stewards H'Cap Chase 3m	Cowboy	Mr J. W. Gregg	Owner	Mr R. H. Walker
Crockafotha Flat H'Cap 1m 3f	Most Noble	Mr R. Courtney	Owner	S. Donoghue
Legganhall Mdn. Chase 2m 1f.	Venetian Mast	Mr P. Rogers	Owner	Mr M. Langan

1908
July 1
Race	Winner	Owner	Trainer	Jockey
Hill H'Cap Hurdle 1 ½ m	Dublin Fusilier	Mr D. P Coady	M. Dawson	Mr T. Price
Hilltown Flat H'Cap 1m	Double Saint	Mr J. C. Lyons	P.F. Hartigan	M. Colbert
Conyngham Cup Chase 3m	Sheepstown	Mr G.B Tunstall-Moore	H. Matthews	Mr C. Brabazon
Drogheda Tradesmen's Chase 2m	St. Conan	Mr G. W. Lushington	J. Hunter	A Anthony
Meath Selling Flat Race 2m	Final Effort	Mr P. J. Brophy	J.J. Parkinson	Mr J. W. Widger
Corporation Chase 3m	Armida	Count Stolberg	Private	Count Stolberg

July 2
Race	Winner	Owner	Trainer	Jockey
Legganhall Hurdle 1 ½ m	Sore Toes	Mr B.W. Carew	G.L. Walker	Mr R.H. Walker
Tally Ho Welter Flat H'Cap 2m	Ranulphus	Mr J. C. Lyons	P.F. Hartigan	Mr T.J. Hartigan
His Majesty's Plate 2 ¼ m	Georgetown	Mr W.W. Bailey	M. Arnott	J. Thompson
Grand Stand Chase 2 ¼ m	Just in Time II	Baron F. de Tuyll	M. Arnott	G. Brown
Crockafotha Flat H'Cap 1m 3 f	Dublin Fusilier	Mr. D.P. Coady	M. Dawson	John Doyle
Stewards H'Cap Chase 3m	Guy	Mr P. Maynard	J.P. Maher	T. Dowdall

1909
July 7
Race	Winner	Owner	Trainer	Jockey
Hill H'Cap Hurdle 1 ½ m	Hampton Lad	Mr H. Matthews	M. Dawson	Mr T. Price
Hilltown Flat H'Cap 1m	Finner	Mr N.J. Kelly	P. Behan	S. Donoghue
Conyngham Cup Chase 3m	Void	Void	Void	Void
Drogheda Tradesmen's Chase 2m	Pleasure Garden	Baron F. de Toyll	M. Arnott	G. Brown
Meath Selling Flat Race 2m	Bill Dell	Mr J. W. Gregg	Owner	Mr L. Brabazon
Corporation Chase 3m	Bally Hackle	Mr K.F. Malcolmson	J.J. Maher	J. Walsh

July 8
Race	Winner	Owner	Trainer	Jockey
Legganhall Hurdle 1 ½ m	Hamperley II	Mr Silver	M. Arnott	G. Brown
Tally Ho Welter Flat H'Cap 2m	Dear Sonny	Mr H.L Fitzpatrick	G.L. Walker	Mr R.H. Walker
His Majesty's Plate 2 ¼ m	Georgetown	Mr W.W. Bailey	M. Arnott	J. Thompson
Grand Stand Chase 2 ¼ m	Red Orchid	Hon. E. O'Brien	M. Arnott	P. Cowley
Crockafotha Flat H'Cap 1m 3 f	Hampton Lad	Mr H. Matthews	M. Dawson	A Sharples
Stewards H'Cap Chase 3m	Small Polly	Mr R.H. Walker	G.L. Walker	Mr R.H. Walker

1910
July 6
Race	Winner	Owner	Trainer	Jockey
Hilltown Flat H'Cap 1m	Balscadden	Mr J. Maher	J.J.Byrne	C. Symes
Hill Chase 2m	Jim May	Mr P. Cullinan	L. Hope	J. Lynn

	Race	Winner	Owner	Trainer	Jockey
	Drogheda Tradesmen's Chase 2m	Sundance	Mr T.C. Moore	M. Dennehy	C. Green
	Conyngham Cup Chase 3m	Pat Cullinan	Mr H.M. Hartigan	R. Moss	R. Moss
	Meath Flat H'Cap 2m	Galoshes	Baron F de Tuyll	M. Arnott	Mr R.H. Walker
July 7	Demesne H'Cap Chase 3m	Small Polly	Mr R.H. Walker	G. Walker	Mr R. H. Walker
	Harbourstown Flat H'Cap 1m	Scillot	Sir T. Dixon	J. Ruttle	Mr J. Barron
	Leggan Hall Chase 2m	Jim May	Mr P. Cullinan	L. Hope	J. Lynn
	His Majesty's Plate 2 ¼ m	Knight of Honour	Mr J.J. Parkinson	Owner	J. Thompson
	Nanny Chase 2 ¼ m	Swift Hack	Mr P. Cullinan	L. Hope	J. Lynn
	Tally Ho Flat Race 2m.	Thimblerigger	Mr A. Lowry	L. Hope	Mr P. Nugent
1911					
July 5	Hilltown Flat H'Cap 1m	Robinstown	Mr R. O'Reilly	J. Smith	J. Hogan
	Hill Chase 2m	Tory Hill II	Mr J.J. Stafford	H. Ussher	R. Trudgill
	Drogheda Tradesmen's Chase 2m	Piccaninny II	Mr R. G. Hope	C. Hope	B. Ellis
	Conyngham Cup Chase 3m	No Saint	Mr J.B. McRoberts	L. Hope	Mr P. Nugent
	Corporation Chase 2 ½ m	Strangegate	Mr J. Ryan	H. Ussher	R. Trudgill
	Meath Welter Flat H'Cap 2m	Chocolate Soldier	Baron F. de Tuyll	M. Arnott	Mr R.H. Walker
July 6	Crockafotha Flat H'Cap 1m 3Fur	Castle Jewel	Sir G. Abercromby	M. Arnott	John Doyle
	Leggan Hall Chase 2m	Tory Hill II	Mr J.j. Stafford	H. Ussher	R. Trudgill
	His Majesty's Plate 2 ¼ m	Spectral	Mr H. Moore	H. Ussher	J. Thompson
	Grandstand Chase 2 ½ m	Simonoff	Mrs Hollins	M. Arnott	Mr L. Brabazon
	Tally Ho Flat Race 2m.	Cresswell	Mr H.M. Hartigan	M. Arnott	Mr H.M. Hartigan
	Stewards H'Cap Chase 3m.	Small Polly	Mr R.H. Walker	G. Walker	Mr R. H. Walker
1912					
July 3	Hilltown Flat H'Cap 1m	Never Again	Mr P. Rogers	P. Behan	J. Thompson
	Hill Chase 2m	Killallon	Mr C. Hope	R.G. Hope	T. Dowdall
	Corporation Flat Race 2 ¼ m.	Heather Decre	Mr E.J. Hope	C. Brabazon	Mr L. Brabazon
	Drogheda Tradesmen's Chase 2m	Cooldreen	Mr P. McLoughlin	Owner	Mr J. Manley
	Meath Flat Race 1m.	Land Agent	Mr P. Cullinan	J. Dunne	John Doyle
	Conyngham Cup Chase 3m	Swallow Hawk	Lord Dudley	M. Arnott	T. Sheridan
July 4	Crockafotha Flat H'Cap 1m 3Fur	Mrs A	Mr C.T. Lewis	M. Dawson	G. Maynard
	Leggan Hall Chase 2m	Lady Fitz	Mr P. Rogers	M. Arnott	T. Sheridan
	His Majesty's Plate 2 ¼ m	Royal Hackle II	Mr P. Cullinan	J. Dunne	John Doyle
	Grandstand Chase 2 ½ m	Squeal	Mr J. Ferzen	M. Arnott	G. Brown
	Bellewstown Flat Race 1m 3 Fur.	Addinstown Prize	Mr H.M. Hartigan	M. Arnott	Mr B.H. Nicholson
	Stewards H'Cap Chase 3m.	Mallusk	Mr J. Barron	Owner	Mr J. Barron
1913					
July 2	Hilltown Flat H'Cap 1m	Faria	Mr W. A. Wallis	R. Harrison	John Doyle
	Hill Chase 2m	Irish Hot	Mr A. Buckley	A. Anthony	Capt P. O'B. Butler
	Corporation Flat Race 2 ¼ m.	Dysie	Mrs N. J. Kelly	G.L. Walker	Mr R.H. Walker
	Drogheda Tradesmen's Chase 2m	Cathal	Mr W. Jackson	M. Dawson	E. Houlihan
	Meath Flat Race 1m	Rosey Ina	Mr J. G. Evans	R. Harrison	John Doyle
	Conyngham Cup Chase 3m	Merry Point	Mr R.H. Walker	G.L. Walker	Mr R.H. Walker

	Race	Winner	Owner	Trainer	Jockey
July 3	Crockafotha Flat H'Cap 1m 3Fur	Halley's Comet	Mr C.T. Lewis	M. Dawson	Jos Canty
	Leggan Hall Chase 2m	Bruce	Mr H.M. Hartigan	Mr Nicholson	Mr B.H. Nicholson
	His Majesty's Plate 2 ¼ m	Royal Hackle II	Mr P. Cullinan	J. Dunne	John Doyle
	Grandstand Chase 2 ½ m	Dysie	Mrs N.J. Kelly	G.L. Walker	Mr R. H. Walker
	Bellewstown Flat Race 1m 3 Fur.	Persian Chief	Mr H.M. Hartigan	Mr Nicholson	G. Duller
	Stewards H'Cap Chase 3m.	Giacomo	Mr P. Rogers	M. Arnott	B. Twombley
1914					
July 1	Hilltown Flat H'Cap 1m	Enchanted Prince	Mr R. Courtney	Owner	P. Hughes
	Hill Chase 2m	Turkish Maiden	Mr R. Downes	R.G. Cleary	W. Lynn
	Corporation Flat Race 2 ¼ m.	Persian Chief	Ms Garth	M. Arnott	Mr H.M. Hartigan
	Drogheda Tradesmen's Chase 2m	Suffragette Sally	Mr H.M. Hartigan	B. Nicholson	Mr B. M. Nicholson
	Meath Flat Race 1m	Rathleague	Mr P. Rogers	M. Arnott	C. Barrett
July 2	Conyngham Cup Chase 3m	Alice Rockthorn	Major Honner	Owner	W. Lynn
	Crockafotha Flat H'Cap 1m 3Fur	Double Ditch	Mr T.H. Hartigan	Owner	C. Barrett
	Leggan Hall Chase 2m	Miss Devlin	Mr B. Kirby	Owner	M. Colbert
	His Majesty's Plate 2 ¼ m	Ballyneety	Mr H. F. Malcolmson	W. Ussher	Mr L. Brabazon
	Grandstand Chase 2 ½ m	Clonmeen	Mr S. Grehan	M. Arnott	F. Hunter
	Bellewstown Flat Race 1m 3 fur.	First O'May	Mr T.J. Daly	C. Brabazon	F. Pike
		Spoofer	Mr G. Edwarde	T.J. Hartigan	Mr W.J. Parkinson
	Stewards H'Cap Chase 3m.	NeverFear	Mr T. Nolan	G.L. Walker	F. Morgan
1915					
July 7	Hilltown Flat H'Cap 1m	Opportuna	Mr D.J. Power	B. Kirby	P. Lynch
	Hill Chase 2m	Mabestown	Mr C. Hope	Owner	John Gleeson
	Meath Flat Race 1m	Bee Fast	Lord Saville	M. Arnott	Mr W.J. Parkinson
	Drogheda Tradesmen's Chase 2m	Turkish Prince	Lady E. Ainsworth	M. Arnott	M. Farragher
	Bellewstown Flat Race 1m 3Fur.	Symont	Mr. D.M. Gant	J. McKenna	D. McKenna
	Conyngham Cup Chase 3m	German	Mr E. Delany	T. Matthews	Mr J. Manley
July 8	Crockafotha Flat H'Cap 1m 3Fur	Raw Material	Mr J. O'Callaghan		F. Hunter
	Match Race Chase	Night Out	Mr T. Byrne	M. Arnott	M. Farragher
	Leggan Hall Chase 2m	St. Agatha	Mr P. Fox	R. Fetherston	C. Hawkins
	His Majesty's Plate 2 ¼ m	Royal Weaver	Mr P. Cullinan	R. Fetherston	John Doyle
	Grandstand Chase 2 ½ m	Crove Derg	Mrs Croft	H. Ussher	Mr L. Brabazon
	Corporation Flat Race 2 ¼ m.	Cello	Mr M. Arnott	M. Arnott	Mr L. Brabazon
	Stewards H'Cap Chase 3m.	Alice Rockthorn	Mr J. Nugent	A Anthony	Mr P. Nugent
1916					
July 5	Hilltown Flat H'Cap 1m	Pamerine	Mr A. Anthony	A Anthony	W. Williams
	Hill Chase 2m	Golden Fleece	Mr L.S. Ward	W. Ward	Mr L.S. Ward
	Meath Flat Race 1m	Le Connetable	Mr W. F. Egerton	R. Armstrong	R. Crisp
	Drogheda Tradesmen's Chase 2m	Shaun Spadah	Mr F. Barbour	R.H. Walker	Mr H.S. Harrison
	Bellewstown Flat Race 1m 3Fur.	Trepam	Mrs N.J. Kelly	J.T. Rogers	Mr J. Manley
	Conyngham Cup Chase 3m	Genus	Mr E. Delany	E. Delany	B. Twombley
July 6	Crockafotha Flat H'Cap 1m 3Fur	Bachelor's Trick	Mr A. Lowry	J.J. Parkinson	Jos. Harty

	Race	Winner	Owner	Trainer	Jockey
	Leggan Hall Chase 2m	Sultan	Mr T.S. Kirk	Mr T.S. Kirk	W. Smith
	His Majesty's Plate 2 ¼ m	Noham	Mr T. McMahon	M. Dawson	T. Burns
	Grandstand Chase 2 ½ m	Albany Beef	Mr F. Hickman	A. Poole	S. Avila
	Corporation Flat Race 2 ¼ m.	Henriette	Mr J.J. Parkinson	J.J. Parkinson	Mr W.J. Parkinson
	Stewards H'Cap Chase 3m.	Golden Fleece	Mr L.S. Ward	W. Ward	Mr L.S. Ward
1917					
July 4	Hilltown Flat H'Cap 1m	Desmond M	Mr E. Clark	Jas Burns	T. Burns
	Hill Chase 2m	War Flour	Mr C. Odlum	J.A.B. Trench	J. Cahalin
	Meath Flat Race 1m	Carrigacurra	Mr P. Murphy	J.J. Parkinson	W. Barrett
	Drogheda Tradesmen's Chase 2m	Shaun Spadah	Mr F. Barbour	RFetherstonhaugh	C. Hawkins
	Bellewstown Flat Race 1m 3Fur.	Royal Truce	Mr P. Cullinan	J.J. Parkinson	Mr W. J. Parkinson
	Conyngham Cup Chase 3m	The Last	Mr B.W. Parr	M. Arnott	F. Morgan
July 5	Crockafotha Flat H'Cap 1m 3Fur	Distinguished	Mr D.M. Gant	W. Rankin	J. Clark
	Leggan Hall Chase 2m	Irish Field	Mr D. O'M Leahy	J.J. Parkinson	M. Connors
	His Majesty's Plate 2 ¼ m	Parley	Mr D. M. Gant	W. Rankin	J. Clark
	Grandstand Chase 2 ½ m	Meridian	Mr H.M. Hartigan	H.M. Hartigan	Mr A. Stubbs
	Corporation Flat Race 2 ¼ m.	St. Fanshea	Mr P.J. Byrne	P.J. Byrne	Mr C. Brabazon
	Stewards H'Cap Chase 3m.	Privit	Major McCalmont	M. Arnott	F. Morgan
1918					
July 3	Hilltown Flat H'Cap 1m	Metallic	Mr A. Christie	W. Rankin	J. Dines
	Hill Chase 2m	Flying Lady	Mr. P. Cullinan	R. H. Walker	M. Dowdall
	Bellewstown Flat Race 2m	Adequate	Mr T.D. McKeever	R. H. Walker	Mr. H.S. Harrison
	Drogheda Tradesmen's Chase 2m	Roman General	Mr T. Byrne	T. Byrne	F. Morgan
	Meath Flat Race 2m.	Good Health	Mr H.S. Harrison	R.H. Walker	Mr H.S. Harrison
	Conyngham Cup Chase 3m	Meridian	Mr H.R. West	J.H. Burke	A Stubbs
July 4	Crockafotha Flat H'Cap 1m 3Fur	Gemsbok	Mr H.M. Hartigan	M. Arnott	D. Ward
	Leggan Hall Chase 2m	Swordknot	Mr L. Brabazon	L. Brabazon	N. Hayes
	His Majesty's Plate 2 ¼ m	Jenny Jones	Mr J.C. McKeever	R.H. Walker	W. Barrett
	Stewards H'Cap Chase 3m.	Privit	Major McCalmont	M. Arnott	F. Morgan
	Corporation Flat Race 2 ¼ m.	Flavia	Mr. Jos. Kelly	G.S. Kirk	Mr F.F. Tuthill
	Grandstand Chase 2 ½ m	Gerard L.	Major Scott Murray	H. Ussher	J. Hogan
	Summer Flat Race 1m.	Good Health	Mr H.S. Harrison	R.H. Walker	Mr H. S. Harrison
1919					
July 2	Hilltown Flat H'Cap 1m	Vagabond	Mr R. McGarry	R.R. Mahon	J. Killalee
	Hill Chase 2m	Temple Bar	Mr W.P. Gill	J.A. B. Trench	J. Cahalin
	Bellewstown Flat Race 1m	Mayhap	Mr H. M. Hartigan	H.M. Hartigan	Jos. Canty
	Drogheda Tradesmen's Chase 2m	Ben Cruachan	Mr H.H. McGill	R.H. Walker	W. S. Smith
	Meath Flat Race 1m	Privit	Mr M. Arnott	M. Arnott	H. Harty
	Conyngham Cup Chase 3m	Faricate	Mr H.S. Harrison	R.H. Walker	W. Barrett
	Grandstand Chase 2 ½ m	Gay Damsel	Mr T. O'Rourke	T. O'Roarke	N Hayes
July 3	Crockafotha Flat H'Cap 1m 3Fur	Saxham Prince	Mr T.D. McKeever	R.H. Walker	W. Barrett
	Leggan Hall Chase 2m	Rather Dark	Capt. Morgan	A Anthony	W. Smith

Year	Date	Race	Winner	Owner	Trainer	Jockey
1920		His Majesty's Plate 2 ¼ m	Cellar Glen	Mrs M. Scott	C. Brabazon	J. Patman
		Stewards H'Cap Chase 3m.	St. Pam	Mr E. Delany	S. Matthews	D. Colbert
		Corporation Flat Race 2 ½ m.	Fire Screen	Sir G. Abercromby	H.M. Hartigan	Jos. Canty
		Grandstand Chase 2 ½ m	St Enda's	Mr L. Ward	W. Ward	B. Twombley
	July 7	Meath Hurdle 2m	Aimless	Mr B.W. Parr	M. Arnott	M. Dillon
		Hilltown Flat H'Cap 1m	Ballyfore	Mr C. Hope	C. Hope	C. Aylin
		Drogheda Tradesmen's Chase 2m	Hawker	Mr T.B. Bennett	R. Moss	J. Moylan
		Bellewstown Flat Race 2m	Ellen Gibby	Mr W. Duffy	C. Prendergast	Mr F.F. Tuthill
		Hill Chase 2m	Dowdstown	Mr H. Loughran	L. Brabazon	N. Hayes
		Conyngham Cup Chase 3m	SouthSea	Baron de Tuyll	H.M. Hartigan	Jos Canty
	July 8	Crockafotha Flat H'Cap 1 ½ m	Silver Morsel	Mr F. Burke	M. Dawson	Jos Canty
		Corporation Flat Race 1m.	Kilcruttin	Mr JM Prior-Kennedy	C. Brabazon	H. Beasley
		Steward's H'Cap Chase 3m	Aegean	Mr E.L. Lloyd	R. Moss	J. Moylan
		His Majesty's Plate 2 ¼ m	Vagabond	Mr C. Prendergast	C. Prendergast	M. Beary
		Leggan Hall Chase 2m	Kilcullen	Mr J. Fox	J. Fox	P. Powell
		Grandstand Chase 2 ½ m	Pam Nut	Mr E. Delany	E. Delany	C. Aylin
1921	July 6	Meath Hurdle 2m	The Trade	Mr L.H. Reynolds	J. Banahan	J. Banahan
		Hilltown Flat H'Cap 1m	Enchanted Duke	Mr R. Courtney	R. Courtney	M. Colbert
		Drogheda Tradesmen's Chase 2m	Zenon	Mr C.O'Reilly	R.H. Walker	C. Aylin
		Bellewstown Flat Race 2m	Quai d'Orsai	Mr J.L. McGlew	J.L. McGlew	F. Hunter
		Hill Chase 2m	Ayesha	Mr B. L. Coleman	B. L. Coleman	P. Powell
		Conyngham Cup Chase 3m	Speculation II	Major Beamish	Major Beamish	P. Rogers
	July 7	Crockafotha Flat H'Cap 1 ½ m	The Tatler	Mr F.B. O'Toole	M. Dawson	J. Hogan Jnr
		Corporation Flat Race 1m.	Charabanc	Mr T. Mullen	T. Mullen	P. Mullen Jnr
		Steward's H'Cap Chase 3m	Ben Cruachan	Mr F. Barbour	R.H. Walker	C. Aylin
		His Majesty's Plate 2 ¼ m	Tiermourne	Mr G.H. Lowry	M. Dawson	H. Jameson
		Leggan Hall Chase 2m	Hester Island	Mr J. Rolleston	J.A.B. Trench	M. Connors
		Grandstand Chase 2 ½ m	Battle Royal	Mr P. Wilkinson	P. Wilkinson	T. Carbery
1922		July meeting abandoned due to Civil War				
	Sept 1	Crockafotha H'Cap Hurdle 1m 5fur	Graystown	Mr J.J. Kennedy	R.G. Cleary	J. McCarthy
		Hilltown Flat H'Cap 1m	Merry Miner	Mr T.D. McKeever	R.H. Walker	C. Aylin
		Drogheda Tradesmen's Chase 2m	Zenon	Mr C.O'Reilly	R.H. Walker	C. Aylin
		His Majesty's Plate 2 ¼ m	Crock Hill	Capt. J. Collins	R.H. Walker	C. Aylin
		Conyngham Club Chase 3m	Drinmond	Mr P. Rogers	M. Arnott	D. Ward
		Bellewstown Flat Race 2m	Shannon Fairy	Mr F.F. McDonagh	F.F. McDonagh	Mr P.J. Osborne
		Hill Chase 2m	Helmet	Mr J. Magee	J. Farrell	P. Powell
1923	July 4	Meath Hurdle 1m 5fur	Trayeen Trisough	Mr H.M. Hartigan	H.M. Hartigan	T. Burns
		Hilltown Flat H'Cap 1m	Sunny Bird	Col. Croft	H. Ussher	H. Beasley

	Race	Winner	Owner	Trainer	Jockey
	Drogheda Tradesmen's Chase 2m	Helmet	Mr J. Magee	C. Brabazon	W. Horan
	Bellewstown Flat Race 2m	Ellen's Beau	Mr P. Rogers	M. Arnott	Mr C. Brabazon
	Hill Chase 2m	Chatillon	Mr E. Kennedy	J. Hayde	J. Moloney
	Conyngham Cup Chase 3m	Harry Hart	Mr C.A. Rogers	M. Arnott	G. Brown
July 5	Crockafotha Flat H'Cap 1m 5 fur	Trayeen Trisough	Mr H.M. Hartigan	H.M. Hartigan	A. Escott
	Leggan Hall Chase 2m	Double B.	Mr E.J. Hope	R.H. Walker	T. Kelly Jnr
	His Majesty's Plate 2 ¼ m	Doublefirst	Mr P. Rogers	M. Arnott	D. Ward
	Steward's H'Cap Chase 3m	Brendan's Glory	Mr D. Quinlish	R.H. Walker	A. Escott
	Corporation Flat Race 1m.	Marchaway	Mr J. Fullam	M. Arnott	D. Ward
	Grandstand Chase 2 ½ m	Silver Hackle	Mr P. Cullinan	R.H. Walker	T. Kelly Jnr
1924					
July 2	Meath Hurdle 1m 5 fur	Happy Release	Col. Croft	H. Ussher	J. Hogan Jnr
	Hilltown Flat H'Cap 1m	Sunny Bird	Col. Croft	H. Ussher	T. Morgan
	Drogheda Tradesmen's Chase 2m	Goffee	Mrs Croft	H. Ussher	J. Hogan Jnr
	Bellewstown Flat Race 2m	Treble Applause	Mr. P. Rogers	M. Arnott	Mr C. Brabazon
	Hill Chase 2m	Menelaus	Mr R. Power	H. Ussher	J. Hogan Jnr
	Conyngham Cup Chase 3m	Ischevaha	Mr. E.W. Hope Johnstone	M. Arnott	D. Ward
July 3	Crockafotha Flat H'Cap 1 m 5 fur	Knight Templar	Mr H.M. Hartigan	H.M. Hartigan	Jos Canty
	Leggan Hall Chase 2m	Take Notice	Sir T. Ainsworth	H.C. Alexander	W. Horan
	His Majesty's Plate 2 ¼ m	Blue Fish	Mr P. Rogers	M. Arnott	D. Ward
	Steward's H'Cap Chase 3m	Golden Street	Mrs Croft	H. Ussher	J. Hogan Jnr
	Corporation Flat Race 2m.	Commandant Dan	Mr C. McLaughlin	T. Taaffe	A. Barrett
	Grandstand Chase 2 ½ m	Glass Island	Mrs Croft	H. Ussher	J. Hogan Jnr
1925					
July 1	Meath Hurdle 1m 5 fur	Lutoi	Mr D. J. Cogan	M. Rice	D. Ward
	Hilltown Flat H'Cap 1m	Flying Prince	Mr T.P. O'Neill	J. Lenehan	W. Redmond
	Drogheda Tradesmen's Chase 2m	Goffee	Mrs Croft	H. Ussher	J. Hogan Jnr
	Bellewstown Plate 2m Bumper	Letham	Mrs J.D. Wilkinson	H.M. Hartigan	Major R.H. Scott
	Conyngham Club Cup Chase 3m	Nurney	Mr J. Fitzsimons	D. Malone	Mr F.J. Malone
	Hill Novice Chase 2m	Blancona	Mr F. Barbour	C. Brabazon	C. Donnelly
July 2	Crockafotha Flat H'Cap 1 m 5 fur	Kildarra Boy	Mr W. O'Driscoll	M.Dawson	Jos Canty
	Leggan Hall Novice Chase 2m	Puri	Mr A.D. Comyn	H. Ussher	J. Hogan Jnr
	His Majesty's Plate 2 ¼ m	Blue Fish	Mr P. Rogers	M. Arnott	D. Ward
	Steward's H'Cap Chase 3m	Rising Moon	Mr E.W. Hope Johnstone	M. Arnott	D. Ward
	Corporation Maiden Plate 1m.	Beddgelert	Mr R.J. Duggan	M. Arnott	M. Wing
	Grandstand H'Cap 2 m Flat	Bri Leith	Mr P. Kenny	T. O'Roarke	Mr T. O'Roarke
1926					
July 7	Meath Hurdle 1m 5 fur	Grosvenor's Reward	Mr J. J. Parkinson	J.J. Parkinson	J. Moylan
	Hilltown Flat H'Cap 1m	Ambrose	Mr J.J. Parkinson	J.J. Parkinson	E.M. Quirke
	Drogheda Tradesmen's H'Cap 2m	Burgomaster	Mr J. Leech	E. Delany	M. Hynes
	Bellewstown Plate 2m Bumper	Irish Destiny	Mr T.D. McKeever	T.D. McKeever	Major R.H. Scott
	Hill Novice Chase 2m	Anillab	Mr E. Donnelly	T. Taaffe	J. Hogan Jnr

	Race	Winner	Owner	Trainer	Jockey
July 8	Conyngham Club Cup Chase 2 ½ m	Oliver's Mint	Mr T. O'Roarke	T.O'Roarke	J. McNeill
	Crockafotha H'Cap Hurdle 1 m 5 fur	Kildarra Boy	Mr W. O'Driscoll	M. Dawson	J. Moloney
	Duleek Novice Chase 2m	Anillab	Mr E. Donnelly	T. Taaffe	J. Hogan Jnr
	His Majesty's Plate 2 ¼ m	Louvixen	Mr T.P. O'Neill	J.J. Parkinson	E. M. Quirke
	Annagor H'Cap Chase 3m	Stage Management	Mr P. Dunne Cullinan	P. Dunne Cullinan	J. Moylan
	Shallon Maiden 1m	Petit Beau	Capt. Maher	M. Dawson	Jos Canty
		Lord Burdon	Mr C. Fagan	C. Brabazon	J.H. Harty
	Grandstand H'Cap 2 m Flat	Striped Silk	Mr R. Power	H. Ussher	Mr J. H. de Bromhead
1927					
July 6	Meath Hurdle 1m 5 fur	Buster	Mr T. D. McKeever	T.D. McKeever	Mr F.E. McKeever
	Hilltown Flat H'Cap 1m	Ebb Tide	Mr A.D. Comyn	H. Ussher	J. Moylan
	Drogheda Tradesmen's Chase 2m	Odd Cat	Mr T. Ray	T. Ray	J. McNeill
	Bellewstown Plate Bumper 2m	Prickly	Major D. St.G. Daly	H. Ussher	Mr T.B. Cullinan
	Hill Novice Chase 2m	Toitive	Mrs R.H. Walker	R.H. Walker	W. Beasley
	Conyngham Club Cup Chase 2 ½ m	Orby's Beau	Mr T. O'Roarke	T. O'Roarke	J. McNeill
July 7	Crockafotha H'Cap Hurdle 1 m 5 fur	Bachelor's Hobby	Mr A. Lowry	M. Dawson	Jos Canty
	Leggan Hall Novice Chase 2m	Tramon Lad	Capt. J.R. Collins	R.H. Walker	J. Moloney
	His Majesty's Plate 2 ¼ m	Lomond's Lake	Mr P.W. Shaw	J.J. Parkinson	J. Moylan
	Steward's H'Cap Chase 3m	Catriona	Mr T.J. Taaffe	T.J. Taaffe	J. McNeill
	Corporation Maiden 1m.	Duratoi	Mr R.H. Walker	R.H. Walker	J. Moylan
	Grandstand H'Cap Flat 2 m	Brugh	Mr E. Delany	E. Delany	Mr T.B. Cullinan
1928					
July 4	Meath Hurdle 1m 5 fur	Tiranogue	Mr W.W. Ashe	W.W. Ashe	T.B. Cullinan
	Hilltown Flat H'Cap 1m	Argentan	Mr R.H. Walker	R.H. Walker	John Doyle
	Drogheda Tradesmen's Chase 2m	Carlovia	Mr W.E. Melbourne	W.W. Ashe	T.B. Cullinan
	Bellewstown Plate Bumper 2m	Crafty Maid	Mr A. Lowry	C. Brabazon	Mr C. Brabazon
	Hill Novice Chase 2m	Lloydie	Mr J. Laverty	M. Arnott	Mr T. Nugent
	Conyngham Club Cup Chase 2 ½ m	Orby's Beau	Mr T. O'Roarke	T. O'Roarke	J.McNeill
July 5	Crockafotha H'Cap Hurdle 1 m 5 fur	Orby's Beau	Mr T. O'Roarke	T. O'Roarke	J.McNeill
	Leggan Hall Novice Chase 2m	Southern Witch	Col. Sir G. Abercromby	H. Hartigan	J.H. Harty
	His Majesty's Plate 2 ¼ m	Striped Silk	Mr R. Power	H. Ussher	J. Moylan
	Steward's H'Cap Chase 3m	Lisworney	Ms M. Feore	M. Dawson	J. Lynn Jnr
	Corporation Maiden 1m.	Brushlight	Mr E Bellaney	H. Ussher	J. Moylan
	Shallon H'Cap Flat 2 m	Bathoi	Mr R. O'Neill	J. Turner	Mr T. Nugent
1929					
July 3	Meath Hurdle 1m 5 fur	Liscarroll Castle	Mr B.W. Purdon	M. Arnott	D.Ward
	Hilltown Flat H'Cap 1m	Helena's Gem	Mr E.J. Hope	C. Brabazon	M. Wing
	Drogheda Tradesmen's Chase 2m	Mintsprig	Sir T. Dixon	M. Arnott	D. Ward
	Bellewstown Plate Bumper 2m	Culnagor	Mr J. Laverty	M. Arnott	Mr T. Nugent
	Hill Novice Chase 2m	Slater	Mr M. Arnott	M. Arnott	D. Ward
	Conyngham Club Cup Chase 2 ½ m	Orby's Beau	Mr T. O'Roarke	T. O'Roarke	J.McNeill
July 4	Crockafotha H'Cap Hurdle 1 m 5 fur	Carmenita	Mr J. Brennan	F. Mitchell	M. Hynes

	Race	Winner	Owner	Trainer	Jockey
	Leggan Hall Novice Chase 2m	Laudamus	Mr E.J. Kieran	M. Arnott	D.Ward
	His Majesty's Plate 2 ¼ m	Pucka Ranee	Mr J.A. Mangan	J.A. Mangan	E.M. Quirke
	Steward's H'Cap Chase 3m	South Louth	Major H.D. Beamish	Major Beamish	Mr F.E. McKeever
	Corporation Maiden 1m.	Misterin Lad	Mr F. Rogers	W. Hilliard	W. Beasley
	Grandstand H'Cap Flat 1m 5 fur.	Liscarroll Castle	Mr B.W. Purdon	M. Arnott	Mr T. Nugent
1930					
July2	Meath Hurdle 1m 5 fur	Matador	Lady Brooke	M. Arnott	Mr T. Nugent
	Hilltown Flat H'Cap 1m	Rush Point	Lieut. Col. Fenwick Palmer	H. Ussher	J. Moylan
	Drogheda Tradesmen's Chase 2m	Culnagor	Mr J. Laverty	M. Arnott	Mr T. Nugent
	Bellewstown Plate Bumper 2m	Aeolus	Mr W.J. Hilliard	W.J. Hilliard	Mr W.J. Hilliard
	Hill Novice Chase 2m	Hakeen	Major Gerard	H. Hartigan	Mr F.E. McKeever
		The Black Fellow	Mr C. Brady	J. Osborne	M. Hynes
	Duleek Chase 3m	Groundsheet	Sir T. Ainsworth	M. Arnott	J.McNeill
July 3	Crockafotha H'Cap Hurdle 1 m 5 fur	Koscie's Star	Mr H.C. McNally	R. H. Walker	Mr F.E. McKeever
	Leggan Hall Novice Chase 2m	Partesian	Mr J.D. Wilkinson	J.D. Wilkinson	Mr I.R. Alder
	His Majesty's Plate 2 ¼ m	Pucka Ranee	Mr J.A. Mangan	J.A. Mangan	E.M. Quirke
	Steward's H'Cap Chase 3m	South Louth	Major H. Beamish	Major Beamish	Mr F.E. McKeever
	Corporation Maiden 1m.	Clear Note	Mr J.P. Maher	M. Arnott	E.M. Quirke
	Shallon H'Cap Flat 1 m 5 fur.	Knuckleduster	Major Beamish	Major Beamish	Mr F.E. McKeever
1931					
July1	Meath Hurdle 1m 5 fur	Knuckleduster	Major Beamish	Major Beamish	Mr F.E. McKeever
	Hilltown Flat H'Cap 1m	Son's West	Mr J.J. Parkinson	J.J. Parkinson	M. Barrett
	Drogheda Tradesmen's Chase 2m	Old Bachelor	Mrs B.M. Webster	C.A. Rogers	S. Magee
	Bellewstown Plate Bumper 2m	Essexhall	Mrs B.M. Webster	C.A. Rogers	Mr W.J. Hillirad
	Hill Novice Chase 2m	Black Willow	Mrs J. Cunningham	T. J. Taaffe	J.McNeill
	Duleek Chase 3m	Thomond II	Duke de Stacpoole	R.H. Walker	Mr F.E. McKeever
July 2	Crockafotha H'Cap Hurdle 1 m 5 fur	Knight's Battle	Mr A.D. Comyn	H. Ussher	J. Moylan
	Leggan Hall Novice Chase 2m	Tennessee	Mr J.E. Ryan	M. Arnott	Mr T. Nugent
	His Majesty's Plate 2 ¼ m	Nice Token	Mr J.T. Rogers	J.T. Rogers	E.M. Quirke
	Steward's H'Cap Chase 3m	Groundsheet	Sir T. Ainsworth	M. Arnott	Mr T. Nugent
	Corporation Maiden 1m.	Orange Girl	Mgt. Lady Nelson	J. Ruttle	M.Wing
	Shallon H'Cap Flat 1 m 5 fur.	Priory Prince	Mr C.J. Wall	M. Arnott	Mr T. Nugent
1932					
July 6	Meath Hurdle 1m 5 Fur	One More	Mr E. Delany	E. Delany	S. Regan
	Hilltown Flat H'Cap 1m	Orange Girl	Mr E.J. Hope	J. Ruttle	John Doyle
	Drogheda Tradesmen's Chase 2m	Sherdoon	Mrs M. Dawson	J. Dawson	J. Costello
	Bellewstown Plate Bumper 2m	Biddles	Mr B.L. Coleman	H. Ussher	Mr I.R. Alder
	Hill Novice Chase 2m	Lady Bremen	Mr D. Murray	D. Murray	Jos Doyle
	Duleek Chase 3 m	Ballymoe	Mr J.M. Ennis	J.M. Ennis	Mr I.R. Alder
July 7	Crockafotha Flat H'Cap 1 m 5 Fur	Lady Frivol	Lady H. McCalmont	H. Hartigan	T. Burns
	Leggan Hall Novice Chase 2m	Jack's Fancy	Mr J.B. Richards	M. Arnott	T. McNeill

Year	Date	Race	Winner	Owner	Trainer	Jockey
		His Majesty's Plate 2 ¼ m	Rada	Mr G.F. Gillespie	J.A Mangan	Jos Canty
		Steward's H'Cap Chase 3m	Flying Dale	Mr R.J. Power	T.J. Taaffe	Mr R.J. Power
		Corporation Maiden 1 m	Chieftain	Mr R.S. Croker	C. Brabazon	T. Burns
		Shallon H'Cap Flat 1 m 5 Fur	Modest Study	Mr N. Kelly	J.A. Mangan	Mr J.A. Mangan
1933	July 5	Meath Hurdle 1m 5 Fur	South Louth	Major H. Beamish	Major Beamish	Mr F. E. McKeever
		Dardistown Novice Chase 2m	Bowmint	Mr Bowes Daly	Fetherstonhaugh	S. Magee
		Drogheda Tradesmen's Chase 2m	Lady Bremen	Mr D. Murray	D. Murray	P.J. Murray
		Bellewstown Plate Bumper 2m	Speakeasy II	Mr E. Delany	E. Delany	Mr P. Sleator
		Hill Chase 2m	Lacatoi	Lady Nugent	R.H. Walker	Mr F. E. McKeever
		Hilltown Flat H'Cap 1m	Three Star	Mr J.J. Sullivan	J.J.Parkinson	M. Barrett
	July 6	Crockafotha Flat H'Cap 1 m 5 Fur	Silver Work	Mr R. Collen	R.Collen	W. Gilmour
		Corporation Maiden 1 m	If You Please	Sir J. Nelson	J. Ruttle	E.M. Quirke
		Ardcath H'Cap Chase 3m	Lerida	Mr J.S. Leonard	T.R. McKeever	Mr T.R.McKeever
		Naul H'Cap Flat 1m 5 Fur	Cairn Lassie	Mr J. O'Brien	J.J. Parkinson	Mr E. Parkinson
		Leggan Hall Novice Chase 2m	Crockafotha	Mr T.R. McKeever	T.R. McKeever	Mr T.R. McKeever
		His Majesty's Plate 2 ¼ m	Santaria	Sir J. Nelson	J. Ruttle	E.M. Quirke
1934	July 4	Meath Hurdle 1m 5 Fur	Decant	Mr W.J. Hilliard	R.H. Walker	F. E. McKeever
		Duleek Novice Chase 2m	Magnum II	Mr E. Delany	E. Delany	T. Regan
		Drogheda Tradesmen's Chase 2m	Mollison	Mrs J. Bennett	R.H. Walker	F. E. McKeever
		Bellewstown Plate Bumper 2m	Poolgowran	Sir J. Nelson	J. Ruttle	R. Everett
		Hill Chase 2m	Lady Lustre	Mr D.J. Cogan	W. Magee	Mr D.L. Moore
		Hilltown H'Cap Flat 1m	Strolling Witch	Mrs M. O'Regan	J. Kirwan	A Thompson
	July 5	Crockafotha Flat H'Cap 1 m 5 Fur	Spanish Red	Mr T.R. McKeever	T.R. McKeever	T. Burns
		Corporation Maiden 1 m	Slanthe	Mr E. Delany	E. Delany	T. Regan
			Mount Essex	Mrs Shirley	J.T. Rogers	E. Gardner
			Coollattin	Lord Milton	H. Ussher	J. Moylan
		Steward's H'Cap Chase 3m	Cottage Owl	Mr M. McCabe	M. Arnott	W.T. O'Grady
		Shallon H'Cap Flat 1 m 5 Fur	Toga	Mr P.D. Matthews	H. Ussher	Mr J.H. de Bromhead
		Leggan Hall Novice Chase 2m	Biddles	Mrs Croft	H. Ussher	W.T. O' Grady
		His Majesty's Plate 2 ¼ m	High Prestige	Mr H.G. Wellesley	H.G. Wellesley	P. Maher
1935	July 3	Meath Hurdle 1m 5 Fur	Yellow Furze	Lt. Col. S. Hill-Dillon	Fetherstonhaugh	T. Regan
		Duleek Novice Chase 2m	Mollison	Mrs J. Bennett	R.H. Walker	F. E. McKeever
		Hilltown Flat H'Cap 1m	Moleskin Joe	Mr D. Malone	D. Malone	W. Howard
		Drogheda Tradesmen's Chase 2m	Markington	Major H.C. Robinson	R.H. Walker	F. E. McKeever
		Hill H'Cap Chase 2m	Suir View	Mr Jos McGrath	H. Ussher	W.T. O'Grady
		Bellewstown Plate Bumper 2m	Viva France	Mr J.J. Parkinson	J.J. Parkinson	Mr E. Parkinson
	July 4	Crockafotha Flat H'Cap 1 m 5 Fur	Golden Dragon	Mrs Croft	H. Ussher	W.T. O'Grady
		His Majesty's Plate 2 ¼ m	Delightful	Mr W. Johns	H.G. Wellesley	Peter Maher
		Steward's H'Cap Chase 3m	Water Gipsy	Sir T. Ainsworth	M. Arnott	W.T. O'Grady

Race	Winner	Owner	Trainer	Jockey
1936				
Shallon H'Cap Flat 1m 5 Fur	Drucetown	Lady Nelson	Major Scott	Major Scott
Leggan Hall Chase 2m	Little Ant	Mr T. Plunkett	T. Plunkett	J. McCarthy
Corporation Maiden 1m	Miss Honour	Mrs R.C. Dawson	H.G. Wellesley	Peter Maher
July 1				
Meath Hurdle 1m 5 Fur	Bard of Meath	Mr C.H. Nicholson	T.R. McKeever	F. E. McKeever
Duleek Novice Chase 2m	Speakeasy II	Mr E. Delany	E. Delany	T. Regan
Hilltown Flat H'Cap 1m	Derryormonde	Mr D.V. Morris	M. Arnott	W. Barrett
Drogheda Tradesmen's Chase 2m	Magnum II	Mr E. Delany	E. Delany	T. Regan
Bellewstown Plate Bumper 2m	Mountain Breeze	Capt. J.A. Hornsby	T.R. McKeever	Mr M.JO'H. McArdle
Hill Handicap Chase 2m	Little Thrill	Mr J. Cox	J. Cox	M.C. Prendergast
July 2				
Crockafotha H'Cap Hurdle 1m 5 Fur	Embattle	Mr C.J. Pope	R.H. Walker	F. E. McKeever
His Majesty's Plate 2¼ m	Axle	Sir P. Lorraine	R. More O'Ferrall	E.M. Quirke
Steward's H'Cap Chase 3m	Water Gipsy	Sir T. Ainsworth	M. Arnott	W.T. O'Grady
Shallon H'Cap Flat 1m 5 Fur	Clatterbox	Mr E. Delany	E. Delany	Mr P. Sleator
Leggan Hall Chase 2m	Southern Era	Mr M. McCabe	M. Arnott	F. E. McKeever
Corporation Maiden 1m	Glendine	Mr J.P. Kennedy	W.W. Ashe	W. Howard
1937				
June 30				
Meath Hurdle 1m 5 Fur	Opticien II	Mr J.V. Rank	Fetherstonhaugh	P. Murray
Duleek Novice Chase 2m	Mar-Din	Mr T. Morrow	J. Turner	M.C. Prendergast
Hilltown Flat H'Cap 1m	Golden Toff	Mrs Croft	H. Ussher	J. Moylan
Drogheda Tradesmen's Chase 2m	Vesuvian	Mr P. Dunne Cullinan	M. Arnott	F. E. McKeever
Bellewstown Plate Bumper 2m	Baybush	Ms H. Ball	J. W. Osborne	Mr P. Sleator
Hill H'Cap Chase 2m	Decant	Mr W.J. Hilliard	W.J. Hilliard	Jerry Fitzgerald
July 1				
Crockafotha H'Cap Hurdle	Embattle	Mr C.J. Pope	R.H. Walker	F. E. McKeever
His Majesty's Plate 2¼ m	Foxie	Mr J.H. Whitney	H. Ussher	J. Moylan
Steward's H'Cap Chase 3m	Golden Star	Mr. W. Ronaldson	R.H. Walker	F. E. McKeever
Shallon H'Cap Flat 1m 5 Fur	Currock	Mr B. Kerr	P.J. Lenehan	Mr P.J. Lenehan
Leggan Hall Chase 2m	Mar Din	Mr T. Morrow	J. Turner	M.C. Prendergast
Corporation Maiden 1m	Hammock	Mr J.J. Parkinson	J.J. Parkinson	M. Wing
1938				
July 6				
Meath Hurdle 1m 5 Fur	Serpolette	Mr E. Delany	E. Delany	W.T. O'Grady
Duleek Novice Chase 2m	Golden Fizz	Mr J. Leech	E. Delany	W.T. O'Grady
Hilltown Flat H'Cap 1m	African Queen	Mrs Shirley	B. Rogers	H. Holmes
Drogheda Tradesmen's Chase 2m	Golden Toff	Mrs Croft	H. Ussher	W.T. O'Grady
Bellewstown Plate Bumper 2m	Pride of Rheims	Sir A. Maguire	H. G. Wellesley	Mr P.J. Lenehan
Hill H'Cap Chase 2m	Triple Alliance	Mr M. Arnott	M. Arnott	V. Mooney
July 7				
Crockafotha H'Cap Hurdle 1m 5 Fur	Savota	Mr E.G. Reed	T.R. McKeever	J. Tiernan
His Majesty's Plate 2¼ m	Bulletin	Mr J.T. Rogers	B. Rogers	H. Beasley
Wintergrass H'Cap Chase 3m	Little Ant	Mr T. Plunkett	T. Plunkett	M.C. Prendergast
Shallon H'Cap Flat 1m 5 Fur	Senville	Mr T.R. McKeever	T.R. McKeever	F. E. McKeever
Leggan Hall Chase 2m	West Point	Mr P. Dunne Cullinan	M. Arnott	F. E. McKeever
Corporation Maiden 1m	Painter's Song	Major Shirley	B. Rogers	H. Beasley

Race	Winner	Owner	Trainer	Jockey
1939				
July 5				
Hill H'Cap Chase 2m	Brittas	Mrs S. Hare	J. Ruttle	J. Brogan
Crockafotha H'Cap Hurdle 2m	Shanagarry	Mr S.J. Duffy	S.J. Duffy	T.McNeill
Hilltown Flat H'Cap 1m	Fortune's Favourite	Mr J.J. Parkinson	J.J. Parkinson	M. Wing
Drogheda Tradesmen's Chase 2m	Golden Toff	Mrs Croft	H. Ussher	W.T. O'Grady
Bellewstown Plate Bumper 2m	Vesuvian	Mr P. Dunne Cullinan	M. Arnott	J. Brogan
Duleek Novice Chase 2m	Young Queen	Mr J.J. Parkinson	J.J. Parkinson	Mr E. Parkinson
	Bistro	Lady Brooke	M. Arnott	J. Brogan
July 6				
Meath Hurdle 1m 5Fur	Hearty Welcome	Mr R.F. Coonan	J. Burke	F. Maxwell
His Majesty's Plate 2 ¼ m	Fisherman's Prayer	Major Shirley	B. Rogers	H. Holmes
Wintergrass H'Cap Chase 3m	My Branch	Mrs N.J. Kelly	T.W. Dreaper	E. Dempsey
Shallon H'Cap Flat 1 m 5 Fur	Bridgewater	Mr V.A. Cartwright	M. Arnott	Mr P. Sleator
Leggan Hall Chase 2m	St. James's Gate	Lady Elveden	M. Arnott	J. Brogan
Corporation Maiden 1 m	Bonnie Blue	Mr J.H. Whitney	H. Ussher	J. Moylan
1940				
July 3				
Hill H'Cap Chase 2m	Minstrel Boy	Miss M. Gaisford St Lawrence	M. Arnott	V. Mooney
Crockafotha H'Cap Hurdle 2m	Smerwick's Nephew	Mrs R.H. Walker	R.H. Walker	D.L. Moore
Hilltown Flat H'Cap 1m	Dandy Boy	Mr D. Malone	D. Malone	T. Whitehead
Drogheda Tradesmen's Chase 2m	Atco	Ms D. Paget	C.A. Rogers	T. Molony
Bellewstown Plate Bumper 2m	Swindon Beauty	Mr J.A. Mangan	J.A. Mangan	Mr P. Sleator
Duleek Novice Chase 2m	Knight of the Border	Ms D. Paget	C. A. Rogers	D.L. Moore
July 4				
Meath Hurdle 1m 5Fur	Little Step	Mr J. Cox	J. Cox	Mr J. Cox, jnr
His Majesty's Plate 2 ¼ m	Red Shaft	Col. D.W. Daly	R. More O'Ferrall	E.M. Quirke
Wintergrass H'Cap Chase 3m	Prince Tozzi	Mr M. Kelly	C.P. Kelly	P. O'Loughlin
Shallon H'Cap Flat 1 m 5 Fur	Swing Fro	Mr J.H. Nicholl	N. Kelly	Mr J. Cox Jnr.
Leggan Hall Chase 2m	Brown Admiral	Mr A.D. Comyn	M. Arnott	V. Mooney
Corporation Maiden 1 m	Diamond Link	Mrs T. McCairns	J. Ruttle	W. Howard
1941				
July 2				
Hill H'Cap Chase 2m	Charon	Mrs N.T. Atkinson	M. Arnott	J. Brogan
Crockafotha H'Cap Hurdle 2m	Silver Fizz	Mr J. Leech	E. Delany	T.McNeill
Hilltown Flat H'Cap 1m	Fumble	Mr J.V. Rank	Fetherstonhaugh	J. Moylan
Drogheda Tradesmen's Chase 2m	Brown Admiral	Mr A.D. Comyn	M. Arnott	J. Brogan
Bellewstown Plate Bumper 2m	Crafty Prince	Mr A.D.H. Cooke	A.D.H. Cooke	Mr G.V. Malcolmson
Duleek Novice Chase 2m	My Cherry	Mr T.K. Baker	T.W. Dreaper	E. Dempsey
Meath Hurdle 1m 5Fur	Crafty Prince	Mr A.D.H. Cooke	A.D.H. Cooke	J. Lenehan
July 3				
His Majesty's Plate 2 ¼ m	Lemon and Grey	Lord Adare	M.C. Collins	M. Wing
Wintergrass H'Cap Chase 3m	Golden Ivy	Mr P.J. O'Hagan	F. Ward	J. Brogan
Shallon H'Cap Flat 1 m 5 Fur	Guardroom	Mr T.J. Taaffe	T T.J. Taaffe	Mr T. Nugent
Leggan Hall Chase 2m	Silver Fizz	Mr J. Leech	E. Delany	T. McNeill
Corporation Maiden 1 m	Hazel Fair	Mr J.A. Farrell	J.A. Farrell	G. Wells

Race	Winner	Owner	Trainer	Jockey
1946				
July 3				
Meath Hurdle (2m Nov H)	Penny Plain	Mrs Davey	MJ Webster	D McCann
Amateur Hurdle (2m H'cap H)	Indecision	Mrs Foley	J Kirwan	Mr PP Hogan
Drogheda Tradesmen's Chase (2m H'cap Ch)	Smiling Marcus	Mrs D Cullinan	M Arnott	M Gordon
Hilltown Plate (1m Fl H'cap)	Wrong Note	Mr R McIlhagga	B Nugent	T Burns
Bellewstown Plate (2m Bumper)	Hattons Grace	Commdt D Corry	R O'Connell	Owner
Duleek S'Chase (2m Nov Ch)	Colehill	Mr RH Walker	Owner	A Brabazon
July 4				
Crockafotha Chase (2m H'cap H)	Sweet Haven	Mr S McGrath	Owner	J Walshe
His Majesty's Plate (2 ¼m Flat)	Lady Antoinette	Mrs AP Reynolds	RJ McCormick	G Wells
Wintergrass Steeplechase (3m H'cap)	Senria	Mr A Craigie	TW Dreaper	E Newman
Shallon Plate (2M Bumper)	Freebooter	Mr J Johnson	R O'Connell	Mr JR Cox Jnr
Legganhall Chase (2m Nov)	Clare Man	Mr PJ Prendergast	Owner	M Molony
Corporation Plate (1m Fl H'cap)	Conkers	Mrs VH Parr	CA Rogers	G Wells
1947				
July 2				
Meath Hurdle (2m Nov H)	Drumbuoy	Mr H Wilson	B Nugent	M Molony
Amateur Hurdle (2m H'cap H)	Wervina	Mr J Jeffers	JW Osborne	Mr JA Osborne
Drogheda Trad. Chase (2m H'cap)	New Pyjamas	Mr GF Annesley	H Ussher	A Brabazon
Hilltown Plate (1m Fl H'cap)	Northern Dandy	Mrs M Keogh	B Nugent	W Howard
Bellewstown Plate (2m Bumper)	Grey Point	Mr JJ Davy	MJ Webster	Mr AO Scannell
Duleek S'Chase (2m Nov)	My Twig	Mr T K Baker	TW Dreaper	T Hyde
July 3				
Crockafotha Hurdle (2m Nov)	Sir Gabriel	Mr PJ Ryan	Owner	M Browne
His Majesty's Plate (2 ¼ m flat)	Lorimer	Mr AP Reynolds	RJ McCormick	J Power
Wintergrass S'Chase (3m H'cap)	Cadamstown	Mr P McIlhagga	P Nugent	D Morgan
Shallon Plate (1m 5f flat)	Come And Go	Mr JJ Parkinson	Owner	Mr W Willis
Leggan Hall S'Chase (2m Nov) *Dead Heat	His Eminence	Mr M Owens	RH Walker	J Brogan
*Dead Heat	Confucious	Mr JV Rank	TW Dreaper	E Newman
Corporation Plate (1m Handicap)	Teretania	H.H. Aga Khan	HM Hartigan	G Cooney
1948				
June 30				
Meath Hurdle (2m Nov H)	Dab	Mr H Surman	Owner	M Gordon
Amateur Hurdle (2m H'cap)	Sir Gabriel	Mr PJ Ryan	Owner	Mr J Ryan
Drogheda Tradesmen's Chase (2m H'cap)	Astra	Mr WJ Hutchinson	J Kirwan	T Foran
Hilltown H'cap(1m Fl H'cap)	Dawros	Mrs G Robinson	G Robinson	J Eddery
Bellewstown Plate (2m Bumper)	Moss Trooper	Mr AJ Fitzsimons	JJ Long	Mr T O'Connell
Duleek S'Chase (2m Nov)	Smiling Marcus	Mr WM White	M Arnott	M Gordon
July 1				
Crockafotha Hurdle (2m H'cap)	Gay Rosalinda	Mr T Morrow	P Sleator	C Sleator
His Majesty's Plate (2 ¼ m flat)	Fanny's Way	Miss F Lowry	C Brabazon	TP Burns
Wintergrass S'Chase (3m H'cap)	West Wind	Ms DN Lawlor	P Connolly	M Gordon
Shallon Plate (1m 5f flat)	Murrisk	Mrs K Coonan	RF Coonan	Mr JA Osborne
Leggan Hall S'Chase (2m Nov)	Lonely Boy	Mr C Lawless	Owner	B O'Neill
Corporation Plate (1m F)	Count Gabriel	Mr C Dowdall	M Arnott	M Gordon
1949				
July 6				
Meath Hurdle (2m Nov H)	Jack Loo	Ms D Paget	CA Rogers	TP Burns

	Race	Winner	Owner	Trainer	Jockey
	Amateur Hurdle (2m H'cap)	Ice Flow	Ms D Paget	CA Rogers	Mr PP Hogan
	Drogheda Tradesman Chase (2m H'cap)	Crafty Prince	Mr PJ Lenehan	Owner	M Molony
	Hilltown H'cap(1m Fl H'cap)	Solifa	Mr J McVey	G Robinson	P Canty
	Bellewstown Plate (2m Bumper)	Prince Resenda	Mr CA Rogers	CA Rogers	Mr PP Hogan
	Duleek S'Chase (2m Chase)	Wuhu	Mr TJ Taaffe	Owner	Mr P Taaffe
July 7	Crockafotha H'cap Hurdle (2m)	Gangster	Mr J Grow	J Cox	Mr JR Cox
	His Majesty's Plate (2 ¼ m)	Anthony Wakefield	Mr WM Chapman	B Nugent	P Cowley
	Wintergrass H'cap Chase (3m)	Pastime	Brig. R Critchley	JW Osborne	M Molony
	Shallon Flat H'Cap (1m)	Statistic	Mr WM White	M Arnott	L Ward
	Leggan Hall Chase (2m)	Dark Ivy	Mrs C Stronach	Maj. J Carson	M Browne
	Corporation Plate (1m F)	Hyland Dew	Mr AW Hawkins	PJ Prendergast	P Powell Jnr
1950					
	Race	Winner	Owner	Trainer	Jockey
July 5	Meath Hurdle (2m)	Cloncan	Mr G Dunwoody	RG Patton	Owner
	Ardcath Maiden (1m 5f)	Golden Strand	Visc. Bury	H Ussher	J Tyrell
	Drogheda Tradesmen's Chase (2m)	Bright Cherry	Mr TK Baker	TW Dreaper	P Taaffe
	Hilltown H'cap(1m)	Ladastra	Mr J McGrath	S McGrath	J Eddery
	Bellewstown Plate	Embarkation	Mr P McCarthy	DL Moore	Mr JR Cox
	Duleek S'Chase (2m)	Buy Me	Mr DL Moore	DL Moore	Mr R Knowles
July 6	Crockafotha H'cap Hurdle (2m)	Murrisk	Mrs K Coonan	RF Coonan	P Taaffe
	His Majesty's Plate (2 ¼ m)	Radiant Guinea	Mr E Higgins	G Robinson	J Eddery
	Wintergrass H'cap Chase (3m)	Lucky Sprig	Mr PJ Lenehan	Owner	M Molony
	Shallon H'Cap (1m 5f)	Statistic	Mr WM White	M Arnott	W Howard
	Leggan Hall Nov Chase (2m)	Scrambler	Mr R Richards	JW Osborne	M Molony
	Corporation Plate (1m)	Garry Ro	Mr B Kerr	PJ Higgins	J Eddery
1951					
July 4	Meath Hurdle (2m)	Mountrath	Mr PJ Kilmartin	CA Rogers	M Molony
	Ardcath Maiden (1m 5f)	Still Waters	Sir R Brooke	RJ McCormick	PF Conlon
	Drogheda Tradesmen's Chase (2m)	Still Prudent	Mr RJ McIlhagga	DJ Morgan	E Newman
	Hilltown H'cap(1m)	Free Entry	Mr D Kirwan	Owner	J Eddery
	Bellewstown Plate (2m)	Persian Lad	Ms D Paget	CA Rogers	Mr PP Hogan
	Duleek S'Chase (2m)	Noble Scion	Capt. R Elwes	Capt. D Baggally	E Newman
July 5	Crockafotha H'cap Hurdle (2m)	Court Idol	Mrs AW Riddle Martin	DL Moore	TP Burns
	His Majesty's Plate (2 ¼ m)	Rose Dentelle	Mr AL Hawkins	PJ Prendergast	J Mullane
	Wintergrass H'cap Chase (3m)	St. Kathleen II	Mrs A Bell	WT O'Grady	PJ Doyle
	Shallon H'Cap (1m 5f)	Statistic	Mr D Steel	G Flood	A Duff
	Corporation Maiden Plate (1m)	Fijian	Mr T Gray	M Hurley	G Wells
	Leggan Hall Nov Chase (2m)	Knight's Harp	Ms D Paget	CA Rogers	M Molony
1952					
July 2	Meath Hurdle (2m)	Dovetail	Mr IE Levy	JW Osborne	T Taaffe
	Ardcath Maiden (1m 5f)	Orange Torney	Mrs EJ Lewis	AW Riddle Martin	F McMahon
	Drogheda Tradesmen's Chase (2m)	Royal Bridge	Ms E Shortiss	J Brogan	C Grassick

	Race	Winner	Owner	Trainer	Jockey
	Duleek Chase (2m)	Noble Scion	Capt. R Elwes	Capt. DAR Baggallay	E Newman
	Hilltown H'cap(1m)	Rathregan	Mr J Grow	J Cox	TP Burns
	Bellewstown Plate (2m)	La Tinta	Mr R Patton	R Patton	Mr S Patton
July 3	Crockafotha H'cap Hurdle (2m)	Little Roger	Mr J Cox	J Cox	PJ Doyle
	Her Majesty's Plate (2 ¼ m)	Excelsa	Capt. C Boyd-Rochfort	RN Fetherstonhaugh	H Holmes
	Wintergrass H'cap Chase (3m)	Grange Silvia	Mr D Kirwan	D Kirwan	Jos. P Kelly
	Shallon H'Cap (1m 5f)	Third Estate	Mrs N Cosgrave	G Robinson	J Eddery
	Corporation Maiden Plate (1m)	Mighty High	Mr SJ Parr	M Hurley	J Flanagan
	Leggan Hall Nov Chase (2m)	Baby Power	Mr WT McKeever	Owner	Owner
1953					
July 1	Meath Hurdle (2m)	Le Plaisant	Mr S Scheftel	B Nugent	P Cowley
	Ardcath Maiden (1m 5f)	Sir Norman	Mr B Kerr	K Kerr	J Mullane
	Drogheda Tradesmen's Chase	Nas Na Riogh	Mrs BM Lawlor	TJ Taaffe	P Taaffe
	Duleek Chase (2m)	Nice Work	Mrs G Verney	TW Dreaper	P Taaffe
	Hilltown H'cap(1m)	Lady Gracefield	Mr JG Jones	WJ Byrne	P Powell Jnr
	Bellewstown Plate (2m)	Little Horse	MR LL Ball	Owner	Mr EJ Kelly
July 2	Crockafotha H'cap Hurdle (2m)	Fair Bachelor	Mrs E Doyle	JT Doyle	Mr MR Magee
	Her Majesty's Plate (2 ¼ m)	Foxella	Mr AL Hawkins	PJ Prendergast	L Ward
	Shallon H'Cap (1m 5f)	Flandria	Mrs PW McGrath	S McGrath	John J Eddery
	Wintergrass H'cap Chase (3m)	Rambling Gold	Mr C Blackmore	D Kirwan	T O'Brien
	Corporation Maiden Plate (1m)	Stalenger	Mrs EJ King	C Sheridan	N Brennan
	Leggan Hall Nov Chase (2m)	Bell Wave	Mr D Kirwan	D Kirwan	T O'Brien
1954					
July 7	Meath Hurdle (2m)	In View	Mr L Brand	DL Moore	PJ Doyle
	Ardcath Maiden (1m 5f)	Pearl Chariot	Mr NW Waddington	H Hartigan	G Cooney
	Duleek H'cap Chase (2m)	Southern Town	Capt. E Gargan	WJ Magnier	EL McKenzie
	Drogheda Tradesmen's Chase (2m)	Soir	Mr PJ Byrne	M Dawson	CF McCormick
	Hilltown H'cap(1m) Dead Heat*	Keimaneigh	Mr Jos McGrath	S McGrath	J Eddery
	Dead Heat*	Rathregan	Mr J Grow	T O'Sullivan	TP Burns
	Bellewstown Plate (2m)	Artic Flame	Mr P Rooney	P Rooney	Mr J R Cox
July 8	Crockafotha H'cap Hurdle (2m)	Little Roger	Mr J Cox	J Cox	Mr J Cox
	Her Majesty's Plate (2 ¼ m)	Itaiassu	Mr De Castro	PJ Prendergast	T Wallace
	Shallon H'Cap (1m 5f)	Reinstated	Mrs J Bourke	G Robinson	TP Burns
	Wintergrass H'cap Chase (3m)	Game Toi	Mr RP O'Connell	RP O'Connell	J Lehane
	Corporation Maiden Plate (1m)	Scroll	Ms D Paget	CA Rogers	P Canty
	Leggan Hall Nov Chase (2m)	Spicey	Mrs JW Lyons	TJ Taaffe	T Taaffe
1955					
July 6	Meath Hurdle (2m)	Kilkilogue	Mr RG Patton	RG Patton	P Crotty
	Ardcath Maiden (1m 5f)	Low Cloud	Lt. Col. E Shirley	PJ Prendergast	TM Burns
	Duleek H'cap Chase (2 1/2m)	Belrobin	Mr L Gottlieb	J Cox	T Taaffe
	Drogheda Tradesmen's Chase (2m)	Camofly	Mr P Purfield	GA Barry	ME Regan
	Hilltown H'cap(1m)	Rocint	Capt. W Townend	CL Weld	TP Burns

	Race	Winner	Owner	Trainer	Jockey
Div I	Bellewstown Plate (2m)	Royal Courier	Mr P McCann	DL Moore	Mr B Lenehan
Div II	Do.	Irish Tara	Mrs H Ross	WT McKeever	Mr EP Harty
July 7	Crockafotha H'cap Hurdle (2m)	Merry Rock	Lord Bicester	TW Dreaper	M Murray
	Her Majesty's Plate (2 ¼ m)	Itaiassu	Mr De Castro	PJ Prendergast	L Ward
	Shallon H'Cap (1m 5f)	Master Melody	Mrs AW RiddleMartin	AW RiddleMartin	G Carroll
	Wintergrass H'cap Chase (3m)	Rosegg	Mrs V Vanden Berg	JW Osborne	MR Magee
	Corporation Maiden Plate (1m)	Dusty Bridge	Mr WF Pinnington	JM Rogers	W Burke
	Leggan Hall Nov Chase (2m)	Waterview	Mr HJ Kirwan	M Dawson	CF McCormick
1956					
July 4	Meath Hurdle (2m)	Nicholaus' Dream	Mr Omer Vanlandegham	TW Dreaper	P Taaffe
	Ardcath Maiden (1m 5f)	Duckling	Lt. Col. E Shirley	PJ Prendergast	TM Burns
	Duleek H'cap Chase (2 1/2m)	Caduceus	Mr R Dreaper	TW Dreaper	T Taaffe
	Drogheda Tradesmen's Chase (2m)	Honor's Ray	Mr R Dunne	TJ Taaffe	T Taaffe
	Hilltown H'cap(1m)	Eleanor M	Mr D Kirwan	D Kirwan	H Holmes
	Bellewstown Plate (2m)	No Surprise	Mr PJ Lawlor	P Sleator	Mr F Flood
July 5	Crockafotha H'cap Hurdle (2m)	Soir	Mr JJ McDowell	HG McDowell	P Taaffe
	Her Majesty's Plate (2 ¼ m)	Infidel	Mrs R More O'Farrell	M Dawson	L Ward
	Shallon H'Cap (1m 5f)	Tracassin	Mr L Brand	DL Moore	F McKenna
	Wintergrass H'cap Chase (3m)	New Hope	Mr WL Cullen	WL Cullen	D Kinane
	Corporation Maiden Plate (1m)	Corraith	Mrs J Thursby	JM Rogers	P Powell Jnr
	Leggan Hall Nov Chase (2m)	French Sky	Capt. GAJ Wilson	G Wells	Mr GW Robinson
1957					
July 6	Meath Hurdle (2m)	Regal Token	Mr TJ Good	C Magnier	D O'Donovan
	Ardcath Maiden (1m 5f)	Lime Cordial	Mr R McIlhagga	G Robinson	GW Robinson
	Duleek H'cap Chase (2 1/2m)	Another Jungle	Mr C Ronaldson	C Ronaldson	Owner
	Drogheda Tradesmen's Chase (2m)	French Sky	Capt. GAJ Wilson	G Wells	J Magee
	Hilltown H'cap(1m)	Cheer Up	Mr B Kerr	PJ Lenehan	EJ Fordyce
	Bellewstown Plate (2m)	Mr Wain	Mrs J Burke	G Robinson	Mr F Prendergast
July 7	Crockafotha H'cap Hurdle (2m)	Turkish Princess	Mr R McIlhagga	G Wells	J Magee
	Her Majesty's Plate (2 ¼ m)	Steel Flash	Mr AO Dietz	PJ Prendrgast	TM Burns
(Firm)	Shallon H'Cap (1m 5f)	By-Passed	Mr C McCarthy	G Robinson	GW Robinson
	Wintergrass H'cap Chase (3m)	Villain of Lyons	MR HJ Montgomery	TW Dreaper	P Taaffe
	Corporation Maiden Plate (1m)	Scented Slipper	Mrs B Aitken	J Oxx	J Power
	Leggan Hall Nov Chase (2m)	Captain Hanley	Mr J McManus	D Brennan Jnr	WJ Brennan
1958					
July 2	Meath Hurdle (2m)	Villain of Lyons	Mr Omar Vanlandegham	TW Dreaper	P Taaffe
(Yielding)	Ardcath Maiden (1m 5f)	Ancient Silver	Mr C Lawless	WJ Byrne	J Mullane
	Duleek H'cap Chase (2 1/2m)	Cuilapuca	Mr RW Hall-Dare	J Brogan	J Lehane
	Drogheda Tradesmen's Chase (2m)	The Big Hindu	Mr TT Streeter	TW Dreaper	P Taaffe
	Hilltown H'cap(1m)	Brogeen Oir	Mr R O'Loghlem	P Kearns	D Page
	Bellewstown Plate (2m)	Nurney	Mr P Rooney	P Rooney	Mr JR Cox

	Race	Winner	Owner	Trainer	Jockey
July 3	Crockafotha H'cap Hurdle (2m)	Havasnack	Mr P Meehan	P Sleator	H Beasley
(Yielding)	Her Majesty's Plate (2 ¼ m)	Tula Riona	H.E. The President	J Oxx	J Power
	Shallon H'Cap (1m 5f)	Good Score	Mr J Cox	J Cox	L Browne
	Wintergrass H'cap Chase (3m)	Passfriend	Mr P McCarthy	P Sleator	H Beasley
	Corporation Maiden Plate (1m)	My Prayer	Mr ND O'Mahony	K Bell	L Ward
	Leggan Hall Nov Chase (2m)	Clane Beau	Mr MJ Fanning	MJ Fanning	GW Robinson
1959					
July 1	Meath Hurdle (2m)	Headwave	Mr AWS Adams	J Cox	H Beasley
(Firm)	Ardcath Maiden (1m 5f)	King's Charter	Lt. Col. TW Clarke	J Oxx	J Power
	Duleek H'cap Chase (2 1/2m)	Wild Cherry	Mr G Ansley	TW Dreaper	P Taaffe
	Drogheda Tradesmen's Chase (2m)	The Big Hindu	Mr TT Streeter	TW Dreaper	P Taaffe
	Hilltown H'cap(1m)	Good Spelling	Mr TP Gallagher	RJ McCormick	J Mullane
	Bellewstown Plate (2m)	Ill Wind	Ms S Gorey	WJ Purcell	Mr John Cash
July 2	Crockafotha H'cap Hurdle (2m)	West Bank	Mr MJ Taggart	P Sleator	H Beasley
(Firm)	Her Majesty's Plate (2 ¼ m)	Maid of Galloway	MR EP Douglas	C Weld	TP Burns
	Shallon H'Cap (1m 5f)	Mesroor	Mr G Ansley	TW Dreaper	M Kennedy
	Wintergrass H'cap Chase (3m)	Digby Diver	Lord Donoughmore	TW Dreaper	Mr M Hely Hutchinson
	Corporation Maiden Plate (1m)	Barslipper	Mrs EJ King	Sir H Nugent	P Powell Jnr
	Leggan Hall Nov Chase (2m)	Hall Star	Mr RR Clarke	WE Rooney	Mr WE Rooney
1960					
July 6	Meath Hurdle (2m)	Sparkling Flame	Mr C Balding	P Sleator	H Beasley
(Firm)	Ardcath Maiden (1m 5f)	Celtic Park	Mr B Kerr	KR Kerr	M Kennedy
	Collierstown H'cap (2m)	Snow Trix	Mr J Cox	J Cox	M Kennedy
	Duleek H'cap Chase (2 1/2m)	Little Champ	Mr H Catherwood	G Dunwoody	C Kinane
	Hilltown H'cap(1m)	Cheer Up	Mr B Kerr	PJ Lenehan	M Kennedy
	Bellewstown Plate (2m)	Blueville	Mr RA Hoey	RA Hoey	Mr K Prendergast
July 7	Crockafotha H'cap Hurdle (2m)	Blueville	Mr RA Hoey	RA Hoey	C Finegan
(Firm)	Her Majesty's Plate (2 ¼ m)	Deal Sma	Mrs G St J Nolan	M Geraghty	P Matthews
	Shallon H'Cap (1m 5f)	Clane Beau	Mr MJ Fanning	P Sleator	R Moylan
	Wintergrass H'cap Chase (3m)	Little Champ	Mr H Catherwood	G Dunwoody	C Kinane
	Corporation Maiden Plate (1m)	Peter's Town	Mr JF Kearns	DJ Morgan	TP Burns
	Leggan Hall Nov Chase (2m)	Hyseller	MR RA Murray	DL Moore	GW Robinson
1961					
July 5	Meath Hurdle (2m)	Copper Cottage	Maj. TW Hughes	E Ahern	F Carroll
(Firm)	Jos. Bellew H'cap Hurdle (2m)	Spanish Hawk	Col. J Thompson	TW Dreaper	P Taaffe
	Collierstown H'cap (2m)	Narcotic Nora	MR PJ O'Hagan	E Delany	T Regan
	Duleek H'cap Chase (2 1/4m)	Hall Star	Mr RR Clarke	WE Rooney	Mr G Rooney
	Hilltown H'cap(1m)	Last Count	Lt. Col, R FenwickPalmer	TD Ainsworth	P Powell Jnr
	Ardcath Maiden (1m5f)	His Shoes	Mr J Nugent	Sir H Nugent	P Powell Jnr
July 6	Crockafotha H'cap Hurdle (2m)	Breaker's Hill	Mrs A Masters	J Cullen	P Powell Jnr
(Firm)	Her Majesty's Plate (2m)	Dante's Hope	Mrs J Dunlop	J Oxx	P Sullivan
	Shallon H'Cap (1m 5f)	Mesroor	Mr G Ansley	TW Dreaper	M Kennedy

	Race	Winner	Owner	Trainer	Jockey
	Wintergrass H'cap Chase (3m)	Lucky Touch	Mr F Yorke	F Yorke	A Redmond
	Corporation Maiden Plate (1m)	Chignon	Mrs C Magnier	C Magnier	D Page
	Leggan Hall Nov Plate (2m)	Straight Lady	Mr A Watson	J Woods	Mr A Watson
1962					
July 4	Meath Hurdle (2m)	Erindale Boy	Mr E Delany	E Delany	Mr E D Delany
Firm	Jos. Bellew H'cap Hurdle (2m)	Killykeen Star	Mrs Rochfort-Hyde	Private	F Shortt
	Collierstown Flat H'cap (2m)	Duffcarrig	Mr G Ansley	TW Dreaper	P Taaffe
	Duleek H'cap Chase (2 1/2m)	Tax Law	Mrs DJ Morgan	DJ Morgan	TE Hyde
	Hilltown H'cap(1m)	Donora	Mr W Moore	C Weld	P Powell Jnr
	Ardcath Maiden (1m5f)	Illustrious	Ms P O'Connor	B Fetherstonhaugh	P Boothman
July 5	Crockafotha H'cap Hurdle (2m)	Thorny Path	Mrs E Delany	E Delany	T Regan
Firm	Her Majesty's Plate (2m)	Medusa III	Lord Harrington	C Chute	N Brennan
	Shallon H'Cap (1m 5f)	Sandshoes	Mrs EJ King	Sir H Nugent	M Kennedy
	Wintergrass H'cap Chase (3m)	Yonder He Goes	Mr O Eustace Duckett	Private	GW Robinson
	Corporation Maiden Plate (1m)	Elle-Meme	Mr EP Douglas	C Weld	P Powell Jnr
	Leggan Hall Plate (2m)	Artic Find	Mr P Rooney	P Rooney	Mr JR Cox
1963					
July 3	Meath Hurdle (2m)	Prarie Wolf	Mr CA Rogers	DL Moore	T Carberry
Good	Jos. Bellew H'cap Hurdle (2m)	Duffcarrig	Mr G Ansley	TW Dreaper	P Taaffe
	Collierstown Flat H'cap (2m)	Kilcrohane	Mr JM Coughlan	DJ Morgan	P Powell Jnr
	Duleek H'cap Chase (2 1/2m)	Tax Law	Mrs DJ Morgan	DJ Morgan	TE Hyde
	Hilltown H'cap(1m5f)	Sedandun	Mr P O'Donoghue	P Norris	T Enright
	Ardcath Maiden (1m)	Green Minstrel	Mr EM Quirke	S Quirke	N Brennan
July 4	Crockafotha H'cap Hurdle (2m)	Great Time	Mrs J McElroy	Private	R McElroy
Good	Her Majesty's Plate (2m)	Baymoon	Mrs A Burke	TD Ainsworth	N Brennan
	Shallon H'Cap (1m)	Steel	Mrs M Cowley	C Grassick	O Weldon
	Wintergrass H'cap Chase (3m)	Burton Brown III	MrP Dunny	P Murphy	F Shortt
	Corporation Maiden (1m)	Panama Mail	Lord Donoughmore	J Oxx	P Sullivan
	Leggan Hall Plate (2m)	Tralee Bay	Mr FN Shane	M Dawson	Mr K Prendergast
1964					
July 1	Meath Hurdle (2m)	Celdado	Lt. Col. TC Wilkinson	TW Dreaper	P Woods
Firm	Jos. Bellew H'cap Hurdle (2m)	Duffcarrig	Mr G Ansley	TW Dreaper	P Taaffe
	Collierstown H'cap (2m)	Kitty Sick	Ms S Dowley	C Magnier	J Larkin
	Duleek H'cap Chase (2 1/2m)	Titus	Mr J H Thursby	TW Dreaper	P Taaffe
	Hilltown H'cap(1m5f)	Cool Pace	Mr TI Breen	K Bell	V Kennedy
	Ardcath Maiden (1m)	Royal Graney	Mr MJ King	K Bell	TP Burns
July 2	Crockafotha H'cap Hurdle (2m)	Clancy Junior	Mrs TK Cooper	DL Moore	T Carberry
Firm	Her Majesty's Plate (2 m)	Tarmac	Mrs J McGrath Jnr	S McGrath	J Roe
	Shallon H'Cap (1m)	Talgo Abbess	Mr PJ Conlon	K Prendergast	P Black
	Wintergrass H'cap Chase (3m)	Proud Glen	Mr T Mahon	LJ Mahon	L McLoughlin
	Corporation Maiden Plate (1m5f)	King's Highway	Mrs W MacAuley	D Auld	N Brennan
	Leggan Hall Plate (2m)	King's Ribbon	Mr CA Metcalfe	J Cox	Mr JR Cox

Race	Winner	Owner	Trainer	Jockey
1965				
July 7				
Meath Hurdle (2m)	Scoil	Mr AWS Adams	J Cox	B Hannon
Firm				
Jos. Bellew H'cap Hurdle (2m)	Ronan	Gen. RK Mellon	TW Dreaper	P Taaffe
Preston 10 Stakes (1m)	Miss Sherluck	Mrs ME Whitney Tippett	K Prendergast	D Dunn
Duleek H'cap Chase (2 1/2m)	Celdado	Lt. Col. TC Wilkinson	T.W. Dreaper	P Woods
Collierstown H'cap(5f)	Abbey Liffey	Mr PJ Conlon	K Prendergast	N Brennan
Hilltown H'cap (1m5f)	Migoli Slipper	Sir H Nugent	Sir H Nugent	M Kennedy
July 8				
Crockafotha H'cap Hurdle (2m)	The Hedger	Mr FC Ffrench Davis	B Nugent	B Hannon
Her Majesty's Plate (2 ¼ m)	Musical Chairs	Mr BF Dunne	C Magnier	J O'Grady
Regency Sherry H'Cap (5f)	Whistling Lady	Mr JF Kelly	P Norris	TP Burns
Wintergrass H'cap Chase (3m)	Arkloin	Mr G Ansley	TW Dreaper	P Taaffe
Corporation Maiden Plate (1m5f)	Pinard	Mr LM Gelb	P Prendergast	P Matthews
Leggan Hall Plate (2m)	East Wind	Mr E Delany	E Delany	Mr ED Delany
1966				
July 20				
Meath Hurdle (2m)	Appollon	Mrs A Sobell	DL Moore	T Carberry
Firm				
Mount Hanover Am. H'cap Hurde (2 1/4m)	Flaxen King	Mrs S Catherwood	J Cox	Mr F Flood
Preston 10 Stakes (1m)	Ballysax Kuda	Mrs E Perkins Maguire	B Alexander	P Sullivan
Duleek H'cap Chase (2 1/2m)	Felspar	Capt. TJW Till	T Taaffe	B Hannon
Collierstown H'cap (5f)	Tic Tac	Lady Nugent	Sir H Nugent	J Larkin
Hilltown H'cap(1m 5f)	Terossian	Mr R McIlhagga	GH Wells	TP Burns
July 21				
Crockafotha H'cap Hurdle (2m)	A.S.R.	Mr RA Palfreyman	P Murphy	F Shortt
Her Majesty's Plate (2m)	Irish Independent	Mr B Kerr	M Connolly	G McGrath
Firm				
Regency Sherry H'Cap (5f)	Star Clipper	Mr PJ O'Regan	M Connolly	J Roe
Wintergrass H'cap Chase (3m)	Arkloin	Mr G Ansley	TW Dreaper	P Taaffe
Corporation Maiden Plate (1m 5f)	Mr World	Mr WJ Kavanagh	M Hurley	JV Smith
Leggan Hall Plate (2m)	Most Seen	Mr I Williams	D Kinane	Mr I Williams
1967				
July 19				
Meath Hurdle (2m)	Around The World	Mr HJ Boylan	J Sherwin	P McDonnell
Firm				
Mount Hanover Am. H'cap Hurde (2 1/4m)	Hydra-Z	Mr WA Tellright	C Magnier	Mr W McLernon
Preston 10 Stakes (1m)	Telling	Col. JD Clague	C Magnier	J Murtagh
Duleek H'cap Chase (2 1/2m)	Marvellous Tack	Mr J O'Connell	J O'Connell	R Coonan
Collierstown H'cap (5f)	Sweet Chupati	Mrs JR Lucas	C Weld	LW Johnson
Hilltown H'cap(1m 5f)	Migoli Slipper	Sir H Nugent	Sir Hugh Nugent	J Roe
July 20				
Crockafotha H'cap Hurdle (2m)	Peaceful Pat	Mr JF Tormey	JF Tormey	Mr T Tormey
Her Majesty's Plate (2m)	Pawn Office	Mr O Lambe	K Prendergast	LW Johnson
Firm				
Regency Sherry H'Cap (5f)	Star Clipper	Mr PJ O'Regan	M Connolly	J Roe
Wintergrass H'cap Chase (3m)	Fairy Pack	Mrs K Harper	P McCreery	A Redmond
Corporation Maiden Plate (1m 5f)	Tangleberry	Mr J Muldoon	P Prendergast Jnr	P Matthews
Leggan Hall Plate (2m)	After Eight	Mr WD O'Neill	V Keane	Mr C Ronaldson
1968				
July 3				
Meath Hurdle (2m)	Treasure Time	Mr N Galway Greer	P Sleator	R Coonan
Firm				
Mount Hanover Am. H'cap Hurde (2 1/4m)	Kilcoo	Mr AS Robinson	DL Moore	Mr A Moore

	Race	Winner	Owner	Trainer	Jockey
	Ardcath Maiden (1m)	Persian Tiger	Comte. A de Laubespin	M Hurley	WG McMahon
	Duleek H'cap Chase (2 1/2m)	Home Alone II	Mr TJ Murphy	C McCartan Jnr	C Finnegan
	Collierstown H'cap (5f)	Lucky Plum	Mrs B de Mulder	John Murphy	J Roe
	Hilltown H'cap (1m 5f)	Gay Bruce	Mr JA O'Connor	M Connolly	C Roche
July 4	Crockafotha H'cap Hurdle (2m)	Night Assault	Mr ALT Moore	B Alexander	Mr A Moore
Firm	Her Majesty's Plate (2m)	Copper Gamble	Mrs PJ Hughes	K Prendergast	LW Johnson
	Shallon H'Cap (5f)	Wild Bee	Mr S McGrath	S McGrath	G McGrath
	Wintergrass H'cap Chase (3m)	Fairy Pack	Mrs K Harper	P McCreery	F Shortt
	Corporation Maiden Plate (1m 5f)	Fantastic Lady	Mrs K Prendergast	K Prendergast	LW Johnson
	Leggan Hall Plate (2m)	Eau de Vie	Mr L Winters	Mrs Nolan	Mr ND Winters
1969					
July 2	Meath Hurdle (2m)	Cincinatti	Mr GS Smith	CB Harty Jnr	JP Harty
Firm	Mount Hanover Am. H'cap Hurdle (2 1/4m)	Autumn Girl	Mrs TC O'Brien	V Keane	Mr E Collins
	Ardcath Plate (1m)	Lodola	Comte. A de Laubespin	M Hurley	WG McMahon
	Duleek H'cap Chase (2 1/2m)	Struell Park	Ms KR Payne	TL Crawford	T Kinane
	Collierstown H'cap (5f)	Gold Spot	Mr MA O'Toole	MA O'Toole	MC Nolan
	Hilltown H'cap (1m 5f)	Aldave	Mr D Prentice Jnr	GR Dunwoody	P Boothman
July 3	Crockafotha H'cap Hurdle (2m)	Trentina	Mr R Guest	DL Moore	T Carberry
Firm	Her Majesty's Plate (2m)	Eternal Hope	Mr E Goring	K Prendergast	M O'Shaughnessy
	Shallon H'Cap (5f)	Arctic Talisman	Mr J Dynes	K Prendergast	G Curran
	Wintergrass H'cap Chase (3m)	Indian War	Mr D Ryan	D Ryan	B Hannon
	Corporation Maiden Plate (1m 5f)	Khailas	Mr ER More O'Farrell	K Prendergast	G Curran
	Leggan Hall Plate (2m)	Red How	Mr MA O'Toole	MA O'Toole	Mr J Fowler
1970					
July 1	Meath Hurdle (2m)	Fortina's Dream	Mr Omer Vanlandegham	TW Dreaper	P Taaffe
Firm	Mount Hanover Am. H'cap Hurdle (2 1/4m)	Ballydesmond	Mrs J Corrigan	J Woods	Mr E Rice
	Ardcath Maiden (1m)	Welcome Home	Mrs TE Kelly	S McGrath	G McGrath
	Duleek H'cap Chase (2 1/2m)	Black Secret	Mrs J Watney	TW Dreaper	Mr J Dreaper
	Collierstown H'cap (5f)	Black Gnat	Mrs C Magnier	C Magnier	M Teelin
	Hilltown H'cap (1m 5f)	Vector	Lady H Svejdar	GH Wells	T Carberry
July 2	Crockafotha H'cap Hurdle (2m)	Nobska	Mrs RK Mellon	TW Dreaper	P Taaffe
Firm	Her Majesty's Plate (2m)	Copper Gamble	Mrs PJ Hughes	K Prendergast	G Curran
	Shallon H'Cap (5f)	Galesian	Mr M Gallagher	C Grassick	G Curran
	Wintergrass H'cap Chase (3m)	Carriglea Lady II	Mrs S Catherwood	DL Moore	T Carberry
	Corporation Maiden Plate (1m 5f)	Credulous	Mr S Sanger	K Prendergast	G Curran
	Leggan Hall Plate (2m)	Parthian Ranger	Mrs S Catherwood	MA O'Toole	Mr DK Weld
1971					
June 30	Meath Hurdle (2m)	Dicasee	Mr ML Marsh	P Sleator	L O'Donnell
Firm	Mount Hanover Am. H'cap Hurdle (2 1/4m)	Credulous	Mrs HF Williams	HF Williams	Mr I Williams
	Ardcath Maiden (1m)	Bert Satin	Mrs MA O'Toole	MA O'Toole	AC Brennan
	Duleek H'cap Chase (2 1/2m)	Little Tom	Mrs H Ferris	WE Rooney	T Carberry
	Collierstown H'cap (5f)	Black Gnat	Mrs C Magnier	C Magnier	M Teelin

Race	Winner	Owner	Trainer	Jockey
July 1 *Firm*				
Hilltown H'cap (1m 5f)	Big Jack	Mr T McDonnell	JA O'Connell	P Mooney
Crockafotha H'cap Hurdle (2m)	Sapphire Star	Mr B Lawless	JA O'Connell	P Mooney
Her Majesty's Plate (2m)	Le Levanhot	Col. M de Gregorio	K Prendergast	G Curran
Shallon H'Cap (5f)	Mezlam Prince	Mrs KA Wilby	MA O'Toole	P Sullivan
Wintergrass H'cap Chase (3m)	Rosinver Bay	Mr AW RiddleMartin	AW Riddle Martin	M McNeill
Corporation Maiden Plate (1m 5f)	Paul Revere	Mr JR Mullion	PJ Prendergast	C Roche
Leggan Hall Plate (2m)	Veni Vici	Mr Omer Vanlandegham	TW Dreaper	Mr J Dreaper

1972

Race	Winner	Owner	Trainer	Jockey
June 28 *Good*				
Meath Hurdle (2m)	Shevatroon	Mrs PJ Foley	P Mullins	MA Brennan
Mount Hanover Am. H'cap Hurde (2 1/4m)	Journalist	Mr WJ Brennan	WJ Brennan	Mr T Jones
Ardcath Maiden (1m)	Fledgeling	Mrs OM Alexander	C Magnier	T Murphy
Duleek H'cap Chase (2 1/2m)	Truly Merry	Mr T Nicholson	Private	Mr JW Nicholson
Collierstown H'cap (5f)	Snow Moss	Mr D O'Donnell	D O'Donnell	Martin Kinane
Hilltown H'cap(1m 5f)	Saucy Society	Mr J Dowling	P Mullins	RF Parnell
June 29 *Good*				
Crockafotha H'cap Hurdle (2m)	Lisheen	Mrs BOE Scott	P Norris	Mr H Scott
Her Majesty's Plate (2m)	Census	Mrs RL Johnson	JR Bryce-Smith	C Roche
Shallon H'Cap (5f)	Paul's Pet	Mr PJ Quinn	P Prendergast Jnr	B Marsh
Wintergrass H'cap Chase (3m)	Westland Boy	Mr A Murphy	T Costello	J Cullen
Corporation Maiden Plate (1m 5f)	High Beech	Mrs S Johnson	C Magnier	T Murphy
Leggan Hall Plate (2m)	Connin Beg	Mr JJ Howlett	PM Berry	Mr W McLernon

1973

Race	Winner	Owner	Trainer	Jockey
June 27 *Firm*				
Meath Hurdle (2m)	Wadi Halfa	Ms A Buggle	Private	B Hannon
Mount Hanover Am. H'cap Hurde (2 1/4m)	Brissago	Mr JA Duffy	J Dreaper	Mr M Murray
Ardcath Maiden (1m)	Bouquet	Mabel, Lady Brooke	D Weld	RF Parnell
Duleek H'cap Chase (2 1/2m)	Native Clover	Mrs CP Smith	JA O'Connell	P Mooney
Collierstown H'cap (5f)	Spruce Street	Mr E Behan	L Browne	E Downey
Hilltown H'cap(1m 5f)	Bilbo Baggins	Mr JJ O'Connor	K Prendergast	G Curran
June 28 *Firm*				
Crockafotha H'cap Hurdle (2m)	Lady Aylmer	Mr RJ McKenna	A Geraghty	J O'Gorman
Her Majesty's Plate (2m)	Meadow Manor	Mrs Parker Poe	PJ Prendergast	C Roche
Shallon H'Cap (5f)	Supercede	Mrs P Prendergast Jnr	P Prendergast Jnr	N O'Toole
Wintergrass H'cap Chase (3m)	Rough Silk	Mrs PG McCrea	EJ O'Grady	Mr M Morris
Corporation Maiden Plate (1m 5f)	Caralgo	Mr B Donnelly	D Weld	RF Parnell
Leggan Hall Plate (2m)	Rosaveal	Mr JJ Reilly	Private	Mr JJ Reilly

1974

Race	Winner	Owner	Trainer	Jockey
June 26 *Firm*				
Meath Hurdle (2m)	Coniff	O Freaney	J Dreaper	T Carberry
Mt. Hanover Am. H'cap Hurdle (2 1/2m)	Kilmore Boy	PP Dalton	R Walsh	Mr TM Walsh
Ardcath Maiden (1m)	Nakilts	MJ O'Brien	C Grassick	M Kennedy
Duleek Chase (2 ½m)	Glittering Gold	Mrs K Harper	P McCreery	J Bracken
Collierstown Handicap (5f)	Wild Boquet	J Corcoran	M Connolly	RM Connolly
Hilltown H'cap (1m 6f)	La Grissette	BP Geoghegan	JA O'Connell	C Roche

	Race	Winner	Owner	Trainer	Jockey
June 27	Crockafotha H'cap Hurdle (2m)	Colonial Prince	Mrs JL White	DL Moore	T Carberry
Firm	Her Majesty's Plate (2m)	Baltic Star	Mrs R McGrath	S McGrath	G McGrath
	Shallon H'cap (5f)	Ruysch	S Cohn	M Hurley	W Swinburn
	Wintergrass H'cap Chase (3m)	Casquette	W Bell	TL Crawford	S Shields
	Corporation Maiden (1m 6f)	Surcingle	Jos McGrath	S McGrath	G McGrath
	Legganhall Plate (2m)	Philipine Hill	PR Lyons	P Woods	Mr E Woods
Aug 23	Beaumond Maiden Hurdle (2m)	Saucy Slave	T Murray	DL Moore	T Carberry
Good to Firm	Carnes 2 y/o Plate (5f)	Spare Slipper	Sir H Nugent	Sir H Nugent	RF Parnell
	Bolies Chase (2 1/2m)	Colonial Prince	Mrs JL White	DL Moore	T Carberry
	Lisdornan Maiden (1m 6f)	Kitty O'Shea	Mrs PW McGrath	S McGrath	G McGrath
	Dardistown H'cap (1m)	Carol Barnett	J Muldoon	John Murphy	T Carmody
	Kilsharvan Plate (2m)	Gay Boris	Jos McGrath	P McCreery	Mr TM Walsh
1975					
June 25	Meath Hurdle (2m)	Auburn	Mrs D Gillam	PM Berry	C Seward
	Mt. Hanover Am. H'cap Hurdle (2 1/2m)	Yellow Sam	Mr B Curley	WJ Brennan	Mr M Furlong
	Ardcath Maiden (1m)	Lee Brook Lass	E McGillycuddy	L Browne	T Carmody
	Duleek Chase (2 ½m)	Drop Even	MJ Redmond	PM Berry	F Berry
	Collierstown Handicap (5f)	National Note	RN Webster	P Prendergast Jnr	C Roche
	Hilltown H'cap (1m 6f)	Le Gaulois	R Annesley	R Annesley	W Swinburn
June 26	Crockafotha H'cap Hurdle (2m)	Colonial Prince	Mrs JL White	DL Moore	T Carberry
	Her Majesty's Plate (2m)	Safari	GP Corcoran	K Prendergast	J McCutcheon
	Shallon H'cap (5f)	Nuaguese	Sir D Clague	C Magnier	R Carroll
	Wintergrass H'cap Chase (3m)	Escari	JJ McDowell	JR Cox	P Black
	Corporation Maiden (1m 6f)	We Robin	WH Shaw	K Prendergast	G Curran
	Legganhall Plate (2m)	Mersheen	J Fowler	J Fowler	Mr J Fowler
Aug 27	Beaumond Maiden Hurdle (2m)	Mariners Barge	JP Keane	P McCreery	J Bracken
	Bolies Chase (2 1/2m)	Own's Mill	JJ Prendrgast	F Prendergast	F Berry
	Dardistown H'cap (1m) Div I	Festive Diplomat	Mrs R Gallagher	GW Robinson	TP Burns
	Do. Div II	Thorn Proof	C McCarthy	F Ennis	P Clarke
	Lisdornan Maiden	Duetto	Comre A de Laubespin	R Annesley	W Swinburn
	Kilsharvan Plate (2m)	Wurrabi	Mr R Beaumont	JF Tormey	Mr T Tormey
1976					
June 23	Meath Hurdle (2m)	Three Million	MJ McNally	D Kinane	R Coonan
Firm	Mt. Hanover Am. H'cap Hurdle (2 1/2m)	Perfect Blue	J MacAuley	J MacAuley	Mr D MacAuley
	Ardcath Maiden (1m) Div I	Irish Advocate	GP Corcoran	K Prendergast	G Curran
	Do. Div II	Ballyglass	Mrs PJ Lally	PJ Lally	W Swinburn
	Duleek Chase (2 ½m)	Kiltotan	J Gavin	P Mullins	F Murphy
	Collierstown Handicap (5f)	Pierre The True	MD Thorp	D Weld	RF Parnell
	Hilltown H'cap (1m 6f)	Serissa	Mrs M Delolaux	D Weld	KF Coogan
June 24	Crockafotha H'cap Hurdle (2m)	Bamber's Security	JB Lusk	JB Lusk	MF Morris
Firm	Shallon H'cap (5f)	Borsalindo	Mrs A BoydRochfort	D Weld	W Swinburn
	Wintergrass H'cap Chase (3m)	Gone Out	J Horgan	F Flood	F Berry

	Race	Winner	Owner	Trainer	Jockey
	Corporation Maiden (1m 6f)	Moctezuma	Mrs PW McGrath	S McGrath	N Cassidy
	Her Majesty's Plate (2m)	Whistle for Gold	DB O'Meara	J Oxx	R Carroll
	Legganhall Plate (2m)	King or Country	A Cameron	RA Hoey	Mr J Fowler
Aug 25	Bolies Chase (2 1/2m)	Collins	Mrs JM Walsh	G Hogan	F Murphy
Firm	Beamond Maiden Hurdle (2m)	Intervention	JJ Gleeson	A Redmond	P Russell
	Carnes 2 y/o Plate (5f)	Jean Fabre	S McGrath	S McGrath	G McGrath
	Dardistown H'cap (1m)	Fickle City	Mrs J McGrath	S McGrath	M Kennedy
	Lisdornan Maiden (1m 6f)	Emperor's Twinkle	W Joyce	J Power	M Kennedy
	Kilsharvan Plate (2m)	Bar You Forgot	P Griffin	P Woods	Mr E Woods
1977					
June 22	Meath Hurdle (2m) Div I	Cocoboy	Ms EM Galvin	John Murphy	RS Townend
Firm	Do. Div II	Knocknarea	P Flanagan	A Redmond	F Berry
	Mt. Hanover Am. H'cap Hurdle (2 1/2m)	Autumn Wonder	Mrs JP McGuinness	RA Hoey	Mr J Fowler
	Ardcath Maiden (1m)	Gigitipoke	FP Glennon	DK Weld	W Swinburn
	Duleek Chase (2 ½m)	Mayfield Grove	T Donohoe	F Ennis	RS Townend
	Collierstown Handicap (5f)	Strip Light	NF Glynn	P Russell	KF Coogan
	Hilltown H'cap (1m 6f)	Melody Music	OBP Carroll	C Grassick	R Eddery
June 23	Crockafotha H'cap Hurdle (2m)	Gallop'n Inflation	PS Gallagher	C Grassick	R Coonan
	Wintergrass H'cap Chase (3m)	Little Bug	RL Poots	Private	M Cummins
Firm	Shallon H'cap (5f)	Always Late	Mr C o'Reilly	L Browne	D Gillespie
	Corporation Maiden (1m 6f)	Surely-A-Boyo	Ms C Clements	J Oxx	R Carroll
	Her Majesty's Plate (2m)	Borallez	CA Gamberill	PM Berry	T Murphy
	Legganhall Plate (2m) Div I	Readypenny	CF Cronin	JR Cox	Mr R King
	Do. Div II	Artic Sunset	Mrs P Norris	P Norris	Mr A Tyrell
Aug 24	Bolies Chase (2 1/2m)	Millgrange	P Smyth	P Smyth	JP Byrne
Good to Firm	Beamond Maiden Hurdle (2m)	Gougan Barra	P McCarthy	P Mullins	Mr P McCarthy
	Carnes 2 y/o Plate (5f)	Real Character	Mrs P Poe	PJ Prendergast	C Roche
	Dardistown H'cap (1m) Div I	Love Child	Mrs J Alexander	R Annesley	G McGrath
	Do. Div II	Engage	LE Cabrera	K Prendergast	G Curran
	Lisdornan Maiden (1m 6f)	Lady Lantern	Mrs S Prentice-Porter	S Quirke	D Hogan
	Kilsharvan Plate (2m)	Sneem	Mrs M Flanagn	K Prendergast	G Curran
1978					
June 20	Beaumond Mn. Hurdle (2m)	Red Due	JJ Smurfitt Jnr	C Magnier	T Carberry
Firm	Carnes 2 y/o Maiden (5f)	Sparkling Kitty	Mrs M Connolly	M Connolly	J Corr
	Dardistown H'cap (1m)	Windy Dee Dee	Ms M Dooley	P Norris	DJ Murphy
	Kilsharvan Maiden (5f)	Mariko	N Griffin	C Magnier	B Coogan
	Bolies Flat H'cap (2m+)	Lady Annie	EJ Cunningham	JM Kennedy	P Lowry
	Lisdornan Flat race (2m+)	Buck Royale	JJ McNicholl	Private	Mr J Queally
June 21	Meath Hurdle (2m+)	Legal Swith	RA Keogh	A Moore	A Moore
Firm	Mt. Hanover Am. H'cap (2 1/2m)	King Herbert	Mrs B Brady	F Oakes	Mr F Codd
	Ardcath Maiden (1m)	Water Witch	Mrs RW Furber	K Prendergast	G Curran
	Bellewstown Mares Hurdle (2m+)	Wallis	F Oakes	F Oakes	P McCormack

	Race	Winner	Owner	Trainer	Jockey
	Collierstown H'cap (5f)	Soul Train	Mrs P Mullins	P Mullins	MJ Murphy
	Hilltown H'cap (1m 6f)	Pollardstown	AD Brennan	K Prendergast	G Curran
June 22	Crockafotha H'cap Hurdle (2m+)	Kingstown Pride	P McAteer	F Flood	F Berry
Good	Shallon 2 y/o Maiden (1m)	Derelett	T Laverty	A Redmond	TA Quinn
	Drogheda H'cap (1m)	Passing Glory	ADH Cooke	A Brabazon	D Gillespie
	Corporation Maiden (1m 6f)	Tudor Earl	JP Foy	S Murless	T Carberry
	Her Majesty's Plate (2m)	Lovely Bio	F McDonell	C Magnier	T Carberry
	Legganhall Flat Race (2m+)	What A Pleasure	Mrs JB O'Callaghan	R Walsh	Mr TM Walsh
1979					
June 19	Carnes 2 y/o Maiden (5f)	Sunderland	MW Smurfitt	DK Weld	J Deegan
Firm	Beaumond Mn. Hurdle (2m)	Joann's First	Mrs A Sweeney	W Bourke	JP Harty
	Dardistown H'cap (1m)	Hutnage	W Richardson	TJR Walls	PV Gilson
	Bolies H'cap Hurdle (3m)	Delightful Buck	RG Patton	D Patton	G Newman
	Kilsharvan Maiden (5f)	Carriglen	LP Greene	LP Greene	PV Gilson
	Lisdornan Flat race (2m+) Div I	A While	Maj. GT Ponsonby	J Dreaper	Mr E Woods
	Do. Div II	Three Clouds	C Ronaldson	C Ronaldson	Mr C Ronaldson
June 20	Her Majesty's Plate (2m)	Nice Client	S McGrath	S McGrath	G McGrath
Firm	Hilltown H'cap (1m 6f)	Hodelsing	JR Bryce Smith	JR Bryce Smith	RF Parnell
	Sean Graham Am. H'cap Hurdle (2 1/2m)	Accipiter	JC Roche	C Magnier	Mr CP Magnier
	Ardcath Maiden (1m)	Captain Birdseye	N O'Callaghan	K Prendergast	G Curran
	Bellewstown Mares Md. Hurdle (2m+) Div I	Greenane Prince	Mrs M Farrell	T Kinane	T Kinane
	Meath Hurdle (2m+)	Clanrouge	Ms G Byrne	M Connolly	C Roche
	Collierstown H'cap (5f)	Sound Reality	BR Firestone	DK Weld	J Deegan
June 21	Shallon 2 y/o Maiden (5f)	An Tig Gaélige	Mrs RA Keogh	RA Keogh	P Parnell
Firm	Corporation Maiden (1m 6f)	Valace	Mrs CP Smith	CP Smith	P Mooney
	Crockafotha H'cap Hurdle (2m+)	Up Front	Mrs TP Kelly	RJ McCormick	MJ Murphy
	Drogheda H'cap (1m)	Zarina Lady	PJ Beggan	PJ Beggan	T Carberry
	Bellewstown Mares Md. Hurdle (2m+) Div I	Hazelwell	Mrs H Robinson	J Fowler	Mr M Lynch
	Do. Div II	French Trail	B Brindley	B Brindley	Mr B Brindley
	Legganhall NH Flat Race (2m+)				
1980					
July 1	Carnes 2 y/o Maiden (5f)	Singing My Song	Dr. J Tornsey	A Redmond	G McGrath
Firm	Beaumond Mn. Hurdle (2m)	The Downs	Mrs T Silvey	A Geraghty	F Berry
	Dardistown H'cap (1m) Div I	Collector's Item	CS Gaisford St.Lawrence	M Kauntze	MJ Kinane
	Do. Div II	Palmalina	Mrs B Lynch	N Meade	S Craine
	Bolies H'cap Hurdle (3m)	Laurentino	R Nevin	R Nevin	JJ Maher
	Kilsharvan Maiden (5f)	Restless dancer	OBP Carroll	C Grassick	D Gillespie
	Lisdornan Flat race (2m+)	New Harbour	Lord Hemphill	C Magnier	Mr CP Magnier
July 2	Corporation Maiden (1m 6f)	Castleshane Pat	AD Brennan	K Prendergast	G Curran
Good	Ardcath Maiden (1m)	Balmy Grove	P Kelly	Paul Kelly	J Deegan
	Sean Graham Am. H'cap Hurdle (2 1/2m)	Welsh Thorn	F McDonnell	C Magnier	Mr CP Magnier
	Her Majesty's Plate (2m)	Weaver's Pin	S McGrath	S McGrath	J Corrigan
	Meath Hurdle (2m+)	Old Matt	M Fanning	R Coonan	Martin Kinane

	Race	Winner	Owner	Trainer	Jockey
July 3	Collierstown H'cap (5f)	Muscari	LP Greene	LP Greene	MJ Kinane
	Shallon 2 y/o Maiden (5f)	Royal Hobbit	S McGrath	S McGrath	J Corrigan
Good to Firm	Drogheda H'cap (1m)	Boogie Woogie	M Waldheim	K Prendergast	G Curran
	Crockafotha H'cap Hurdle (2m+)	Ailwee Caves	Mrs F Burke	WJ Brennan	M Drake
	Hilltown H'cap (1m 6f)	Public Opinion	Mrs Gainsford St.Lawrence	M Kauntze	MJ Kinane
	Bellewstown Mares Md. Hurdle (2m+) Div I	Marand	TM Flynn	PA Brennan	P Gill
	Do. Div II	Moss Fairy	MP Lafferty	MP Lafferty	G McGlinchey
	Legganhall NH Flat Race (2m+)	Miss Jordan	B Malone	B Malone	Mr M Lynch
1981					
June 30	Carnes 2 y/o Maiden (5f)	Songoli	M Soudaver	K Prendergast	G Curran
Good	Beaumond Mn. Hurdle (2m)	Charfran	Mrs CP Smith	CP Smith	P Mooney
	Dardistown H'cap (1m)	High Hollow	Mrs JA Walsh	A Geraghty	PV Gilson
	Bolies H'cap Hurdle (3m)	Belassie	ME McAuley	J Dreaper	K Morgan
	Kilsharvan Maiden (5f)	Real Torque	FN Groves	TG Curtin	D Hogan
	Lisdornan Flat race (2m+) Div I	Blazing Wind	Mrs A Redmond	A Redmond	Mr CP O'Toole
	Do. Div II	Conduction	Mrs K Urquhart	F Flood	Mr A Powell
July 1	Meath Hurdle (2m+)	Casanova Kid	Mrs MA O'Toole	MA O'Toole	N Madden
Good	Ardcath Maiden (1m) Div I	Bridewell Belle	Maj. JH de Burgh	A Moore	T Murphy
	Bradain Maiden (1m 6f)	Polish Prince	B Dunne	M Connolly	C Roche
	Sean Graham Am. H'cap Hurdle (2 1/2m)	Fitzwell	A Crowther	F Flood	Mr A Powell
	Collierstown H'cap (5f)	Waiting Knight	NB Hunt	TG Curtin	D Hogan
	Hilltown H'cap (1m 6f)	Triumphal March	BR Firestone	DK Weld	W Swinburn
	Bradain Maiden (1m 6f)	Persian Wanderer	Brig. A Wingfield	J Dreaper	Mr TM Walsh
July 2	Shallon 2 y/o Maiden (5f)	Nora's Mark	Mrs E McMahon	JS Bolger	D Gillespie
Good to Firm	Drogheda H'cap (1m)	Dancing Light	RE Sangster	K Prendergast	MA Cooney
	Crockafotha H'cap Hurdle (2m+)	Track Scout	JA Harte	A Geraghty	T Morgan
	Corporation Maiden (1m 6f)	Airbus	W Haefner	DK Weld	MJ Kinane
	Bellewstown Mares Md. Hurdle (2m+) Div I	Gift Seeker	Mrs T Beattie	A Moore	T McGivern
	Do. Div II	Highway's last	WR Donaldson	P Woods	E Woods
	Legganhall NH Flat Race (2m+)	Sicilian Answer	Lt. Commdr. G Lennox-Cotton	F Shortt	Mr P Gallagher
1982					
July 6	Carnes 2 y/o Maiden (5f)	The Flying Sputnik	L Browne	L Browne	MJ Kinane
Good	Beaumond Mn. Hurdle (2m)	Sinead's Princess	PC Boyd	A Redmond	F Berry
	Dardistown H'cap (1m)	Truculent Scholar	Dr. J Tornsey	EJ O'Grady	PV Gilson
	Bolies H'cap Hurdle (3m)	Gallant Prince	Mrs PJ O'Connor	P Mullins	A Mullins
	Kilsharvan Maiden (5f)	Rioting	FN Groves	TG Curtin	W Swinburn
	Lisdornan Flat race (2m+)	Rugged Maid	IJ Keeling	IJ Keeling	Mr IJ Keeling
July 7	Meath Hurdle (2m+)	Northern Sky	J Feerick	P Hughes	F Berry
Good to Firm	Ardcath Maiden (1m) Div I	Electra Glide	D Prentice	K Prendergast	G Curran
	Do. Div II	Flamante	ND Biddle	K Prendergast	G Curran
	Sean Graham Am. H'cap Hurdle (2 1/2m)	Half Shot	J Curran	P Rooney	Mr T McCourt
	Collierstown H'cap (5f)	Senta's Girl	Lady S Barry	H de Bromhead	D Gillespie

	Race	Winner	Owner	Trainer	Jockey
	Hilltown H'cap (1m 6f)	Sanmarr	JS Bolger	JS Bolger	D Gillespie
	Bradain Maiden (1m 6f)	H Harry	EJ Cunningham	MF Morris	Mr J Queally
July 8	Crockafotha H'cap Hurdle (2m+)	Tamers Belle	PJ Donavan	F Flood	F Berry
Firm	Shallon 2 y/o Maiden (5f)	Sept	JF Kelly	DK Weld	W Swinburn
	Drogheda H'cap (1m)	Loose Goose	MJ Heaslip	M Cunningham	D Gillespie
	Corporation Maiden (1m 6f)	Behroz	JM Egan	L Browne	D Parnell
	Bellewstown Mares Md. Hurdle (2m+)	Ballymacarrett	Marquess of Donegall	J Fowler	Mr J Fowler
	Legganhall NH Flat Race (2m+)	Wingate	P Griffin	P Griffin	Mr RJ Beggan
1983					
July 5	Carnes 2 y/o Maiden (5f)	Nosey	D Prentice	K Prendergast	G Curran
Firm	Beaumond Mn. Hurdle (2m)	Sir Lee	F Conroy	A Redmond	F Berry
	Dardistown H'cap (1m)	Persian Potamia	TP Donahue	TA Regan	B Coogan
	Bolies H'cap Hurdle (3m)	Daltmore	N Coburn	N Meade	T Carmody
	Kilsharvan Maiden (5f)	Two Touches	J Dunne	N Meade	S Craine
	Lisdornan Flat race (2m+)	Ballycahan Boy	A Mooney	R Coonan	Mr J Shortt
July 6	Meath Hurdle (2m+)	Pasquinal	S McGrath	S McGrath	JP Byrne
Firm	Ardcath Maiden (1m)	Tetradracham	NB Hunt	TG Curtin	K Moses
	Hilltown H'cap (1m 6f)	Wingate	P Griffin	P Griffin	J Deegan
	Duleek Am. H'cap Hurdle (2 1/2m)	Wren's Lass	D O'Hagan	JR Cox	Mr J Queally
	Collierstown H'cap (5f) Div I	Gulf Girl	Mrs EM Burke	M Kauntze	MJ Kinane
	Do. Div II	Waiting Knight	NB Hunt	TG Curtin	K Moses
	Bradain Maiden (1m 6f)	Little Mills	B Daly	JR Cox	Mr J Queally
July 7	Bellewstown Mares Md. Hurdle (2m+)	Dual Express	Mrs E Birchall	V Bowens	MM Lynch
Firm	Shallon 2 y/o Maiden (5f)	Gallant Deer	FP Glennon	M Connolly	C Roche
	Drogheda H'cap (1m)	The Chancey Man	J Sweeney	JS Bolger	D Gillespie
	Crockafotha H'cap Hurdle (2m+)	Roaminer	J Farrell	PB Farrell	JN Brady
	Corporation Maiden (1m 6f)	Private Opinion	Mrs Gaisford St.Lawrence	M Kauntze	JC Barker
	Legganhall NH Flat Race (2m+)	Zaratino	C Gould	C Gould	Mr TM Walsh
1984					
July 3	Kilsharvan Maiden (5 fur)	Recent Events	AD Brennan	P Norris	G Curran
(Firm)	Beaumond Maiden Hurdle (2ml)	Ballyglunin	N Hogan	JR Bryce Smyth	M Cummins
	Carnes Fillies 2y/o Race (5f)	Wolverine Wonder	P Leon	K Prendergast	G Curran
	Bolies H'Cap Hurdle (3m)	Retinue Dual	D McParland	C Kinane	M J Byrne
	Dardistown H'Cap (1ml)	Divine Aspara	Ms C Anthony	K Prendergast	A J Nolan
	Lisdornan INH Flat Race (2ml)	Paupers Spring	Capt JP Roche	F Flood	Mr M Phelan
July 4	Meath Hurdle (2 ml)	The Centaur	C P Magnier	C Magnier	Mr CP Magnier
(Firm)	Ardcath Maiden (1 ml)	Miss Racine	Dr JF Miller	K Prendergast	G Curran
	Hilltown H'Cap (1 ml.6f)	Commanding Height	P McKeever	M Kauntze	D Parnell
	Duleek Am. H'cap Hurdle (2ml)	Deputy's Pass	G Dobbs	J Dreaper	Mr DH O'Connor
	Collierstown H'Cap (5f)	Libby Jayne	J W Cuthbert	P Norris	M Kinane
	Bradain Maiden (1 m.6f)	Black Economy	Ms T Matthews	J R Cox	Mr J Shortt
July 5	Shallon 2y/0 Maiden (5f)	Torresol	Ms M. Brennan	M Connolly	MJ Kinane

	Race	Winner	Owner	Trainer	Jockey
(Firm)	Drogheda H'Cap (1m)	Jaflora	WJ Hamilton	M Connolly	MJ Kinane
	Crockafotha H'Cap Hurdle (2m)	Prince Constance	RG Philliphs	F Ennis	PA Farrell
	Corporation Maiden (1m1.6f)	Michaela	CAB St George	K Prendergast	G Curran
	Bellewstown Mares Maiden Hurdle (2m)	Call Me Anna	G Halford	P McEntee	M. Halford
	Leggan Hall N/H Flat Race	North Brigade	TM Walsh	R Walsh	Mr TM Walsh
1985					
July 2	Kilsharvan Maiden (5f)	Winds Light	Ms S McCarthy	P Mullins	S Craine
(Good)	Beamond Maiden Hurdle (2ml)	Helens Birthday	C Carr	JR Bryce Smith	T.J Taaffee
	Carnes Fillies 2 y/0 Plate (5 f)	Pollete	NB Hunt	TG Curtin	K Moses
	Potato Growers H'Cap Hurdle (3m)	Fort Invader	C Murdock	JR Cox	Mr J Shortt
	Drogheda H'Cap (Div I) 1m	Silver Lark	Ms EP Lynam	E Lynam	D Manning
	Drogheda H'Cap (Div II)	Aqualon	Ms. S Hickey	T Casey	D Gillespie
	Lisdornan INH Flat Race (2m)	Bonnie Buskins	Ms JP Daly	JP Daly	Mr PP Larkin
July 3	Meath Hurdle (2ml)	Pitch Hitter	B Carolan	N Meade	P Leech
(Good)	Five Roads Maiden (1m)	Secundus	O Brady	TA Regan	D J Murphy
	Hilltown H'Cap (1m 6f)	Joe Denby	Tl Duggan	Tl Duggan	D Manning
	Jack Penny Mem H'Cap Hurdle 2 m	Hasty Prince	MP Farrell	T Carberry	F Berry
	Collierstown H'Cap (Div I) 5 f	Another Deb	Ms DP Magnier	A Redmond	S Craine
	Collierstown H'Cap (Div II)	Formalist	Ms MA O'Toole	MA O'Toole	D Manning
	Bradain Maiden (1m6f)	Polar Bee	G Mayers	C Magnier	Mr CP Magnier
July 4	Shallon 2y/0 Maiden Div I (1m)	Song An'DanceMan	Ms KPrendergast	K Prendergast	G Curran
Good to Firm	Shallon 2y/0 Maiden Div II (1m)	Caroline Anne	B Malone	B Malone	J Coogan
	Bellewstown Mares Maiden Hurdle (2m)	Call Me Kiri	Ms A Bergin	PJ Molloy	Mr M McNulty
	Crockafotha H'Cap Hurdle (2ml)	Cuban Crisis	MV Manning	MV Manning	PMcCormick
	Dardistown EBF H'Cap (1m)	Irish Folly	M Fustok	JM Oxx	D Hogan
	Corporation Maiden (1m 6f)	Rage In The Cage	F Conroy	EJ O'Grady	S Craine
	V Keating INH Flat Race (2m)	Four Trix	JR Cox	JR Cox	Mr J Shortt
1986					
July 1	Kilsharvan Maiden (5f)	Island Danny	D Brosnan	TF Lacy	D Gillespie
Good	Beaumond Maiden Hurdle (2m)	McKillop	Ms. M Halford	M Halford	T Carmody
	Carnes Fillies 2y/o Maiden (5f)	African Cousin	G Mullins	P Mullins	CF Swan
	Potato Growers H'Cap Hurdle (3m)	Bavamour	E McKeever	P Martin	Mr. J Queally
	Drogheda H'Cap Div I (1m)	Classic Times	N Carter	DK Weld	MJ Kinane
	Drogheda H'Cap Div II (1m)	Dancer's Shoe	Ms MJ Waldron	RM Connolly	R Hillis
	Drogheda/Dundalk Dairies INH Flat (2m)	Turf'Side VI	TH Moore	RM Connolly	Mr CP Magnier
July 2	Five Roads Maiden (1m)	Royal Celerity	RM Rennick	JR Cox	JM Hunter
Good	J. Penny Mem. H'Cap Hurdle (2m)	Four Trix	Ms S Catherwood	JR Cox	M Flynn
	S. Mulvany Hurdle (2.1/2m)	Winning Nora	DJ Reddan	M Hourigan	KF O'Brien
	Hilltown H'Cap (1m 6f)	Magic Deer	FP Glennon	M Connolly	R Hillis
	Collierstown H'Cap Div.I (5f)	Zinzi	JP Costelloe	JP. Costelloe	D Parnell
	Collierstown H'Cap Div II (5f)	Miami High	TR Smith	TA Regan	R Hillis

	Race	Winner	Owner	Trainer	Jockey
July 3	Bradain Race (1m 6f)	Windy Harbour	JJ Byrne	T Carberry	Mr. J Queally
	Bellewstown Mares Maiden Hurdle Div 1	Ewood Park	Ms EJ Hogan	JM Kennedy	P Leech
Good	Bellewstown Mares Maiden Hurdle Div II	Ella Rosa	Ms E Hackett	T Carberry	D Geraghty
	Corporation Maiden (1m 6f)	Carogrove	Lord Iveagh	K Prendergast	G Curran
	Crockafotha H'Cap Hurdle (2m)	Crohane Chieftain	Ms N Hayden	E Hayden	P Gill
	Dardistown E.B.F. H'Cap (1m)	Majestic Wolf	P Cusssen	D McDonagh	JF Egan
	Shallon 2y/o Maiden (1m)	Leszko Le Noir	A Mutchnik	DK Weld	MJ Kinane
	V Keating INH Flat Race (2m)	Harrington	DJ Reddan	M Hourigan	Mr E Bolger
1987					
June 30	Carnes Fillies 2y/o Maiden (5 f)	Pas Du Tout	JD Clague	M Kauntze	MJ Kinane
Good	Potato Growers H'Cap Hurdle (3m)	New Sister	R McCarthy	N Meade	P Leech
	Kilsharvan Maiden (5f)	Power and Red	MJ O'Meara	A Leahy	JM Hunter
	S Mulvaney Hurdle (2.5m)	Pargan	Ms P Mullins	P Mullins	A Mullins
	Drogheda H'Cap Div. I (1m)	Fletcher Christian	AerohorseracingLt	RM Connolly	R Carroll
	Drogheda H'Cap Div. II (1m)	Tokyo Joe	Ms PAMcLernon	M Halford	PV Gilson
	T.J Molloy (Coal) INH Flat Race (2m)	Atlantic Angel	Ms B McKeown	M Cunningham	Mr. AJ Martin
July 1	Five Roads Maiden (1m)	Absence	BR Firestone	DK Weld	MJ Kinane
Good	M Moore (Car Sales) Maiden Hurdle (2m)	Saintfield	SMawhinney	JP Harty	TG McCourt
	J Penny Memorial H'Cap Hurdle (2m)	Timber Creek	Ms J Wade	JP Byrne	JP Byrne
	Hilltown H'Cap (1m6f)	Cooliney Chimes	JM O'Malley	M Cunningham	D Gillespie
	Collierstown H'Cap Div I (5f)	Haulboulder	J Sheridan	P Russell	D Parnell
	Collierstown H'Cap Div II (5f)	FlowerFromHeaven	W Granville	C Kinane	MJ Kinane
	SP Graham Flat Race (1m6f)	Never Be Great	Ms K Urquhart	F Flood	Mr JA Berry
	Bellewstown Maiden Hurdle (2m)	Black Trix	JR Cox	JR Cox	J Shortt
July 2	Corporation Maiden (1m6f)	Montagnard	Lord Iveagh	K Prendergast	G Curran
Good/Firm	Crockafotha H'Cap Hurdle (2.5m)	Fane Prince	N Coburn	N Meade	P Leech
	Shallon 2y/o Maiden (1m)	Top Cut	Ms MJ Comer	V Bowens	CN Bowens
	Dardistown EBF H'Cap (1m)	Hazy Bird	JM Cusack	P Mullins	S Craine
	V Keating (Oil) INH Flat Race (2m)	Mid-day Run VI	FM O'Brien	FM O'Brien	Mr JP O'Brien
1988					
July 5	PB Gunne 2y/o Fillies Maiden (5f)	Country Clover	MJ Cleary	P Hughes	S Craine
Good/Firm	Potato Growers H'Cap Hurdle (3m)	Sandymount	Ms D Tarrant	FM O'Brien	KF O'Brien
	Balbriggan Shopping Centre Maiden (5f)	Sweet Hollow	FN Groves	TG Curtin	JF Egan
	Seamus Mulvaney Hurdle (2.5m)	Gallant Boy	Ms J Harrington	Ms J Harrington	A Powell
	Murphy Sand & Gravel H'Cap Div I (1m)	Persian Valley	P Pender	M Grassick	N McCullagh
	Murphy Sand & Gravel H'Cap Div II (1m)	Mr Mystery	SJ Murphy	P Martin	P Gilson
	Betaway INH Flat Race (2m)	Dalus Dawn	N Treacy	WP Treacy	Mr N Kennedy
July 6	M Moore Car Sales Hurdle (2m)	Gemini Way	F Corrigan	P Norris	B Sheridan
Firm	PB Gunne Maiden (1m)	Nec Precario	TD Tieken	JP Harty	EA Leonard
	Ladies Day H'Cap Hurdle (2m)	Valtron Lad	AD Evans	AD Evans	DT Evans
	Murphy's Irish Stout H'Cap (1m6f)	Profligate	FJ Hardy	RM Connolly	C Roche
	Cock Tavern H'Cap (5f)	Flower from Heaven	W Granville	C Kinane	MJ Kinane

	Race	Winner	Owner	Trainer	Jockey
July 7	Sean Graham Amateur Flat Race (1m.6f)	Innocent Choice	Ms J Byrne	P Mullins	Mr. WP Mullins
Firm	Drogheda Town Centre Maiden Hurdle	Golden Wood	Ms W Cunningham	M Halford	T Carmody
	PB Gunne Maiden (1m6f)	Mizuna	TD Tieken	JP Harty	D Gillespie
	Bernard Barry H'Cap Hurdle (2.5m)	Trouville Lady	P O'Leary	P O'Leary	N O'Toole
	Water Jump EBF 2y/o Maiden (1m)	Evana's Pride	P McCutcheon	JC Hayden	D Gillespie
	Heineken EBF H'Cap (1m)	Ballatico	F Cullen	O Finnegan	DV Smith
	V Keating Oil Dist INH Flat Race (2m)	Slaney Queen	Ms M Hayes	P Martin	Mr J Queally
1989					
July 4	Kilsharvan 2y/o Fillies Maiden (5f)	Bold Starlet	Ms MA O'Toole	MA O'Toole	JP Murtagh
Good	Gunne's Carnaross Mart H'Cap Hurdle 3m	Black Trix	JR Cox	JR Cox	C O'Dwyer
	Balbriggan Shopping Centre (5f)	Saint Joachim	DM Rooney	M Kauntze	P Shanahan
	Seamus Mulvaney Hurdle (2.5m)	Pargan	Ms P Mullins	P Mullins	A Mullins
	Murphy Sand & Gravel H'Cap Div I (1m)	Expensive Lad	MB Moore	DK Weld	MJ Kinane
	Murphy Sand & Gravel H'Cap Div II (1m)	Grand Weather	AA McCloskey	DK Weld	MJ Kinane
	Betaway INH Flat Race (2m)	Bee Friend	Ms AF Mee	JT Dreaper	Mr M McNulty
July 5	M Moore Car Sales Hurdle (2m)	Toohami	Ms M Tierney	WP Mullins	A Mullins
Good	Gunne Monaghan Marts Maiden (1m)	Killiney Graduate	V O'Reilly	V Kennedy	PV Gilson
	Potato Growers H'Cap Hurdle (2m)	Derrynap	Ms S Purcell	R Donoghue	R Byrne
	Ladies Day H'Cap (1m6f)	Orembo	Ms RW Hanson	M Kauntze	MJ Kinane
	Cock Tavern H'Cap (5f)	Littlepace	Ms J Keaney	T Keaney	JP Murtagh
	Bellewstown Race (1m4f)	Picture Perfect	BR Firestone	DK Weld	MJ Kinane
	Foran's Equine Products Flat Race (1m 6)	Coolcullen	Ms U Bolger	JS Bolger	Mr AP O'Brien
July 6	John Ward Novice Hurdle (2.5m)	Profligate	PJ Hardy	T Carberry	T Carmody
Good	Gunne Carrickmacross Mart Maiden (1m6f)	Newton John	N Schibbye	JM Oxx	JP Murtagh
	Bernard Barry Crockafotha HCap Hdle	Corporate Raider	East Meath RC	TG McCourt	N Byrne
	Hilltown 2y/o Maiden (1m)	Albakht	H-AlMaktoum	DK Weld	MJ Kinane
	Amstel H'Cap (1m)	Turbo Rose	R Lewis	P Hughes	JP Murtagh
	DR Enterprises Maiden Hurdle (2m)	Dance On Lady	Ms K Prendergast	K Prendergast	CF Swan
	V Keating Oil Dist. INH Flat Race (2m)	Sunset Travel	Ms A Healy	P Martin	Mr FJ Flood
1990					
July 3	Balbriggan Shopping Centre Maiden (5f)	Hitchin A Ride	Ms PV Doyle	Mrs PV Doyle	M Fenton
Good	Forans Equine Products H'Cap Hurdle (3m)	Sam Weller	Ms C Taaffe	PA McCartan	P Clarke
	Derrinstown Stud Sprint 2y/o Series (5f)	Downeaster Alexa	G McNulty	K Prendergast	WF Harris
	Seamus Mulvaney Hurdle (2.5m)	Never Be Great	P McAteer	F Flood	C O'Dwyer
	Murphy Sand & Gravel H'Cap Div I (1ml)	Nukonnen	Pollardstown RS	PA McCartan	JP Murtagh
	Murphy Sand & Gravel H'Cap Div II (1ml)	Slightly Shy	J Andrews	JT Gorman	AJ Nolan
	Betaway INH Flat Race (2m)	Bel Slipper	P Grimes	M Murray	Mr C McCann Jun
July 4	M Moore Car Sales Hurdle (2m)	Saygoodbye	P Reynolds	John Murphy	M Flynn
Yielding	Ardcath Maiden (1m)	Burella	Ms D Grant	PJ Finn	G Curran
	Potato Growers H'Cap Hurdle (2m)	Orbis	Ms C Shubotham	JS Bolger	LP Cusack
	Ladies Day H'Cap (1m6f)	Montezuma	CAB St George	K Prendergast	RM Burke
	Cock Tavern H'Cap (5f)	Majesty's Nurse	F Towey	PA McCartan	R Hughes

	Race	Winner	Owner	Trainer	Jockey
	Bellewstown Inn Race (1m4f)	Gaze Upon	S O'Shea	DK Weld	MJ Kinane
	Duleek QR Race (1m6f)	Latin Quarter	Ms M Heffernan	JS Bolger	Mr AP O'Brien
July 5	Drogheda Novice Hurdle (2.5m)	Gentle Lad	C Kinane	C Kinane	Mr CT Kinane
Soft	Garristown Race (1m6f)	Arabian Nights	Y Akazawa	DK Weld	MJ Kinane
	B Barry Crockafotha H'Cap Hurdle (2.5m)	Hero to Zero	P Smyth	Ms SB Duffy	PD Carey
	Tattersalls 2y/o Maiden (1m)	Nordic Sun	Hde Kwiatkowski	JS Bolger	C Roche
	Heineken EBF H'Cap (1m)	Blue Sceptre	CS GSt Lawrence	M Kauntze	WJ O'Connor
	DR Enterprises Maiden Hurdle (2m)	The Ridge Boreen	T Farrell	G Farrell	T Carmody
	V Keating Oil Distributors INH Flat Race	Pit Runner	Mrs P. Mullins	P Mullins	Ms S McCarthy
1991					
July 2	Kilsharvan EBF Maiden (5f)	Lute And Lyre	DrRTornseyDurkin	EJ O'Grady	T J O'Sullivan
Good	Collierstown Hurdle (2.5m)	Viola Quay	J Doody	J Coogan	PA Davey
	Balbriggan Shopping Centre Maiden (5f)	Siwana	Aga Khan	JM Oxx	JP Murtagh
	Seamus Mulvaney H'Cap Hurdle (3m)	Twilight Gale	PA Glynn	K Riordan	D Leahy
	Murphy Sand & Gravel H'Cap Div I (1m)	Morris Dancer	Ms EJ O'Grady	EJ O'Grady	NG McCullagh
	Murphy Sand & Gravel H'Cap Div II (1m)	Mejive	Dr PF Lynch	BV Kelly	S Craine
	McLoughlin Oil INH Flat Race (2m)	Heloonium	DE Finn	Ms E Finn	Mr DE Finn
July 3	M Moore Car Sales Hurdle (2m)	Cellatica	AF Gleeson	JP Byrne	JP Byrne
Good	Ashbourne House Hotel Maiden (1m)	Mutarijam	H-AlMaktoum	K Prendergast	RJ Griffiths
	Potato Growers H'Cap Hurdle (2m)	Harristown Lady	A Comerford	A Redmond	PMcWilliams
	Anglo Print H'Cap (1m6f)	Prince Yaza	A Comerford	A Redmond	MJ Kinane
	Cock Tavern H'Cap (5f)	Simply Amber	ST McElligot	P Prendergast	DV Smith
	Bellewstown Inn Race (1m4f)	News Headlines	Classic T'Breds	MV O'Brien	PV Gilson
	Kepak Clonee QR Race (1m.6f)	Judicial	M Duffy	M Grassick	Mr R Neylon
July 4	Drogheda Novice Hurdle (2m4f)	Katesville	L Bowles	BV Kelly	Mr A J Martin
Good	Stamullen Maiden Hurdle (2m)	Pylon Sparks	Ms DA Breen	EP Harty	M Flynn
	Heineken H'Cap (1m)	Radley	TG Curtin	TG Curtin	JP Murtagh
	Tattersalls 2y/o Maiden (1m)	Penine Pass	FW Lynch	D Gillespie	S Craine
	S Mulvaney Crockafotha H'Cap Hurdle	Kayrawan	D McDonagh	D McDonagh	D Bromley
	Bambury Bookmakers Race (1m6f)	Banour	Aga Khan	JM Oxx	JP Murtagh
	V Keating Oil Dist INH Flat Race (2m)	Moresque	Timberlake Ltd	TG Curtin	Mr TM Walsh
1992					
June 30	M McAuley Fingal Contr 2y/o Maiden (5f)	Gate Lodge	Maj V McCalmont	M. Kauntze	MJ Kinane
Good	Oldbridge Concrete Hurdle (2m4f)	Head of Chambers	Ms M Watt	MA O'Toole	JP Banahan
	Balbriggan Shopping Centre Maiden (5f)	Imprimatur	Ms MA O'Toole	MA O'Toole	MJ Kinane
	Bambury Bookmakers H'Cap (1m6f)	Mariyda	Aga Khan	JM Oxx	DG O'Shea
	S Mulvaney H'Cap Hurdle (3m)	Harristown Lady	A Comerford	A Redmond	A Powell
	Murphy Sand & Gravel H'Cap (1m)	Happy Rover	Ms E McMahon	F Dunne	RM Burke
	McLoughlin's Oil INH Flat Race (2m)	Turnings Lass	Ms A Keane	M Halford	Mr C Farrell
July 1	Tattersalls 2y/o Auction Race (1m)	Earl of Barking	Ms C McNulty	KPrendergast	RJ Griffiths
Good	M Moore Car Sales Hurdle (2m)	Tymoole	R P Gogan	N Meade	H Rogers

	Race	Winner	Owner	Trainer	Jockey
	Ashbourne House Hotel Maiden (1m)	Damisters Pet	M Fennessy	DK weld	MJ Kinane
	Carrolls Festival H'Cap Div I (1m)	Drumaaler	Nineties RC	E Lynam	M Fenton
	Carrolls Festival H'Cap Div II (1m)	Tombara	Ms B Howard	J Coogan	B Coogan
	Tayto Growers H'Cap Hurdle (2m)	Beau Beauchamp	D Kinsella	N Meade	CF Swan
	Anglo Printers H'Cap (5f)	Osvaldo	JP Gleeson	JS Bolger	C Roche
	Bellewstown Inn QR Race (1m6f)	Enqelaab	Kildare RC	MA O'Toole	Mr D Marnane
July 2	John D's 2y/o Maiden (1m)	Lantasia	H-Al Maktoum	D Weld	MJ Kinane
Good	Bookmakers Maiden Hurdle (3m)	Oatfield Lad	PJ Lohan	D Gillespie	M Flynn
	Heineken H'Cap (1m)	Classic Match	P Yan-yeund	DJ Murphy	PV Gilson
	Tipperary Water Novice Hurdle (2m4f)	El Bae	BH Leneghan	A Moore	TJ Taaffe
	S Mulvaney Crockafotha H'CapHurdle	Pearl Twist	JJ O'Neil	JJ O'Neill	PL Malone
	Derek Plant Race (1m 6f)	Clivden Gail	Int TheBreeders	DK Weld	MJ Kinane
	V Keating Oil Dist INH Flat Race (2m)	Bellecarra	W Moore	P Casey	Mr PJ Casey
1993					
July 6	Kilsharvan EBF 2y/o Maiden (5f)	Nurmi	Ms A Doyle	PJ Flynn	JF Egan
Good/Firm	Hilltown Hurdle (2m6f)	Cabra Towers	JG Cosgrave	JG Cosgrave	MM Mackin
	Maurice McAuley Memorial M/n (5f)	Killeen Star	R Fabrizius	M Grassick	R Hughes
	Oldbridge Concrete H'cap (1m6f)	Angareb	Lone Star Syndicate	M Halford	PV Gilson
	Bolies H'Cap Hurdle (3m)	Pearl Twist	JJ O'Neill	JJ O'Neill	PL Malone
	Murphy Sand &Gravel H'Cap (1m)	Happy Rover	Ms EM McMahon	F Dunne	J P Murtagh
	McLoughlin Oil INH Flat Race (2m)	First Session	JA Mernagh	WP Mullins	Ms JM Mullins
July 7	Michael Moore Car Sales Hurdle (2m)	His Way	R Scott	K Prendergast	M Flynn
Good/Firm	Tattersalls 2y/o Auction Race (1m)	Summerhill Special	P Beirne	P Beirne	Ms J Morgan
	Ashbourne House Hotel Maiden (1m)	What A Pleasure	Ms K Prendergast	K Prendergast	BJ Walsh
	Carrolls Festival H'Cap Div I (1m)	Mejeve	Ms M Cahill	BV Kelly	S Craine
	Carrolls Festival H'Cap Div II)1m)	The Bower	Ms C Collins	C Collins	RM Burke
	Tayto Growers H'Cap Hurdle (2m)	Aquinas	W Hennessy	A Mullins	RA Hennessy
	Anglo Printers H'Cap (5f)	Afterglow	Ms J Magnier	CP Magnier	L O'Shea
	Bellewstown Inn QR Race (1m6f)	Hackett's Cross	F Heffernan	N Chance	Mr JA Nash
July 8	Shallon 2y/o E.B.F. Maiden (1m)	Oliver Messel	Ms C McNulty	K Prendergast	WJ Supple
Firm	Bookmakers Maiden Hurdle (2m)	Open Market	S Creaven	DK Weld	B Sheridan
	Heineken H'Cap (1m)	Desert Calm	Ms C McNulty	K Prendergast	BJ Walsh
	Tipperary Water Novice Hurdle (2.5m)	Morning Dream	D Hassett	D Hassett	GM O'Neill
	S Mulvaney Crockafotha H'Cap Hurdle	SongOfCaedmon	Ms T Moriarty	D Hughes	CF Swan
	Derek Plant Race (1m6f)	Safe Conduct	F Dunne	F Dunne	JP Murtagh
	V Keatings Oil Dist NHF Flat Race (2m)	Cloghans Bay	Mrs P. Prendergast	P Prendergast	Mr JA Nash
1994					
July 5	Kilsharvan 2y/o EBF Maiden (5f)	Double Risk	McLorc Synd	J Coogan	B Coogan
Good	Michael Moore Car Sales Hurdle (2m)	LakeOf Loughrea	BezwellFixingsLtd	KPrendergast	J Shortt
	Maurice McAuley Mem. Maiden (5f)	Tourandot	Ms T Stack	T Stack	S Craine
	Oldbridge Concrete H'Cap (1m6f)	Wesbet	Ms S McCullagh	M McCullagh	D McCullagh
	Agrifert H'Cap Hurdle (3m)	Merry People	K Casey	J Queally	T Horgan

	Race	Winner	Owner	Trainer	Jockey
	Murphy Sand & Gravel H'Cap (1m)	Nordic Colours	Ms JS Bolger	JS Bolger	JA Heffernan
	McLoughlins Oil INH Flat Race (2m)	Lancastrians Dream	Bracken Synd	AP O'Brien	Mr. GF Ryan
July 6	Hilltown 4y/0 Hurdle (2m)	LaCenerentola	Ms M Hunt	N Meade	Paul Carberry
Good	Tattersalls 2y/o Auction Race (1m)	Hero's Honour	Ms JM Ryan	AP O'Brien	JA Heffernan
(Soft after	Ashbourne House Hotel Maiden (1m)	Nun's Island	Fun Synd	J Coogan	PV Gilson
4th Race)	Durham's Miners Gala Fest H'Cap DivI	Blake's Hotel	W McDonald	MA O'Toole	JF Egan
	Durham's Miners Gala Fest H'Cap DivII	Noble Choice	JJ McLoughlin	JJ McLoughlin	PJ Smullen
	Tayto Growers H'Cap Hurldle (2m)	Dashing Rose	F Towey	N Meade	Paul Carberry
	Anglo Printers H'Cap (5f)	Matchless Prince	Ms P O'Reilly	PJ Flynn	M Duffy
	Mullagh Quarries QR Race (1m6f)	Rockfield Native	MF McKeon	AP O'Brien	Mr AP O'Brien
July 7	Shallon 2y/o E.B.F. Maiden (1m)	Blue Kestrel	D Fagan	K Prendergast	WJ Supple
Yielding/soft	Bookmakers Maiden Hurdle (2m)	Stevie Be	SJ Fahy	M Hourigan	KF O'Brien
	Heineken H'Cap (1m)	General Chaos	JN Anthony	C Collins	S Craine
	Tipperary Water Nov Hurdle (2.5m)	Push The Button	Ms G Maher	MJ PO'Brien	DJ Finnegan
	S Mulvaney Crockafotha H'Cap Hurdle	Coin Machine	P Hughes	P Hughes	Paul Carberry
	Derek Plant H'Cap (1m6f)	Huncheon Chance	A McAleese	I Ferguson	AP McCoy
	V Keating Oil Dist INH Flat Race (2m)	Waterloo Ball	J Smyth	AP O'Brien	Mr GF Ryan
1995					
July 4	Kilsharvan 2y/o EBF Maiden (5fur)	Almaty	P Savill	C Collins	PV Gilson
Good	Agrifert H'Cap Hurdle (3m)	DerravaraghGale	L Gilsenan	C Ross	F Woods
	Oldbridge Concrete H'Cap (1m6f)	Multy	MsKPrendergast	K Prendergast	WJ Supple
	Maurice McAuley Mem Maiden (5f)	Violets Wild	MsA RiddleMartin	C Collins	PV Gilson
	M Moore Car Sales Hurdle (2m)	CullenstownLady	P Hughes	P Hughes	CF Swan
	Murphy Sand & Gravel H'Cap (1m)	Dance Academy	M Haga	M Kauntze	WJ O'Connor
	McLoughlin's Oil INH Flat Race (2m)	Harry Heaney	KP Heaney	P Martin	Mr K Whelan
July 5	Potato Protection 4y/o Hurdle (2m)	Better Style	Becks Synd	T O'Neill	CF Swan
Good to Firm	Tattersalls 2y/o Maiden (1m)	MagicCombination	RJ Cullen	K Prendergast	WJ Supple
	Ashbourne House Hotel H'Cap (1m)	Zico	RP Behan	E Lynam	DA O'Sullivan
	Durham's Miners Gala Fest H'Cap (1m)	Royal Crimson	Ms MA O'Toole	MA O'Toole	JF Egan
	Tayto Growers H'cap Hurdle (2m)	Turning Point	R Jordan	A Moore	F Woods
	Anglo Printers H'Cap (5f)	Coolowen Flash	B McSweeney	JJ Walsh	RM Burke
	Mullagh Quarries QR Race (1m6f)	Brave Fountain	Ms C Conroy	AP O'Brien	Ms F Crowley
July 6	Shallon 2y/o EBF Maiden (1m)	Sholam	ShMohammad	M Kauntze	W J O'Connor
Good to Firm	Sam Dennigan Maiden Hurdle (2m)	WelcomeExpress	TAD Enterprises	M Flynn	DT Evans
	Heineken H'Cap (1m)	Kilconnel	Ms MaxwellMoran	DK Weld	MJ Kinane
	Tipperary Water Nov Hurdle (2m)	No Dunce	Ms P Mullins	P Mullins	DJ Casey
	S Mulvaney Crockafotha H'Cap Hurdle	Maid Of Glenduragh	RC Irvine	JF Maxwell	B Sheridan
	Derek Plant H'Cap (1m6f)	TouchingMoment	MS J McGettigan	A Moore	F Woods
	V Keating Oil Dist INH Flat Race (2m())	Cladaha Rose	Ms P Ryan	AP O'Brien	Ms FCrowley
1996					
July 2	Kilsharvan EBF 2y/o Maiden (5f)	On Bended Knee	Last Grand Synd	JS Bolger	KJ Manning
Good/Firm	Agrifert H'Cap Hurdle (3m)	Arctic Kate	Ms PD Richards	J O'Haire	C O'Dwyer

Race	Winner	Owner	Trainer	Jockey
Maurice McAuley Mem Maiden (5f)	Cuddles	GS RC	AP O'Brien	JA Heffernan
Oldbridge Concrete H'Cap (1m 6f)	MagicCombinationm	RJ Cullen	K Prendergast	WJ Supple
Murphy Sand & Gravel 3 y/o Maiden(1m)	Forsake Me Not	Ms H Norton	C Collins	P Shanahan
McLoughlin's Oil INH Flat Race (2m)	MoonlightEscapade	P Shanahan	A Mullins	Mr P Fenton
M Moore Car Sales Hurdle (2m)	Siberian Tale	Ms P Casey	P Casey	MrPJ Casey
July 3 Potato Protection 4 y/o Nov Hurdle (2m)	Wesperada	Ms A McAleer	N Meade	Paul Carberry
Good/Firm Tattersalls 2y/o Maiden (1m)	Burtown	MsK Prendergast	K Prendergast	WJ Supple
McDermott Communications H'Cap (1m)	Gerry Dardis	DPK Synd	JP Kavanagh	PJ Smullen
Shotfirers H'Cap (1m)	Bajan Queen	C Johnston	P Martin	JJ Behan
Tayto Growers H'Cap Hurdle (2m)	Near Gale	PF Kehoe	P Mullins	TP Treacy
Anglo Printers H'Cap (5f)	BestBeforeDawn	Ms AM O'Brien	A P O'Brien	JA Heffernan
Branagans QR Race (1m6f)	Celtic Lore	M Smurfitt	DK Weld	Mr D Marnane
July 4 Shallon EBF 2y/o Maiden (1m)	Mystic Magic	Ms Lauterpacht	C Collins	PV Gilson
Good Sam Dennigan Maiden Hurdle (2m)	Red Glitter	W Godfrey	JA Quinn	CF Swan
Heineken H'Cap (1m)	BoldandGorgeous	F Sheedy	AP O'Brien	JA Heffernan
Tipperary Water Maiden Hurdle (3m)	Kilcaramore	PJ Healy	PJ Healy	Mr PJ Healy
SV Mulvaney Crockafotha H'Cap Hurdle	Shorewood	L Thompson	EJ O'Grady	F Woods
Derek Plant H'Cap (1m6f)	NotComplainingBut	Ms CA Moore	P Mullins	T P Treacy
V Keating Oil Dist INH Flat Race (2m)	Supreme Charm	DM O'Meara	M O'Meara	Mr P Fenton
1997				
July 1 Kilsharvan EBF 2y/o Maiden (5f)	Dress Design	Y Akazawa	J Muldoon	WJ Supple
Good/Yielding Agrifert H'CapHurdle (3m)	Kilcar	JH Patton	T Carberry	Paul Carberry
Maurice McAuley Mem Maiden (1m)	Burnt Toast	Ms T Stack	T Stack	JP Murtagh
Oldbridge Concrete H'Cap (1m6f)	Jawah	Sheikh Ahmed	DK Weld	DP McDonagh
M Moore Car Sales Hurdle (2.5m)	Welcome Parade	Ms N O Callaghan	T Taaffe	C O'Dwyer
Murphy Sand & Gravel 3 y/o Maiden (1m)	I Have To Go	P Cluskey	P Cluskey	WJ Smith
McLoughlin's Oil INH Flat Race (2m)	Hi Jamie	Ms D Reddan	AJ Martin	Mr AJ Martin
July 2 Potato Protection 4 y/o Nov Hurdle (2m)	Snow Falcon	Falcon Synd	T Taaffe	N Williamson
Yielding/Soft Tattersalls 2y/o Maiden (1m)	Precise Direction	Ms K Magnier	AP O'Brien	JA Heffernan
McDermott Comm H'Cap Div I (1m)	Shahnad	Ms M Behan	DP Kelly	WJ Smith
McDermott Comm H'Cap Div II (1m)	Aurliano	Ms M McWey	JT Gorman	P Shanahan
Billy McShane Mem H'Cap (1m)	Bolero Dancer	Arlington RS	T O'Neill	PJ Smullen
Bambury Bookmakers QR Race (1m6f)	Born To Win	TB Conroy	MJP O'Brien	TP Rudd
Tayto Growers H'Cap Hurdle (2m)	Tinker Amelia	JG McDonnell	JG McDonnell	G Moylan
Xcess Ind Contract Staff H'Cap (5f)	Valley Erne	SAM Syndicate	M Cunningham	Mr P Fenton
July 3 Blooms Hotel Maiden (1m4f)	Hamamelis	Hon S Lawson	MJP O'Brien	E Aherne
Soft Sam Dennigan Maiden Hurdle (2m)	Alambar	Ms G O'Brien	N Meade	Paul Carberry
Heineken H'Cap (1m)	Eternal Joy	M Tabor	AP O'Brien	JA Heffernan
Tipperary Water Maiden Hurdle (3m)	Kinnegad Girl	L Bowles	L Bowles	JM Maguire
S Mulvaney Crockafoth H'Cap Hurdle	Roseaustin	M Donohoe	M Donohoe	D McCullagh
Derek Plant H'Cap (1m6f)	Sambara	Demure Synd	WP Mullins	JP Murtagh
Vincent & Nancy Keating INH Flat Race	Jackpot Johnny	T Farrell	G Farrell	Mr G Farrell

	Race	Winner	Owner	Trainer	Jockey
1998					
July 1	Kilsharvan EBF 2y/o Maiden (5f)	The Flying Pig	Ms M Horan	P Prendergast	S Craine
Good	Agrifert H'Cap Hurdle (3m)	Native Status	T Carberry	T Carberry	Mr PA Carberry
	Maurice McAuley Mem Maiden (5f)	Sarigor	Aga Khan	JM Oxx	JP Murtagh
	Oldbridge Concrete H'Cap (5f)	Generous Lady	J McKay	GA Cusack	FM Berry
	P Fallon Civil Eng Hurdle (2m4f)	Daisy A Day	J Bowe	J Bowe	D McCullagh
	Murphy Sand & Gravel 3y/o Maiden (1m)	Night Scout	M Morrin	K Prendergast	S Craine
	McLoughlin's Oil INH Flat Race (2m)	Townley Hall	GA Kingston	F Flood	Mr JP Byrne
July 2	Potato Protection 4y/o Nov Hurdle (2m)	Mumaris	PC Byrne	P Hughes	A Maguire
Good/Firm	Tattersalls 2y/o Maiden (1m)	Alabama Jacks	J McEvoy	K Prendergast	S Craine
	Old Mill H'Cap Div I (1m)	New Legislation	M Bergin	M Halford	JP Murtagh
	Old Mill H'Cap Div II (1m)	Eloquent Way	P Cluskey	P Cluskey	SJ Crawford
	Billy McShane Mem H'Cap (1m)	Luminoso	GP Moore	P Mooney	DR McCabe
	Tayto Growers H'Cap Hurdle (2m4f)	Southern Man	P O'Connor	Ms F Crowley	CF Swan
	ONC Contract Staff H'Cap (5f)	Burnt Toast	Ms T Stack	T Stack	JP Spencer
	Bambury Bookmakers QR Race (1m6f)	Galletina	TC Stewart	D Hanley	Mr A Coonan
July 3	Thatch Bar Maiden (1m4f)	Chaina	Sheik Mohammed	JM Oxx	JP Murtagh
Good/Firm	Sam Dennigan Maiden Hurdle Div I (2m)	Fawn Prince	JP McManus	CF Swan	CF Swan
	Sam Dennigan Maiden Hurdle Div II (2m)	Treasure Dome	Ms R Polly	N Meade	B Geraghty
	Heinken H'Cap (1m)	Golden Fact	Golden Sand Syn	M McElhone	P Shanahan
	Tipperary Water Maiden Hurdle (3m)	Mulligans Boy	Ms M McNamee	SM Cox	G Cotter
	S Mulvaney Crockafotha H'CapHurdle	Rice's Hill	AT Battersby	O Finnegan	PL Malone
	Derek Plant H'Cap (1m 6f)	No Avail	Ms P Mullins	P Mullins	SW Kelly
	Vincent&Nancy Keating Mem INH Flat	Colins Double	C McCarthy	C McCarthy	Mr RP McNally
1999					
June 30	Kilsharvan EBF 2y/o Maiden (5f)	Newpark Lady	Sax Syncicate	KF O'Brien	J P Murtagh
Good/Firm	Agrifert H'Cap Hurdle (3m)	Rice's Hill	AT Battersby	O Finnegan	PL Malone
	Maurice McAuley Mem Maiden (5f)	Black Paddy	Ms AM Hanley	D Hanley	E Ahern
	Oldbridge Concrete H'Cap (1m6f)	Undaunted	Woodpecker Syn	SJ Mahon	K Manning
	P Fallon Civil Eng Hurdle (2m4f)	Twin Gale	CKC Synd	SJ Tracey	SP McCann
	Murphy Sand & Gravel (3y/o Maiden(1m)	Sarraaf	H Al Makotum	K Prendergast	S Craine
	McLoughlin Oil INH Flat Race (2m)	MissDale	N Doyle	DT Hughes	Mr RM Walsh
July 1	Potato Protection 4y/o Nov Hurdle (2m)	Abuhail	Raglan Road Syn	DG McArdle	CF Swan
Good/Yielding	Tattersalls 2y/o Maiden (1m)	Neutron	Eight Hill Synd	Ms F Crowley	P Shanahan
	Old Mill H'Cap Div I (1m)	Gers Gold	ML Keating	J Harley	AP Fagan
	Old Mill H'Cap Div II (1m)	Treora	Ms L Carberry	WT Bourke	DA Stamp
	Bambury Bookmakers H'Cap (1m)	Society Queen	Ms P Casey	P Casey	O Casey
	Tayto Growers H'Cap Hurdle (2m)	Cheeky Harry	BM Reilly	G Keane	SP McCann
	ONC Recruitment H'Cap (5f)	Magic Annmarie	Impact II RS	P Martin	E Ahern
	Navan Shopping Centre QR Race (1m6f)	Monty's Fancy	J Cronin	WT Bourke	Mr CA Cronin
July 2	Dessie Kavanagh Mem Maiden (1m4f)	Prince Valiant	P Wetzel	DK Weld	PJ Smullen
Yielding/Soft	Sam Dennigan Maiden Hurdle (2m)	Okay Ocee	JJ O'Connor	EJ O'Grady	JF Titley

Race	Winner	Owner	Trainer	Jockey
Tipperary Water H'Cap (1m)	Gates	Sam Maguire Sy	DK Weld	PJ Smullen
Thatch Bar Maiden Hurdle (3m)	Outrigger	P Evans	Ms F Crowley	B Geraghty
S Mulvaney Crockafotha H'Cap Hurdle Div I	Duinin	M Kavanagh	P Hughes	CF Swan
S Mulvaney Crockafotha H'Cap Hurdle DivII	Savu Sea	M Doran	M Doran	R Walsh
Derek Plant H'Cap (1m 6f)	Snow Falcon	Falcon Synd	N Meade	FM Berry
Vincent & Nancy Keating Mem INH Flat	Scary Spice	Ms C O'Toole	WT Bourke	Mr JPByrne
2000				
July 5				
Kilsharvan EBF 2y/o Maiden (5f)	Stokesie	BJ Stokes	E Lynam	KJ Manning
Good/ Agrifert Handicap Hurdle (3m)	Star Club	Range Synd	M Halford	K Whelan
Firm in Places Maurice McAuley Mem Maiden (5f)	Indian Mystery	Ms CO'Reilly	DK Weld	PJ Smullen
Oldbridge Concrete H'Cap (1m6f)	Goldenhalo	CrockofGoldSyn	Ms F Crowley	C O'Donoghue
Seamus Murphy Balbriggan Hurdle (2.5m)	Miners Run	J Cox	WP Mullins	R Walsh
Murphy Sand & Gravel 3y/o Maiden (1m)	Copper Express	Ms AP-Ramos	DK Weld	PJ Smullen
McLoughlin's Oil INH Flat Race Div I (2m)	Mandalink	F Fitzsimons	CF Swan	Mr JF O'Meara
McLoughlin's Oil INH Flat Race Div II 2m	Galahoo Wonder	C Byrnes	C Byrnes	Mr P Fenton
July 6 Potato Protection 4y/o Novice Hurdle (2m)	Macabeo	Ms P Hunt	N Meade	Paul Carberry
Tattersalls 2y/o Maiden (1m)	Like A Dream	MJ Tynan	MJ Tynan	JA Heffernan
Good Irelands Own Annual H'Cap Div I (1m)	Illusions Tom	Ms BM Kirwan	AD Evans	WJ Smith
Irelands Own Annual H'Cap Div II (1m)	SpringfieldGuest	Ms M Flannery	DP Quinn	JA Heffernan
Bambury Bookmakers H'Cap (1m)	Helen Bach	SchoonerB Synd	M Halford	TP O'Shea
Tayto Growers H'Cup Hurdle (2m)	Lord Grey	Ms B Marchant	DP Kelly	KA Kelly
ONC Recruitment H'Cap (5f)	Gossie Maderia	LT Reilly	LT Reilly	JA Heffernan
Bellewstown Festival IV QR Race (1m6f)	Dante's Battle	Ms M Cahill	N Meade	Mr D Russell
July 7 Citroen Xsara Picasso Autopoint Maiden 1	Spicebird	Ms S Rogers	C Collins	P Shanahan
Sam Dennigan Maiden Hurdle (2m)	Clan Royal	JP McManus	A Moore	C O'Dwyer
Good/Firm Tipperary Water H'Cap (1m)	Headfort Rose	JO'R Synd	M Cunningham	JA Heffernan
Thatch Bar Maiden Hurdle (3m)	Whatchowillie	J Crowley	Ms F Crowley	DN Cullinane
S Mulvaney Crockafotha H'Cap Hurdle Div I	Shereevagh	Run for Fun Syn	T McCourt	BM Cash
S Mulvaney Crockafotha H'Cap Hurdle Div II	Malacca Hill	JJ Ramsbottom	WP Mullins	R Walsh
Derek Plant H'Cap (1m6f)	Fraser Carey	Ms E Chay	D Gillespie	M Hussey
Vincent &Nancy Keating Mem INH Flat	Garrick	Hill Synd	D Hassett	Mr DP. Hassett
2001				
July 4 Kilsharvan EBF 2y/o Maiden (5f)	Real Delight	Pat Carey	Pat Carey	JA Heffernan
Good / Firm Farrington's Agri H'Cap Hurdle (3m)	Muskerry King	Model Farm Syn	TJ O'Mara	RP O'Brien
Mount Hanover Maiden (5f)	Seychelles	M Tabor	C O'Brien	FM Berry
Oldbridge Concrete H'Cap (1m6f)	Berkley Boy	Berkley RS	M Halford	TP O'Shea
Seamus Murphy Property Hurdle (2m4f)	Goldenhalo	CrockofgoldRS	Ms FM Crowley	R Walsh
Murphy Sand & Gravel 3y/o Maiden(1m)	Arboreta	CSG StLawrence	WM Roper	JA Heffernan
McLoughlin's Oil INH Flat Race Div I(2m)	Drom Wood	Ms T Hyde	A Mullins	Mr P Fenton
McLoughlin's Oil INHF Flat Race DivII	Sardakan	PJ Fallon	MsJH Harrington	Mr G Elliott
July 5 Potato Protection 4y/o Nov Hurdle(2m)	Gold Street	Crockofgold Syn	Ms FM Crowley	R Walsh
Good / Firm Tattersalls Ireland 2y/o Maiden (1m)	Sir Azzaro	Cameron ExpInc	F Mourier(USA)	E Ahern

	Race	Winner	Owner	Trainer	Jockey
	Tote Ireland H'Cap (Div I) (1m)	Queen For ADay	JJ Maps Syn	PJ Flynn	TP Queally
	Tote Ireland (H'Cap (DivII) (1m)	Illusions Tom	Ms. BM Kirwan	AD Evans	WJ Smith
	Bambury Bookermakers H'Cap (1m)	In The Dusk	K Duffy	M Halford	Rachel Costello
	Bracken Court Hotel H'Cap Hurdle (2m)	Moorside River	Beechwood Syn	P Morris	MP Madden
	ONC Recruitment H'Cap (5f)	Queen Sarabi	D Shine	P Martin	E Aherne
	Bellewstown Festival IV QR Race (1m6f)	DerravarraSunset	EJ Fagan	D Wachman	Mr M Grant
July 6	Citreon CS Autopoint Maiden (1m4f)	Glass Note	Ms J Donnelly	T Stack	W Lordan
Good/Firm	Tipperary Water 3y/o H'Cap (1m)	Latin Quarter	R Evans	P Martin	Cathy Gannon
	Sam Dennigan Maiden Hurdle (2m)	Brierfield Lady	StopAtTheTopSy	T Carberry	Philip Carberry
	Derek Plant H'Cap (1m6f)	Breathonme	R Wood	Ms J Harrington	WJ Smith
	Thatch Bar Maiden Hurdle (3m)	The GipsyBaron	SJP Syndicate	M Halford	Paul Carberry
	S Mulvaney Crockafotha H'Cap Hurdle DivI	Lantern Leader	Ms M Farrell	M Hourigan	W Callaghan
	Mulvaney Crockafotha H'Cap Hurdle DivII	Ask The Moon	Maggy Boys Syn	M Halford	Paul Carberry
	Eddie's Hardware INH Flat Race (2m)	LordEdward'sArmy	P M Brady	P Mullins	Mr M Grant
2002					
July 3	Kilsharvan EBF 2y/o Maiden (5f)	New Design	JackofTrumpsRC	D Wachman	TP O'Shea
Good	Duleek H'Cap Hurdle (3m)	Uncle Arthur	Ms G McDonald	M Halford	B Geraghty
	Mount Hanover Maiden (5f)	AlexanderBallot	N O'Callaghan	M Grassick	JA Heffernan
	Oldbridge Concrete H'Cap (1m6f)	Patsy Veale	MA Ryan	J Queally	FM Berry
	Seamus Murphy Properties Hurdle (2m4f)	Hobart Frisby	MB Moore	K Prendergast	K Kelly
	Murphy Sand & Gravel Maiden (1m)	Irish Style	CM Ryan	DK Weld	PJ Smullen
	McLoughlin's Oil INH Flat Race Div I (2m)	Artane Boys	JP McManus	C Roche	Mr A Crowe
	McLoughlin's Oil INH Flat Race Div II 2m	Rendari	Last Chance Syn	P Cashman	Mr P Cashman
July 4	Potato Protection 4y/o Nov Hurdle (2m)	Carlesmio	Ms P Towey	N Meade	Paul Carberry
Good / Firm/	Tattersalls Ireland 2y/o Maiden (1m)	Culcabock	WJ Purcell	Ms FMCrowley	Jayne Mulqueen
Yielding after	Tote Account H'Cap Div I (1m)	BlueRussian	L Vambeck	D Hassett	DJ Condon
3rd race	Tote Account H'Cap Div II (1m)	Celtic Project	EC Sexton	E Sexton	Helen Keohane
	Bet Bambury H'Cap (1m)	Heemanela	Winning Post RS	Ms S Bramell	DP McDonagh
	Redz / Lucky Ned Peppers H'Cap Hurdle	Bob What	Ms P Mullins	P Mullins	R Walsh
	Hilltown H'Cap (5f)	CarrieMeHome	MS E Hamilton	E Byrne	JJ Gooney
	Bellewstown Festival IV Cup (1m6f)	Ostjessy	Ms B Schluter	D Gillespie	Mr T Gillespie
July 5	Stamullen Maiden (1m4f)	Little Linnet	J Hennessy	JG Burns	Philip Carberry
Yielding	Sam Dennigan Maiden Hurdle (2m)	Mac's Valley	Ms M McManus	WP Mullins	R Walsh
	Leggan Hall 3y/o H'Cap (1m)	MarkTheBeginning	JT Burns	P Carey	TM Houlihan
	Thatch Bar Maiden Hurdle (3m)	Gli Gli	JG McDowell	N Meade	Paul Carberry
	SMulvaney Crockafotha H'Cap Hurdle DivI	Cappaduff	M Burke	L Whitmore	Paul Carberry
	Mulvaney Crockafotha H'Cap Hurdle Div II	Digyourheelsin	G Hatchard	T Carmody	R Walsh
	Derek Plant H'Cap (1m6f)	Fluttery Dancer	S Foran	T McCourt	D Condon
	Eddie's Hardware INH Flat Race (2m)	Liberman	PJ O'Donovan	P Mullins	Mr. K Mercer
2003					
July 2	Irish Stallion Farms E.B.F. 2 y/o Maiden 5f	PinkieDinkieDoo	F. McLaughlin	D. Weld	P.J. Smullen
Good	Tote Exacta H'Cap Hurdle 3m	Craughwell Aris	J. Gannon	F.J. Bowles	D.J. Casey

	Race	Winner	Owner	Trainer	Jockey
	Mount Hanover Maiden 5f	Penny Rye	A. Lyons	P. Beirne	J.A. Heffernan
	Oldbridge Concrete H'Cap 1m6f	Estival Park	D.Kinsella	D. Kinsella	T.P. Queally
	Seamus Murphy Prop Consultants 3 y/o Maidn	Banasan	S. Mulryan	MJ O'Brien	R. Walsh
	Milton Properties Consultants 3 y/o Mdn 1m	Sandtrap	Onefornothingatall Synd	K.F. O'Brien	C O'Donoghue
	McLoughlins Oil INH Flat Race Div 1	Electric Flower	F.N. Doyle	A. Mullins	Mr P.G. Murphy
	Ditto Div II	Father of the Bride	J.P. Mangan	J. Crowley	Mr G.J. Power
July 3	Potato Protection 4 y/o Nov. Hurdle 2m	Mirpour	A.J. Mulvey	E. Griffen	B. Geraghty
Good to firm	Tattersalls Ireland 2 y/o Maiden 1m	Alabama Blues	J. Monaghan	T. Doyle	W. Lordan
	Anglo Printers H'Cap Div I 1m	The Red Fellow	A. Hoey	H. Rogers	F.M. Berry
	Ditto Div II	Okay	Mrs V. Cross	J. Gorman	Cathy Gannon
	Derek Plant Farm Mach H'Cap 1m	Instant Hit	Range Synd.	R.P. Burns	W. Lordan
	Tote Jackpot H'Cap Hurdle 2m	Balla Time	P. Challoner	H. Rogers	B. Geraghty
	Shuler Black Hilltown H'Cap 5f	Solo Solero	Maine Synd.	B. Lawlor	M. Hussey
	Bellewstown Festival I.V. Cup 1m6f	Kadoon	Hon S Lawson	M.J. O'Brien	Mr D. Cullen
July 4	Murphy Sand and Gravel Maiden 1 ½ m	Brogella	MJ Hanrahan	J. G. Burns	T. Houlihan
	Sam Dennigan Maiden Hurdle 2m	Love Ditty	S.O'Driscoll	W. Mullins	R. Walsh
Good to firm	Clarke Telehandlers 3y/o H'Cap 1m	Soft Mist	P.M. Kennedy	G. Lyons	H.A. Heffernan
	Thatch Bar Maiden Hurdle 3m	Chain	J.P. Kelly	D. Hughes	K. Kelly
	S. Mulvaney Crockafotha H'Cap Hdle 2 ½ m	Symboli Bay	Haven's Hopers	E.J. O'Grady	B. Geraghty
	Derrinstown Stud Apprentice H'Cap Div I	Sanadja	P.G.C. Synd.	R. Donoghue	S. Curling
	Ditto Div II 1m6f	Zamnah	Mrs C. Connolly	F.J. Bowles	Rachel Costello
	Eddies Hardware INH Flat Race 2m	Miss Congeniality	J. Martin Smith	W. Mullins	Mr J.A. Nash
2004					
June 30	Irish Stallion Farms EBF 2y/o Maiden (5f)	Humble Dream	McGann	P Carey	F Berry
Good	Glebe House Stud Jul'town H'CapHurdle	San Diego	Ms P Madden	N Madden	Mr NP Madden
	Mount Hanover Maiden (5f)	Cupid's Ray	Ms H Johnson	M Halford	TP O'Shea
	Oldbridge Concrete H'Cap (1m6f)	Lily Shing Shang	DJ Power	P Hughes	Cathy Gannon
	Seamus Murphy Properties Hurdle (2m4f)	Fairwood Present	RJ Bagnall	P Rothwell	DJ Casey
	Sullivan Property 3y/o Maiden (1m)	Sans Reserve	Ms HM Smith	Ms J Morgan	JA Heffernan
	McLoughlin's Oil INHS Flat Race (2m)	Chapel Man	EP Heffernan	Ms F Crowley	Mr JJ Feane
July 1	Potato Protection 4yr/o Nov Hurdle (2m)	Complete Circle	Fox Cover RC	M Halford	Paul Carberry
Good	Tattersalls Ireland 2y/old Maiden (1m)	Fearless Flyer	P Gately	T Stack	W Lordan
	Anglo Printers H'Cap Div I (1m)	Coolnaharan	Loughcraig RS	P Rothwell	TP O'Shea
	Anglo Printers H'Cap Div II (1m)	Monroe Gold	C Wilkinson	C Wilkinson	SM Gorey
	Derek Plant H'Cap (1m)	Rookwith	P Jordan	T McCourt	PB Beggy
	Boyne Valley Hotel H'Cap Hurdle (2m)	BouncingBowdler	J Gough	S Mahon	Paul Carberry
	HB Dennis H'Cap (5f)	Paris Sue	PC Conroy	M Callaghan	J Moriarty
	Thatch Bar IV Cup Race (1m6f)	Amid The Chaos	MW Smurfit	DK Weld	Mr K O'Ryan
July 2	Murphy Sand & Gravel Maiden (1m4f)	Crested Pochard	Ms KPrendergast	K Prendergast	DP McDonagh
Good	Sam Dennigan Maiden Hurdle (2m)	Quintet	Ms JP Duffy	JA O'Connell	Paul Carberry

Race	Winner	Owner	Trainer	Jockey
Duleek Credit Union 3y/o H'Cap (1m)	Benwilt Gold	Annalee Synd	G Lyons	P Cosgrave
AIB Bank Maiden Hurdle (3m)	Saor Go Deo	Ms S Fahey	PG Fahey	Mr P Fahey
SMulvaney Crockafotha H'Cap Hurdle 2m4f	Ursumman	Ms P Madden	N Madden	Mr NP Madden
Capital Eyes International H'Cap Div I	Ashlawn	T Tully	H Rogers	RP Cleary
Capital Eyes International H'Cap Div II	Anonymity	B Keane	GT Lynch	CD Hayes
Eddies Hardware INH Flat Race (2m)	Cherry Valley	Ms L Austin	W Austin	Mr NP Madden

2005

Race	Winner	Owner	Trainer	Jockey
June 29				
Irish Stallion Farms EBF 2y/o Maiden (5f)	Bye Bye Ben	Ms EM McCann	PJ Prendergast	DP McDonagh
Good				
Bluegrass Horse Feed H'Cap Hurdle (3m)	Laragh House	Gone West RS	EJ O'Grady	J Culloty
Cassely's Fun Fair Maiden (5f)	Miss Isabella	Jack of Trumps	Ms F Crowley	FM Berry
Castleview Homes H'Cap (1m6f)	Carlesimo	Ms P Towey	N Meade	FM Berry
S Murphy, Yellow Sam 30thAniv Hurdle	Princess Comm	M Lane	S Mahon	RC Colgan
AIB Bank 3y/o Maiden (1m)	Clonard	SS Murphy	PA Fahey	PJ Smullen
McLoughlin's Oil INH Flat Race (2m)	Amber Trix	PP Cullen	AJ Black	Mr AE Lynch
June 30				
Sean McManus Tyres 4y/o Nov Hurdle	Grand Lili	P Gilsenan	JC McConnell	BC Byrnes
Good				
Tattersalls Ireland 2y/o Maiden (1m)	Crosshaven	Ms B Miley	PJ Prendergast	C O'Donoghue
Anglo Printers H'Cap Div I (1m)	Pretty Posh	P Grimes	T Doyle	Cathy Gannon
Anglo Printers H'Cap Div II (1m)	Groves Royal	MJ Smith	H Rogers	CD Hayes
Derek Plant H'Cap (1m)	Tin Town Boy	F Oliver	H Rogers	CD Hayes
Boyne Valley Hotel H'Cap Hurdle (2m)	On Your Way	On Your Side Sy	Ms E Doyle	B Geraghty
HB Dennis H'Cap (5f)	Tango Step	Maine Syndicate	B Lawlor	MJ Lane
Inter Vintners Cup QR Race (1m6f)	Kinger Rocks	T Michael	DK Weld	Ms N Carberry
July 1				
Murphy Sand & Gravel Maiden (1m4f)	Charlies First	B Sweeney	P Casey	N P Madden
Good/Firm				
Sullivan Properties Cons Mdn Hurdle (2m)	Perugino's Shad	Lucky 15 Synd	JA O'Connell	TP Treacy
Duleek Credit Union 3y/o H'Cap Div I (1m)	Head & Shoulder	Good Luck Synd	KJ Condon	DJ Condon
Duleek Credit Union 3y/o H'Cap Div II	At the Helm	L Lillingston	JG Burns	TP O'Shea
Sam Dennigan Maiden Hurdle (3m)	Toulon Toulose	PA Kinsella	PA Kinsella	MP Watts
S Mulvaney Crockafotha H'Cap Hurdle	Persian Return	Eastern RS	P Martin	RC Colgan
Capital Eyes International H'Cap (1m6f)	Flames Last	Ms PF O'Kelly	M Grassick	TP O'Shea
Aug 17				
Eddies Hardware INH Flat Hace (2m)	Crenaun Bridge	T Gilligan	WP Mullins	Ms K Walsh
Good				
Tally-Ho Stud 2y/0 Maiden (1m)	Lightening Hit	Ms J Magnier	T Stack	W Lordan
Dunsany Construction Hurdle (2m)	Ease the Way	Dr M Smurfit	DK Weld	Paul Carberry
Irish Stallion Farms EBF 3y/o Maiden (1m)	Maria's Dream	L Rowley	E Tyrell	JJ Behan
Ulster Bank NE Business H'Cap Div I (1m)	Star of Russia	B Kerr	C Collins	P Shanahan
Ulster Bank NE Business H'Cap Div II (1m)	Dalwich	Give Her Sally S	T McCourt	FM Berry
Tote Ireland 75th Aniv H'Cap Hurdle (2m)	Chemin D'or	OBP Carroll	M Brassil	R Walsh
Kelly Green Laytown Maiden Hurdle (3m)	Sorry Al	T & C Synd	CF Swan	R Walsh
Aug 18				
Ray White Auctioneers QR Race (1m6f)	Red Damson	WE Sturt	Sir M Prescott	Mr P Fahey
Good				
Glebe House Stud 2y/o Nursery (5f)	Seven Gold Rings	EJ Donegan	Ms J Morgan	WJ Lee
C&M Construction H'Cap Div I (5f)	Paris Sue	PC Conroy	M Callaghan	PB Beggy

	Race	Winner	Owner	Trainer	Jockey
	C&M Construction H'Cap Div II (5f)	Belle Child	RJ Lynch	M Halford	E Butterley
	McCabe Garage Drog Mares Maiden Hurdle	Couture Daisy	M Bennett	Ms V Keately	NJ O'Shea
	Murphy Env Mullacurry Cup H'Cap Hurdle	Blue Corrig	R Forrristal	J Crowley	R Walsh
	Farmvale 3y/o H'Cap (1m)	Peculiar Prince	A Gannon	L McAteer	VR deSouza
	Local Trainers Supp B'town 3y/o Mdn Hdle	Battle Dress	Ashton Synd	KC Conlon	Paul Carberry
	ID Technology Ladies INH Flat Race (2m)	Dream River	Measured Leap Synd	P Martin	Ms N Carberry
2006					
July 5	Irish Stallions Farms EBF 2y/o Maiden (5f)	Just For Mary	A Doyle	L McAteer	VR deSouza
Firm	Bluegrass Horse Feeds H'Cap Hurdle (3m)	Silver Pat	Butlersgrange RS	P Rothwell	Mr SW Jackson
	Cassellys Fun Fair Maiden (5f)	Smitten Kitten	Ms T Mahon	G Lyons	JP Murtagh
	Seamus Murphy Properties Hurdle (2m4f)	Classic Approach	MA Ryan	J Queally	JR Barry
	Castleview Homes H'Cap (1m)	Distant Piper	Celtic Goose Syn	A McGuinness	DP McDonagh
	Ray White Auctioneers 3y/o Maiden (1m)	Sweet Spot	M McLoughlin	E Tyrell	M Hussey
	McLoughlins Oil INH Flat Race Div 1 (2m)	Silver Adonis	Professional Syn	P Rothwell	Mr D O'Connor
	McLoughlins Oil INH Flat Race Div II (2m)	Trade War	B Connell	P Fenton	Mr B Connell
July 6	Derek Plant 4y/o Nov Hurdle(2m)	Jubilant Note	Chron Croyns Sy	MD Murphy	DN Russell
Firm	Tattersalls Ireland 2y/o Maiden (1m)	Dal Cais	P Carney	F Ennis	RP Cleary
	Anglo Printers H'Cap Div I (1m)	Breaker Morant	Coill Dubs Synd	A McGuinness	DP McDonagh
	Anglo Printers H'Cap Div II (1m)	Appraise	Short Cut Synd	C O'Brien	WJ Lee
	Riverstown H'Cap (1m6f)	Ardalan	Aga Khan	JM Oxx	FM Berry
	Boyne Valley Hotel H'Cap Hurdle (2m)	Oyez	F Rushe	MJ Kelly	BC Byrnes
	Chris Curtis Menswear H'Cap (5f)	La Motta	Whats the Story	A McGuinness	CD Hayes
	Inter Vintners Cup QR Race (1m 4f)	Bernabeau	Ms AC Ryan	EJ O'Grady	Mr J King
July 7	Murphys Sand & Gravel Maiden (1m4f)	House of Bourbon	Sh Mohammed	JM Oxx	FM Berry
Firm	C & M Construction Maiden Hurdle (2m)	Mission Possible	PF Shanahan	P Rothwell	Philip Carberry
	Glebe House Stud 3y/o H'Cap (1m)	Angels Camp	Ms P K Cooper	G Lyons	WJ Supple
	Sam Dennigan Maiden Hurdle (3m)	Mr Blacktie	N O'Farrell	P Rothwell	AJ McNamara
	S Mulvaney Crockafotha H'cap Hurdle	Spare Change	West Man Synd	P Rothwell	AJ McNamara
	The wwwtote.ie H'Cap Div 1 (1m6f)	Monahullan Prin	Ms E Keane	G Keane	CD Hayes
	The wwwtote.ie H'Cap Div II (1m6f)	Lagniappe	Who Syndicate	RP Burns	W Lordan
	Eddies Hardware INH flat Race (2m)	Cobham	New Court Synd	WP Mullins	Ms K Walsh
Aug 23	Tally-Ho Stud 2y/o Maiden (1m)	Impetious	M McLoughlin	E Tyrell	WJ Supple
Good/Firm	Kilsaran Concrete Hurdle (2m)	DavenportDemo	PM RS	W P Mullins	R Walsh
	Castleview Homes H'Cap (1m)	Poppy Field	Ms E Rogers	H Rogers	WJ Supple
	Ulster Bank NE Business Centre H'Cap D I	Dapple Dawn	M McLoughlin	E Tyrell	E Butterley
	Ulster Bank NE Business Centre H'Cap II	Send Me Home	Just Two Synd	A McGuinness	PB Beggy
	Rennicks Signs H'Cap Hurdle (2m)	Abow	D Kinsella	L Winters	RM Power
	Kelly Green Laytown Maiden Hurdle (3m)	Whataboutya	J Shaughnessy	N Meade	Paul Carberry
Aug 24	Rivendell International 2y/o Nursery (5f)	Maid Of Iron	River Valley Syn	M Quigley	SM Gorey
Firm	Cumiskey's Real Estate H'Cap (5f)	Lilly Be	Ms K Kelly	P Magnier	FF deSilva

	Race	Winner	Owner	Trainer	Jockey
	McCabe Garage Drogheda Mares Mdn Hdle	GloriousMoment	Ms C Hyde	CF Swan	D Hogan
	Irish Stallion Farms EBF 3y/o Maiden (1m)	Tikraar	HamAl Maktoum	DK Weld	SM Gorey
	Murphy Env Mullacurry Cup H'Cap Hurdle	Portant Fella	Port Fella Synd	Ms J Morgan	DN Russell
	Bellewstown Golf Club H'Cap Hurdle (3m)	Coin Man	AMG O'Neill	Eoin Doyle	JR Barry
	AIB Ladies INH Flat Race (2m)	For The Big One	Ms F Weisz	M Brassil	Ms K Ferris
2007					
July 5	Irish Stallion Farms EBF 2y/o Maiden (5f)	Cherry Picked	Ms PK Cooper	G Lyons	WJ Supple
Soft Yielding to	Bellewstown Golf Course Maiden (5f)	Nanotech	Ms MM Kelly	J Fahey	WJ Lee
Soft in places	Leaseplan H'Cap Hurdle (3m)	Spring Charm	PSN Synd	Ms I Monahan	AB Joyce
	Ray White Auct EBF 3y/o Maiden (1m)	Hum The Tune	K Abdullah	DK Weld	PJ Smullen
	Riverstown QR H'Cap (1m6f)	Kasimali	P Wilmott	EJ O'Grady	MrP McNamara
	Balbriggan Retail Park Hurdle (2m4f)	Aldahar Beepers	A Abdel Khaleq	M Phelan	D Casey
	McLoughlin's Oil INH Flat Race (2m)	Grace's Choice	KB Munnelly	WP Mullins	Mr P Mullins
July 6	Tattersalls Ireland 2y/o Maiden (1m)	ChevalierCountr	RF Larkin	JT Gorman	CD Hayes
Good	Derek Plant Maiden Hurdle (2m)	Salt Lake	Pacmen Synd	EJ O'Grady	A McNamara
Yielding to	AIB H'Cap (5 f)	Zhukhov	B Doyle	T McCourt	Amy Parsons
Soft in places	Kilsaran Concrete 3y/o H'Cap (5f)	Johnstown Lad	L Cox	N Moran	WJ Supple
	Sam Dennigan H'Cap Hurdle (2m)	Zanderi	JJ Brennan	P Nolan	AP Crowe
	Anglo Printers H'Cap Div I (1m)	Desert Mile	Ms A Cassidy	E Lynam	FM Berry
	Anglo Printers H'Cap Div II (1m)	Sheer Dance	Ms C Grassick	M Grassick	RP Cleary
	C & M Construction QR Race (1m4f)	Rocket Ship	Ms P Sloan	N Meade	Ms N Carberry
July 7	Murphy Sand & Gravel Maiden (1m4f)	Winners Toast	Toast Synd	D Wachman	W Lordan
Yielding	Sherry Fitzgerald 4y/o Nov Hurdle (2m)	Impudent	Pleasant Boy Syn	W P Mullins	R Walsh
Soft in places	Glebe House Stud H'Cap (1m6f)	Show Blessed	S Breen	Ms J Morgan	PJ Smullen
	Eddie's Hardware INH Flat Race (2m)	Uncle Junior	Ms MM McMahon	WP Mullins	Mr P Mullins
	D Hotel H'Cap (1m)	Cupid's Bow	P Coffey	P Martin	C Geoghegan
	Casseley's Fun Fair Maiden Hurdle (3m)	Sher One Moor	Last Call Synd	J Crowley	R Walsh
	S Mulvaney Crockafotha H'Cap Hurdle	G'day Molly	FTB Synd	J Crowley	JM Allen
August 29	Tally-Ho Stud 2y/o Maiden (1m)	CasablancaJewel	Dr D Harron	D Wachman	W Lordan
Good	Track Bookmakers Hrdle (2m)	Paramount	FM Moriarty	TM Walsh	R Walsh
To firm	Ulster Bank NE Bus Centre H'Cap Div I 1m	Fields Of Green	Mortal R.C	M Halford	JP Murtagh
	Ulster Bank NE Bus Centre H'CapDivII	Send Me Home	Never Better Syn	A McGuinness	PB Beggy
	Castleview Homes H'Cap (1m)	The God of Love	Ms IO'Sh'nessy	G Lyons	JP Murtagh
	Rennicks Signs H'Cap Hurdle (2m)	Our Monty	DJ Reddan	KF O'Brien	G Hutchinson
	Kelly Green Laytown Maiden Hurdle (3m)	Coppet	Pegasus P'Ship	MJP O'Brien	AE Lynch
	Riverside Fiat Drogheda QR Race (1m6f)	Summer Soul	Dr M Surfitt	DK Weld	Mr MM O'Connor
August 30	Cumisky's Real Estate 2y/o Nursery (5f)	Princess Zoe	W Durkin	PJ Prendergast	C O'Farrell
Firm	Gerard Tuite Plant Hire H'Cap (5f)	Doorock	JP Prunty	M Halford	RP Cleary
	McCabe Garage Drogheda Mares Mdn Hdle	Sally's Dream	DJ Reddan	M Hourigan	Paul Carberry
	Irish Stallions Farms EBF 3y/o Maiden	De La Grandera	Ms J Magnier	D Wachman	W Lordan

	Race	Winner	Owner	Trainer	Jockey
	Murphy Envir Mullacurry Cup H'Cap Hdl	Lyceum	DA Southside Sy	DT Hughes	R Loughran
	Boyne Valley Hotel H'Cap Hurdle (3m)	Coin Man	AMGO'Neill	Eoin Doyle	JR Barry
	Ir. Portable Cottages Ladies INH Flat Race	Go Dana Le Pras	Ms SM Rice	Ms J Harrington	Ms K Harrington
2008					
July 3	Stallion Farms EBF 2y/o Maiden (5f)	Progresso	T Corden	T Stack	W Lordan
Good	Ray White Auctioneers Maiden (5f)	Anapoly	EJ Barrett	Ms S Finn	WJ Lee
Good/yielding	Bellewstown Golf Course H'Cap Hurdle	DerrymoreDawn	Derbar RP	W Mullins	R Walsh
In places	Irish Stallion Farms EBF 3y/o Maiden (1m)	Nice Style	D Landy	G Lyons	K Latham
	Bambury Bookmakers QR H'Cap (1m6f)	Darenjan	Ms TC Collins	JJ Hanlon	Mr EJ O'Connell
	S Murphy Balbriggan Retail Pk Hurdle	Spiriton	MJ Smiddy	P Cashman	P Townend
	McLoughlin's Oil INH Flat Race Div I (2m)	Pops Hero	AM Roche	RP Rath	Me E Mullins
	McLoughlin's Oil INH Flat Race Div II 2m	Cloone Stream	Ms K Gillane	CF Swan	Ms N Carberry
July 4	D Hotel 2y/o Maiden (1m)	Redera	Ms M McWey	JT Gorman	CD Hayes
Good	Ivor Fitzpatrick & Co Maiden Hurdle (2m)	Cler	P Burke	WP Mullins	R Walsh
Good/Firm	Betfair 'Odds Are Better' H'Cap (5f)	Mt Weather	Don'tLetOn Syn	R Donohue	DP McDonagh
In places	Kilsaran Lifestyle 3y/o H'Cap (5f)	La Sylvia	F Cosgrave	D McDonagh	DP McDonagh
	Sam Dennigan H'Cap Hurdle (2m)	Quai Du Roi	F Gaughran	T McCourt	P Townend
	Anglo Printers Celebrate 25y H'Cap Div I	Joyful Tears	MC Fahey	P Cashman	BA Curtis
	Anglo Printers Celebrate25y H'Cap Div II	Turk	Tanela Invest Ltd	G Lyons	K Latham
	Eddies Hardware QR Race (1m4f)	Paramount	FM Moriarty	TM Walsh	Mr A Duff
	Murphy Sand & Gravel Maiden (1m4f)	Perhelion	Ms AM O'Brien	AP O'Brien	JA Heffernan
July 5	Champion Lettings 4y/o Nov Hurdle (2m)	Jewelofthe West	Munnelly SS Ltd	N Meade	Paul Carberry
Good/Yielding	Glebe House Stud H'Cap (1m6f)	Eritrea	Sammaya synd	PJ Flynn	DM Grant
	C&M Construction H'Cap (1m)	Funatfuntasia	Claret & Blue Sy	Ms J Morgan	DP McDonagh
	Riverside Fiat Maiden Hurdle (3m)	Can'tellyou	MC Fahey	P Cashman	JM Allen
	S Mulvaney Crockafotha H'CapHurdle	Lucky at Last	P Martin	P Martin	JP Byrne
	Eastern Tarmacadam INH Flat Race (2m)	Allez Vite	JM Barcoe	R Donohue	Mr BT O'Connor
Aug 27	Tally-Ho Stud 2y/o Maiden (5f)	Haaf Ok	M O Cullinane	M Halford	M Halford
Good	Ulster NE Bank H'Cap Div I (1m)	Kaitlins Joy	JM Dunne	P Martin	P Martin
Good/Yielding	Ulster NE Bank H'Cap Div II (1m)	Toberogan	SE Quinn	WA Murphy	WA Murphy
In Places	The www.bellewstownraces.ie H'Cap (1m)	Lonesome Maver	D Kinsella	D Kinsella	D Kinsella
	Tully Bookmakers Hurdle (2m)	Quartino	Midas Synd	Ms J Harrington	Ms J Harrington
	AIB H'Cap Hurdle (2m)	Coscorrig	D Corry	A Lynch	A Lynch
	Kelly Green Laytown Maiden Hurdle (3m)	The Rall	TomTonyKarl	D Hughes	D Hughes
	Hireall Marquees QR Race (1m6f)	Bobs Pride	RBlacoe	DK Weld	DK Weld
Aug 28	Cumiskey's Real Estate 2y/o Nursery (5f)	Croisultan	Brunaboinne Syn	L McAteer	L McAteer
Good	Gerard Tuite Plant Hire H'Cap (5f)	Doorock	JP Prunty	ST Nolan	ST Nolan
Good/Yielding	McCabe's Garage Drog. Mares Mdn Hdle	Cabin Point	J Harrington	Ms J Harrington	Ms J Harrington
In Places	Irish Stallion Farms EBF 3y/o Maiden (1m)	El Presidente	Would Ya Synd	M Halford	M Halford
	Murphy Env Mullacurry Cup H'Cap Hdle	Mudslinger	Gigginstown Std	P Nolan	P Nolan

	Race	Winner	Owner	Trainer	Jockey
	Rennicks Signs H'Cap Hurdle Div I (3m)	Mr Joe Platinum	G Ten Syndicate	JJ Hanlon	JJ Hanlon
	Rennicks Signs H'Cap Hurdle Div II (3m)	Lucky At Last	PJ Daly	P Martin	P Martin
2009	Irish Portable Cottage Ladies INH Flat Race	Commons Glory	Glasvale Synd	JC McConnell	JC McConnell
July 2	Stallion Farms EBF 2/yo Maiden (5f)	Arctic	Ms C Collins	C Collins	P Shanahan
Good	Irish Mirror Maiden (5f)	April	Ms CL Weld	DK Weld	PJ Smullen
	Bambury Bookmakers QR H'Cap (1m6f)	Raise the Goblet	Dr M Carmody	P Hughes	Mr C Motherway
	Bellewstown Golf Course H'Cap Hurdle 3m	Third Level Tom	Secret 7 Synd	C Byrnes	D Russell
	Irish Stallion Farms EBF 3y/o Maiden (1m)	Benji's Babes	D Wylie	T Stack	W M Lordan
	S Murphy Balbriggan Hurdle (2m4f)	Dual Gales	Killeedy Synd	W Mullins	R Walsh
	McLoughlins Oil INH Flat Race (2m)	Dumitas	Ms T Hyde	TE Hyde	Ms N Carberry
July 3	James Curran Memorial 2y/o Maiden (1m)	Kimberley Boy	EJ Donegan	JF O'Shea	SM Gorey
Good	Anglo Printers H'Cap (1m)	Napa Starr	Woodfield Synd	C Byrnes	D McDonagh
	D Hotel Maiden Hurdle (2m)	Gallery Man	S O'Brien	VT O'Brien	AE Lynch
	Bar One Racing H'Cap (5f)	Ability'delivery	MJ Browne	MJ Browne	EJ McNamara
	Bar One Racing 3y/o H'Cap (f)	Palazzone	DC Nolan	GM Lyons	EJ McNamara
	Sam Dennigan H'Cap Hurdle (2m)	Lightening Sky	Ms A Fox	J Fox	KT Coleman
	Eddies Hardware QR Race (1m4f)	Star Wood	PGC Syndicate	MJ Fitzgerald	Mr M Fahey
July 4	Murphy Sand & Gravel Maiden (1m4f)	Vivacious Viv	Ms J Kinsella	L Winters	CD Hayes
Good	Champion Lettings 4y/o Nov Hurdle (2m)	HonourtheWorld	JP Byrne	AJ Martin	R Walsh
	O'Neill's Sports H'Cap (1m6f)	Akinspirit	JF Salter	M Butler	WJ Lee
	Irish Mirror H'Cap (1m)	Astonish	Ms J Magnier	D Wachman	W Lordan
	Landmark Estates Maiden Hurdle (3m)	Older and Wiser	Cavan Dev.	O'McKiernan	R. Walsh
	S Mulvaney Crockafotha H'Cap Hurdle	Fingers	Mrs K.F. O'Brien	KF. O'Brien	L. McNiff
August 26	Portable Cottages 2y/o Nursery (5f)	Midnight Mover	Jos M McGrath	K Prendergast	D McDonagh
Heavy	Golf Bag H'Cap (5f)	AbilityN'Deliver	MJ Browne	M J Browne	E J McNamara
	Tally Ho Stud 2y/o Maiden (1m)	Lyle Lady	Lyle House Synd	J McConnell	S Foley
	Thos Jenkinson Mem 3y/o Maiden (1m)	FirmFoundations	L Mulvany	M Mulvany	G Carroll
	The Bet Chronicle Com H'Cap (1m)	Peculiar Prince	L McAteer	L McAteer	N McCullagh
	James Gogarty Stone H'Cap (1m)	Toberogan	JA Murphy	WA Murphy	K Latham
	MF Bourke (Homes) Ltd QR Race (1m6f)	Zaralabad	N O'Flaherty	CF Swan	Mr P Mullins
August 27	McCabes Garage Mares Mdn Hurdle (2m)	Asigh Pearl	JG McDowell	N Meade	Paul Carberry
Soft	The Bet Daq Com Hurdle (2m)	Holy Road	JB O'Connor	A Slattery	EF Power
	Murphy Env Mullacurry Cup H'CapHurdle	On Your Way	FW Doyle	Ms E Doyle	AP Thornton
	AIB H'Cap Hurde (2m)	Deal Or No Deal	PP Byrnes	C Byrnes	D Russell
	Flogas Natural Gas Mdn Hurdle (3m)	Red Hot Poker	Ms A Bish	W Mullins	R Walsh
	Irish Mirror H'Cap Hurdle (3m)	Wellforth	Ms NB Watts	Ms C Hutchinson	AE Lynch
	Gosh Cosmetics Ladies INH Flat Race	St Devote	DubsvCulchies Syn	E Griffin	Ms N Carberry

	Race	Winner	Owner	Trainer	Jockey
2010					
July 2	Irish Stallion Farms EBF 2y/o Maiden (5f)	Cloneylass	Cloneys Magic S	Ms J Harrington	FM Berry
	Essential Drogheda Magazine 3y/o H'cap 5f	BoldThady Quill	Iona Equine Syn	K Condon	S Foley
	Murphy Sand & Gravel 2y/o Maiden (1m)	Vamizi Island	Pension Fund Sy	T Stack	W Lordan
	Paddy Farnan Memorial H'Cap (1m)	SixteenFortyTwo	D Wachman	D Wachman	MA Cleere
	The www.citynorthhotel.com H'Cap Div I	Blue Law	Ms W Callaghan	M Callaghan	W J Lee
	The www.citynorthhotel.com H'Cap Div II	Polly Ella	Ms E Rogers	H Rogers	K Latham
	Meade Potato Co H'Cap (1m6f)	Penolva	Dr J Syndicate	Ms S Dawson	JA Heffernan
	The www.pacon.ie QR H'Cap (1m4f)	Cyborg	P Wilmott	C Byrnes	Mr RP Quinlan
July 3	Irish Stallion Farms EBF 3y/o Maiden(1m)	The SilverCrown	L Mulvany	M Mulvany	G Carroll
Good to firm	Aviva Drogheda Maiden (5f)	Perino	Nova Syndicate	K Condon	DP McDonagh
	Blackstone Motors Renault H'Cap (5f)	That's A Fret	Ms M Cusack	L McAteer	BA Curtis
	Sam Dennigan & Co. Hurdle (2m4f)	Bacher Boy	SF Gallagher	G Elliott	Paul Carberry
	Castleview Homes Maiden (1m4f)	Third Intention	R Klaey	K Condon	DP McDonagh
	Bellewstown Golf Course H'Cap Hurdle 3m	Yours Busy	R O'Gara	JA Nash	AP Crowe
	S Murphy Balbriggan Ret Park QR Race	Salute Him	Byrne Bros Syn	AJ Martin	Mr D O'Connor
July 4	Glebe House Stud 5y/o Maiden Hurdle (2m)	Hamalka	Click Synd	G Elliott	Paul Carberry
	Liz Jenkinson Mem 4y/o Nov Hurdle (2m)	Jerry's Agent	Ms F Sexton	L Walshe	BJ Cooper
	Grangeclare Paddocks Maiden Hurdle (3m)	Russian War	T Howley Jun	G Elliott	Paul Carberry
	S Mulvaney Crockafotha Hurdle (2m4f)	Grey Soldier	Gigginstown Stu	G Elliott	Paul Carberry
	Outsource H'Cap Hurdle (2m)	Mojito Royale	P Holden	Eoin Doyle	MP Butler
	Tote Trifecta Rollover H'Cap Hdl Div I 2m4f	Mr Bones	Ms B Howard	J Coogan	BM Cash
	Tote Trifecta Rollover H'Cap Hdl Div 2	Carutomark	Stablegate RC	P Magnier	C O'Farrell
	McLaughlin's Oil INH Flat Race 2m	Viking Visitor	PJ O'Connell	K Purcell	Mr JE Burns
August 25	Bluegrass Horse Feeds 2y/o Nursery (5f)	Proper Madam	Ms JJ Murphy	JJ Murphy	DM Grant
Good	Lougher Stables H'Cap (5f)	The Hamptons	JP McManus	N Madden	FM Berry
	Irish Racing Post 2y/o Maiden (1m)	Jamesie	D Lavelle	D Marnane	C O'Donoghue
	Irish Stallion Farms EBF 2y/o Maiden (1m)	Slade	BA Heffernan	A Heffernan	FM Berry
	Liam O'Donoghue Mem H'Cap Div I (1m)	Lily's Star	Ms A Donaldson	H Rogers	DC Byrne
	Liam O'Donoghue Mem H'Cap Div II (1m)	Foxillian	TP O'Leary	K Condon	DP McDonagh
	The www.thetote.com.H'Cap (1m6f)	Knight Eagle	JM McGrath	K Prendergast	S James
	Beamish Stout Race (1m6f)	Zaralabad	N O'Flaherty	CF Swan	C O'Farrell
August 26	McCabe's Garage Drogheda Mares Mdn Hdl	Takeyourcapoff	Sport RC	Ms J Harrington	RM Power
Good	Anglo Printers Hurdle (2m)	Pires	Ms EA Lawlor	AJ Martin	R Walsh
	Lougher Stables H'Cap Hurdle (2m)	Rockazar	Tipp Inn RC	Ms D Foster	Mr AT Duff
	Murphy Env Mullacurry Cup H'Cap Hdl(2m4f	GrangeclareGold	DT Hughes	DT Hughes	R Loughran
	King Crisps Maiden Hurdle Div I (3m)	Drop Anchor	E Cawley	E Cawley	PT Enright
	King Crisps Maiden Hurdle Div II (3m)	Talab	FG Kenny	DT Hughes	R Loughran
	Tote Trifecta Rollover H'Cap Hurdle (3m)	DreamChampion	Ms MacP'Ship	AJ Martin	R Walsh
	Buck Mooneys Ladies INH Flat Race (2m)	Smokey Joe	Ms J Purcell	K Purcell	Ms N Carberry

2011

	Race	Winner	Owner	Trainer	Jockey
July 1	Irish Stallion Farms EBF 2y/o Maiden (5f)	RockviewDiamo	Any News Synd	J McConnell	S Foley
Good	Essential Drogheda Magazine 3y/o H'Cap(5f)	Red Army Blues	S Jones	G Lyons	K Latham
Good/Firm In	Beamish Inter Vint Pub Ch H'Cap (5f)	Mt Weather	R Donoghue	R Donoghue	DP McDonagh
Places	Patrick Tallan & Co Solr Maiden (1m 4f)	Tantalising	Ms D Nagle	D Wachman	WJ Lee
	Fast Shipping Ireland QR Race (1m4f)	Table Forty Six	Iona Equine Syn	K Condon	Ms P Ryan
	Irish Stallion Farms EBF 2y/o Maiden (1m)	Dark Passion	S Jones	G Lyons	JP Murtagh
	The www.citynorthhotel.com H'Cap Div.1.1m	Blackn'Brew	Any News Syn	J McConnell	G Carroll
	The www.citynorthhotel.com H'Cap Div II	The Educator	C Ross	C Ross	DJ Benson
July 2	Thejogforjockeys.ie 5y/o Maiden Hdl (2m)	London Bridge	RJ Bagnall	N Meade	Paul Carberry
Good/Firm	Indaver Ireland 4y/o Nov Hurdle (2m)	High Importance	A Collins	AJ Martin	R Walsh
	Sam Dennigan & Co Maiden Hurdle (3m)	Bingo Lady	Killtippford Synd	K Purcell	TJ Doyle
	S Mulvaney Crockafotha H'Cap Hurdle	Original Option	Ms M O'Driscoll	N Meade	Paul Carberry
	Martinstown Opportunity H'cap Hurdle	Promise Maker	A Holland	JP Cahill	EJ O'Connell
	O'Neill's Sports Clubs Challenge H'Cap Hdl	Nivek's Dream	Paleface Sioux S	P Martin	AP Thornton
	McLoughlin's Oil INH Flat Race (2m)	Donatis Comet	T Honniball	P Martin	Mr JP McKeown
July 3	Balbriggan Ret Park Claiming Race (1m)	Maal	Ms M Marnane	D Marnane	S Foley
Good/firm	Irish Stallion Farms EBF 3y/o Maiden (1m)	O What A Kitten	KL Ramsay	DK Weld	PJ Smullen
Good In Places	Glebe House Stud H'Cap (1m)	Elusive Ridge	Nap RS	H Rogers	PJ Smullen
	Castleview Homes H'Cap Div I (1m6f)	Action Master	All Gone West S	DT Hughes	NG McCullagh
	Castleview Homes H'Cap Div II (1m6f)	Green To Gold	T Kavanagh	C Roche	FM Berry
	Bellewstown Golf Course H'Cap Hurdle(3m)	Corrick Bridge	W Moloney	AJ Martin	R Walsh
	Nordman Portable Stables Hurdle (2m4f)	Tom Horn	N Meade	N Meade	Paul Carberry
	The www.pacon.ie QR H'Cap (1m6f)	De Senectude	Monread Stud	WP Mullins	Ms K Walsh
August 17	Irish Stallion Farms EBF 2y/o Maiden 1m	Forces of D'ness	Ms Childray Pshi	D Wachman	W Lordan
Good	Irish Stallion Farms EBF 3y/o Maiden 1m	Boom To Bust	Anamoine Ltd	G Lyons	JP Murtagh
	The jogforjockeys.ie H'Cap Div I (1m)	Secret Hero	SF Gallagher	A McGuinness	WJ Lee
	The jogforjockeys.ie H'Cap Div II (1m)	Fairy Wing	Ms R Vaughan	Ms J Harrington	FM Berry
	Glebe House Stud 2y/o Nursery (5f)	Chocolate Hills	Sh Mohammed	G Lyons	N McCullagh
	Lougher Stable H'Cap (5f)	Eurosmart Lady	DP McConnell	J McConnell	M Monaghan
	The www.thetote.com H'Cap (1m6f)	Zaralabad	N O'Flaherty	CF Swan	FM Berry
	Hilltown QR Race (1m 4f)	Pires	Ms EA Lawlor	AJ Martin	Ms N Carberry
August 18	McCabe's Garage Drog. Mares Mdn Hdle	Bessie Lou	MsJ Fitzgerald	MJ Fitzgerald	B Geraghty
Good to firm	The www.angloprinters.ie Hurdle (2m)	Jackson's Lady	JP Dempsey	JP Dempsey	B Geraghty
	Lougher Stables H'Cap Hurdle (2m)	Magnetic Force	Round Table Syn	RA Hennessy	B Geraghty
	Mullacurry Cup H'Cap Hurdle (2M4F)	Original Option	Ms M O'Driscoll	N Meade	Paul Carberry
	Nick O'Toole Arkle Memo Maiden Hdle	GormanstonCuck	Headers Synd	CA Murphy	D Russell
	Tote Trifecta Rollover H'Cap Hdl (3m)	AhorsecalledMol	T Manning	A Lynch	R C Colgan
	(Dead Heat in above Race)	Cerveza Dinero	Winonesoon Syn	D Hogan	D Hogan
	Foleys Antiques Arkle Statute Fund Mdn	Bullock Harbour	B Connell	Ms J Harrington	C O'Dwyer

	Race	Winner	Owner	Trainer	Jockey
	Lester Piggott B'town Ladies INH Flat	Maller Tree	J Harrington	Ms J Harrington	Ms K Harrington
2012					
July 6	Irish Stallion Farms EBP 2y/o Maiden (5f)	ScreamBlueMurder	Ms G Rupert	T Stack	W Lordan
Heavy	Heineken Inter Vint Pub Chal H'Cap (5f)	StatuteOfDreams	M flynn	JB McCabe	CD Hayes
	Fast Shipping Ireland 3y/o H'Cap (5f)	Faleena	Ms B Cooney	PJ Flynn	DM Grant
	Essential Drog Magazine Maiden (1m4f)	I Have A Dream	Ms J Magnier	AP O'Brien	JP O'Brien
	Meath Farm Machinery QR Race (1m4f)	Blackstair Mtn	Ms S Ricci	WP Mullins	Mr P Mullins
	Irish Stallion Farms EBF 2y/o Maiden (1m)	Lucked Out	JC Harley	K Prendergast	DP McDonagh
	Hibernia Steel Products 3y/o H'Cap (1m)	California Rose	TF Brennan	P Martin	BA Curtis
July 7	Buck Mooney's 5y/o Maiden Hurdle (2m)	Thomas Edison	JP McManus	AJ Martin	M P Walsh
Soft	Bluegrass Resolve Cubes 4y/o Nov Hurdle	Casimir Road	PG McKeon	MJ Grassick	P Townend
	Sam's Potatoes Maiden Hurdle (3m)	Civena	Goforit Synd	JA Berry	P Townend
	S Mulvaney Crockafotha H'Cap Hurdle	Carlingford Loug	JP McManus	JE Kiely	MP Walsh
	Martinstown Opportunity H'Cap Hurdle	Brian Who	E Cawley	E Cawley	RJ Jones
	O'Neill's Sports Club Chal H'Cap Hurdle2m	Our Nana Rose	JA Creanor	P Martin	AP Thornton
	McLoughlin's Oil INH Flat Race (2m)	Pique Sous	Supreme Horse	WP Mullins	Mr P Mullins
July 8	Irish Stallion Farms EBF 3y/o Maiden (1m)	Lord Jim	R Barnes	PJ Prendergast	C O'Donoghue
Soft to heavy	Glebe House Stud H'Cap (1m)	Boom To Bust	Anamoine Ltd	G Lyons	E McNamara
	Tote Jackpot H'Cap (1m)	Happy Aniversar	R Donohoe	R Donohoe	JP O'Brien
	Collierstown H'Cap (1m6f)	Knockcroghery	JW Nicholson	JW Nicholson	P J Smullen
	The jogforjockey's.ie Hurdle (2m4f)	Discoteca	Gigginstown	G Elliott	K Donoghue
	B'town Golf Course H'Cap Hurdle(3m)	Dunroe Boy	PJ Lohan	JG Carr	IJ McCarthy
	Panda QR H'Cap (1m 6f)	OneCoolShabra	Ms R Shah	PO Brady	Mr RP Treacy
August 22	Irish Stallion Farms EBF 2y/o Maiden (1m)	Approval Given	Mrs P Deegan	P. Deegan	CD Hayes
Soft	Niall Collier Mem 3y/o Claiming Mdn 1m	Jpevie	D Kierans	J. McConnell	G Carroll
	Meath H'Cap (1m)	Liberty To Rock	Ms PA Foley	J.T. Gorman	RP Whelan
	Glebe House Stud (2y/o Nursery (5 f)	All Ablaze	JM English	D.J. English	RP Cleary
	Lougher Stables H'Cap Div I (5f)	Speed Dream	P Starr	J.M. Barrett	RP Cleary
	Lougher Stables H'Cap Div II (5f)	Rigid Rock	Ms PA Foley	J.T. Gorman	DP McDonagh
	The www.thetote.com H'Cap (1m6f)	Solo Performer	MsM McGuinnes	H. Rogers	CD Hayes
	Hilltown QR Race (1m4f)	Blackstair Mtn	Ms S Ricci	W. Mullins	Mr P Mullins
August 23	McCabe's Garage Drog. Mares Nov Hdl	Shadow Eile	S Reilly	Mrs D. Love	AJ McNamara
Yielding	The www.angloprinters.ie Hurdle (2m)	PassageVendome	FN Doyle	W. Mullins	E Mullins
Soft in places	Lougher Stables H'Cap Hurdle (2m)	Rawnaq	KJ Smith	R.A. Hennessy	B Geraghty
	CastleviewHomes MullacurryCup H'Cap Hd	Caim Hill	MJ Dempsey	P. Fenton	BT O'Connell
	The www.thetote.com Maiden Hurdle 3m	Upon the Hoof	L Westwood	T.J. Taaffe	B Geraghty
	Indaver H'Cap Hurdle (3 m)	Heaney	Ms O O'Reilly	T.J. Taaffe	P Townend
	Monica Tobin Salon Ladies INH Flat Race	Aranhill Chief	TC Quinn	S.J. Mahon	Ms AB O'Connor